About the Author

Jim Geier is an internationally known consultant, author, and speaker on wireless LAN technologies and implementation strategies. He is currently the director of Network and Software Systems at Monarch Marking Systems, an international leader in providing bar code system solutions. Jim's department develops wireless system tools and application software for companies and organizations worldwide.

Jim is the author of *Wireless Networking Handbook* (1996, New Riders Publishing) and *Network Reengineering* (1996, McGraw-Hill), as well as numerous articles in leading publications, including *Network Magazine* and *Byte*. Jim has instructed courses internationally on computer-related topics, including wireless networking, software development, and project management, for George Washington University and Technology Training Corporation. He speaks regularly at conferences and tradeshows held throughout the world.

Jim served as chairman of the Institute of Electrical and Electronic Engineers (IEEE) Computer Society, Dayton Section, and chairman of the IEEE International Conference on Wireless LAN Implementation. He was an active member of the IEEE 802.11 working group, responsible for developing international standards for wireless LANs.

Jim's past 20 years of experience include a variety of consulting and management positions. At Wright-Patterson Air Force Base in Ohio, Jim managed the design and operational support of numerous LANs and a wide area network that supports over 10,000 users. For the base, he evaluated the effectiveness of wireless network technologies for use in mobile and portable office environments. He led the development of a tool to aid engineers in the installation of wireless networks and evaluated commercial network technologies for use with U.S. government mobile sensor systems.

He was the principal investigator for a small business innovative research grant to develop an automated software tool that assists engineers in planning, upgrading, and maintaining information systems. He managed a test team responsible for testing computer networks throughout the world. He has developed corporate information system standards for companies migrating from mainframe to client/server systems.

Jim holds a B.S. degree from California State University, Sacramento, and an M.S. degree from Air Force Institute of Technology, both in electrical engineering with emphasis in computer networks. As part of his master's thesis, he developed and implemented an adaptive automatic routing algorithm for a worldwide packet radio network.

Jim's hobbies include sailing and amateur radio (KC8KQH). He resides with his wife and four sons in Yellow Springs, Ohio. You can reach him at `jimgeier@aol.com`.

Dedication

I dedicate this book to my wife, Debbie, for her loving support of my writing efforts.

Acknowledgments

When writing this book, I was fortunate to work with an excellent team at Macmillan Technical Publishing, whose contributions vastly improved the presentation of this book. In particular, Tom Cirtin, development editor, did an outstanding job guiding me through the revision of the text. Tom's ideas and his editing enhanced this book's readability and use as a tool for implementing wireless LANs.

I'd also like to give special thanks to Ed Lamprecht for performing the technical review of the book's manuscript. Ed's valuable suggestions greatly refined this book.

Wireless LANs

Implementing Interoperable Networks

Jim Geier

MACMILLAN
TECHNICAL
PUBLISHING
U·S·A

Wireless LANs: Implementing Interoperable Networks

International Standard Book Number: 1-57870-081-7

Library of Congress Catalog Card Number: 98-85498

2001   00   99   98   4   3   2   1

Interpretation of the printing code: The rightmost double-digit number is the year of the book's printing; the rightmost single-digit, the number of the book's printing. For example, the printing code 98-1 shows that the first printing of the book occurred in 1998.

Composed in Bergamo and MCPdigital by Macmillan Computer Publishing

Printed in the United States of America

Trademark Acknowledgments

Warning and Disclaimer

Feedback Information

At Macmillan Technical Publishing, our goal is to create in-depth technical books of the highest quality and value. Each book is crafted with care and precision, undergoing rigorous development that involves the unique expertise of members from the professional technical community.

Readers' feedback is a natural continuation of this process. If you have any comments regarding how we could improve the quality of this book, or otherwise alter it to better suit your needs, you can contact us at networktech@mcp.com. Please make sure to include the book title and ISBN in your message.

We greatly appreciate your assistance.

Publisher
Jim LeValley

Executive Editor
Linda Ratts Engelman

Managing Editor
Caroline Roop

Acquisitions Editor
Karen Wachs

Development Editor
Thomas Cirtin

Project Editor
Laura N. Williams

Copy Editor
Keith Cline

Indexer
Tim Wright

Proofreader
Julie Searls

Acquisitions Coordinator
Amy Lewis

Manufacturing Coordinator
Brook Farling

Book Designer
Gary Adair

Cover Designer
Sandra Schroeder

Production Team Supervisor
Tricia Flodder

Production
Eric S. Miller

About the Technical Reviewers

These reviewers contributed their considerable practical expertise to the entire development process for *Wireless LANs*. As the book was being written, these folks reviewed all the material for technical content, organization, and flow. Their feedback was critical to ensuring that *Wireless LANs* fits our readers' need for the highest quality technical information.

D. Ed Lamprecht is a Senior Systems Engineer at Monarch Marking Systems with 15 years of programming experience in applications and operating systems. He received a bachelor's degree in 1983 from the University of Northern Iowa and started his career with NCR Corporation programming operating systems in assembly for retail computing systems. It was during this time that Ed also developed applications for other platforms, including UNIX and DOS.

In 1988, Ed joined Monarch Marking Systems, a company specializing in bar code printers and labels. Here he developed bar code applications for MS-DOS and Microsoft Windows 2.0 and later, including PC drivers and TSRs and connectivity software. Since 1996, Ed has been involved in data collection systems providing wireless network connectivity solutions of handheld printers and data collection terminals for retail, industrial, manufacturing, and health care markets.

At Monarch, Ed has developed client/server applications, visited customer sites for analysis and problem solving, and provided international training on products and wireless connectivity. Ed holds six patents in bar code software and handheld printer and data collectors.

Ed lives with his wife, Michelle, and his son, Colin, in Dayton, Ohio. When not tinkering with PCs and networks at home, he enjoys model railroading, railroad memorabilia collecting, golfing, traveling, and spending time with his son.

Peter Rysavy is a consultant specializing in wireless communication and other technologies related to personal and mobile communication. His firm, Rysavy Research, assists clients with market research, product and business development, and technology assessment. Peter is the chairman of the standards committee of the Portable Computing and Communications Association (PCCA), a standards group that produces wireless-data standards.

Since 1993, Peter has worked as a consultant with numerous clients on projects involving mobile and wireless communication. Clients include cellular carriers, communications software companies, network hardware companies, investment firms, automotive electronics companies, research organizations, and universities. He also teaches seminars and writes articles about wireless communication.

Peter graduated with an MSEE from Stanford University in 1979, where he was involved in several collaborations between academia and industry. Joining Fluke Corporation in 1979, he designed communications hardware and software for data-acquisition products. From 1981 to 1983, he designed ethernet networking hardware at Time Office Computers in Australia. He rejoined Fluke, and until 1988 managed the development of a family of communication-oriented touch terminals. From 1988 to 1993, Peter was VP of Engineering and Technology at Traveling Software (makers of LapLink). His last major project was LapLink Wireless. He also managed the development of LapLink and connectivity solutions for a broad variety of mobile platforms.

Contents at a Glance

Contents

Introduction

Wireless LAN technology is rapidly becoming a crucial component of computer networks, and its use is growing by leaps and bounds. Thanks to the finalization of the IEEE 802.11 wireless LAN standard, wireless technology has emerged from the world of proprietary implementations to become an open solution for providing mobility as well as essential network services where wireline installations proved impractical. Now companies and organizations are increasingly investing in wireless networks to take advantage of mobile, real-time access to information.

Most wireless LAN suppliers now have 802.11-compliant products, allowing companies to realize wireless network applications based on open systems. The move toward 802.11 standardization is lowering prices and enabling multiple-vendor wireless LANs to interoperate. This is making the implementation of wireless networks more feasible than before, creating vast business opportunities for system implementation companies and consultants.

Many end-user companies and system integrators, however, have little knowledge of, and experience in, developing and implementing wireless network systems. In many cases, there is also confusion over the capability and effectiveness of the 802.11 standard. The implementation of wireless networks is much different from traditional wired networks. In contrast to ethernet, a wireless LAN has a large number of setup parameters that affect the performance and interoperability of the network. An engineer designing the network and the person installing the network must understand these parameters and how they affect the network. To address wireless installation issues, this book is full of implementation notes, especially regarding 802.11-compliant solutions.

To optimize the operation of wireless systems, you need to be familiar with software options for interfacing wireless handheld appliances to application software and databases located on the network. Terminal emulation, direct database connectivity, and middleware are alternatives that provide connectivity depending on system requirements. This book describes each of these in detail, and explains how to choose one over the others.

Altogether, this book provides a practical overview of wireless network technologies, with emphasis on the IEEE 802.11 wireless LAN standard and implementation steps and recommendations.

Who Will Benefit from This Book?

This book is primarily intended for readers having knowledge of networking concepts and protocols. Readers should be familiar with basic communications protocol handshaking processes and ethernet network infrastructures, for example. Readers should also be conversant with basic computer terminology, such as *local area network*, *client/server*, and *application software*. Project managers can also benefit from the book by learning important project-planning steps for wireless network implementations.

This book is aimed at the following audience:

- Information system (IS) staff and system integrators involved with analyzing, designing, installing, and supporting wireless LANs

- Engineers developing wireless LAN products and solutions

- Managers planning and executing projects for developing wireless products or implementing wireless LAN systems

Key Features of This Book

This book contains the following features that make it a practical guide for developing and implementing wireless LANs:

- Roadmaps at the beginning of each chapter clearly summarize the topics addressed in the chapter.

- Various case studies throughout the book anchor the reader in real-life examples.

- Implementation notes provide practical instruction in the concepts described in this book.

- Diagrams throughout the book illustrate technical issues and procedures.

- Tables convey crucial technical information at a glance.

- The glossary defines terms related to wireless network systems. It is a handy reference to use when reading this book or working on a wireless network project.

- A list of all the case studies (on the inside of the cover of this book) provides a handy reference to the examples of real-world implementation.

The Organization of This Book

To expedite the learning process required in mastering wireless LAN technology, this book follows a three-part sequence of related topics—beginning with explanations of essential concepts and culminating in solid implementation procedures. The book's organization is described in detail in the following sections.

Part I: Wireless Networks—A First Look

The first part of this book addresses introductory material as a basis for understanding the remaining elements. This portion will help the reader understand the concepts, benefits, and issues dealing with radio network systems, clearing up confusion of competing wireless solutions.

If you are already familiar with wireless networks, you might want to skip Chapter 1, "Introduction to Wireless Networks," and Chapter 2, "Wireless Network Configurations." In any case, be sure to read Chapter 3, "Overview of the IEEE 802.11 Standard," if you need an introduction to the standard for wireless LANs.

Part II: Inside IEEE 802.11

Part II is more challenging and contains in-depth coverage of the medium access and physical layers of the IEEE 802.11 standard. Chapter 4, "Medium Access Control (MAC) Layer," describes MAC operations and frame structures, and Chapter 5, "Physical (PHY) Layer," explains PHY operations and frame structures and helps readers select the type of 802.11 physical layer that best fits their needs.

Engineers designing wireless LAN solutions will find this part useful for understanding design options and tuning of an 802.11 network. Engineers developing 802.11-compliant products will find the coverage of the 802.11 standard beneficial when specifying new 802.11-compliant products. IS operational support staff will also find this part most useful to understand frame formats when troubleshooting network behavior.

Part III: Deploying Wireless LANs

The final chapters contain all the steps necessary to deploy a wireless LAN. Chapter 6, "Wireless System Integration," explains the technologies and components needed in addition to what 802.11 covers, such as MobileIP and application connectivity software. Chapter 7, "Planning a Wireless LAN," and Chapter 8, "Implementing a

Wireless LAN," describe the steps you should follow when planning, analyzing, designing, and installing a wireless system. A single case study, threaded throughout Chapters 7 and 8, provides details of a real project that help you understand how to implement the ideas presented in the chapters' step-by-step procedures.

In addition, special implementation notes throughout the chapters of Part III enable readers to directly apply what they have read in earlier chapters to solving the needs for wireless networks within their companies or organizations. IS staff, system integrators, and project managers can strongly benefit by using this part of the book as a practical guide that is based on the experiences and lessons learned from many wireless network projects.

Appendices

The appendices provide supplementary information related to wireless networks. Appendix A, "Automatic Identification and Data Capture (AIDC)," gives the reader an understanding of implementing bar code systems—a primary application of wireless LANs.

Appendix B, "Products, Companies, and Organizations," principally identifies the wireless network product suppliers and system integration companies. This appendix is useful to people looking for products and services when implementing a wireless network. It is also a quick reference for the organizations mentioned in this book.

PART I

Wireless Networks—A First Look

CHAPTER 1

Introduction to Wireless Networks

- **The benefits of wireless networking**
  Wireless networks save you time and money over wired networks that utilize twisted pair and optical fiber, such as ethernet (IEEE 802.3) and token ring (IEEE 802.5). This chapter outlines the benefits of wireless networks that increase the efficiency of mobile applications and save users time and money.

- **Wireless network markets and applications**
  Wireless networks can meet the needs of mobile applications, such as handheld data collection and inventory functions. This chapter provides a summary of the markets and applications that can realize benefits from wireless networks.

- **Wireless network concerns**
  Although wireless networks provide benefits associated with mobility, you need to be aware of several issues related to implementing wireless networks.

- **The components of a wireless network**
  A wireless network consists of components similar to other networks. It is important that you understand these components before designing a wireless network.

- **The history of wireless networks**
  The presence of wireless networks today is the result of 40 years of research, production systems, and recently approved standards. The major milestones that deal with wireless networks are summarized.

- **The future of wireless networks**
  Markets are beginning to grasp the benefits of wireless networks. This is fueling the development of more capable wireless products and services, which are becoming widely available.

The Benefits of Wireless Networking

The emergence and continual growth of wireless networks are being driven by the need to lower the costs associated with network infrastructures and to support mobile networking applications that offer gains in process efficiency, accuracy, and lower business costs. The following sections explain the mobility and cost-savings benefits of wireless networking.

Mobility

Mobility enables users to physically move while using an appliance, such as a hand-held PC or data collector. Many jobs require workers to be mobile, such as inventory clerks, healthcare workers, police officers, and emergency-care specialists. Of course, wireline networks require a physical tether between the user's workstation and the network's resources, which makes access to these resources impossible while roaming about the building or elsewhere.

Mobile applications requiring wireless networking include those that depend on real-time access to data—usually stored in centralized databases (see Figure 1.1). If your application requires mobile users to be immediately aware of changes made to data, or if information put into the system must immediately be available to others, you have a definite need for wireless networking. For accurate and efficient price markdowns, for example, many retail stores use wireless networks to interconnect handheld bar code scanners and printers to databases having current price information. This enables the printing of the correct price on the items, making both the customer and the business owner more satisfied.

Another example of the use of wireless networking is in auto racing. Formula-1 and Indy race cars have sophisticated data acquisition systems that monitor the various on-board systems in the car. When the cars come around the track and pass the respective teams in the pit, this information is downloaded to a central computer, thereby enabling real-time analysis of the performance of the race car.

Not all mobile applications require wireless networking, however. Sometimes the business case doesn't support the need for mobile real-time access to information. If the application's data can be stored on the user's device, and changes to the data are not significant, the additional cost of wireless network hardware may not provide enough benefits to justify the additional expense. Keep in mind, however, other needs for wireless networks may still exist.

Cost Savings

Because of the lack of a tether between the user's appliance and a server, wireless networks offer benefits that reduce networking costs. The following sections explain the benefits and their associated cost savings of utilizing wireless networks.

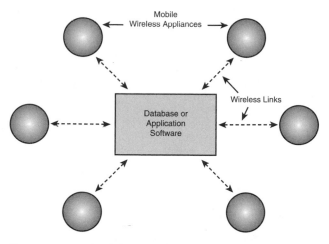

FIGURE 1.1   *A wireless network supports mobile applications by providing access to real-time data.*

Installation in Difficult-to-Wire Areas

The implementation of wireless networks offers many tangible cost savings when performing installations in difficult-to-wire areas. If rivers, freeways, or other obstacles separate buildings you want to connect (see Figure 1.2), a wireless solution may be much more economical than installing physical cable or leasing communication circuits, such as T1 service or 56 Kbps lines. Some organizations spend thousands or even millions of dollars to install physical links with nearby facilities.

If you are facing this type of installation, consider wireless networking as an alternative. The deployment of wireless networking in these situations costs thousands of dollars, but will result in a definite cost savings in the long run.

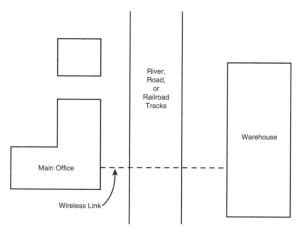

FIGURE 1.2   *Wireless networks make it cost effective to provide network connectivity in situations that are difficult to wire.*

Case Study 1.1:

Replacing a Dial-Up System with a Wireless Network

A grain-handling firm based in Canada trimmed overhead and boosted customer service levels by replacing its slow and expensive modem-based dial-up links to a nearby satellite facility with a low-cost wireless network. This enables remote workstations to swiftly and seamlessly access the company's LAN. The result: Communication costs have dropped dramatically, and customer transactions at a remote facility are completed much faster.

The firm buys wheat, barley, flax, and canola from farmers in several provinces and ships the grains to export markets. The company accepts delivery of the grain from farmers at grain elevators and then, based on the type of grain and its grade, pays for the delivery and logs the transaction into a settlement system.

In a particular city in Canada, farmers deliver large quantities of grain to an inland terminal that also houses business offices; smaller deliveries are made to a smaller grain elevator, called Elevator A, 700 feet away. With twelve staff members at the main business office, and only two at Elevator A, implementing separate networks at each site to support the settlement system was not cost effective.

Faced with the problems of optimizing transaction speed for farmers at Elevator A, enhancing overall network operation control, minimizing capital expenditures, and controlling ongoing communication costs, the firm looked for a way to integrate workers at this remote facility with a new LAN implemented at the main business office. The most obvious solution was a leased telephone line. Because traffic is so light between the two sites, however, the cost could not be justified. Similarly, linking the sites with fiber optic or coaxial cable was also too expensive, due in part to the costs of obtaining permits to lay cable under the railroad lines that separate the facilities. The company then considered utilizing the same frame relay network used to link offices and elevators at its other facilities, but the costs of this option would have been $600 per month and low data speeds.

With no conventional communications alternatives meeting their needs, the firm began a market search for a low-cost, easy-to-install wireless link between the two sites that would not be affected by extreme climatic conditions—including temperatures that vary from 104 degrees Fahrenheit (40 degrees Celsius) in the summer to minus 40 degrees Fahrenheit (minus 40 degrees Celsius) in winter. The firm decided to use Proxim's RangeLINK product. RangeLINK has been operating flawlessly throughout Canada's harsh winter climate at speeds that enable transactions at Elevator A to be completed four times faster than with the modem-based dial-up system that the firm previously used.

The asbestos found in older facilities is another problem that many organizations encounter. The inhalation of asbestos particles is extremely hazardous to your health; therefore, you must take great care when installing network cabling within these areas. When taking necessary precautions, the resulting cost of cable installations in these facilities can be prohibitive.

Some organizations remove the asbestos, making it safe to install cabling. This process is very expensive because you must protect the building's occupants from breathing the asbestos particles agitated during removal. The cost of removing asbestos covering just a few flights of stairs can be tens of thousands of dollars. Obviously, the advantage of wireless networking in asbestos-contaminated buildings is that you can avoid the asbestos removal process, resulting in tremendous cost savings.

In some cases, it might be impossible to install cabling. Some municipalities, for example, may restrict you from permanently modifying older facilities with historical value. This could limit the drilling of holes in walls during the installation of network cabling and outlets. In this situation, a wireless network might be the only solution. Right-of-way restrictions within cities and counties may also block the digging of trenches in the ground to lay optical fiber for the interconnection of networked sites. Again in this situation, a wireless network might be the best alternative.

Case Study 1.2:

A Wireless Solution in an Historic Building

An observatory in Australia has provided stargazing to astronomy enthusiasts for nearly 140 years. Built in 1858, the observatory is classified by the National Trust as one of Australia's historical buildings.

When the observatory began investigating ways to share these views of space with a much broader audience, the obvious solution was to download images to multiple PCs and large screens via a local area network. Due to the historical nature of the building, however, cabling was not an option. Very thick sandstone walls and historic plaster ceilings could not be easily drilled into, and strings of cable would have been unsightly and unsafe to the public. The only feasible solution was a wireless LAN.

The observatory installed Lucent WaveLAN radio cards in each of the their eight PCs and the network server. Telescopic images are downloaded from the Internet or from electronic cameras housed in the observatory's telescopes. These images are then displayed on the various PCs for individual viewing or on larger monitors for group viewing.

Increased Reliability

A problem inherent to wired networks is the downtime that results from cable faults. In fact, cable faults are often the primary cause of system downtime. Moisture erodes metallic conductors via water intrusion during storms and accidental spillage or leakage of liquids. With wired networks, users may accidentally break their network connector when trying to disconnect their PCs from the network to move them to different locations. Imperfect cable splices can cause signal reflections that result in unexplainable errors. The accidental cutting of cables can bring a network down immediately. Wires and connectors can easily break through misuse and even normal use. These problems interfere with the users' ability to utilize network resources, causing havoc for network managers. An advantage of wireless networking, therefore, results from the use of less cable. This reduces the downtime of the network and the costs associated with replacing cables.

Reduced Installation Time

The installation of cabling is often a time-consuming activity. For LANs, installers must pull twisted-pair wires above the ceiling and drop cables through walls to network outlets that they must affix to the wall. These tasks can take days or weeks, depending on the size of the installation. The installation of optical fiber between buildings within the same geographical area consists of digging trenches to lay the fiber or pulling the fiber through an existing conduit. You might need weeks or possibly months to receive right-of-way approvals and dig through ground and asphalt.

The deployment of wireless networks greatly reduces the need for cable installation, making the network available for use much sooner. Therefore, many countries lacking a network infrastructure have turned to wireless networking as a method of providing connectivity among computers without the expense and time associated with installing physical media. This is also necessary within the United States to set up temporary offices and "rewire" renovated facilities.

Case Study 1.3:

Using a Wireless Network for Disaster Recovery

A manufacturer in Sweden distributes auto safety equipment, such as airbags, seat belts, and child seats. With factories in virtually all major European manufacturing countries, the manufacturer has positioned itself as one of the largest suppliers of safety equipment in Europe.

A fire in one of its facilities caused extensive damage to over 6,000 square meters (65,000 square feet) of production and storage facilities. Furthermore, existing network cabling and a majority of the

manufacturing terminals were damaged in the blaze. Given the severity of the fire and the company's dedication to customer satisfaction, a solution was needed to rapidly fulfill existing customer orders.

By incorporating a configuration of Lucent WaveLAN-equipped PCs and WavePOINT access points, the manufacturer was able to successfully and rapidly rebound from the disaster. Within a matter of days, the WaveLAN wireless local area network was installed. The WaveLAN solution helps track approximately 800,000 pieces of equipment delivered to customers daily.

In addition to the swift and easy installation, WaveLAN is providing the company with flexibility and mobility that it lacked with a traditional wired LAN environment. Inventory control, materials tracking, and delivery information are available online from various locations on the production floor. WaveLAN's 2 Mbps data speed helps to further increase productivity by handling this critical information more efficiently than the 9600 bit rate speed of the old system. The cost effectiveness of the wireless LAN is also becoming apparent by helping the company save on reconfiguration and rewiring costs that average nearly 3,500 Swedish Kronas ($500) per terminal.

Long-Term Cost Savings

Companies reorganize, resulting in the movement of people, new floor plans, office partitions, and other renovations. These changes often require recabling the network, incurring both labor and material costs. In some cases, the recabling costs of organizational changes are substantial, especially with large enterprise networks. A reorganization rate of 15 percent each year can result in yearly reconfiguration expenses as high as $250,000 for networks that have 6,000 interconnected devices. The advantage of wireless networking is again based on the lack of cable: You can move the network connection by just relocating an employee's PC.

Case Study 1.4:

Saving Moving Expenses

An oil exploration company operating in Colombia, South America, experienced high expenses when relocating its drilling rigs. The oil drilling setup requires two control rooms in portable sheds located approximately 5,000 feet from the drilling platform to provide 500 Kbps computer communication between the sheds and the drilling rig. The communication system consisted of ethernet networks at each of the three sites. Each shed had four PCs running on the network, and the drilling site had one PC for direct drilling control purposes.

Every time the oil company needed to move to a different drilling site, which occurred four or five times each year, it had to spend $50,000 to $75,000 to reinstall optical fiber over the difficult terrain between the sheds and the drilling platform. With cabling expenses reaching as high as $375,000 per year, the system engineer on site designed a wireless point-to-point system to accommodate the portability requirements and significantly reduce the cost of relocating the drilling operation. The solution includes a spread spectrum radio-based wireless

continues

continued

system that uses point-to-point antennas to direct communication between the sheds and the drilling platform.

The cost of purchasing the wireless network components was approximately $10,000. Whenever the oil company moves its operation, it saves the costs of laying new cable between the sites.

Wireless Network Markets and Applications

Wireless networking is applicable to all industries with a need for mobile computer usage or when the installation of physical media is not feasible. Such networking is especially useful when employees must process information on the spot, directly in front of customers, via electronic-based forms and interactive menus. Wireless networking makes it possible to place portable computers in the hands of mobile front-line workers such as doctors, nurses, warehouse clerks, inspectors, claims adjusters, real estate agents, and insurance salespeople.

The coupling of portable devices with wireless connectivity to a common database and specific applications, as Figure 1.1 illustrates, meets mobility needs, eliminates paperwork, decreases errors, reduces process costs, and improves efficiency. The alternative to this, which many companies still employ today, is utilizing paperwork to update records, process inventories, and file claims. This manual method processes information slowly, produces redundant data, and is subject to errors caused by illegible handwriting. The wireless computer approach using a centralized database is clearly superior.

Retail

Retail organizations need to order, price, sell, and keep inventories of merchandise. A wireless network in a retail environment enables clerks and storeroom personnel to perform their functions directly from the sales floor. Salespeople are equipped with a pen-based computer or a small computing device with bar code reading and printing capability, with the wireless link to the store's database. They are then able to complete transactions—such as pricing, bin labeling, placing special orders, and taking inventory—from anywhere within the store.

When printing price labels that will be affixed to the item or shelves, retailers often utilize a handheld bar code scanner and printer to produce bar coded and/or human readable labels. A database or file contains the price information either located on the handheld device, often called a *batch* device, or a server located somewhere in the store. In batch mode, the price clerk scans the bar code (typically the product code) located on the item or shelf edge, the application software uses the product code to look up the new price, and then the printer produces a new label that the clerk affixes to the item.

In some cases, the batch-based scanner/printer has enough memory to store all the price information needed to effectively perform the pricing function throughout a shift or entire day. This situation makes sense if you update price information in the database once a day, typically during the evening. The clerks load the data on to the device at the beginning of their shifts, and then walk throughout the store continuously pricing items within the store. If the memory in the device is not large enough to store all the data, however, a wireless network is probably necessary. If the handheld unit is equipped with a wireless network connection, the data can be stored in the much larger memory capabilities of a centralized PC server or mainframe and accessed each time the item's bar code is scanned. In addition, a wireless network-based solution has merits if it is too time consuming to download information to a batch device.

Warehouses

Warehouse staff must manage the receiving, putting away, inventory, and picking and shipping of goods. These responsibilities require the staff to be mobile. Warehouse operations have traditionally been a paper-intensive and time-consuming environment. An organization can eliminate paper, reduce errors, and decrease the time necessary to move items in and out, however, by giving each warehouse employee a handheld computing device with a bar code scanner interfaced via a wireless network to a warehouse inventory system.

Upon receiving an item for storage within the warehouse, a clerk can scan the item's bar coded item number and enter other information from a small keypad into the database via the handheld device. The system can respond with a location by printing a put-away label. A forklift operator can then move the item to a storage place and account for the procedure by scanning the item's bar code. The inventory system keeps track of all transactions, making it very easy to produce accurate inventory reports.

As shipping orders enter the warehouse, the inventory system produces a list of the items and their locations. A clerk can view this list from the database via a handheld device and locate the items needed to assemble a shipment. As the clerk removes the items from the storage bins, the database can be updated via the handheld device. All these functions depend heavily on wireless networks to maintain real-time access to data stored in a central database.

Healthcare

Healthcare centers, such as hospitals and doctors' offices, must maintain accurate records to ensure effective patient care. A simple mistake can cost someone's life. As a result, doctors and nurses must carefully record test results, physical data, pharmaceutical orders, and surgical procedures. This paperwork often overwhelms healthcare staff, taking 50–70 percent of their time.

Doctors and nurses are also extremely mobile, going from room to room caring for patients. The use of electronic patient records, with the ability to input, view, and update patient data from anywhere in the hospital, increases the accuracy and speed of healthcare. This improvement is possible by providing each nurse and doctor with a wireless pen-based computer, coupled with a wireless network to databases that store critical medical information about the patients.

A doctor caring for someone in the hospital, for example, can place an order for a blood test by keying the request into a handheld computer. The laboratory will receive the order electronically and dispatch a lab technician to draw blood from the patient. The laboratory will run the tests requested by the doctor and enter the results into the patient's electronic medical record. The doctor can then check the results via the handheld appliance from anywhere in the hospital.

Another application for wireless networks in hospitals is the tracking of pharmaceuticals. The use of mobile handheld bar code printing and scanning devices dramatically increases the efficiency and accuracy of all drug transactions, such as receiving, picking, dispensing, inventory taking, and the tracking of drug expiration dates. Most importantly, however, it ensures that hospital staff can administer the right drug to the right person in a timely fashion. This would not be possible without the use of wireless networks to support a centralized database and mobile data collection devices.

Hospital Uses Wireless LAN to Speed Up Emergency Room Registration*

Methodist Hospital in Indianapolis, Indiana, installed Proxim's RangeLAN2 wireless communications technology to enable faster patient intake in the Emergency Room. The new system gives medical staff the ability to take patients straight back to the treatment rooms, giving them immediate treatment and more privacy when divulging insurance information and medical problems.

Methodist Hospital is an 1,100-bed private hospital with a 45-bed Emergency Room that features a state-approved, Level-1 trauma center. Approximately

85,000 to 90,000 patients pass through the hospital's Emergency Room each year, and many are in need of immediate treatment. For these patients, there's no time to wait in a room full of people while a registration clerk collects information on the reason for the visit, type of insurance coverage, and health history. Sometimes information must be recorded as the patient is being transported to a room, or even while being treated.

To expedite the registration process, Methodist Hospital worked with Datacom for Business, a value-added reseller based in Champaign, Illinois. As a result, the hospital remodeled its 65,000-square-foot Emergency Room, eliminating all but two registration tables and replacing the rest with Compaq Contura notebook computers outfitted with wireless LAN adapters. Now, patients can go directly to treatment rooms, where registration clerks gather the necessary intake data and enter it into the database on the host computer.

Methodist Hospital's wireless communications are made possible by RangeLAN2/ PCMCIA adapters from Proxim, Inc. The wireless PCMCIA adapters enable the Compaq notebook computers running TN3270 terminal emulation to access the clinic's existing wired client/server network or communicate on a peer-to-peer basis with other mobile systems within the same clinic site.

The adapters operate at an average power output of about 100 milliwatts and use advanced power management to minimize the drain on the mobile systems' batteries. RangeLAN2 provides transparent access to standard wired LAN environments, including the hospital's existing TCP/IP network. This is accomplished through the use of three Proxim RangeLAN2/Access Points, which act as wireless bridges and enable mobile users anywhere in the emergency room to send information to the Telnet LAN server. The terminal emulation is then transferred in real time over a TCP/IP enterprise backbone to the hospital's database in the mainframe computer.

Reprinted by permission from Proxim, Inc.

Note

In his war against drugs, President Bill Clinton signed into law the Controlled Substances Act, which pushes hospitals to keep better records of the intake, use, and distribution of controlled drugs. In most cases, the use of handheld computers increases productivity of pharmacy staff by 50–75 percent, enables them to rapidly produce management reports, and eliminates errors in math computations, transcriptions, and accounting.

Real Estate

Real estate salespeople perform a great deal of their work away from the office, usually talking with customers at the property being sold or rented. Before leaving the office, salespeople normally identify a few sites to show a customer, print the Multiple Listing Service (MLS) information that describes the property, and then drive to each location with the potential buyer. If the customer is unhappy with that round of sites, the real estate agent must drive back to the office and run more listings. Even if the customer decides to purchase the property, they must both go back to the real estate office to finish paperwork that completes the sale.

Wireless networking makes the sale of real estate much more efficient. The real estate agent can use a computer away from the office to access a wireless MLS record. IBM's Mobile Networking Group and Software Cooperation of America, for example, make wireless MLS information available that enables real estate agents to access information about properties, such as descriptions, showing instructions, outstanding loans, and pricing. An agent can also use a portable computer and printer to produce contracts and loan applications for signing at the point of sale.

Hospitality

Hospitality establishments check customers in and out and keep track of needs, such as room-service orders and laundry requests. Restaurants need to keep track of the names and numbers of people waiting for entry, table status, and drink and food orders. Restaurant staff must perform these activities quickly and accurately to avoid making patrons unhappy. Wireless networking satisfies these needs very well.

Wireless computers are very useful in the situations where there is a large crowd, such as a restaurant. For example, someone can greet restaurant patrons at the door and enter their names, the size of the party, and smoking preferences into a common database via a wireless device. The greeter can then query the database and determine the availability of an appropriate table. Those who oversee the tables would also have a wireless device used to update the database to show whether the table is occupied, being cleaned, or available. After obtaining a table, the waiter transmits the order to the kitchen via the wireless device, eliminating the need for paper order tickets.

Utilities

Utility companies operate and maintain a highly distributed system that delivers power and natural gas to industries and residences. Utility companies must continually monitor the operation of the electrical distribution system and gas lines, and must check usage meters at least monthly to calculate bills. Traditionally, this means a person must travel from location to location, enter residences and company facilities, record information, and then enter the data at a service or computing center. Today, utility companies employ wireless networks to support the automation of meter reading and system monitoring, saving time and reducing overhead costs.

Kansas City Power & Light operates one of the largest wireless metering systems, serving more than 150,000 customers in eastern Kansas and western Missouri. This system employs a monitoring device at each customer site that takes periodic meter readings and sends the information back to a database that tracks usage levels and calculates bills, avoiding the need for a staff of meter readers.

Case Study 1.5:

Increasing Efficiency and Reducing Paperwork with a Wireless Network

A power utility company in Florida uses a wireless WAN service from the company RAM Mobile Data to save time and reduce paperwork. This system eliminates radio conversations and paperwork between central-site dispatchers and maintenance people, speeding up the service to customers.

The propensity of the company's operating region to experience severe weather conditions forced them to review their reliance on voice radio communications. Storm-force winds, including Hurricane Andrew, caused the loss of wireline service and left up to 80,000 customers without power. These critical periods typically resulted in cellular telephone networks overloading and congesting voice radio systems as storm repair began.

The utility company equipped 38 field service troubleshooters with AST Research Inc.'s GRID 1680 notebook computers, an Ericsson C719 wireless radio modem in conjunction with RAM Mobile Data's service, and TelePartner International Inc.'s Mobi3270 wireless software.

The distribution system restoration process began with the dispatcher taking data from a customer call and generating a repair ticket. Prior to the RAM deployment, the dispatcher alone had access to the information center, and, as a result, had to disseminate the information to the field technicians over the voice radio network. The dispatcher's attempts to contact field technicians were time consuming and wasted the skill of both parties. Storms would only exacerbate the problems.

The RAM Mobile Data system has radically improved the capability of the utility company to respond to severe weather conditions. The dispatcher and the field technicians now have access to the same distribution system restoration information. Field technicians can access information simultaneously and the dispatcher can spend more time answering customer inquiries and redirecting power around trouble spots.

Field service troubleshooters can access key online repair information, such as customer names, phone numbers, meter numbers, transformer locations, and a detailed outline of the problem. Further, dispatchers can determine the status of repairs and the availability and location of troubleshooters in the field, enabling the dispatcher to respond to evolving weather-network problems.

The company has not abandoned its voice radio facilities. The implementation of the RAM Mobile Data service reduced the volume demands on the voice radio, enabling it to be held in reserve for more complex repair tasks.

When the company first implemented the mobile data capability, 66 percent of the repair and maintenance jobs no longer required voice communication between the field technicians and the dispatcher. That figure has since risen to 90 percent as system efficiencies increase.

Field Service

Field service personnel spend most of their time on the road installing and maintaining systems or inspecting facilities under construction. To complete their jobs, these individuals need access to product documentation and procedures. Traditionally, field service employees have had to carry several binders of documentation with them to sites that often lack a phone and even electricity.

In some cases, the field person might not be able to take all the documents with him to a job site, causing him to delay the work while obtaining the proper information. On long trips, this information may also become outdated. Updates require delivery that may take days to reach the person in the field. Wireless access to documentation can definitely enhance field service. A field service employee, for example, can carry a portable computer connected via a wireless network to the office LAN containing accurate documentation of all applicable information.

Field Sales

Sales professionals are always on the move meeting with customers. While on site with a customer, a salesperson needs access to vast information that describes products and services. Salespeople must also place orders, provide status—such as meeting schedules—to the home office, and maintain inventories.

With wireless access to the home office network, a salesperson can view centralized contact information, retrieve product information, produce proposals, create contracts, and stay in touch with home office staff and other salespeople. This contact permits salespeople to complete the entire sale directly from the customer site, which increases the potential for a successful sale and shortens the sales cycle.

Vending

Beverage and snack companies place vending machines in hotels, airports, and office buildings to enhance the sales of their products. Vending machines eliminate the need for a human salesclerk. These companies, however, must send employees around to stock the machines periodically. In some cases, machines might become empty before the restocking occurs because the company has no way of knowing when the machine runs out of a particular product.

A wireless network can support the monitoring of stock levels by transporting applicable data from each of the vending machines to a central database that can be easily viewed by company personnel from a single location. Such monitoring allows companies to be proactive in stocking their machines, because they will always know the stock levels at each machine. Comverse Technology's DGM&S subsidiary licensed software to BellSouth to support a vending machine monitoring service called Cellemetry, which uses the data channels of existing cellular networks.

Wireless LANs for the Home

The HomeRF™ Working Group (HRFWG) is working on the Shared Wireless Access Protocol (SWAP) specification for wireless communications in the home. The SWAP specification is an open standard, enabling PCs, peripherals, cordless telephones, and other consumer electronic devices to communicate and interoperate with one another.

The HRFWG should deliver the final version of SWAP at the end of 1998, with vendors releasing devices based on SWAP during the second half of 1999. For more information about the SWAP specification, visit the HRFWG's Web site at `http://www.homerf.org`.

Wireless Network Concerns

The benefits of a wireless network are certainly welcomed by companies and organizations. Network managers and engineers should be aware, however, of the following concerns that surround the implementation and use of wireless networking:

- Radio signal interference
- Power management
- System interoperability
- Network security
- Connection problems
- Installation issues
- Health risks

Radio Signal Interference

The process of transmitting and receiving radio and laser signals through the air makes wireless systems vulnerable to atmospheric noise and transmissions from other systems. In addition, wireless networks can interfere with other nearby wireless networks and radio wave equipment. As shown in Figure 1.3, interference can take on an *inward* or an *outward* direction.

Inward Interference

A radio-based LAN, for example, can experience inward interference either from the harmonics of transmitting systems or other products using similar radio frequencies in the local area. Microwave ovens operate in the S band (2.4 GHz) that many wireless LANs use to transmit and receive. These signals result in delays to the user by either blocking transmissions from stations on the LAN or causing bit errors to occur in data being sent. These types of interference can limit the areas in which you can deploy a wireless network.

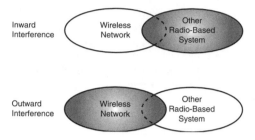

FIGURE 1.3 *Inward and outward interference raises concerns with wireless networks.*

Case Study 1.6:
Radio Interference

When deploying a wireless network at a site located in Washington, D.C., along the Potomac River, a consulting firm occasionally experienced a great deal of delay from stations located on the side of the building facing the river. The implementation team found, through radio propagation tests, that a military base on the opposite side of the river was periodically transmitting radio signals. The interfering signal was strong enough for the LAN stations to misinterpret it as data traffic, forcing the stations to wait an inefficient period.

Note

Most radio-based products operate within public, license-free bands. These products do not require users to obtain FCC licenses, which means the FCC does not manage the use of the products. If you experience interference resulting from another product operating within the public band, you have no recourse. The FCC is not required to step in and resolve the matter, which leaves you with the choice of dealing with delays the interface causes or looking for a different technology to support your needs. This type of interference, however, is rare.

Interference with radio-based networks is not as bad as it might seem. Products using the public radio frequencies incorporate spread spectrum modulation that limits the amount of harm an interfering signal causes. The spread spectrum signal operates over a wide amount of bandwidth, and typical narrow bandwidth interference affects only a small part of the spread information signal, resulting in few or no errors. Therefore, spread spectrum-type products are highly resistant to interference.

Narrowband interference with signal-to-interference ratios of less than 10 dB does not usually affect a spread spectrum transmission. Wideband interference, however, can have damaging effects on any type of radio transmission. The primary source of wideband interference is domestic microwave ovens that operate in the 2.4 GHz band. The typical microwave transmits at 2450 MHz, possibly corrupting the wireless data signal if within 50 feet of the interfering source. Other interference may result from elevator motors, duplicating machines, theft protection equipment, and cordless phones.

Outward Interference

Inward interference is only half of the problem. The other half of the issue, *outward interference*, occurs when a wireless network's signal disrupts other systems, such as adjacent wireless LANs and navigation equipment on aircraft. This disruption results in the loss of some or all of the system's functionality. Interference is uncommon with wireless LAN products operating in the public spread spectrum bands because they operate on such little power (less than 1 watt). The transmitting components must be very close and operating in the same band for either one to experience inward or outward interference.

Techniques for Reducing Interference

When dealing with interference, you should coordinate the operation of radio-based wireless network products with your company's frequency-management organization, if one exists. Government organizations and most hospitals generally have people who manage the use of transmitting devices. This coordination will avoid potential interference problems.

In fact, the coordination with frequency-management officials is a mandatory requirement before operating radio-based wireless devices of any kind on a U.S. military base. The military does not follow the same frequency allocations issued by the FCC. The FCC deals with commercial sectors of the United States, and the military has its own frequency-management process. You must obtain special approval from the government to operate wireless LAN products on military bases and some government locations because they may interfere with some of the military's systems. The approval process can take several months to complete.

Troubleshooting Tip

If no frequency-management organization exists within your company, run some tests to determine the propagation patterns within your building. These tests let you know whether existing systems might interfere with, and thus block and cause delay to, your network. You will also discover whether your signal will disturb other systems. See Chapter 6, "Wireless System Integration," for details on ways to perform propagation tests (site survey).

Power Management

If you are using a portable computer in an automobile, performing an inventory in a warehouse, or caring for patients in a hospital, it is probably too cumbersome or even impossible to plug your computer into an electrical outlet. Therefore, you will depend on the computer's battery. The extra load of the wireless *network interface card (NIC)* in this situation can significantly decrease the amount of time you have available to operate the computer before needing to recharge the batteries. Your operating time, therefore, might decrease to less than an hour if you access the network often or perform other functions, such as printing.

To counter this problem, vendors implement power management techniques in their PCMCIA format wireless NICs. Proxim's wireless LAN product, RangeLAN2/PCMCIA, for example, maximizes power conservation. RangeLAN2 accommodates advanced power-management features found in most portable computers. Without power management, radio-based wireless components normally remain in a receptive state waiting for any information.

Proxim incorporates two modes to help conserve power: the Doze mode and the Sleep mode. The Doze mode, which is the default state of the product, keeps the radio off most of the time and wakes it up periodically to determine whether any messages await in a special mailbox. This mode alone utilizes approximately 50 percent less battery power. The Sleep mode causes the radio to remain in a transmit-only standby mode. In other words, the radio wakes up and sends information if necessary, but is not capable of receiving any information. Other products offer similar power-management features.

System Interoperability

When implementing an ethernet network, network managers and engineers can deploy NICs from a variety of vendors on the same network. Because of the stable IEEE 802.3 standard that specifies the protocols and electrical characteristics that manufacturers must follow for ethernet, these products all speak exactly the same language. This uniformity enables you to select products meeting your requirements at the lowest cost from a variety of manufacturers.

Today, this is not possible with most wireless network products currently deployed. The selection of these wireless products in the past was predominantly single vendor (that is, proprietary), sole-source acquisitions. These products will not interoperate with those from a different company. This raises compatibility problems when adding wireless-based products from different vendors. In the long run, however, the recently approved IEEE 802.11 standard will significantly increase compatibility among multiple-vendor wireless networks.

Network Security

Network security refers to the protection of information and resources from loss, corruption, and improper use. Are wireless networks secure? Among businesses considering the implementation of a wireless system, this is a common and very important question. To answer this question, you must consider the functionality a wireless network performs.

A wireless network provides a bit pipe, consisting of a medium, synchronization, and error control that supports the flow of data bits from one point to another. The functionality of a wireless network corresponds to the lowest levels of the network architecture and does not include other functions, such as end-to-end connection establishment or logon services that higher layers satisfy. Therefore, the only security issues relevant to wireless networks include those dealing with these lower architectural layers, such as data encryption.

Security Threats

The main security issue with wireless networks, especially radio networks, is that they intentionally propagate data over an area that may exceed the limits of the area the organization physically controls. For instance, radio waves easily penetrate building walls and are receivable from the facility's parking lot and possibly a few blocks away. Someone can passively retrieve your company's sensitive information by using the same wireless NIC from this distance without being noticed by network security personnel (see Figure 1.4). This requires, though, that the intruder obtain the network access code necessary to join the network.

This problem also exists with wired ethernet networks, but to a lesser degree. Current flow through the wires emits electromagnetic waves that someone could receive by using sensitive listening equipment. They must be much closer to the cable, though, to receive the signal.

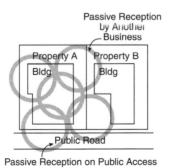

Passive Reception on Public Access

FIGURE 1.4 *The passive reception of wireless network data is much easier than with wired networks.*

Another security problem is the potential for electronic sabotage, in which someone maliciously jams the radio-based network and keeps you from using the network. Remember, most wireless networks utilize a carrier sense protocol to share the use of the common medium. If one station is transmitting, all others must wait. Someone can easily jam your network by using a wireless product of the same manufacture that you have within your network and setting up a station to continually resend packets. These transmissions block all stations in that area from transmitting, thereby making the network inoperable. In such cases, the company stands to incur a loss.

Security Safeguards

Wireless network vendors solve most security problems by restricting access to the data. Most products require you to establish a network access code and set the code within each workstation. A wireless station will not process the data unless its code is set to the same number as the network. Proxim's RangeLAN, for example, can utilize over two billion possible network IDs. If the code is kept secret, it becomes much more difficult for someone to receive and process your data.

Some vendors also offer encryption as an option. Lucent's WaveLAN, for example, has two options for encryption. One version encrypts according to the Data Encryption Standard (DES) as defined by the U.S. Department of Commerce, National Institute of Standards and Technology (NIST), formerly called the National Bureau of Standards (NBS). The other version implements a proprietary method called Advanced Encryption Scheme (AES).

The DES and AES algorithms both use a 16-hexadecimal digit key for encryption, as shown in Figure 1.5. The key is loaded into the security chip when the adapter is configured at installation. When a message is received or sent, the security chip uses the key to encrypt or decrypt the message. Only those workstations in the network with the same security chip and key will be able to understand the messages. Other users of WaveLAN who do not have the key will be unable to decrypt any messages. Both DES and AES perform the encryption in one continuous stream of bits that pass through the system's modulator without affecting performance.

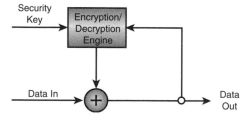

FIGURE 1.5 *A data encryption process improves the security of wireless networks.*

The Department of Commerce limits export of DES devices outside the United States. The purpose of the AES is to provide an alternative for DES to those users of WaveLAN needing a secure air interface, but who are not allowed to use DES due to export limitations. AES implements a proprietary algorithm that has been approved for export.

Connection Problems

The use of traditional wired-based protocols over wireless networks introduces problems with maintaining connections between the user's appliance and the application residing on a server. TCP/IP, for example, provides very reliable connections over wired networks, such as ethernet and token ring. Over wireless networks, however, TCP/IP is susceptible to losing connections, especially when the appliance is operating in an area with marginal wireless network coverage.

In addition, the mobile nature of wireless networks can offer addressing problems. Most networks require the IP address loaded in the user's appliance to be within a specific address range to maintain proper connections with applications. When a user roams with a wireless appliance from one IP subnet to another, the appliance and the application may lose the capability to connect with each other. To learn more about these connection problems and corresponding solutions, refer to Chapter 6, "Wireless System Integration."

Installation Issues

With wired networks, planning the installation of cabling is fairly straightforward. You can survey the site and look for routes where installers can run the cable. You can measure the distances and quickly determine whether cable runs are possible. If some users are too far away from the network, you can design a remote networking solution or extend the length of the cable by using repeaters. After the design is complete, installers can run the cables, and the cable plant will most likely support the transmission of data as planned.

A radio-based wireless LAN installation is not as predictable. It is difficult, if not impossible, to design the wireless system by merely inspecting the facility. Predicting the way in which the contour of the building will affect the propagation of radio waves is difficult. Omnidirectional antennas propagate radio waves in all directions if nothing gets in the way. Walls, ceilings, and other obstacles attenuate the signals more in one direction than the other, and even cause some waves to change their paths of transmission. Even the opening of a bathroom door can change the propagation pattern. These events cause the actual radiation pattern to distort, taking on a jagged appearance, as shown in Figure 1.6.

Wireless MANs also are difficult to plan. What looks like a clear line-of-sight path between two buildings separated by 1,500 feet might be cluttered with other radio transmitting devices.

To avoid installation problems, an organization should perform propagation tests to assess the coverage of the network. Neglecting to do so may leave some of the users outside of the propagation area of wireless servers and access points. Propagation tests give you the information necessary to plan wired connections between access points, allowing coverage over applicable areas. Refer to Chapter 8, "Implementing a Wireless LAN," for identifying the location of access points.

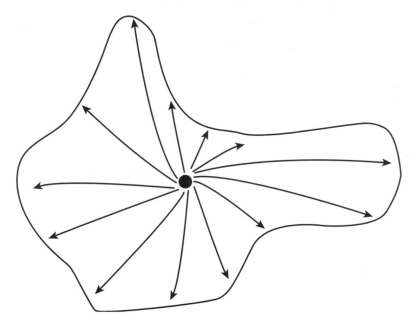

FIGURE 1.6 *The resulting radiation pattern of an omnidirectional antenna within an office building is irregular and unpredictable.*

Health Risks

Another common concern is whether wireless networks pose any form of health risk. So far, there has been no conclusive answer. Radio-based networks, however, appear to be just as safe or safer than cellular phones. There is little or no risk in using cellular phones, which operate in frequency bands immediately below wireless networks. Wireless network components should be even safer than cellular phones because they operate at lower power levels, typically between 50 and 100 milliwatts, compared to the 600 milliwatts to 3 watt range of cellular phones. In addition, wireless network components usually transmit for shorter periods of time.

Laser-based products, found in both wireless LANs and MANs, offer very little or no health risks. In the United States, the Center for Devices and Radiological Health (CDRH), a department of the U.S. Food and Drug Administration, evaluates and certifies laser products for public use. The CDRH categorizes lasers into four classes, depending on the amount of harm they can cause to humans.

Supermarket scanners and most diffused infrared wireless LANs satisfy Class I requirements, where there is no hazard under any circumstance. Class IV specifies devices, such as laser-scalpels, which can cause grave danger if the operator handles them improperly. Most long-range, laser-based wireless networks are rated as Class III devices, whereby someone could damage his eyes if looking directly at the laser beam. Therefore, care should be taken when orienting lasers between buildings.

The Components of a Wireless Network

Wireless networks perform similar functions as their wired ethernet and token ring counterparts. In general, networks perform the following functions to enable the transfer of information from source to destination:

1. The medium provides a bit pipe (path for data to flow) for the transmission of data.

2. Medium access techniques facilitate the sharing of a common medium.

3. Synchronization and error control mechanisms ensure that each link transfers the data intact.

4. Routing mechanisms move the data from the originating source to the intended destination.

5. Connectivity software interfaces an appliance, such as pen-based computer or bar code scanner, to application software hosted on a server.

A good way to depict these functions is to specify the network's architecture. This architecture describes the protocols, major hardware, and software elements that constitute the network. A network architecture, whether wireless or wired, may be viewed in two ways, physically and logically.

Physical Architecture of a Wireless Network

The physical components of a wireless network implement the Physical, Data Link, and Network Layer functions (see Figure 1.7) to satisfy the functionality needed within local, metropolitan, and wide areas. The following sections explain the various components of a wireless LAN.

End-User Appliances

As with any system, there needs to be a way for users to interface with applications and services. Whether the network is wireless or wired, an *end-user appliance* is an interface between the user and the network. Following are the classes of end-user devices that are most effective as appliances for wireless networks:

- Desktop workstations
- Laptop computers

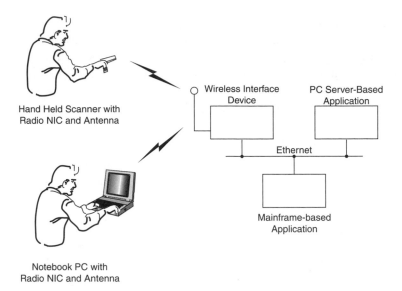

Hand Held Scanner with
Radio NIC and Antenna

Wireless Interface
Device

PC Server-Based
Application

Ethernet

Mainframe-based
Application

Notebook PC with
Radio NIC and Antenna

FIGURE 1.7   *The physical components of a wireless network extend the capability of ethernet and token ring.*

- Palmtop computers

- Handheld PCs

- Pen-based computers

- Personal digital assistants (PDA)

- Handheld scanners and data collectors

- Handheld printers

Today, the handheld PC, introduced by Microsoft (but developed and manufactured by other companies), is the primary hardware platform for Windows CE, which makes an excellent handheld wireless appliance. The main goals in developing the handheld PC include long battery life, affordable price (around $500), compactness and light weight, familiar interfaces, easy PC connection, and effective keyboard input.

Note

Microsoft, being mostly a software house, signed up seven partners to develop a variety of handheld PCs that provide common functionality and vendor-specific features that support Windows CE. These partners are Casio, Compaq, Hewlett-Packard, Hitachi, Phillips Electronics, NEC, and LG Electronics.

Common features of handheld PCs include the following:

- Embedded QWERTY keyboard with alphanumeric keys, standard punctuation, a Ctrl key, an Alt key, and two Shift keys. Other vendor-specific keys are optional. A word of warning: If you have large fingers, you may have a difficult time pressing keys. Japanese and Chinese versions do not have keyboards; they have handwriting recognition as input.

- Embedded touch screen with resolutions of 480×240 or 640×240 pixels, four gray scales (2-bit pixel depth).

- Styles that acts like a mouse when tapped on the touch screen.

- Docking cradle to recharge the machine's batteries and connect it to your desktop PC.

- One PC Card (PCMCIA) slot, one serial connector, and one infrared port (IrDA).

- At least 2 MB RAM and 4 MB of ROM.

PalmPilot

As an example of handheld PCs, consider the PalmPilot by 3Com. It is a pocket-size organizer designed to connect seamlessly with a Windows-based or Macintosh computer. This combination of portability and one-touch connectivity provides a practical way to carry personal data anywhere. The PalmPilot fits in a shirt pocket and contains a suite of personal information management (PIM) applications.

A touchscreen and physical buttons provide one-finger data access. The compact Palm Connected Operating System switches screens and launches applications instantly, yet is efficient enough that two AAA batteries can power the device for several months. The organizer contains a memory module that the user can replace to add memory or upgrade the device. In addition, users will be able to attach communications add-on products,

such as modems and pagers as they become available.

The PalmPilot drops into a docking station that is connected to the desktop by a serial cable. Pressing the HotSync button on the cradle automatically backs up and synchronizes data with the desktop. Because the desktop synchronization software runs in the background, the user does not need to manage the process on the desktop and viewer. As a result, synchronizing data requires less user interaction than printing a document.

The PalmPilot includes Microsoft Windows or Macintosh OS companion versions of applications. Desktop software serves as the gateway between PalmPilot and desktop applications. For example, a mail merge between the PalmPilot Address Book and Microsoft

continues

continued

Word is accomplished with a simple click-and-drag operation.

Because wireless network appliances are often put into the hands of mobile people who work outdoors, the appliance must be tough enough to resist damage resulting from dropping, bumping, moisture, and heat. Some companies offer more durable versions of the portable

computer. Itronix, for example, sells the X-C 6000 Cross Country portable computer. The X-C 6000's case is built from strong, lightweight magnesium and includes a elastomer covering that protects the unit from weather and shock. The unit is impervious to rain, beverage spills, and other work environment hazards.

Note

When evaluating appliances for use with a mobile application, be certain to consider the ergonomics of the unit. You certainly won't be able to realize any of the benefits of a wireless network if users don't use the system because of appliances that weigh too much or are difficult to use.

Network Software

A wireless network consists of software that resides on different parts of the network. A network operating system (NOS), such as Microsoft NT Server, hosted on a high-end PC provides file, print, and application services. Many NOS's are server oriented, as shown in Figure 1.8, where the core application software and databases reside. In most cases, the appliances will interface via TCP/IP with application software or a database running on the NOS.

Client software, located on the end-user's appliance, directs the user's commands to the local appliance software, or steers them out through the wireless network. The software residing on a wireless appliance is very similar to software that runs on a wired appliance. The main difference is that it is important to develop the wireless software to optimize the use of the wireless network's relatively small amount of bandwidth.

The software performing application functions can run on a server/host, the appliance, or a combination of both. In some cases, such as with applications running on an IBM mainframe, IBM AS/400, or UNIX-based hosts, the wireless appliances may need to run terminal emulation. This makes the appliance act as a dumb terminal, just interfacing the keyboard, screen, printer, and so on, with the application running on the host. With client/server systems, the software on the appliance may perform part or all of the application's functionality and merely interface with a database located on a server, such as Microsoft NT Server. Chapter 6, "Wireless System Integration," covers this in more detail.

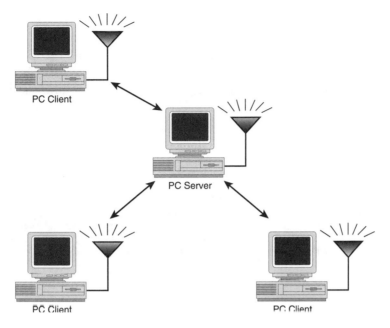

FIGURE 1.8 *The server-based network operating system provides a centralized platform for applications and data storage for mobile users.*

Note

A wireless network appears transparent to application software and operating systems on the network. As a result, applications written for a wired network can generally run without changes over a wireless network.

In some cases, a gateway running *middleware* is necessary to provide an interface between the appliance and the application software running on the server. The appliances communicate with the host/server through the gateway. The gateway acts as a proxy for the various appliances. The advantages of using the gateway are as follows:

- *Better RF throughput:* With the presence of a transport and application gateway, the appliances communicate with the gateway by using a "lightweight" protocol that is wireless friendly, unlike TCP/IP.

- *Reliability:* Because the gateway proxies all the appliances, any outages in communication due to the appliances roaming out of range are transparent to the host/server.

- *Longer battery life:* When the appliances are idle, the network software does not have to periodically send out keep-alive packets to keep the connection to the host/server open. The gateway does this.

Wireless Network Interface

Computers process information in digital form, with low direct current (DC) voltages representing data 1s and 0s. These signals are optimum for transmission within the computer, not for transporting data through wired or wireless media. A wireless network interface couples the digital signal from the end-user appliance to the wireless medium, which is air, to enable an efficient transfer of data between sender and receiver. This process includes the modulation and amplification of the digital signal to a form acceptable for propagation to the receiving location.

Note

Modulation is the process of translating the baseband digital signal used in the appliance to an analog form suitable for transmission through the air. This process is very similar to the common telephone modem, which converts a computer's digital data into an analog form within the 4 KHz limitation of the telephone circuit. The wireless modulator translates the digital signal to a frequency that propagates well through the atmosphere. Of course wireless networks employ modulation by using radio waves and infrared light.

The wireless network interface generally takes the shape of a wireless NIC or an external modem that facilitates the modulator and communications protocols. These components interface with the user appliance via a computer bus, such as ISA (Industry Standard Architecture) or PCMCIA (Personal Computer Memory Card International Association). The ISA bus comes standard in most desktop PCs. Many portable computers have PCMCIA slots that accept credit card-sized NICs. PCMCIA specifies three interface sizes: Type I (3.3 millimeters), Type II (5.0 millimeters), and Type III (10.5 millimeters). Some companies also produce wireless components that connect to the computer via the RS-232 serial port.

The interface between the user's appliance and NIC also includes a software driver that couples the client's application or NOS software to the card. The following driver standards are common:

- *NDIS (Network Driver Interface Specification):* Driver used with Microsoft network operating systems

- *ODI (Open Datalink Interface):* Driver used with Novell network operating systems

- *PDS (Packet Driver Specification):* A generic DOS-based driver developed by FTP Software, Inc. for use with TCP/IP-based implementations

---

Note

Be sure to investigate the existence of suitable (NDIS, ODI, PACKET) drivers for the wireless NIC, and fully test its functionality with your chosen appliance before making large investments in wireless network hardware.

Radio cards traditionally come in a two-piece version configuration—that is, a PCMCIA card that inserts into the appliance and an external transceiver box. This setup is okay for some applications, such as forklift-mounted appliances; however, it is not ergonomic for most handheld appliances. Some vendors, especially with their newest radio cards, offer one-piece units having an integrated radio and transceiver assembly that all fits within the PCMCIA form factor.

Antenna

The antenna radiates the modulated signal through the air so that the destination can receive it. Antennas come in many shapes and sizes and have the following specific electrical characteristics:

- Propagation pattern

- Gain

- Transmit power

- Bandwidth

The *propagation pattern* of an antenna defines its coverage. A truly omnidirectional antenna transmits its power in all directions; whereas, a directional antenna concentrates most of its power in one direction. Figure 1.9 illustrates the differences.

A directional antenna has more *gain* (degree of amplification) than the omnidirectional type and is capable of propagating the modulated signal farther because it focuses the power in a single direction. The amount of gain depends on the directivity of the antenna. An omnidirectional antenna has a gain equal to one; that is, it doesn't focus the power in any particular direction. Omnidirectional antennas are best for indoor wireless networks because of relatively shorter range requirements and less susceptibility to outward interference.

Directional antennas will best satisfy needs for interconnecting buildings within metropolitan areas because of greater range and the desire to minimize interference with other systems.

The combination of *transmit power* and gain of an antenna defines the distance the signal will propagate. Long-distance transmissions require higher power and directive radiation patterns; whereas, shorter distance transmissions can get by with less power and gain. With wireless networks, the transmit power is relatively low, typically one watt or less.

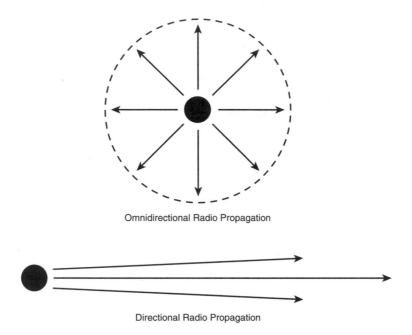

Omnidirectional Radio Propagation

Directional Radio Propagation

FIGURE 1.9   *An omnidirectional antenna broadcasts radio waves in all directions; whereas, a directional antenna focuses the power in a particular direction.*

Note

Most spread spectrum radio vendors sell the following types of antennas:

- Snap-on antenna: *Connects directly to the radio card and provides relatively low gain via an omni-directional radio propagation pattern. This relatively small antenna is best for highly mobile applications when a larger antenna is impractical.*

- Dipole antenna: *Sits on a desk or table and connects to the radio card via a short antenna cable. This approach provides relatively low gain. This antenna is best for portable applications.*

- High gain antenna: *Attaches to a wall or antenna pole/tower and connects to the radio card or access point via a relatively long antenna cable. This approach provides relatively high gain and is best for access points and permanent stations.*

Bandwidth is the effective part of the frequency spectrum that the signal propagates. The telephone system, for example, operates over a bandwidth roughly from 0 to 4 KHz. This is enough bandwidth to accommodate most of the frequency components within our voices. Radio wave systems have greater amounts of bandwidths located at much higher frequencies. Data rates and bandwidth are directly proportional: the higher the data rates, the more bandwidth you will need.

Note

If you're considering integrating a radio NIC into a particular PCMCIA-based appliance, such as a hand-held data collector, you may have to redesign the antenna mounting hardware to accommodate the construction of the appliance.

The Communications Channel

All information systems employ a communications channel along which information flows from source to destination. Ethernet networks may utilize twisted-pair or coaxial cable. Wireless networks use air as the medium. At the earth's surface, where most wireless networks operate, pure air contains gases, such as nitrogen and oxygen. This atmosphere provides an effective medium for the propagation of radio waves and infrared light.

Troubleshooting Tip

The communications channel offers unforeseen obstacles to wireless systems. Always perform a site survey to investigate the effects of physical structures and atmospheric conditions on the propagation of wireless signals before finalizing the design and purchase of a wireless system. (See "Identifying the Location of Access Points" in Chapter 8, "Implementing a Wireless LAN," for information on conducting a site survey.)

Rain, fog, and snow can increase the amount of water molecules in the air, however, and can cause significant *attenuation* to the propagation of modulated wireless signals. Smog clutters the air, adding attenuation to the communications channel as well. Attenuation is the decrease in the amplitude of the signal, and it limits the operating range of the system. The ways to combat attenuation are to either increase the transmit power of the wireless devices, which in most cases is limited by the FCC, or incorporate special amplifiers called *repeaters* that receive attenuated signals, revamp them, and transmit downline to the end station or next repeater.

Logical Architecture of a Wireless Network

A *logical architecture* defines the network's protocols, which ensures a well-managed and effective means of communication. PCs, servers, routers, and other active devices must conform to very strict rules to facilitate the proper coordination and transfer of information.

One popular standard logical architecture is the seven-layer Open System Interconnect (OSI) Reference Model, developed by the International Standards Organization (ISO). OSI specifies a complete set of network functions, grouped into layers. Figure 1.10 illustrates the OSI Reference Model.

End User A   End User B

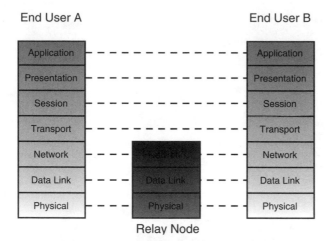

Relay Node

FIGURE 1.10   *The Open System Interconnect Reference Model illustrates all levels of network functionality.*

The OSI layers provide the following network functionality:

- *Layer 7—Application Layer:* Establishes communications with other users and provides such services as file transfer and email to the end users of the network.

- *Layer 6—Presentation Layer:* Negotiates data transfer syntax for the Application Layer and performs translations between different data types, if necessary.

- *Layer 5—Session Layer:* Establishes, manages, and terminates sessions between applications.

- *Layer 4—Transport Layer:* Provides mechanisms for the establishment, maintenance, and orderly termination of virtual circuits, while shielding the higher layers from the network implementation details. Such protocols as TCP operate at this layer.

- *Layer 3—Network Layer:* Provides the routing of packets though routers from source to destination. Such protocols as IP operate at this layer.

- *Layer 2—Data Link Layer:* Ensures synchronization and error control between two entities.

- *Layer 1—Physical Layer:* Provides the transmission of bits through a communication channel by defining electrical, mechanical, and procedural specifications.

Note

Each layer of OSI supports the layers above it.

Does a wireless network offer all OSI functions? No, not in a theoretical sense. As shown in Figure 1.11, wireless networks operate only within the bottom three layers. Only wireless wide area networks, however, perform Network Layer functions.

In addition to the wireless network functions, a complete network architecture needs to include such functions as end-to-end connection establishment and application services to make it useful. Chapter 3, "Overview of the IEEE 802.11 Standard," provides details on the architecture of 802.11-compliant LANs which only covers the Network and Physical Layers of OSI. Chapter 6, "Wireless System Integration," explains other components necessary to design and implement a complete system.

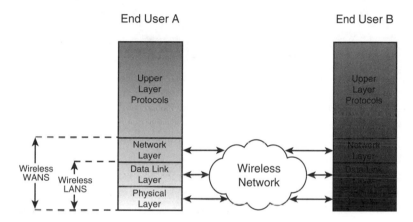

FIGURE 1.11 *Wireless LANs and MANs fulfill Data Link and Physical Layer functionality; whereas, wireless WANs also include functions at the Network Layer.*

The History of Wireless Networks

Network technologies and radio communications were brought together for the first time in 1971 at the University of Hawaii as a research project called ALOHANET. The ALOHANET system enabled computer sites at seven campuses spread out over four islands to communicate with the central computer on Oahu without using the existing unreliable and expensive phone lines. ALOHANET offered bidirectional communications, in a star topology, between the central computer and each of the remote stations. The remote stations had to communicate with one another via the centralized computer.

In the 1980s, amateur radio hobbyists, *hams,* kept radio networking alive within the United States and Canada by designing and building *terminal node controllers* (TNCs) to interface their computers through ham radio equipment (see Figure 1.12). TNCs act much like a telephone modem, converting the computer's digital signal into one that a ham radio can modulate and send over the airwaves by using a packet-switching technique. In fact, the American Radio Relay League (ARRL) and the Canadian Radio Relay League (CRRL) have been sponsoring the Computer Networking Conference since the early 1980s to provide a forum for the development of wireless WANs. Thus, hams have been utilizing wireless networking for years, much earlier than the commercial market.

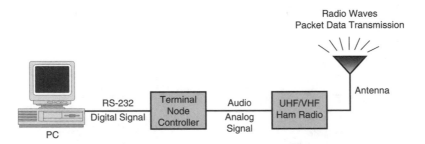

FIGURE 1.12 *Terminal node controllers enable a PC to interface with a ham radio to form a packet radio network.*

In 1985, the Federal Communications Commission (FCC) made the commercial development of radio-based LAN components possible by authorizing the public use of the Industrial, Scientific, and Medical (ISM) bands. This band of frequencies resides between 902 MHz and 5.85 GHz, just above the cellular phone operating frequencies. The ISM band is very attractive to wireless network vendors because it provides a part of the spectrum upon which to base their products, and end users do not have to obtain FCC licenses to operate the products. The ISM band allocation has had a dramatic effect on the wireless industry, prompting the development of wireless LAN components. Without a standard, however, vendors began developing proprietary radios and access points.

In the late 1980s, the Institute for Electrical and Electronic Engineers (IEEE) 802 Working Group, responsible for the development of LAN standards, such as ethernet and token ring, began development of standards for wireless LANs. Under the chairmanship of Vic Hayes, an engineer from NCR, the IEEE 802.11 Working Group developed the Wireless LAN Medium Access Control and Physical Layer specifications.

The IEEE Standards Board approved the standard on June 26, 1997, and the IEEE published the standard on November 18, 1997. The finalizing of this standard is prompting vendors to release 802.11-compliant radio cards and access points throughout 1998. Other vendors new to the wireless market are sure to develop and release 802.11-compliant products based on the standard blueprint provided by the 802.11 standard.

Another widely accepted wireless network connection, however, has been wireless WAN services, which began surfacing in the early 1990s. Companies such as ARDIS and RAM Mobile Data were first in selling wireless connections between portable computers, corporate networks, and the Internet. Companies then began introducing Cellular Digital Packet Data (CDPD) services, which enable users to send and receive data packets via digital transmission services. These services enable employees to access email and other information services from their personal appliances without using the telephone system when meeting with customers, traveling in the car, or staying in a hotel.

The Future of Wireless Networks

Where is wireless networking going? What will the future bring? Predicting what the state of this technology and its products will be five years from now, or even a year from now, is impossible. The outlook for wireless networks, however, is very good. The maturation of standards should motivate vendors to produce new wireless products and drive the prices down to levels that are much easier to justify.

The presence of standards will motivate smaller companies to manufacture wireless components because they will not need to invest large sums of money in the research and development phases of the product. These investments already will have been made and embodied within the standards, which will be available to anyone interested in building wireless network components.

CHAPTER 2

Wireless Network Configurations

- **Wireless LANs**
  It is important to understand the various types of wireless LANs to choose the best alternative technology and select the right components for use within a local area. You learn about the different configurations of a wireless LAN and how they operate.

- **Wireless point-to-point networks**
  While providing network connectivity—mostly outdoors—wireless point-to-point networks offer additional challenges that are different from wireless LANs. Understanding how to maximize the use of wireless point-to-point network technologies is crucial to implementing their solutions.

- **Wireless WANs**
  Wireless WANs can solve your wide area mobile network connectivity needs, but you need to use the technology that is going to provide the necessary coverage. You learn to differentiate the choices you have for wireless wide area networks.

Wireless LANs

Most wireless LANs operate over unlicensed frequencies at near-ethernet speeds (10 Mbps) using carrier sense protocols to share a radio wave or infrared light medium. The majority of these devices are capable of transmitting information up to 1,000 feet between computers within an open environment, and their costs per user range from $150 to $800. In addition, most wireless LAN products offer Simple Network Management Protocol (SNMP) to support network management through the use of SNMP-based management platforms and applications. Figure 2.1 illustrates the concept of a wireless local area network interfacing with a wired network.

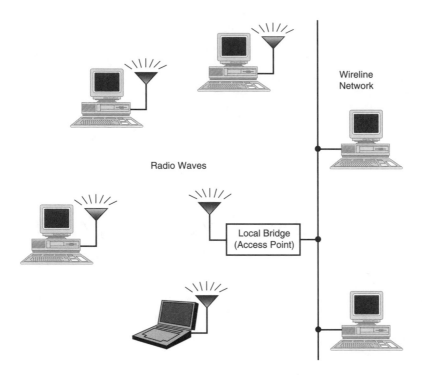

Figure 2.1 *A wireless local area network provides connectivity over the airwaves within a local area, such as a building.*

The components of a wireless LAN consist of a wireless NIC and a wireless local bridge, which is often referred to as an *access point*. The wireless NIC interfaces the appliance with the wireless network, and the access point interfaces the wireless network with a wired network. Most wireless NICs interface appliances to the wireless network by implementing a carrier sense access protocol and modulating the data signal with a spreading sequence.

The following sections describe three approaches to wireless networking within a local environment. These methods include the following:

- Radio waves
- Infrared light
- Carrier currents

Radio-Based Wireless LANs

The most widely sold wireless LAN products use radio waves as a medium between computers and peripherals. An advantage of radio waves over other forms of wireless connectivity is that they can interconnect users without line of sight and propagate through walls and other obstructions with fairly little attenuation, depending on the type of wall construction. Although several walls might separate the user from the server or wireless bridge, users can maintain connections to the network. This supports true mobility. With radio-LAN products, a user with a portable computer can move freely through the facility while accessing data from a server or running an application.

A disadvantage of using radio waves, however, is that an organization must manage them along with other electromagnetic propagation. Medical equipment and industrial components may utilize the same radio frequencies as wireless LANs, which could cause interference. An organization must determine whether potential interference is present before installing a radio-based LAN. Because radio waves penetrate walls, security might also be a problem. Unauthorized people from outside the controlled areas could receive sensitive information; however, vendors often scramble the data signal to protect the information from being understood by inappropriate people.

This section discusses the following topics that explain the operation and configuration of radio-based wireless LANs:

- Medium access control
- Spread spectrum modulation
- Narrowband modulation
- Wireless local bridges
- Single-cell wireless LANs
- Multiple-cell wireless LANs

Medium Access Control

Medium access control, which is a Data Link Layer function in a radio-based wireless LAN, enables multiple appliances to share a common transmission medium via a carrier sense protocol similar to ethernet. This protocol enables a group of wireless computers to share the same frequency and space.

As an analogy, consider a room of people engaged in a single conversation in which each person can hear if someone speaks. This represents a fully connected bus topology (where everyone communicates using the same frequency and space) that ethernet and wireless networks, especially wireless LANs, utilize.

To avoid having two people speak at the same time, you should wait until the other person has finished talking. Also, no one should speak unless the room is silent.

This simple protocol ensures that only one person speaks at a time, offering a shared use of the communications medium. Wireless systems operate in a similar fashion, except the communications are by way of radio signals. Figure 2.2 illustrates the generic carrier sense protocol, commonly known as *Carrier Sense Multiple Access with Collection Detection* (CSMA/CD).

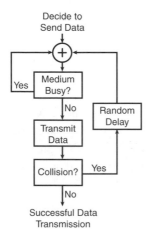

FIGURE 2.2   *The operation of the carrier sense protocol works very similar to a business meeting: You take turns talking when the room is quiet.*

Wireless networks handle error control by having each station check incoming data for altered bits. If the destination station does not detect errors, it sends an acknowledgment back to the source station. If the station detects errors, the data link protocol ensures that the source station resends the packet. To continue the analogy, consider two people talking to each other outside. If one person is speaking and a disruption occurs, such as a plane flying overhead, the dialog might become distorted. As a result, the listener asks the speaker to repeat a phrase or two. (Chapter 4, "Medium Access Control (MAC) Layer," covers the IEEE 802.11 standard for MAC functions in wireless LANs.)

Note

Some manufactures of such devices as power meter readers, medical instruments, point-of-sale devices, and order-entry equipment, have interest in incorporating wireless data communications into their product lines. Many of the wireless network companies can support this need by offering original equipment manufacturer (OEM) versions of their products.

Proxim, for example, sells the RangeLAN2 6300 Mini-ISA that measures under four inches long. RangeLAN2 6300 is an integrated hardware/software OEM package that enables developers to easily incorporate wireless networking capabilities into their products. It is especially well suited for integration into portable computer platforms for mobile data applications.

Another company, Digital Wireless Corporation, offers an OEM product called WIT2400 Frequency Hopping Transceiver. The WIT2400 operates over the 2.4 GHz ISM band at up to 2,000 feet with data rates of 250 Kbps.

Spread Spectrum Modulation

Modulation, which is a Physical Layer function, is a process in which the radio transceiver prepares the digital signal within the NIC for transmission over the airwaves. *Spread spectrum* "spreads" a signal's power over a wider band of frequencies (see Figure 2.3), sacrificing bandwidth to gain signal-to-noise performance (referred to as *process gain*). This contradicts the desire to conserve frequency bandwidth, but the spreading process makes the data signal much less susceptible to electrical noise than conventional radio modulation techniques. Other transmission and electrical noise, typically narrow in bandwidth, will only interfere with a small portion of the spread spectrum signal, resulting in much less interference and fewer errors when the receiver demodulates the signal.

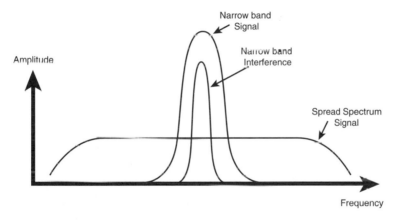

FIGURE 2.3 *Because spread spectrum spreads the signal over a wider frequency range, common narrowband interference affects less of the spread spectrum signal than the narrowband signal.*

Spread spectrum modulators use one of two methods to spread the signal over a wider area: frequency hopping or direct sequence.

Frequency Hopping Spread Spectrum

Frequency hopping works very much like its name implies. It takes the data signal and modulates it with a carrier signal that hops from frequency to frequency as a function of time over a wide band of frequencies (see Figure 2.4). A frequency hopping radio, for example, will hop the carrier frequency over the 2.4 GHz frequency band between 2.4 GHz and 2.483 GHz.

A hopping code determines the frequencies the radio will transmit and in which order. To properly receive the signal, the receiver must be set to the same hopping code and listen to the incoming signal at the right time and correct frequency. FCC regulations require manufacturers to use 75 or more frequencies per transmission channel with a maximum *dwell time* (the time spent at a particular frequency during any single hop) of 400 ms. If the radio encounters interference on one frequency, the radio will retransmit the signal on a subsequent hop on another frequency. Because of the nature of its modulation technique, frequency hopping can achieve up to 2 Mbps data rates. Faster data rates are susceptible to an overwhelming number of errors.

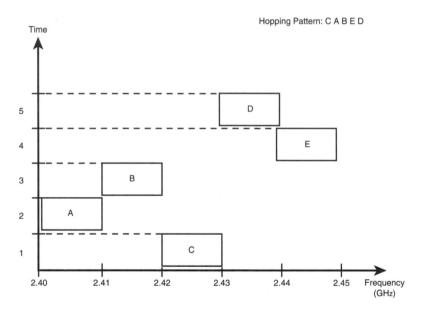

FIGURE 2.4 *With frequency hopping spread spectrum, the carrier frequency changes periodically.*

The frequency hopping technique reduces interference because an interfering signal from a narrowband system will affect the spread spectrum signal only if both are transmitting at the same frequency at the same time. Therefore, the aggregate interference will be very low, resulting in little or no bit errors.

It is possible to have operating radios use spread spectrum within the same frequency band and not interfere, assuming they each use a different hopping pattern. While one radio is transmitting at one particular frequency, the other radio is using a different frequency. A set of hopping codes that never use the same frequencies at the same time are considered *orthogonal*. The FCC's requirement for the number of different transmission frequencies allows frequency hopping radios to have many non-interfering channels. Chapter 5, "Physical (PHY) Layer," covers the IEEE 802.11 standard for frequency hopping wireless LANs.

Troubleshooting Tip

Some vendors allow the user to choose the channel (a particular hopping code) through software that the radio will operate on; however, all users within the same local network have to use the same code. This does give you the ability, however, to have wireless LANs within close proximity to each other operate within the same band and not interfere with each other, so long as you assign them orthogonal hopping codes. Therefore, if your appliances are not connecting with any of the access points, ensure that the hopping codes are equal.

Direct Sequence Spread Spectrum

Direct sequence spread spectrum combines a data signal at the sending station with a higher data rate bit sequence, which many refer to as a *chipping code* (also known as *processing gain*). A high processing gain increases the signal's resistance to interference. The minimum linear processing gain that the FCC allows is 10, and most commercial products operate under 20. The IEEE 802.11 Working Group has set its minimum processing gain requirements at 11. In comparison to frequency hopping, direct sequence can achieve much higher than 2 Mbps data rates.

Figure 2.5 shows an example of the operation of direct sequence spread spectrum. A chipping code is assigned to represent logic 1 and 0 data bits. As the data stream is transmitted, the corresponding code is actually sent. For example, the transmission of a data bit equal to 1 would result in the sequence 00010011100 being sent.

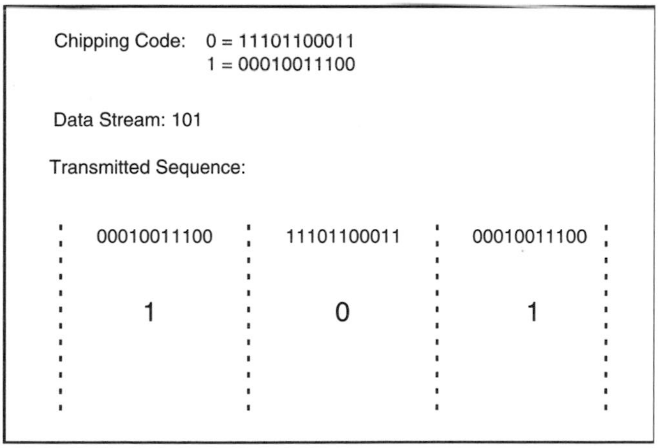

```
Chipping Code:   0 = 11101100011
                 1 = 00010011100

Data Stream: 101

Transmitted Sequence:


    00010011100    :    11101100011    :    00010011100


         1         :         0         :         1
```

FIGURE 2.5 *Direct sequence spread spectrum sends a specific string of bits for each data bit sent.*

In most cases, frequency hopping is the most cost-effective type of wireless LAN to deploy if needs for network bandwidth are 2 Mbps or less. Direct sequence, having higher potential data rates, would be best for bandwidth-intensive applications.

ISM Frequency Bands

In 1985, as an attempt to stimulate the production and use of wireless network products, the FCC modified Part 15 of the radio spectrum regulation, which governs unlicensed devices. The modification authorized wireless network products to operate in the *Industrial, Scientific, and Medical (ISM) bands*. The ISM frequencies are shown in Figure 2.6.

The FCC allows users to operate wireless products without obtaining FCC licenses if the products meet certain requirements, such as operation under 1 watt transmitter output power. This deregulation of the frequency spectrum eliminates the need for user organizations to perform costly and time-consuming frequency planning to coordinate radio installations that will avoid interference with existing radio systems. This is even more advantageous if you plan to move your equipment frequently, because you can avoid the paperwork involved in licensing the product again at the new location. As you can see, more bandwidth is available within the higher-frequency bands, which will support higher data rates.

Implementing ISM Band Frequencies

All commercial companies can deploy wireless networks that operate within the ISM bands; however, be sure to coordinate the use of ISM frequencies with the company's frequency manager if one exists. This is especially important with hospitals, where medical instruments may be using ISM frequencies as well. This coordination will significantly reduce the possibility of interference.

Also be aware that the U.S. military manages frequencies by special non-FCC organizations. If you plan to operate a wireless network on a military base, you must first contact the base frequency manager and obtain a special operating license. If the radio LAN frequencies might interfere with radio equipment used on base, you probably will not be granted a license.

Many wireless LANs deployed today in the United States operate at 902 MHz, but this frequency is not available throughout the world. Figure 2.7 identifies those countries that allow wireless LAN operation in the 902 MHz and 2.4 GHz ISM bands. The 2.4 GHz is the only unlicensed band available worldwide. This band was approved in North and South America in the mid-1980s and was accepted in Europe and Asia in 1995. Companies first began developing products in the 902 MHz band because manufacturing costs in this band were cheaper. The lack of availability of this band in some areas and the need for greater bandwidth, however, drove these companies to migrate many of their products to the 2.4 GHz band.

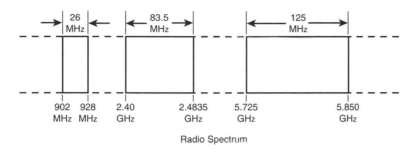

FIGURE 2.6 *The Industrial, Scientific, and Medical (ISM) frequency bands offer greater bandwidth at higher frequencies.*

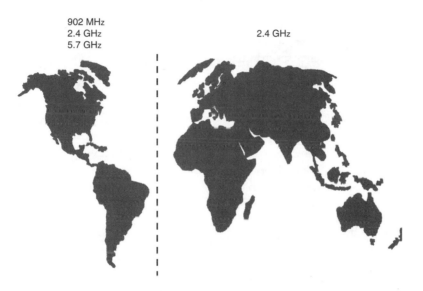

FIGURE 2.7 *The 2.4 GHz ISM frequency band is the only one acceptable worldwide.*

Table 2.1 depicts the tradeoffs between 902 MHz and 2.4 GHz operating frequencies, indicating that 2.4 GHz is the better choice of operating frequency for wireless LANs.

TABLE 2.1 TRADEOFFS BETWEEN 902 MHz AND 2.4 GHz OPERATING FREQUENCIES

902 MHz	2.4 GHz
Lower cost	Higher cost
Longer range	Shorter range
Limited bandwidth	Wider bandwidth
Not compliant with the 802.11 standard	Compliant with the 802.11 standard
Available mostly in North America	Available worldwide
Comprises most of the currently installed base in North America	Comprises most new installations within North America and abroad

The 5.7 GHz band offers more bandwidth than either the 902 MHz and 2.4 GHz bands, enabling data rates above 10 Mbps. Systems operating at 5.7 GHz are less susceptible to interference too. Issues with 5.7 GHz, however, include less range, higher multiple-path propagation, and nonconformance with the existing version of the 802.11 standard. The 802.11 Working Group, however, is working on extending the standard to include 5.7 GHz frequencies (refer to the section titled "Future of the IEEE 802.11 Standard" in Chapter 3, "Overview of the IEEE 802.11 Standard").

Narrowband Modulation

Conventional radio systems, such as television and AM/FM radio, utilize *narrowband modulation*. These systems concentrate all their transmit power within a narrow range of frequencies, making efficient use of the radio spectrum in terms of frequency space. The idea behind most communications design is to conserve as much bandwidth as possible; therefore, most transmitted signals utilize a relatively narrow slice of the radio frequency spectrum.

Other systems using the same transmit frequency, however, will cause a great deal of interference because the noise source will corrupt most of the signal. To avoid interference, the FCC generally requires users of narrowband systems to obtain FCC licenses to properly coordinate the operation of radios. Narrowband products, then, can have a strong advantage because you can be fairly assured of operating without interference. If interference does occur, the FCC will generally resolve the matter. This makes narrowband modulation good for longer links traversing cities where significant interference may result.

Tip

When operating radio-based wireless LAN devices, always follow these safety tips:

- *Avoid touching the antenna when transmitting.*
- *Do not operate the transmitter near areas where unshielded blasting caps reside.*
- *Ensure the antenna or a dummy load is connected to the radio before transmitting. Radio waves will reflect back into the radio if no load is connected, which could result in damaging the radio.*

Wireless Local Bridges

Network bridges are an important part of any network: They connect multiple LANs at the Medium Access Control (MAC) Layer to produce a single logical network. The MAC Layer, which provides medium access functions, is part of IEEE's architecture describing LANs. The functionality of the MAC Layer, along with the Logical Link Control (LLC), fits within the Data Link Layer of ISO's OSI Reference Model. Bridges interface LANs together, such as ethernet to ethernet or ethernet to token ring, and also provide a filtering of packets based on their MAC Layer address. This enables an organization to create segments within an enterprise network.

If a networked station sends a packet to another station located on the same segment, the bridge will not forward the packet to other segments or the enterprise backbone. If the packet's destination is on a different segment, however, the bridge will allow the packet to pass through to the destination segment. Thus, bridges ensure that packets do not wander into parts of the network where they are not needed. This process, known as *segmentation*, makes better use of network bandwidth and increases overall performance.

There are two types of bridges:

- *Local bridges:* These connect LANs within close proximity.

- *Remote bridges:* These connect sites that are separated by distances greater than the LAN protocols can support.

Figure 2.8 illustrates the differences between local and remote network bridges. Traditionally, organizations have used leased digital circuits, such as T1 and 56 Kbps, to facilitate the connections between a pair of remote bridges.

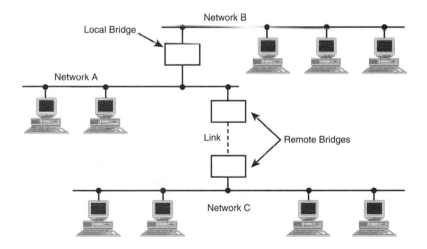

FIGURE 2.8 *Local bridges connect LANs within a local area; whereas, remote bridges connect LANs over a wider area.*

Most companies that develop wireless LAN NICs also sell a wireless local bridge referred to as an *access point* that makes available connections to wired network-based servers and enables multiple wireless cell configurations. Proxim, for example, sells the RangeLAN2 7500 Access Point that interfaces the wireless RangeLAN2 family products to an IEEE 802.3 ethernet network. RangeLAN2 7500 operates in the 2.4–2.4835 GHz ISM band using frequency hopping spread spectrum modulation.

RangeLAN2 7500 optimizes the network's performance and reliability by filtering local packets and only forwarding packets meant for other network segments. RangeLAN2 7500 automatically learns source addresses by monitoring network traffic. Once identified, the address information is stored and forwarded within the network, resulting in an overall reduction in network traffic.

The filtering process of a local bridge (whether it is a wireless or wired type) is critical in maintaining a network configuration that minimizes unnecessary data traffic. WavePOINT, a wireless local network bridge that is part of the Lucent Technologies WaveLAN product family, has a filter table that contains MAC Layer addresses mapped to either the WaveLAN or ethernet side of the bridge. When the bridge receives a packet, it creates a record containing the MAC address (which differentiates the bridge from other network devices) and the physical port on which it receives the frame in a dynamic table.

WavePOINT also enables you to enter static associations between addresses and ports in the static filter table. These entries cannot be overwritten by the WavePOINT bridge. When the bridge receives a frame, it looks at the frame's destination MAC address, and then checks both the dynamic and static filter tables. Then, the WavePOINT forwards all broadcast frames. Next, if the destination MAC address is not in either filter table, the WavePOINT forwards the frame to the opposite port.

A frame coming from the ethernet side that does not have an entry in the tables, for example, will be sent across to the WaveLAN network segment. If the destination MAC address is found in either filter table, the WavePOINT decides whether to forward the frame based on what it finds in the table. The WavePOINT, for example, will not forward a frame coming in from the ethernet side and having an association corresponding to the ethernet side. It will forward the frame, however, if it has an association with the WaveLAN side.

WavePOINT also enables you to enter static associations between addresses and ports in the static filter table. These entries cannot be overwritten by the WavePOINT. When the bridge receives a frame, it looks at its destination MAC address, and then checks both the dynamic and static filter tables. The following situations may occur:

1. The WavePOINT will forward all broadcast frames.

2. If the destination MAC address is not in either filter table, the WavePOINT will forward the frame to the opposite port. A frame coming in from the ethernet side that does not have an entry in the tables, for example, will be sent across to the WaveLAN network segment.

3. If the destination MAC address is found in either filter table, the WavePOINT will decide whether to forward the frame based on what it finds in the table. The WavePOINT, for example, will not forward a frame coming in from the ethernet side and having an association corresponding to the ethernet side. It will forward the frame, however, if it has an association with the WaveLAN side.

The combination of wireless NICs and bridges gives network managers and engineers the ability to create a variety of network configurations. A wireless LAN can assume two main configurations: single-cell and multiple-cell.

Peer-to-Peer Wireless LANs

For small single-floor offices or stores, a peer-to-peer wireless LAN might suffice. Peer-to-peer wireless LANs require only wireless NICs in the devices connected to the network, as shown in Figure 2.9. Access points are not necessary unless users will need connections to wired network-based resources such as servers. Xircom's Netwave wireless LAN product, for example, as with most other wireless LAN products, allows several configurations. You can create a spontaneous LAN easily using Netwave-equipped portables without the use of any access points to form a peer-to-peer network. Any time two or more PCMCIA adapters are within range of each other, they can establish a peer-to-peer network. This enables an organization to form an ad hoc network for temporary use.

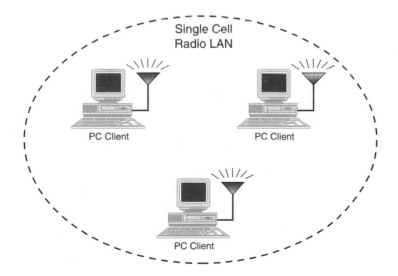

FIGURE 2.9 *A single-cell wireless LAN provides connectivity within radio range, and no access point is required unless there is a need to interface with a wired network.*

With Xircom's Netwave products, the area covered by stations within a peer-to-peer network is called a *basic service area* (BSA), which covers approximately 150 feet between all units in a typical office environment (650 feet in open areas). A single radio-based wireless LAN segment, such as the BSA, can support 6–25 users and still keep network access delays at an acceptable level. These networks require no administration or preconfiguration.

Case Study 2.1:
Wireless Bar Code System

A manufacturer in North America is a leading provider of bar code printers and supplies. As part of the company's goal to streamline processes within its manufacturing plant and warehouse, a process improvement team applied the use of mobile handheld bar code scanning and printing devices with the support of a wireless LAN within its central distribution center (CDC).

Before implementing the system, the CDC was experiencing inefficiencies because clerks needed to walk back and forth between stacks of finished goods and a desktop terminal used to determine a warehouse storage location for the items. The clerks would collect information from the finished goods by writing it down on a piece of paper, and then walk to the terminal to query the company's warehouse-management system for a recommended storage location. The clerk would write this location information on a large label, walk back to the product, and affix the label to the product's container. Later, a forklift operator would come by and place the container in the correct location on the warehouse floor. The process of walking back and forth between the products and the terminal made inefficient use of the clerk's time, which slowed the movement of products through the plant.

The solution to this problem consists of Monarch Marking System's DOS-based Pathfinder Ultra RF handheld bar code scanner and printer, equipped with an Aironet 2.4 GHz frequency hopping radio. Only one radio cell was necessary to cover the area used to stage the finished goods. An Aironet 2.4 GHz access point was needed, however, to provide an interface for the existing ethernet network, which led to the mainframe computer running the warehouse-management system. With this collection of components, the clerk can now scan the finished product's bar code, which is used to query the warehouse management system for a valid put-away location, and then print a label indicating the applicable location information.

Through the use of the scan, print, and apply function, the solution eliminates the need to walk back and forth to the terminal, increasing productivity by 50 percent. In addition, the solution provides significant gains in accuracy through the elimination of human error.

With Netwave, there are two types of peer-to-peer networks: public and named. *Public networks* use a default domain, enabling any Netwave user within range to join the network. If you need more privacy, you can create a *named network* by having users configure the Netwave adapters with a specific domain ID. With this configuration, only stations having the same domain ID can join the network.

The optional data scrambling feature requires participants to know the scrambling key the network is using to decode data packets from other stations on the network. In addition, the domain ID specifies a unique hopping code that minimizes interference between adjacent wireless networks. Most vendors utilize similar approaches.

Multiple-Cell Wireless LANs

If an organization requires greater range than the limitations of a single-cell configuration, you can utilize a set of access points and a wired network backbone to create a multiple-cell configuration (see Figure 2.10). Such a configuration can cover larger multiple-floor buildings, warehouses, and hospitals. In this environment, a handheld PC or data collector with a wireless NIC can roam within the coverage area while maintaining a live connection to the corporate network.

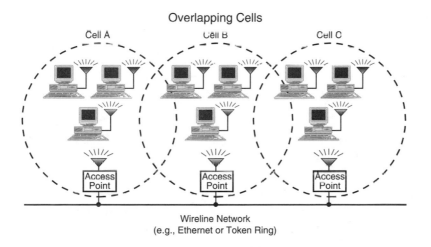

FIGURE 2.10 *A multiple-cell wireless LAN provides continuous network connectivity when the area exceeds the range of a single-cell wireless LAN.*

Designers can configure multiple-cell wireless LANs to satisfy different connectivity requirements. You could configure cells A, B, and C (refer to Figure 2.10) identically, for example, to enable users to roam anywhere within range of any access point to maintain seamless connections throughout a facility. If you have various functional groups that you want to keep separate, you could set up cell A with one set of parameters and establish cells B and C with common parameters. This would be of benefit, for example, if cell A covered the area of manufacturing and cells B and C covered the area of the warehouse.

The ideal wireless LAN configuration for your organization depends primarily on user requirements and geography. If you have a relatively small group that requires wireless connectivity within the immediate group, a single-cell configuration may do the job. If users are spread throughout the entire facility, however, you might need a multiple-cell configuration. In either case, bridges may be necessary to support user access to resources located on the wired infrastructure. Chapter 6, "Wireless System Integration," covers various proprietary and standard methods for roaming.

Infrared Light–Based Wireless LANs

Infrared light is an alternative to using radio waves for wireless LAN connectivity. The wavelength of infrared light is longer (lower in frequency) than the spectral colors, but much shorter (higher in frequency) than radio waves. Under most lighting conditions, therefore, infrared light is invisible to the naked eye. Infrared light LAN products operate around 820 nanometer wavelengths because air offers the least attenuation at that point in the infrared spectrum.

Note

Sir William Herschel discovered infrared light in 1800 when he separated sunlight into its component colors with a prism. He found that most of the heat in the beam fell in the spectral region where no visible light existed, just beyond the red.

In comparison to radio waves, infrared light offers higher degrees of security and performance. These LANs are more secure because infrared light does not propagate through opaque objects, such as walls, keeping the data signals contained within a room or building. Also, common noise sources such as microwave ovens and radio transmitters do not interfere with the light signal. In terms of performance, infrared light has a great deal of bandwidth, making it possible to operate at very high data rates. Infrared light, however, is not as suitable as radio waves for mobile applications because of its limited coverage.

An infrared light LAN consists mainly of two components:

- *Adapter card or unit:* The adapter card plugs into the PC or printer via an ISA or PCMCIA slot (or connects to the parallel port).

- *Transducer:* The transducer, similar to the antenna with a radio-based LAN, attaches to a wall or office partition.

The adapter card handles the protocols needed to operate in a shared-medium environment, and the transducer transmits and receives infrared light signals.

There are two types of infrared light LANs:

- Diffused
- Point-to-point

Diffused Infrared-Based LAN Technique

You have probably been using a diffused infrared device for years—the television remote control—that enables you to operate your TV from a distance without the use of wires. When you depress a button on the remote, a corresponding code modulates an infrared light signal that is transmitted to the TV. The TV receives the code and performs the applicable function. This is fairly simple, but infrared-based LANs are not much more complex. The main difference is that LANs utilize infrared light at slightly higher power levels and use communications protocols to transport data.

When using infrared light in a LAN, the ceiling can be a reflection point (see Figure 2.11). This technique uses carrier sense protocols to share access to the ceiling. Imagine, for example, that there is a room containing four people who can only communicate via flashlights. To send information, they can encode letters that spell words using a system such as Morse Code. If someone wants to send information, he first looks at the ceiling to see whether someone is currently transmitting (shining light off the ceiling). If a transmission is taking place, the person wanting to send the information waits until the other person stops sending the message. If no one is transmitting, the source person will point his flashlight to the ceiling and turn the light on and off, according to the code that represents the information being sent.

To alert the destination person of an incoming message, the sender transmits the proper sequence of code words that represent the destination person's name. All people in the room will be constantly looking at the ceiling, waiting for light signals containing their addresses. If a person sees his name, he will pay attention to the rest of the transmission. Through this method, each person can send and receive information.

Diffused infrared light LANs work similarly to the preceding analogy. The LANs, however, operate much faster. Typical data rates are 1 to 4 Mbps versus the 5 bps the average person can send using flashlights and Morse Code. Prices for these types of wireless adapters range from $200 to $500 each.

Troubleshooting Tip

Due to geometry, diffused infrared light stations are limited in separation distance, typically 30 to 50 feet. The lower the ceiling, the less range between stations. Ceiling heights of 10 feet will limit the range to around 40 feet. To extend the operating range, you can utilize infrared access points to connect cells together via a wired backbone.

Because they depend on ceilings and walls, diffused infrared LANs will not operate outdoors.

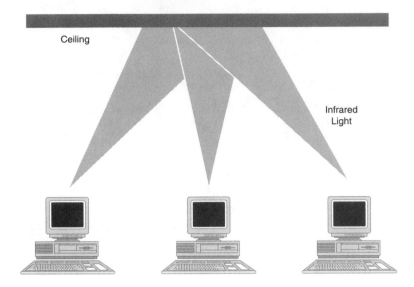

FIGURE 2.11   *A diffused infrared-based wireless LAN system uses the ceiling as a reflection point.*

Note

The Infrared Data Association (IrDA) is a group of more than 80 computer and telecommunications hardware and software firms including Hewlett-Packard, AMP, Apple Computer, AST, Compaq, Dell, IBM, Intel, Lexmark, Motorola, National Semiconductor, Northern Telecom, Novell, Photonics, and Sharp. IrDA has adopted a standard covering three levels of a network's architecture: Serial Infrared Physical Layer Link (IrDASIR), Ir Link Access Protocol (IrLAP), and Ir Link Management and Transport Protocols (IrLMP).

This standard specifies a 115.2 Kbps point-to-point infrared transmission between computers, laptops, printers, and fax machines. Other higher-speed standards of 1.15 Mbps and 4 Mbps that will be more suitable for backups and offline storage are currently being considered by IrDA. Chapter 5, "Physical (PHY) Layer," covers the IEEE 802.11 standard for infrared wireless LANs and goes into more detail about IrDA.

Point-to-Point Infrared LAN System

Currently only one vendor, InfraLAN Technology, Inc., produces a product, InfraLAN, that implements a point-to-point LAN system. InfraLAN consists of a pair of transducers, one for transmitting and one for receiving, that you configure, as shown in Figure 2.12. InfraLAN replaces the cable in the token–ring network with infrared light that can reach distances of up to 75 feet.

At each station, the InfraLAN interfaces with an IEEE 802.5 (token ring) interface board. Token-ring protocols ensure that only one station transmits at a time through the use of a token. The token, which is a distinctive group of bits, circulates the ring. If a station wishes to transmit data, it must first wait its turn to receive the token, and then transmit its data. The capturing of the token ensures that no other station will transmit. The data circulates the ring and the appropriate destination will sense its address and process the data. Once finished, the sending station will forward the token to the next station downline.

Point-to-Point Infrared LAN System

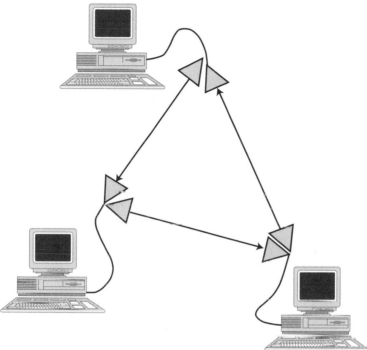

FIGURE 2.12 *A point-to-point infrared LAN system uses a directed light beam to connect token-ring–based computers.*

The advantages of using InfraLAN are the performance and security it offers. Because of the focused infrared beam, the system can match performance requirements of either 4 or 16 Mbps token-ring protocols. InfraLAN is the only wireless LAN system on the market today that can support that type of performance.

Tip

InfraLAN is immune to electrical noise and is difficult to tap. Electrical signals do not interfere with the extremely high frequencies of infrared light, and an information thief would have to place himself within the path of the beam to receive the signal.

continues

The disadvantage with this approach, however, is that it does not accommodate mobility. It might be suitable, however, in such environments as conference rooms or factories, where electrical noise would interfere with radio signals..

Also, be sure to mount the InfraLAN devices to preclude blockage of the light beams. Someone setting a plant on a desk or a forklift raising its cargo in line with the path the light travels could disrupt transmission.

Carrier Current LANs

A quasi-wireless LAN technique, called *carrier current*, is the use of power lines as a medium for the transport of data. This technique is very similar to using an analog modem to communicate over telephone wires.

Note

Although a carrier current LAN is not really wireless, it is worth mentioning because it does not require the installation of network cabling. In the next year or so, you should begin seeing products that implement this approach.

Designers of the telephone system did not plan to accommodate computer communications, but people use modems every day to communicate their data. The telephone system is capable of supporting analog signals with the range of 0 to 4 KHz. Telephone modems convert the computer's digital waveform to an analog signal within this range and transmit to the computer you choose. The modem at the distant end receives the "telephone signal" and converts the data back into a digital signal that is understood by the computer.

Power-line circuits within your home and office provide enough bandwidth to support 1 to 2 Mbps data signals. Utility companies and others designed these circuits to carry 60 Hz alternating current, typically at voltages of 110 volts. It is possible, then, to have a *power-line* modem that interfaces a computer to the power circuitry (see Figure 2.13). The interface acts much like a telephone modem and converts the digital data within your computer to an analog signal for transmission through the electrical wires.

The 110-volt alternating current in the circuit does not affect the signal (or vice versa) because the signals are at different frequencies. The interface has filters that will prevent the lower 60 Hz frequency from being received.

Note

Several vendors have had home-automation products on the market for decades that utilize carrier current signals. Radio Shack, for example, sells a master console that enables you to control various types of devices, such as coffee pots, lamps, heating systems, and so on, via carrier currents sent through the electrical power lines in the home. The master console and the appliances interface to the system via inexpensive modules that plug into a wall outlet and communicate to the master console.

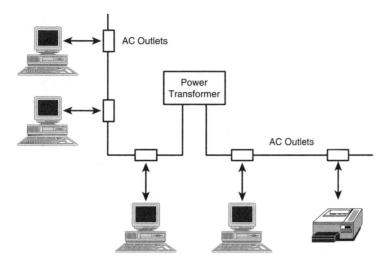

FIGURE 2.13 *A carrier current LAN system provides network connectivity via the electrical wires.*

The advantages of this technique are ease of installation and low-cost products. A disadvantage of the power-line approach is that the presence of electrical transformers, designed to electrically couple signals at 60 Hz, will block higher-frequency data signals. Most homes and smaller facilities will not have this problem because usually only one side of the transformer is available; however, larger buildings, especially industrial centers, will have multiple electrical wire legs connected by transformers. The presence of transformers, therefore, will limit connectivity among sites.

Wireless Point-to-Point Networks

Do you need to network sites within the same metropolitan area? Organizations often have requirements for communications between facilities in a semi-local area, such as a city block or metropolitan area. A hospital, for example, might consist of several buildings within the same general area, separated by streets and rivers. A utility company also might have multiple service centers and office buildings within a metropolitan area.

Traditionally, companies utilize physical media—such as buried metallic wire or optical fiber, or leased 56 Kbps or T1 circuits—to provide necessary connections. These forms of media, however, might require a great deal of installation time and can result in expensive monthly service fees. A cable installation between sites several thousand feet apart can cost thousands of dollars or more, and leasing fees can easily be hundreds of dollars per month. In some cases, leased communications lines might not even be available.

This section explains the applications of wireless point-to-point networks and covers applicable radio and laser-based technologies and products.

Point-to-point wireless networks use technologies very similar to wireless LANs; therefore, this section concentrates on technological aspects differing from wireless LANs.

Wireless Point-to-Point Network Applications

Before getting into the technologies and products, you should understand what drives the need for wireless point-to-point network connectivity. These networks provide communications links between buildings, avoiding the costly installation of cabling or leasing fees and the down-time associated with system failures. The city of Macon, Georgia, for example, uses Cylink's wireless products to provide links for traffic control at 10 consecutive intersections over a four-mile stretch of state highway. This system avoids the installation of wiring along the roadway. Other organizations, such as hospitals and government centers, use wireless point-to-point network components to avoid digging trenches and routing cabling around rivers and roads.

**Case Study 2.2:
Cost Savings with a Wireless
Point-to-Point Network**

A wireless point-to-point network results in tangible cost savings rather quickly. A manufacturer in Texas, for example, installed this type of system between its existing plant and a new plant under construction about 12 miles away. The alternative was to install and lease a digital line between the facilities. The company recovered all the installation costs in less than two years and is now gaining positive returns on its investment. Many other companies are also realizing these types of benefits.

Another application of wireless point-to-point network components is to facilitate a backup in case a primary leased line becomes inoperative. An organization can store the wireless equipment at a strategic location, such as the computing center, to have on hand if a primary link goes down. If a primary link fails, an organization can quickly deploy a wireless link to restore operations.

A wireless point-to-point network, as illustrated in Figure 2.14, utilizes either radio waves or infrared light as a transport for the transmission of data up to 30 miles. These systems work in a point-to-point configuration, much like that of leased lines. Wireless point-to-point systems interface easily and match the data rates of existing LANs. The cost of connecting two sites in a wireless point-to-point network ranges from $1,500 to $20,000, depending on data rate and type of transport. The following sections explain each of these techniques.

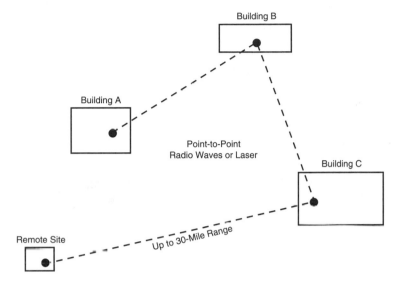

FIGURE 2.14   *A wireless point-to-point network is a flexible way of connecting buildings spread throughout a city.*

Radio-Based Wireless Point-to-Point Networks

A radio-based wireless point-to-point network is currently the most common method for providing connectivity within a metropolitan area. These products have highly directional antennas to focus the signal power in a narrow beam, maximizing the transmission distance. As a result, spread spectrum products operating under one watt of power can reach single hop transmission distances of 30 miles. The actual transmission distance of a particular product, however, depends on environmental conditions and terrain. Rain, for example, causes resistance to the propagation of radio signals, decreasing the effective range. A mountainous area will also hamper the transmission range of the signals.

Radio-based, wireless point-to-point network data rates are 4–5 Mbps for the shorter range products operating over two–three-mile links. Applicable products operate over a 30-mile link; however, they will transmit at much lower data rates to obtain the longer range. In addition, these products use either spread spectrum or narrowband modulation.

Radio-Based, Wireless Point-to-Point Network Components

As shown in Figure 2.15, radio-based, wireless point-to-point networks consist of transceivers that modulate the data being sent across the link with a carrier that will propagate the signal to the opposite site. As with wireless LANs, the modulation transposes the computer's digital data into a form suitable for transmission through the air. Radio-based, wireless point-to-point network products often include an interface to ethernet or token-ring networks, as well as bridging or routing functionality.

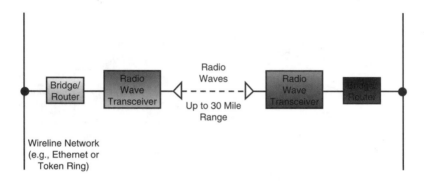

FIGURE 2.15 *Radio-based, wireless point-to-point networks connect ethernet or token-ring networks separated by up to 30 miles.*

Wireless point-to-point network bridges, also called *wireless remote network bridges*, segment data traffic by filtering each packet according to its final destination address. This form of segmentation blocks packets from crossing the wireless link unless they need to reach a destination on the opposite side. As with local bridges, this makes better use of bandwidth and increases network performance.

The router versions of these products work very much like traditional routers that are dependent on physical media: They forward packets based on the final destination address. This makes it possible to create a more intelligent network having alternative routes. In fact, a collection of these components would constitute the functionality of a WAN limited to a large metropolitan area. The greatest difference, however, is that the wireless point-to-point network will not support mobile users—it provides only wireless connections between fixed sites.

Spread Spectrum Wireless Point-to-Point Networks

As with wireless LANs, wireless point-to-point networks using spread spectrum in the ISM bands do not require user licensing with the FCC. The advantage of not dealing with licenses is easy and rapid installation. The installation time of spread spectrum products can take a few hours, for instance, saving the two-month wait-time for obtaining FCC licensing.

Spread spectrum resists interference from traditional narrowband radio systems, enabling systems using both modulation techniques to coexist in the same space. The only signals likely to cause serious interference originate from other spread spectrum devices. The disadvantage, then, is the possible interference with others operating similar wireless point–to–point networks nearby. With wireless LANs, interference is normally not a problem because the radio waves are kept indoors, within the confines and management of the organization.

Radio waves traveling between buildings, perhaps across a large city, will be beyond the organization's jurisdiction and control, possibly receiving interference from other unknown systems. The owning organizations of the wireless point–to–point network equipment, therefore, will probably not be able to do anything about the interference.

Internet Access for Every School!*

The White House has issued this mandate, but implementing Internet access for all students remains an economic challenge for most school districts. The Union Endicott school district (Endicott, New York) met this challenge, brought the Internet to every building, and found a way to save the district money.

The Union Endicott school district obtained a grant from the State of New York to implement an Internet project. The project was initiated by Bert Lawrence, Coordinator of Computer and Library Services, and Gary Burns, Data Processing Manager for the school district. The Union Endicott school district had a 56 Kbps WAN operating among 10 buildings using leased lines. This network did not have the capacity needed to rapidly transmit the growing amount of administrative applications at the remote sites. For this reason alone, Union Endicott needed to implement a higher capacity WAN. And with the data requirements for the Internet, a faster network was definitely needed. The main issue was to get higher capacity without breaking the budget.

The solution was to utilize the Aironet BR2000-E Wireless Bridge. The bridge operates using direct sequence spread spectrum radio in the 24 GHz band. An Aironet bridge pair equipped with high-gain directional antennas can create a 2 Mbps wireless link between ethernet networks in buildings up to 12 miles apart and a 1 Mbps link with buildings up to 25 miles apart. With Aironet Wireless Bridges, all the networks in all the buildings can be connected, sharing one high-speed link to the Internet without using cables or dedicated lines.

Anixter, an Aironet reseller, arranged a field demonstration between two of the schools in the district. Lawrence and Burns were attracted to the possibility of eliminating their leased telephone line expenses by utilizing wireless bridging, but were still skeptical. The demonstration was successful and proved that a wireless link could reliably transmit data at a much greater rate than the current

continues

continued

leased lines. Union Endicott decided to pursue a wireless WAN and procurement was done through the state's Board of Cooperative Education Services equipment purchasing advisory group.

A total of 11 Aironet BR2000-E Wireless Bridges were installed in seven buildings in the district. The leased 56 Kbps lines remained in two building because line-of-sight could not be established. Two other schools were within 800 feet of each other, and they were connected using fiber-optic cable.

The WAN includes six elementary schools, the administration building, a high school, a middle school, and a bus garage. The Internet access is provided directly by Board of Cooperative Education on a fiber-optic link at a T1 data rate to the high school, which functions as a hub. Four remote sites are bridged directly from the high school, while the middle school bridges to two other remote sites. Bridged distances range between 0.33 and 1.2 miles with radio propagation at all sites provided by Yagi directional antennas.

The conversion to Aironet Wireless Bridges will save $25,000 per year in leased line telephone expenses, even with the new Internet access costs added in. In addition, the bridges provide data throughput up to 20 times faster than the prior systems. Because the costs of the bridges were covered by a grant, the project saved money from the start. Similar grants are available in other states and typically cover hardware, like wireless bridges, but not services like phone lines.

This is reprinted with permission from Aironet, Inc.

Narrowband Wireless Point-To-Point Network

The FCC and comparable regulatory agencies in other countries regulate the use of narrowband frequencies. This regulation offers both an advantage and disadvantage. The governmental communications regulatory agency licenses each user site to operate on an assigned frequency, often a 25 KHz slice of bandwidth, which gives the user specific rights for operating on the assigned frequency at a specific location. If interference occurs, for example, the FCC will intervene and issue an order for the interfering source to cease operations. This is especially advantageous when operating wireless point-to-point networks in areas having a great deal of operating radio-based systems.

The disadvantage is that the licensing process can take two or three months to complete. You must complete an application, usually with the help of a frequency consultant, and submit it to the FCC for approval. Therefore, you can't be in a hurry to establish the wireless links. And, you will probably have to coordinate with the FCC when making changes to the wireless point-to-point network topology.

Multipoint Networks sells one of the very few wireless point-to-point network products that operates on narrowband frequencies. Multipoint produces both point-to-point and point-to-multipoint narrowband wireless systems. All Multi-point products operate within the 400–512 MHz and 820–960 MHz frequencies and have a range of 30 miles or more. The point-to-point product, called radio area network (RAN), operates in full-duplex mode ranging in data rates from 9.6 to 125 Kbps. The main applications of RAN are for the replacement of leased lines and wireline modems within metropolitan areas.

Multipoint's transparent point-to-multipoint product, waveNET 2500, is an intelligent hub that supports X.25 connectivity to remote locations. In a point-of-sale or automatic teller machine (ATM) application, you can use Multipoint's LaunchPAD to interface the POS terminal to the waveNET 1000. waveNET's Radio Access Protocol (RAP) manages the data traffic between LaunchPADs and the hub.

Laser-Based Wireless Point-to-Point Networks

Another class of wireless point-to-point networks utilizes laser light as a carrier for data transmission. A laser, which is now a common term for Light Amplification by Stimulated Emission of Radiation, contains a substance in which applied electricity causes the majority of its atoms or molecules to be in an excited energy state. As a result, the laser emits coherent light at a precise wavelength in a narrow beam. Most laser point-to-point networks utilize lasers that produce infrared light.

As with other wireless techniques, a laser modem in this type of system modulates the data with a light signal to produce a light beam capable of transmitting data. With light, these data rates can be extremely high. Most laser links can easily handle ethernet (10 Mbps), 4/16 Mbps token ring, and higher data rates. Figure 2.16 illustrates a laser point-to-point network.

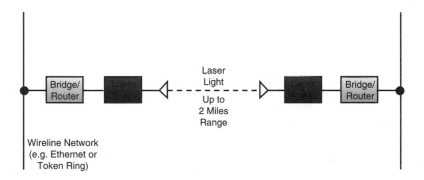

FIGURE 2.16 *A laser-based wireless point-to-point network provides very secure connections between ethernet or token-ring networks separated by up to two miles.*

To maintain safe operation, laser links typically range less than a mile. These devices comply with the Center for Devices and Radiological Health standards and most operate at Class III, which can cause eye damage under some circumstances. Much longer distances are possible, but you would have to increase the power to a level that would damage buildings and injure living things.

Weather is also an influence on the transmission distance of laser systems. A nice, clear day with very little smog will support the one-mile operating distance. Snow, rain, fog, smog, and dust, however, causes attenuation, which could limit the effective range to a half mile or less. A fairly heavy rain shower (3–4 inches per hour), for example, will introduce approximately 6 dB of attenuation per kilometer. As a result, you need to plan the link according to potential changes in the weather.

Why use laser-based point-to-point network technology over radio types? One reason is the need for high-speed data transmission. A laser point-to-point system is the only way to effectively sustain 10 Mbps and higher data rates, which may be necessary for supporting the transfer CAD (Computer Assisted Drawing) files and X-ray images. Also, you do not have to obtain FCC licensing. The FCC doesn't manage frequencies above 300 GHz; therefore, you can set up a laser system as quickly as you can set up a license-free spread spectrum radio system.

When using a laser, very few other systems can cause interference. Even at high microwave frequencies, radio signals are far from the spectral location of laser light, which eliminates the possibility of interference from these systems. Also, an interfering laser beam is unlikely because it would have to be pointed directly at your receiving site. Sure, someone might do this to purposely jam your system, but otherwise it won't occur.

Troubleshooting Tip

Sunlight consists of approximately 60 percent infrared light and can cause interference. The rising or setting sun might emit rays of light at an angle that the laser transducers can receive, causing interference in the early morning and late afternoon. Therefore, an organization should avoid placing laser links with an east-west orientation.

Generally, laser-based point-to-point networks are highly resistant to interference. Therefore, laser links might be the best solution in a city full of radio-based devices, especially for applications where you must minimize downtime. Be careful, however, to plan the installation of laser systems in cities with the assumption that someone may decide to erect a high-rise building directly in the laser's path.

To accommodate a line-of-sight path between source and destination, the best place to install the laser link is on top of a building or tower. This avoids objects blocking the beam, which can cause a disruption of operation. Birds are generally not a problem because they can see infrared light and will usually avoid the beam. A bird flying through the beam, however, will cause a momentary interruption. If this occurs, higher-level protocols, such as ethernet or token ring, will trigger a retransmission of the data. The infrared beam will not harm the bird.

Laser-based systems offer more privacy than radio links. Someone wanting to receive the laser data signal would have to physically place himself directly in the beam's path (see Figure 2.17). Also, the eavesdropper would have to capture the light to obtain the data, significantly attenuating or completely disrupting the signal at the true destination. This means that he would have to put himself next to the laser modem at either end of the link by standing on top of the building or climbing to the top of a tower. Physical security, such as fences and guards, can effectively eliminate this type of sabotage.

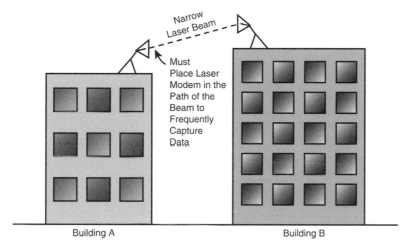

FIGURE 2.17 *It is very difficult to capture data in an unauthorized manner from a laser-based wireless point-to-point network.*

Wireless WANs

Do your professionals on the road need to have access to email and other computing resources at their home office? The traditional solution is to equip the person's portable computer with a wireline modem and access online services and other resources via the *plain old telephone system* (POTS). The user can interface his modem to the telephone line and dial in to the services and resources the user wishes to utilize. This solution works well, assuming the professional has access to a telephone line.

Most hotels and office facilities can accommodate a temporary POTS connection; however, other places do not. Many travelers spend a great deal of time in airports, for example, waiting for plane connections that are often delayed. Unfortunately, there is no place to plug your computer into the POTS at an airport. In addition, you don't typically find POTS connections at archaeological dig sites or environmental survey sites. Some hotels and office buildings also might not have a telephone line that you can use. For these situations, a wireless WAN might be the solution for effectively connecting people to the computing resources they need.

It is important to understand the various wireless WAN technologies and services before choosing a solution. This section describes the following technologies, services, and products that provide wireless WAN connectivity:

- Packet radio WANs
- Analog cellular WANs
- Cellular digital packet data WANs
- Satellite communications
- Meteor burst communications
- Combining location devices with wireless WANs

Packet Radio WANs

A packet radio WAN uses packet switching to move data from one location to another. In general, a user wanting to utilize packet radio networking purchases a radio modem for his portable computer and leases access to a packet-based wireless network from a service provider, such as ARDIS or BellSouth Mobile Data (formally RAM Mobile Data).

The main advantage of packet radio is its capability to economically and efficiently transfer short bursts of data that you might find in systems such as short messaging, dispatch, data entry, and remote monitoring. Packet radio systems do not yet have worldwide coverage, however; today, coverage is limited to large cities. In the next few years, this coverage should be near 100 percent.

Packet Radio Architecture

A packet radio network performs functions relating to the Physical, Data Link, and Network Layers of the OSI Reference Model. Therefore, this type of network provides a physical medium, synchronization, and error control on links residing between nodes or routers and also performs routing.

If more than one hop is necessary to transfer data packets from source to destination, the intermediate packet radio nodes relay the data packets closer to the destination, very much like a router does in a traditional wire-based WAN.

Packet Radio Components

To utilize a packet radio network, the user must equip his notebook or palmtop computer with a radio modem and applicable communications and application software, and lease a packet radio network service from one of several service providers (see Figure 2.18).

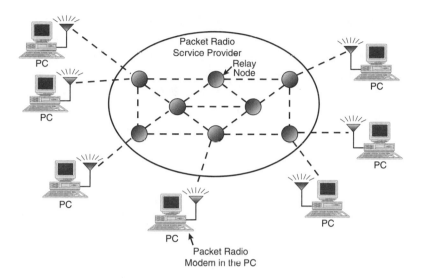

FIGURE 2.18 *A packet radio network consists of relay nodes having a topology that may change depending on atmospheric conditions.*

Packet Radio Modems

A radio modem provides an interface between end-user devices and radio relays, using air as the medium. These modems can transmit and receive radio waves at user throughput rates up to 20 Kbps. They usually do not require licensing, making it easy to move them from one location to another. Most radio modems transmit omnidirectional radiation patterns.

As long as connectivity exists, a pair of radio modems establishes a channel for data transmission between sites. The main condition for proper connectivity is that the destination must be able to correctly receive data from the source at a specified minimum data rate. If the reception of data on a particular channel results in a number of bit errors exceeding the maximum error rate for that link, for example, connectivity is lost.

Note

Due to node separation, transmit power, and irregular terrain, most packet radio networks cannot maintain full connectivity. That is, not every user access device and radio relay node have connectivity with each other.

Node separation affects the connectivity of a radio network because the power of a radio signal decreases exponentially as the distance between the nodes increases. If the distance becomes too great, the signal-to-noise ratio decreases and produces too many transmission errors, causing the two stations to become disconnected.

The transmit power of the source node affects link connectivity because higher transmit powers will keep the signal-to-noise ratio higher, resulting in fewer errors and connectivity. Certain types of terrain, such as mountains and buildings, can affect connectivity because they will attenuate and sometimes completely block radio waves. The attenuation will decrease the signal power, resulting in shorter transmission distances. A packet radio network, therefore, must perform routing to move data packets from the source user device, through a number of intermediate radio relays, and to the destination user device or network.

Tip

Several companies, such as IBM, sell radio modems that will interface with packet radio network services provided by various companies. These modems are specific to the service provider, such as BellSouth Mobile Data or ARDIS, and use different frequencies.

Relay Nodes

The radio relay nodes, which implement a routing protocol that maintains the optimum routes for the routing tables, forward packets closer to the destination. The routing table contains an entry for each possible destination relay node. A relay node uses a routing table to address the packet to the next node that is closer to the destination:

Destination Address	Next Hop (Relay Node)
Node 1	Node 2
Node 2	Node 4
Node 3	Node 4
Node 4	Node 6
Node 5	Node 3
Node 6	Node 5

Packet Radio Operation

To carry packets from source to destination, a packet radio network must do the following:

1. Transmit data packets
2. Update routing tables at the relay nodes

Transmitting Data Packets

When the application software at a user's appliance requests the transfer of data through the network, communications software prepares the data for transmission by wrapping it with a header that primarily contains the destination address and some trailer bits that represent a checksum. The relay nodes will use the address to determine whether to forward the packet to the next relay node or send it to the final destination. A receiving node will utilize the checksum to detect whether the packet encountered any transmission errors. If errors are not present, the receiver will send back an acknowledgment; otherwise, the source will retransmit the packet.

Each station, whether it is the user's access device or a relay node, uses a carrier sense protocol to access the shared air and radio medium. Ethernet and radio-based wireless LANs operate in a very similar pattern. The primary difference is that a packet radio network operates in a partially connected rather than fully-connected topology (see Figure 2.19). The propagation boundary of a particular node defines that node's operating range. Nodes A and C, for example, can communicate direct-ly with each other.

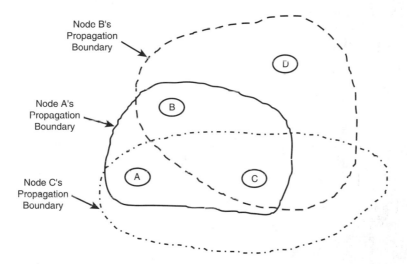

Node B's
Propagation
Boundary

Node A's
Propagation
Boundary

Node C's
Propagation
Boundary

FIGURE 2.19 *The topology of a packet radio network is usually partially connected, which imposes requirements for Network Layer routing functions.*

A packet radio station wanting to send a data packet must first listen to determine whether another station is transmitting. If no other transmission is heard, the sending station will transmit the packet in a broadcast mode using its omnidirectional anten-na. With most packet radio networks, the first station to receive the packet will be the neighboring relay node. This relay will look in its routing table to determine which node to send the packet to next, based on the final destination address. If the destination is located within range, the relay node will broadcast the packet again and the destination will receive it. If the final destination is not close by, the relay node will obtain the address and broadcast the packet to the next relay node closer to the destination. This process will continue until the packet reaches the destination.

Updating Routing Tables

As with wireline WANs, a packet radio topology may change over time. Relay nodes might become inoperative, new relay nodes might appear, and atmospheric conditions, such as rain and sunspots, might affect radio connectivity between stations. These connectivity changes can alter the topology; therefore, the efficient operation of a packet radio network depends on an effective routing protocol capable of updating the routing tables at each relay node.

There are several approaches to updating routing tables; however, the distributed protocol is most common with the Internet and packet radio networks. Wireline WANs utilize routing protocols, such as Routing Information Protocol (RIP) and Open Shortest Path First (OSPF). These protocols enable each router within the network to gain a complete picture of the network's topology. Packet radio routing protocols have the same goal.

More specifically, distributed routing protocols make it possible for each relay node to determine the next path to send a packet by operating as follows: Each relay node periodically sends a status packet that announces its presence to all neighboring relay nodes within range. Each node, then, periodically learns the presence of its immediate neighbors. A router can use this information to update its routing table. When a relay node sends its status message, it also sends a copy of its routing table.

Each relay node also sets timers for each neighbor, and if the relay node does not receive a status message within a certain time period, the relay node will delete the neighbor from the routing table. Other relay nodes will hear of the deletion via the periodic status messages. Through this process, each relay node will eventually obtain a complete picture of the network in terms of connectivity.

Packet Radio Service Providers

Several packet radio service providers have constructed networks that implement the radio relay nodes. The process of establishing packet radio networking is to lease the service from one of several packet radio access providers. This service is very economical, costing pennies to send small email messages. These companies usually supply the software for no charge; however, users must purchase a radio modem.

The following sections provide an overview of several packet radio network providers.

ARDIS

ARDIS is a company that leases access to its wireless WAN, which is based on packet radio technology. The ARDIS network covers 410 top metropolitan areas in the United States, Puerto Rico, and the U.S. Virgin Islands. This encompasses more than 80 percent of the population and 90 percent of the business areas. ARDIS uses two different protocols—MDC4800 at a data speed of 4,800 bps, and Radio Data-Link Access Protocol (RDLAP) at a speed of 19,200 bps. ARDIS was originally developed for IBM service technicians who worked indoors. As a result, ARDIS was designed to have good in-building coverage.

In addition to basic wireless WAN connectivity, ARDIS offers the following wireless WAN applications that enable you to communicate with other ARDIS and Internet users, as well as implement some specific applications:

- *ARDIS PersonalMessaging:* Enables users to send and receive messages to ARDIS and Internet users.

- *ServiceExpress:* A wireless communications solution that makes it easier for field service organizations to incorporate wireless communications. ServiceExpress provides field service engineers with access to corporate information systems using handheld computers.

  ARDIS offers this service with a low monthly payment per field engineer. The payment covers the cost of all hardware, ARDIS air time, training, equipment repair, maintenance, and a 24-hour help desk. In most cases, ServiceExpress will work with a company's existing field service management software.

- *TransportationExpress*: Combines all the components of a wireless dispatch solution including dispatch hardware and software, ARDIS wireless air time, handheld wireless computers for pickup and delivery drivers, project management, installation, training, and a 24-hour help desk.

BellSouth Mobile Data

BellSouth Mobile Data is another alternative for wireless WAN connectivity. BellSouth covers the top 266 United States metropolitan areas, airports, and major transportation corridors. This includes more than 92 percent of the urban business population. BellSouth is committed to providing 100 percent coverage through BellSouth's Strategic Network initiative. For example, a BellSouth user will be able to maintain connectivity through the use of circuit-switched cellular and satellite when traveling beyond BellSouth's wireless WAN coverage area. To provide the Strategic Network, BellSouth has linked up with satellite service providers and telecommunications carriers to ensure a complete and seamless solution.

BellSouth Mobile Data utilizes *Mobitex* technology, which is an established and proven packet radio system for the transmission of data. Mobitex infrastructure was originally developed by L.M. Ericsson in 1983 in cooperation with Sweden's Postal Telegraph and Telephone national communications authority. Mobitex today is seen as a de facto standard for packet-based wireless WANs. The Mobitex Operators Association (MOA) now manages Mobitex standards. There are currently 17 other wireless WANs throughout the world that use Mobitex technology, with more planned for 14 other countries.

BellSouth Mobile owns and operates its network and has licensed frequencies from the FCC with the 896 through 901 MHz and 935 through 940 MHz bands. BellSouth parcels these frequencies to give each metropolitan area up to 30 channels. Each channel supports a data transmission speed of 8 Kbps. BellSouth provides wireless connectivity to mobile users within specific service areas, and then uses a regional switch to tie the service areas together. Users of the system do not have to obtain FCC licenses.

The BellSouth Mobile Data network provides nationwide, transparent and seamless roaming. Subscribers do not have to manually intervene when moving from one service area to another. Each service area uses a different frequency, and the BellSouth Mobile modem automatically locates the best available channel and local switch. In addition, BellSouth Mobile does not charge fees for roaming.

BellSouth Mobile offers an email service for sending and receiving messages with other BellSouth Mobile and Internet users. The service also enables you to utilize many other email products. In fact, over 80 percent of all email products have been BellSouth Mobile–enabled, meaning they will interface with the BellSouth Mobile wireless network. Lotus cc:Mail, Microsoft Mail Remote for Windows, and Novell Groupwise, for example, support the BellSouth Mobile network.

Analog Cellular WANs

The analog cellular telephone system has made it possible for millions of people to make phone calls using portable cellular phones while away from the home or office. Many who start using cell phones can't imagine life without them. The general idea of an analog cellular WAN is to make use of the cell phone's mobility and employ it as a means of transferring data, much like the use of traditional wire-based plain old telephone system (POTS). You can use the analog cellular phone system to dial in to your corporate network to access applications and send email, just like you can when using POTS.

If you need to send large files, such as engineering drawings, this cellular phone approach might be the way to go. It effectively provides data rates up to 14.4 Kbps, which is similar to conventional POTS telephone modems. The idea of this technology is to connect your computer to a cellular telephone via a modem and then with a remote system through a dial-up connection. This provides a relatively easy way to obtain wireless data transfer wherever cellular telephone service exists, which covers most of the world.

Note

The cellular approach does have some drawbacks. For one, the usage costs are relatively high. The cost of sending data is based on the length of the call and the distance to the destination. You also pay more as you roam from one location to another. Roaming within three different regions in one day, for example, can cost approximately $10, not counting the standard air time.

Another problem is the occasional transmission errors you receive that will cause retransmissions to occur. The cellular telephone system was built primarily to transmit voice, which can generally stand more transmission errors than data.

Analog Cellular Technology

The analog cellular telephone system uses FM (Frequency Modulation) radio waves to transmit voice grade signals. To accommodate mobility, this cellular system switches your radio connection from one cell to another as you move between areas. Every cell within the network has a transmission tower that links mobile callers to a mobile telephone switching office (MTSO). The MTSO, which is owned and operated by the cellular carrier in your area, provides a connection to the public switched telephone network. Each cell covers several miles. Figure 2.20 illustrates the general topology of the cellular telephone system.

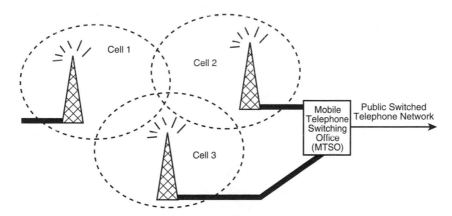

FIGURE 2.20 *The general topology of a circuit-switched cellular telephone system includes multiple cells.*

Most modems that operate over wireline telephone services will also interface and interoperate with cellular phones; however, modem software optimized to work with cellular phones minimizes battery usage. MobileWare, for example, is software that enables you to communicate over cellular or regular wireline phones. MobileWare minimizes the cost of cellular service usage by making a connection only during actual information transmissions. MobileWare prepares the information for transmission and then transmits whenever possible. Thus, you can prepare correspondence such as email messages and faxes while on an airplane, and then MobileWare will send the information after you land. MobileWare also "mobilizes" the Lotus cc:Mail, meaning it enables you to effectively utilize cc:Mail on a wireless connection.

Note

A major problem is that there is no standard connector to interface your portable computer's serial interface to a cellular phone. Therefore, be sure you can find a cable to connect between the modem and the phone.

Cellular Digital Packet Data (CDPD) WANs

To establish a dedicated wireless data network for mobile users, a consortium of companies in the United States developed the Cellular Digital Packet Data (CDPD) standard. CDPD overlays the conventional analog cellular telephone system, using a channel-hopping technique to transmit data in short bursts during idle times in cellular channels. CDPD operates full duplex, meaning simultaneous transmission in both directions, in the 800 and 900 MHz frequency bands, offering data rates up to 19.2 Kbps.

What is the advantage of using CDPD versus analog cellular systems? Recall that the main advantage of the analog cellular system is widespread coverage. Because CDPD piggybacks on this system, it will also provide nearly worldwide coverage. The main plus with CDPD, however, is that it uses digital signals, making it possible to enhance the transmission of data. With digital signaling, it is possible to encrypt the data stream and provide easier error control.

CDPD is a robust protocol that is connectionless and utilizes Reed-Salomon forward error correction (FEC). FEC is an error control technique that corrects errors at the receiver without asking the source to retransmit the errored packet. Security with CDPD, which is accomplished using an encrypted key-passing technique, is very good. Also with CDPD, you pay only for the amount of data actually sent, which is less than the amount you would spend on an analog cellular call if sending the same data.

CDPD is available today in large cities within the United States only, but it is spreading to other areas as well. However, many visualize CDPD as an interim solution until digital cellular telephone service becomes available.

CDPD Design Goals and Objectives

The Wireless Data Forum (formally CDPD Forum) is an industry association with over 90 companies interested in developing and promoting CDPD products and services. The Forum's main mission is to develop a technical standard for CDPD, as well as to develop the marketplace and promote the technology.

As part of the development of the CDPD System Specification, the companies agreed on the following design objectives:

- Maintain compatibility with existing data networks, technology, and applications
- Support a wide range of present and future data network services and facilities
- Provide maximal use of existing data network technologies and minimize the impact on existing end-user appliances
- Allow a phased deployment strategy in terms of basic connectivity, security and accounting, network management, and application services
- Provide services that relate to mobile and portable situations
- Support equipment from multiple vendors
- Provide seamless service to all subscribers
- Protect the subscriber's identity
- Protect the subscriber's data from eavesdropping
- Protect the CDPD network against fraudulent use
- Support conservative use of the airlink interface
- Support use of a wide variety of mobile situations

The CDPD Airlink Interface specification defines all procedures and protocols necessary to allow effective use of existing analog cellular channels for data communications. The initial CDPD System Specification was published in July 1993. Release 1.1 provided some updates and was published in January 1995.

CDPD Architecture

Figure 2.21 illustrates the architecture of the CDPD system. The Mobile Data Base Station (MDBS) defines a radio cell that interfaces the Mobile End System (M-ES), such as a portable computer with a CDPD modem, with the Mobile Data Intermediate System (MD-IS). The MD-ISs provide mobility management services for the CDPD network. The MDBS acts as a bridge between the wireless protocols of the M-ES and the landline protocols of the MD-IS. Therefore, the MDBS decodes the data received from mobile devices, reconstructs the data frames, and transfers them to the MD-IS.

At most cellular telephone base sites, digital communications lines tie the MD-ISs back to the cellular telephone system's MTSO. The CDPD architecture includes mobility management and internetworking between separate CDPD network providers, resulting in seamless operations as you move between different cells and providers.

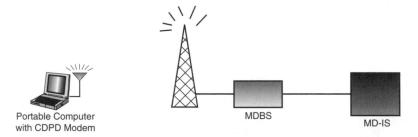

Portable Computer
with CDPD Modem

MDBS

MD-IS

FIGURE 2.21   *The components of the CDPD system are an addition to existing analog cellular infrastructures.*

An M-ES wanting to send data uses the Digital Sense Multiple Access (DSMA) protocol to share radio channels with other M-ESs. This protocol is similar to the common ethernet protocol used in LANs. DSMA, however, has both a forward and reverse channel that supports full-duplex operation. MDBSs transmit on the forward band, and M-ESs transmit on the reverse band.

The forward channel includes transmission of Busy/Idle and Decode Status channel indicators. If an MDBS detects a transmission on the reverse band (coming from a mobile device), it transmits a signal with the Busy/Idle channel status indicator set. An M-ES wishing to send data will first check for this transmission and indicator before transmitting. The M-ES will not transmit until the indicator is set to Idle. The MDBS sends a Decode Status indicator to indicate whether it successfully decoded the received data transmission. If the M-ES does not receive a positive acknowledgment, it will attempt to retransmit the data.

To utilize CDPD, you will need to lease the service through your local provider and purchase a CDPD modem. An example of a CDPD modem is IBM's Cellular Modem, which is housed in two packages: a PCMCIA Type II card and an external transceiver that you connect to the card via a cable. IBM also offers the modem in a tray-mounted version that installs inside the IBM ThinkPad's floppy disk drive. The cellular modem supports three modes of operation: analog voice, analog data, and CDPD.

Satellite Communications

Most wireless WAN services, such as analog cellular, packet radio, CDPD, and paging networks, have fairly good coverage, but offer relatively low data rates. If you are looking for high-speed transmission with complete worldwide coverage for your portable users, satellite communications might be a good alternative.

The main issues with satellite systems are high costs and limited support for mobile users. The monthly service costs are relatively low, but initial equipment costs are very high. The portability aspect of satellite, mainly because of the antenna sizes and point-to-point uplink, requires users to set up the antenna dish and align it with the satellite before sending data.

Satellite systems today support transmission of video, voice, and data for a variety of companies that require global coverage. Figure 2.22 shows the components that make this possible. The satellite is a platform that hosts a series of transponders acting as signal repeaters. The transponders receive directed signals on the uplink from Earth stations and broadcast the signals back to Earth on a downlink frequency where users over a very wide area are able to receive the signal.

A satellite in geostationary orbit has a 24-hour period at an altitude of 22,300 miles over the equator. This type of orbit means the satellite takes one full day to orbit the Earth, which makes the satellite appear to look stationary from the Earth's surface. This enables the Earth station antennas to remain fixed, not having to track the satellite.

Note

Newer, lower Earth-orbiting satellite systems, such as Iridium and Globalstar, offer 2,400 to 9,600 bps data throughput from handheld terminals. Future broadband satellite systems will deliver much higher data rates.

The geostationary orbit puts the satellite directly over the Earth's equator; therefore, Earth stations in the Northern Hemisphere point their antennas toward the southern horizon, and stations near the equator, such as Bogota, Colombia, point their antennas straight up into the sky. Some satellite systems, however, work at lower altitudes to lessen the amount of propagation delay. These lower-altitude satellites are not geostationary and will appear to move across the sky, requiring Earth stations to have tracking antennas.

To utilize a satellite system, you need a satellite station that consists of an antenna, satellite transceiver, and an interface to your computer. Several companies sell these components. California Microwave, for example, has a product called LYNXX Transportable Inmarsat-B Earth Station, providing 64 Kbps throughput for voice, video, fax, and data transmissions. LYNXX can serve as a global wide area gateway into the Internet, as well as corporate networks. The system has a 50-foot interface cable, enabling you to mount the antenna outside and operate the computer from within a building.

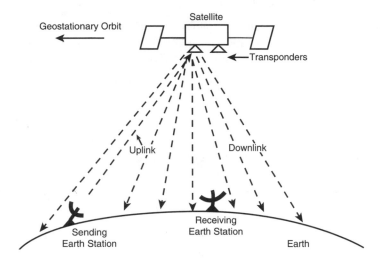

FIGURE 2.22   *A satellite system consisting of a single satellite and applicable Earth stations provides network connectivity over a large area of the Earth's surface area.*

Meteor Burst Communications

Occasionally at night, you can see the burning trail of a meteor as it enters the Earth's atmosphere. Actually, billions of tiny microscopic meteors enter the atmosphere every day. As these meteors penetrate the ionosphere, they leave a trail of ionized gas. Meteor burst communications directs a radio wave, modulated with a data signal, at this ionized gas (see Figure 2.23). The radio signal reflects off the gas and is directed back to Earth in the form of a footprint that covers a large area of the Earth's surface, enabling long-distance operation.

A meteor burst communications system is advantageous because it can reach into remote areas where there is no packet radio or cellular network coverage. In addition, the implementation of a meteor burst system will generally cost less than leasing satellite service. These benefits make meteor burst systems well suited for remote telemetry, water management, environmental monitoring, pipeline regulation, and oceanographic observation.

To use a meteor burst system, you must purchase and implement the equipment yourself. Meteor Communications Corporation (MCC) sells the MCC-520B

Meteor Burst Master Station and the MCC-550C Remote Data Terminal that support data rates up to 8 Kbps over a range of 1,000 miles. These devices operate in the 40 to 50 MHz frequency range.

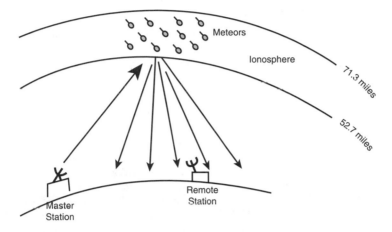

FIGURE 2.23 *A meteor burst communications system works similar to a satellite system, except the meteors reflect the radio signal rather than the satellite.*

The master station is the main component in a meteor burst communications system. It controls the routing of messages and data from hundreds of remote data terminals throughout the system. A remote data terminal collects data from analog and digital sensor inputs and is designed for unattended and automatic operation. When the remote data terminals receive a beam from a master station, they can send data containing information obtained from their sensors. Because of low power consumption, the remote data terminals can operate unattended for a year or more.

Combining Location Devices with Wireless WANs

Location devices identify your position on the Earth's surface in terms of latitude and longitude. Traditionally, products that provide this type of information have been relatively expensive; therefore, they have mainly been used for providing navigation information to aircraft and ships. In the last few years, however, the size and cost of location devices have shrunk dramatically.

Location devices are based on Global Positioning System (GPS) technology—a worldwide, satellite-based radio navigation system providing three-dimensional position, velocity, and time information to users having GPS receivers anywhere on or near the surface of the Earth. Today, you can purchase a handheld position indicator for a couple hundred dollars. With this device and a good map, you are unlikely to get lost. GPS devices tell you your position on Earth within a few meters.

Additionally, many products, such as mapping software, are starting to incorporate GPS technology.

The Global Positioning System (GPS)

The Global Positioning System was developed by the U.S. Department of Defense and provides two levels of service: a Standard Positioning Service (SPS) and a Precise Positioning Service (PPS). SPS is a positioning and timing service available to all GPS users as a continuous, worldwide service with no direct charge. SPS provides the capability to obtain horizontal positioning accuracy within 100 meters and vertical positioning accuracy within 140 meters. The PPS is a highly accurate service used by the military to obtain positioning, velocity, and timing information.

The GPS satellites operate on two L-band frequencies: L1 (1575.42 MHz) for SPS and L2 (1227.6 MHz) for PPS. The system uses spread spectrum modulation and provides a great deal of resistance to interference. Each satellite transmits a navigation message containing its orbital elements, clock behavior, system time, and status messages. A user's GPS receiver can determine its position by obtaining time information from three satellites. Altitude determinations require more than three satellites.

The GPS consists of space, control, and user segments. The space segment consists of 24 satellites in six orbital planes. The satellites operate in circular 10,900 nautical mile (20,200 km) orbits at an inclination angle of 55 degrees and with a 12-hour period. The control segment consists of monitor stations and ground antennas. There are five monitor stations with one located in Hawaii, Kwajalein, Ascension Island, Diego Garcia, and Colorado Springs. There are three ground antennas, one at Ascension Island, Diego Garcia, and Kwajalein. The monitor stations gather range data by tracking all satellites within view. The user segment consists of antennas and receiver processors, providing positioning, velocity, and precise timing to the user.

GPS/Wireless Applications

The combination of wireless WAN technologies and location devices offers some interesting applications. The joining of these technologies makes it possible for a mobile element to communicate its exact location to other elements. Many companies are combining CDPD and paging with the Global Positioning System (GPS) in their products, mainly for vehicle tracking.

ETE has a product, MobileTrak, that is a portable, low-cost, automatic vehicle locating (AVL) system that works with ETE's line of wireless communications products. MobileTrak combines wireless, two-way packet data communications with GPS to create a low-cost, off-the-shelf, AVL system. The MobileTrak system depicts vehicle location on a full-color map on either a laptop, desktop PC, or Macintosh that can be integrated with wireless dispatch products from ETE and other companies.

The MobileTrak system consists of the following three main components:

- *MobileTrak Remote:* A compact, self-contained position tracking and reporting system that includes a wireless digital packet radio and a GPS receiver. You can mount a MobileTrak Remote easily in any vehicle. The system connects to a vehicle's power system or can operate for up to 10 hours with rechargeable nickel-metal hydride batteries.

- *MobileTrak Mapping Display Software:* Displays vehicles or other mobile assets equipped with MobileTrak Remotes on a full-color, real-time, moving map display. The software has many features, such as vehicle tracking, zooming, panning, address location, heading and velocity labels, and two-way chat messaging. The Mapping Display Software can also remotely control a MobileTrak Remote via commands sent over the wireless data communications network.

- *MobileTrak Wireless Agent:* A software product supporting wireless communications between the MobileTrak Mapping display stations and vehicles or assets equipped with MobileTrak Remotes. The MobileTrak Wireless Agent supports up to 100 MobileTrak display stations.

In the United States, the MobileTrak Wireless Agent supports both BellSouth Mobile Data and ARDIS wireless WAN services. Internationally, the MobileTrak Wireless Agent supports DataTAC and Mobitex wireless networks.

CHAPTER 3

Overview of the IEEE 802.11 Standard

- **The importance of standards**
  This chapter begins with an introduction to the types of LAN standards and the primary organization that makes the standards: the Institute for Electrical and Electronic Engineers (IEEE). You learn the important benefits of using the IEEE 802.11 wireless LAN standard.

- **IEEE 802 LAN standards family**
  It is important to know how the IEEE 802.11 standard fits into other LAN protocols to ensure proper interoperability. An overview of the 802 series of LAN standards describes the operation of the 802.2 Logical Link Control that directly interfaces with 802.11.

- **Introduction to the IEEE 802.11 standard**
  An explanation of the scope and goals of the 802.11 standard provides an understanding of the basic functionality of 802.11. Learn the peculiar wireless network issues that were addressed when developing the standard.

- **IEEE 802.11 topology**
  An overview of the physical structure of 802.11-compliant LANs provides an understanding of 802.11 topology. Understand how basic physical 802.11 elements, such as Basic Service Sets (single-cell wireless LANs) and access points, form integrated, multiple-cell wireless LANs that support a variety of mobility types.

- **IEEE 802.11 logical architecture**
  Coverage of the main elements of the 802.11 protocol stack provides an overview of how the 802.11 protocol works. Learn the main functionality of each of the following 802.11 protocol layers: MAC Layer and individual PHY (Physical) Layers (frequency hopping, direct sequence, and infrared).

- IEEE 802.11 services
  802.11-compliant LANs function based on a set of services that relate to stations and distribution systems. Discover how these services offer security equivalent to wired LANs.

- Implications of the IEEE 802.11 standard
  Although the long-awaited 802.11 standard offers several benefits over using proprietary-based wireless LANs, the 802.11 standard still has shortcomings that implementors should be aware of. Learn some of the 802.11 implications, such as relatively low data rates and lack of roaming.

- IEEE 802.11 standard compliance
  The compliance with 802.11 depends on those having the need for wireless networks. Become aware of how vendors are complying with 802.11, what end users need to do to be compliant, and how different regions of the world comply with 802.11 radio frequencies.

- IEEE 802.11 Working Group operations
  Involvement in IEEE 802.11 standards development is open to anyone with a desire to participate, but you need to understand the membership requirements and types of 802.11 members.

- Future of the IEEE 802.11 standard
  When making decisions about wireless LANs, be sure to include what the future holds for the 802.11 standard. Discover the projects IEEE 802.11 members are working on to increase the performance of 802.11-compliant wireless LANs.

The Importance of Standards

Vendors and some end users initially expected markets to dive headfirst into implementing wireless networks. Markets did not respond as predicted, and flat sales growth of wireless networking components prevailed through most of the 1990s. Relatively low data rates, high prices, and especially the lack of standards kept many end users from purchasing the wire-free forms of media.

For those having applications suitable for lower data rates and enough cost savings to warrant purchasing wireless connections, the only choice before 1998 was to install proprietary hardware to satisfy requirements. As a result, many organizations today have proprietary wireless networks for which you have to replace both hardware and software to be compliant with the IEEE 802.11 standard. The lack of standards has been a significant problem with wireless networking, but the first official version of the standard is now available. In response to lacking standards, the Institute for Electrical and Electronic Engineers (IEEE) developed the first internationally recognized wireless LAN standard: IEEE 802.11.

Types of Standards

There are two main types of standards: official and public. An *official standard* is published and known to the public, but it is controlled by an official standards organization, such as IEEE. Government or industry consortiums normally sponsor official standards groups. Official standards organizations generally ensure coordination at both the international and domestic level.

A *public standard* is similar to an official standard, except it is controlled by a private organization, such as the Wireless LAN Interoperability Forum. Public standards, often called *de facto standards*, are common practices that have not been produced or accepted by an official standards organization. These standards, such as TCP/IP, are the result of widespread proliferation. In some cases, public standards that proliferate, such as the original ethernet, eventually pass through standards organizations and become official standards.

Companies should strive to adopt standards and recommended products within their organizations for all aspects of information systems. What type of standards should you use? For most cases, focus on the use of an official standard if one is available and proliferating. This will help ensure widespread acceptance and longevity of your wireless network implementation. If no official standard is suitable, a public standard would be a good choice. In fact, public standards can often respond faster to changes in market needs because they usually have less organizational overhead for making changes. Be sure to avoid nonstandard or proprietary system components, unless there are no suitable standards available.

Case Study 3.1:
802.11 Versus Proprietary
Standards

A large retail chain based in Sacramento, California, had requirements to implement a wireless network to provide mobility within their 10 warehouses located all over the United States. The application calls for clerks within the warehouse to utilize new handheld wireless data collectors that perform inventory-management functions.

The company, already having one vendor's data collection devices (we'll call these brand X), decides to use that vendor's brand Y proprietary wireless data collectors and their proprietary wireless network (the vendor doesn't offer an 802.11-compliant solution). This decision eliminates the need to work with additional vendors for the new handheld devices and the wireless network.

A year passes since the installation, and enhancement requirements begin to pour in for additional mobile appliances that are not available from the brand X

continues

continued

vendor. This forces the company to consider the purchase of new brand Z appliances from a different vendor. The problem, however, is that the brand Z appliances, which are 802.11-compliant, don't interoperate with the installed proprietary brand Y wireless network. Because of the cost associated with replacing their network with one that is 802.11 compliant (the brand Y wireless network has no upgrade path to 802.11), the company can't cost effectively implement the new enhancement.

The company could have eliminated the problem of not being able to implement the new enhancement if it would have implemented the initial system with 802.11-compliant network components, because most vendors offer products that are compatible with 802.11, but not all the proprietary networks. The result would have been the ability to consider multiple vendors for a wider selection of appliances.

Institute for Electrical and Electronic Engineers (IEEE)

The IEEE is a nonprofit professional organization founded by a handful of engineers in 1884 for the purpose of consolidating ideas dealing with electro-technology. In the last 100 plus years, IEEE has maintained a steady growth. Today, the IEEE, which is based in the United States, has over 320,000 members located in 150 countries. The IEEE consists of 35 individual societies, including the Communications Society, Computer Society, and Antennas and Propagation Society.

The IEEE plays a significant role in publishing technical works, sponsoring conferences and seminars, accreditation, and standards development. The IEEE has published nearly 700 active standards publications, half of which relate to power engineering and most others deal with computers. The IEEE standards development process consists of 30,000 volunteers (who are mostly IEEE members) and a Standards Board of 32 people. In terms of LANs, IEEE has produced some very popular and widely used standards. The majority of LANs in the world utilize network interface cards based on the IEEE 802.3 (ethernet) and IEEE 802.5 (token ring) standards, for example.

Before someone can develop an IEEE standard, he must submit a Project Authorization Request (PAR) to the IEEE Standards Board. If the board approves the PAR, IEEE establishes a standards working group to develop the standard. Members of the working groups serve voluntarily and without compensation, and they are not necessarily members of the institute. The working group begins by writing a draft standard, and then solicits the draft to a balloting group of selected IEEE members for review and approval. The ballot group consists of the standard's developers, potential users, and other people having general interest.

Before publication, the IEEE Standards Board performs a review of the Final Draft Standard, and then considers approval of the standard. The resulting standard represents a consensus of broad expertise from within IEEE and other related organizations. All IEEE standards are subjected to review at least once every five years for revision or reaffirmation.

Note

In May 1991, a group of people, led by Victor Hayes, submitted a Project Authorization Request (PAR) to IEEE to initiate the 802.11 Working Group. Victor became Chairman of the working group and led the standards effort to its completion in June 1997.

Benefits of the 802.11 Standard

The benefits of utilizing standards, such as those published by IEEE, are great. The following sections explain the benefits of complying with standards, especially IEEE 802.11.

Appliance Interoperability

Compliance with the IEEE 802.11 standard makes interoperability between multiple-vendor appliances and the chosen wireless network type possible. This means you can purchase an 802.11-compliant PalmPilot from Symbol and Pathfinder Ultra handheld scanner/printer from Monarch Marking Systems, and they will both interoperate within an equivalent 802.11 wireless network, assuming 802.11 configuration parameters are set equally in both devices. Standard compliance increases price competition and enables companies to develop wireless LAN components with lower research and development budgets. This enables a greater number of smaller companies to develop wireless components. As a result, the sales of wireless LAN components should boom over the next few years as the finalization of the IEEE 802.11 standard sinks in.

As shown in Figure 3.1, appliance interoperability avoids the dependence on a single vendor for appliances. Without a standard, for example, a company having a non-standard proprietary Symbol network would be dependent on purchasing only appliances that operate on a Symbol network. This would exclude appliances such as ones from Telxon that only operate on proprietary Aironet networks. With an 802.11-compliant wireless network, you can utilize any equivalent 802.11-compliant appliance. Because most vendors, including Symbol and Telxon, have migrated their products to 802.11, you have a much greater selection of appliances for 802.11 standard networks.

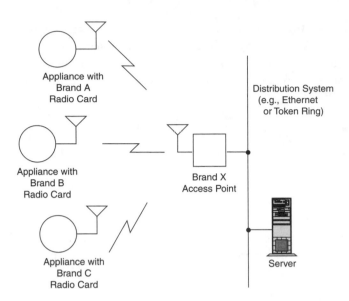

FIGURE 3.1 *Appliance interoperability ensures that multiple-vendor hardware works within equivalent wireless networks.*

Fast Product Development

The 802.11 standard is a well-tested blueprint that developers can use to implement wireless devices. The use of standards decreases the learning curve required to understand specific technologies because the standard-forming group has already invested the time to smooth out any wrinkles in the implementation of the applicable technology. This leads to the development of products in much less time.

Stable Future Migration

Compliance with standards helps protect investments and avoids legacy systems that must be completely replaced in the future as those proprietary products become obsolete. The evolution of wireless LANs should occur in a similar fashion as 802.3, ethernet. Initially, ethernet began as a 10 Mbps standard using coaxial cable media. The IEEE 802.3 Working Group enhanced the standard over the years by adding twisted-pair, optical-fiber cabling, and 100 and 1000 Mbps data rates.

Just as IEEE 802.3 did, the 802.11 Working Group recognizes the investments organizations make in network infrastructure and the importance in providing migration paths that maximize the installed base of hardware. As a result, 802.11 will certainly ensure stable migration from existing wireless LANs as higher performance wireless networking technologies become available.

Price Reductions

High costs have always plagued the wireless LAN industry; however, prices should drop significantly as more vendors and end users comply with 802.11. One of the reasons for lower prices is that vendors will no longer need to develop and support lower-quantity proprietary subcomponents, cutting design, manufacturing, and support costs. Ethernet went through a similar lowering of prices as more and more companies began complying with the 802.3 standard.

Avoiding Silos

Over the past couple of decades, MIS organizations have had a difficult time maintaining control of network implementations. The introduction of PCs, LANs, and visual-based development tools has made it much easier for non-MIS organizations, such as finance and manufacturing departments, to deploy their own applications. One part of the company, for example, may purchase a wireless network from one vendor, and then another part of the company may buy a different wireless network. As a result, *silos*—noninteroperable systems—appear within the company, making it very difficult for MIS personnel to plan and support compatible systems. Some people refer to these silos as *stovepipes*.

Acquisitions bring dissimilar systems together as well. One company having a proprietary system may purchase another having a different proprietary system, resulting in noninteroperability. Figure 3.2 illustrates the features of standards that minimize the occurrence of silos.

Case Study 3.2:

Problems with Mixed Standards

A company located in Barcelona, Spain specializes in the resale of women's clothes. This company, having a MIS group without much control over the implementation of distributed networks in major parts of the company, has projects underway to implement wireless networks for an inventory application and a price-marking application.

Non-MIS project managers located in different parts of the company lead these projects. They have little desire to coordinate their projects with MIS because of past difficulties. As a result, both pro-

ject managers end up implementing noncompatible proprietary wireless networks to satisfy their networking requirements.

The project managers install both systems: one that covers the sales floorspace of their 300 stores (for price marking) and one that encompasses 10 warehouses (for doing inventory functions). Although the systems are noncompatible, all is fine for the users operating the autonomous systems.

The issues with this system architecture, however, are the difficulty in providing

continues

continued

operational support and inflexibility. The company must maintain purchasing and warranty contracts with two different wireless network vendors, service personnel need to acquire and maintain an understanding in the operation of two networks, and the company cannot share appliances and wireless network compo-

nents between the warehouses and the stores.

As a result, the silos in this case make the networks more expensive to support and limit their flexibility in meeting future needs. The implementation of standard 802.11-compliant networks would have avoided these problems.

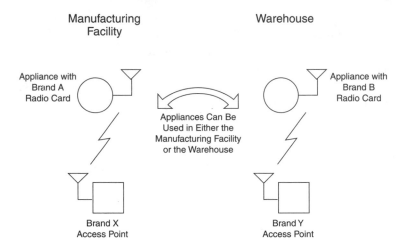

FIGURE 3.2 *Compliance with the IEEE 802.11 standard can minimize the implementation of silos.*

IEEE 802 LAN Standards Family

The IEEE 802 Local and Metropolitan Area Network Standards Committee is a major working group charted by IEEE to create, maintain, and encourage the use of IEEE and equivalent IEC/ISO standards. IEEE formed the committee in February 1980, and has met at least three times per year as a plenary body since then. IEEE 802 produces the series of standards known as IEEE 802.x, and the JTC 1 series of equivalent standards are known as ISO 8802-nnn.

IEEE 802 includes a family of standards, as depicted in Figure 3.3. The MAC and Physical Layers of the 802 standard were organized into a separate set of standards from the LLC because of the interdependence between medium access control, medium, and topology.

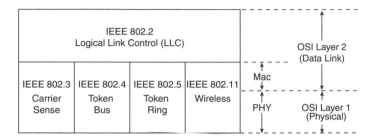

FIGURE 3.3   *The IEEE 802 family of standards falls within the scope of layers 1 and 2 of the OSI Reference Model. The LLC protocol specifies the mechanisms for addressing stations across the medium and for controlling the exchange of data between two stations; whereas, the MAC and PHY Layers provide medium access and transmission functions.*

The IEEE 802 family of standards includes the following:

- *IEEE 802.1: Glossary, Network Management, and Internetworking:* These documents, as well as IEEE 802 Overview and Architecture, form the scope of work for the 802 standards.

- *IEEE 802.2: Logical Link Control (LLC):* This standard defines Layer 2 synchronization and error control for all types of 802 LANs, including 802.11. Refer to the next section, "IEEE 802.2 LLC Overview," for more detail on the features and operation of the LLC.

- *IEEE 802.3: CSMA/CD Access Method and Physical Layer Specifications:* This defines the widely accepted 10, 100, and 1000 Mbps ethernet asynchronous protocol for use over twisted-pair wiring, coaxial cable, and optical fiber.

- *IEEE 802.4: Token-Passing Bus Access Method and Physical Layer Specifications:* This offers a token-passing protocol over a bus topology that can be embedded in other systems.

- *IEEE 802.5: Token-Passing Ring Access Method and Physical Layer Specifications:* This defines a 4 and 16 Mbps synchronous protocol that uses a token for access control over a ring topology.

- *IEEE 802.10: Security and Privacy Access Method and Physical Layer Specifications:* Provides security provisions for both wired and wireless LANs.

- *IEEE 802.11: Wireless Access Method and Physical Layer Specification:* Encompasses a variety of physical media, including frequency hopping spread spectrum, direct sequence spread spectrum, and infrared light for data rates up to 2 Mbps.

IEEE 802.2 LLC Overview

The LLC is the highest layer of the IEEE 802 Reference Model and provides similar functions of the traditional Data Link Control protocol: HDLC (High-Level Data

Link Control). The ANSI/IEEE Standard 802.2 specifies the LLC. The purpose of the LLC is to exchange data between end users across a LAN using a 802-based MAC controlled link. The LLC provides addressing and data link control, and it is independent of the topology, transmission medium, and medium access control technique chosen.

Higher layers, such as TCP/IP, pass user data down to the LLC expecting error-free transmission across the network. The LLC in turn appends a control header, creating an LLC protocol data unit (PDU). The LLC utilizes the control information in the operation of the LLC protocol (see Figure 3.4). Before transmission, the LLC PDU is handed down through the MAC service access point (SAP) to the MAC Layer, which appends control information at the beginning and end of the packet, forming a MAC frame. The control information in the frame is needed for the operation of the MAC protocol.

FIGURE 3.4 *The LLC provides end-to-end link control over an 802.11-based wireless LAN.*

IEEE 802.2 LLC Services

The LLC provides the following three services for a Network Layer protocol:

- Unacknowledged connectionless service
- Connection–oriented service
- Acknowledged connectionless service

These services apply to the communication between peer LLC Layers—that is, one located on the source station and one located on the destination station. Typically, vendors will provide these services as options that the customer can select when purchasing the equipment.

All three LLC protocols employ the same PDU format that consists of four fields (see Figure 3.5). The Destination Service Access Point (DSAP) and Source Service Access Point (SSAP) fields each contains 7-bit addresses, which specify the destination and source stations of the peer LLCs. One bit of the DSAP indicates whether the PDU is intended for an individual or group station(s). One bit of the SSAP indicates whether it is a command or response PDU. The format of the LLC Control field is identical to that of HDLC, using extended (7-bit) sequence numbers. The Data field contains the information from higher-layer protocols that the LLC is transporting to the destination.

8 Bits	8 Bits	8 Bits	Variable
Destination SAP	Service SAP	Control	Data

FIGURE 3.5 *The LLC PDU consists of data fields that provide the LLC functionality.*

The Control field has bits that indicate whether the frame is one of the following types:

- *Information:* Used to carry user data

- *Supervisory:* Used for flow control and error control

- *Unnumbered:* Various protocol control PDUs

Unacknowledged Connectionless Service

The *unacknowledged connectionless service* is a datagram-style service that does not involve any error-control or flow-control mechanisms. This service does not involve the establishment of a Data Link Layer connection (that is, a connection between peer LLCs). This service supports individual, multicast, and broadcast addressing. This service just sends and receives LLC PDUs, with no acknowledgment of delivery. Because the delivery of data is not guaranteed, a higher layer, such as TCP, must deal with reliability issues.

The unacknowledged connectionless service offers advantages in the following situations:

- If higher layers of the protocol stack provide the necessary reliability and flow-control mechanisms, it would be inefficient to duplicate them in the LLC. In this case, the unacknowledged connectionless service would be appropriate. TCP and the ISO transport protocol, for example, already provide the mechanisms necessary for reliable delivery.

- It is not always necessary to provide feedback pertaining to successful delivery of information. The overhead of connection establishment and maintenance can be inefficient—as an example, for applications involving the periodic sampling of data sources, such as monitoring sensors. The unacknowledged connectionless service would best satisfy these requirements.

Case Study 3.3:
Using Unacknowledged
Connectionless Service to
Minimize Overhead

The executive office building of a high-rent advertising agency in Southern California has 20 sensors to monitor temperatures throughout its building as an input to the heating and air conditioning system. These sensors send short information packets every minute to an application on a centralized server that updates a temperature table in a database. The heating and air conditioning system uses this information to control the temperature in different parts of the building.

For this application, the server does not need to acknowledge the reception of every sensor transmission because the information updates are not critical. The system can maintain a comfortable temperature throughout the building even if the system misses temperature updates from time to time.

Additionally, it is not feasible to require the sensors to establish connections with the server to send the short information packets. As a result, designers of the system chose to use the LLC unacknowledged connectionless service to minimize overhead on the network, making the limited wireless network bandwidth available to other applications.

Connection-Oriented Service

The *connection-oriented service* establishes a logical connection that provides flow control and error control between two stations needing to exchange data. This service does involve the establishment of a connection between peer LLCs by performing connection establishment, data transfer, and connection termination functions. The service can only connect two stations; therefore, it does not support multicast or broadcast modes. The connection-oriented service offers advantages mainly if higher layers of the protocol stack do not provide the necessary reliability and flow-control mechanisms, which is generally the case with terminal controllers.

Flow control is a protocol feature that ensures a transmitting station does not overwhelm a receiving station with data. With flow control, each station allocates a finite amount of memory and buffer resources to store sent and received PDUs.

Networks, especially wireless networks, suffer from induced noise in the links between network stations that can cause transmission errors. If the noise is high enough in amplitude, it causes errors in digital transmission in the form of altered bits. This will lead to inaccuracy of the transmitted data, and the receiving network device may misinterpret the meaning of the information.

The noise that causes most problems with networks is usually Gaussian and impulse noise. Theoretically, the amplitude of Gaussian noise is uniform across the frequency spectrum, and it normally triggers random single-bit independent errors.

Impulse noise, the most disastrous, is characterized by long quiet intervals of time followed by high-amplitude bursts. This noise results from lightning and switching transients. Impulse noise is responsible for most errors in digital communication systems and generally provokes errors to occur in bursts.

To guard against transmission errors, the connection-oriented and acknowledged-connectionless LLCs use error-control mechanisms that detect and correct errors that occur in the transmission of PDUs. The LLC ARQ mechanism recognizes the possibility of the following two types of errors:

- *Lost PDU:* A PDU fails to arrive at the other end or is damaged beyond recognition.

- *Damaged PDU:* A PDU has arrived, but some bits are altered.

When a frame arrives at a receiving station, the station checks whether there are any errors present by using a *Cyclic Redundancy Check* (CRC) error detection algorithm. In general, the receiving station will send back a positive or negative acknowledgment depending on the outcome of the error detection process. In case the acknowledgment is lost en route to the sending station, the sending station will retransmit the frame after a certain period of time. This process is often referred to as *Automatic Repeat-Request* (ARQ).

Overall, ARQ is best for the correction of burst errors because this type of impairment occurs in a small percentage of frames, thus not invoking many retransmissions. Because of the feedback inherent in ARQ protocols, the transmission links must accommodate half-duplex or full-duplex transmissions. If only simplex links are available due to feasibility, it is impossible to use the ARQ technique because the receiver would not be able to notify the transmitter of bad data frames.

Note

In cases for which single bit errors predominate or when only a simplex link is available, forward error correction (FEC) can provide error correction. FEC algorithms provide enough redundancy in data transmissions to enable the receiving station to correct errors without needing the sending station to retransmit the data.

FEC is effective for correcting single-bit errors, but it requires a great deal of overhead in the transmissions to protect against multiple errors, such as burst errors. The IEEE LLC, however, specifies only the use of ARQ-based protocols for controlling errors.

The following are two approaches for retransmitting unsatisfactory blocks of data using ARQ.

Continuous ARQ

With continuous ARQ, often called a *sliding window protocol*, the sending station transmits frames continuously until the receiving station detects an error. The sending station is usually capable of transmitting a specific number of frames and maintains a table indicating which frames have been sent.

The system implementor can set the number of frames sent before stopping via configuration parameters of the network device. If a receiver detects a bad frame, it will send a negative acknowledgment back to the sending station requesting that the bad frame be sent over again. When the transmitting station gets the signal to retransmit the frame, several subsequent frames may have already been sent (due to propagation delays between the sender and receiver); therefore, the transmitter must "go back" and retransmit the erred data frame.

There are a couple ways the transmitting station can send frames again using continuous ARQ. One method is for the source to retrieve the erred frame from the transmit buffer and send the bad frame and all frames following it. This is called the *go-back-n technique*. A problem, however, is when *n* (the number of frames the transmitter sent after the erred frame plus one) becomes large, the method becomes inefficient. This is because the retransmission of just one frame means that a large number of possibly "good" frames will also be resent, thus decreasing throughput.

The go-back-n technique is useful in applications for which receiver buffer space is limited because all that is needed is a receiver window size of one (assuming frames are to be delivered in order). When the receive node rejects an erred frame (sends a negative acknowledgment), it does not need to buffer any subsequent frames for possible reordering while it is waiting for the retransmission because all subsequent frames will also be sent.

An alternative to the continuous go-back-n technique is a method that selectively retransmits only the erred frame, and then resumes normal transmission at the point just before getting the notification of a bad data frame. This approach is called *selective repeat*. It is obviously better than continuous go-back-n in terms of throughput because only the erred frame needs retransmission. With this technique, however, the receiver must be capable of storing a number of frames if they are to be processed in order. The receiver needs to buffer data that have been received after an erred frame was requested for retransmission because only the damaged frame will be sent again.

Stop-and-Wait ARQ

With stop-and-wait ARQ, the sending station transmits a frame and then stops and waits for some type of acknowledgment from the receiver on whether a particular frame was acceptable or not. If the receiving station sends a negative acknowledgment, the frame will be sent again. The transmitter will send the next frame only after it receives a positive acknowledgment from the receiver.

An advantage of stop-and-wait ARQ is that it does not require much buffer space at the sending or receiving station. The sending station needs to store only the current transmitted frame. However, stop-and-wait ARQ becomes inefficient as the propagation delay between source and destination becomes large. For example, data sent on satellite links normally experience a round-trip delay of several hundred milliseconds; therefore, long block lengths are necessary to maintain a reasonably effective data rate. The trouble is that with longer frames, the probability of an error occurring in a particular block is greater. Therefore, retransmission will occur often, and the resulting throughput will be lower.

Case Study 3.4:
Using Automatic Repeat-Request
(ARQ) to Reduce Errors

A mobile home manufacturer in Florida uses robots on the assembly line to perform welding. Designers of the robot control system had to decide whether to use ARQ or FEC for controlling transmission errors between the server and the robots. The company experiences a great deal of impulse noise from arc welders and other heavy machinery.

In the midst of this somewhat hostile environment, the robots require error-free information updates to ensure that they function correctly. Designers of the system quickly ruled out the use of FEC because of the likely presence of burst errors due to impulse noise. ARQ, with its capability to detect and correct frames having a lot of bit errors, was obviously the better choice.

Acknowledged Connectionless Service

As with the unacknowledged connectionless service, the *acknowledged connectionless service* does not involve the establishment of a logical connection with the distant station. But the receiving stations with the acknowledged version do confirm successful delivery of datagrams. Flow and error control is handled through use of the stop-and-wait ARQ method.

The acknowledged connectionless service is useful in several applications. The connection-oriented service must maintain a table for each active connection for tracking the status of the connection. If the application calls for guaranteed delivery, but there are a large number of destinations needing to receive the data, the connection-oriented service may be impractical because of the large number of tables required. Examples that fit this scenario include process control and automated factory environments that require a central site to communicate with a large number of processors and programmable controllers. In addition, the handling of important and time-critical alarm or emergency control signals in a factory would also fit this case. In all these examples, the sending stations need an acknowledgment to ensure successful delivery of the data; however, the urgency of transmission cannot wait for a connection establishment.

Note

A company having a requirement to send information to multiple devices needing positive acknowledgment of the data transfer can make use of the acknowledged connectionless LLC service. A marina may find it beneficial to control the power to different parts of the boat dock via a wireless network, for example. Of course, the expense of a wireless network may not be justifiable for this application alone.

Other applications, such as supporting data transfers back and forth to the cash register at the gas pump and the use of data-collection equipment for inventorying rental equipment, can share the wireless network to make a more positive business case. For shutting off the power on the boat dock, the application would need to send a message to the multiple power controllers, and then expect an acknowledgment to ensure the controller receives the notification and that the power is shut off. For this case, the connectionless transfer, versus connection-oriented, makes most sense because it would not be feasible to make connections to the controllers to support such a short message.

LLC/MAC Layer Service Primitives

Layers within the 802 architecture communicate with each other via service primitives having the following forms:

- *Request:* A layer uses this type of primitive to request that another layer perform a specific service.

- *Confirm:* A layer uses this type of primitive to convey the results of a previous service request primitive.

- *Indication:* A layer uses this type of primitive to indicate to another layer that a significant event has occurred. This primitive could result from a service request or from some internally generated event.

- *Response:* A layer uses this type of primitive to complete a procedure initiated by an indication primitive.

These primitives are an abstract way of defining the protocol, and they *do not* imply a specific physical implementation method. Each layer within the 802 model uses specific primitives. The LLC communicates with its associated MAC Layer through the following specific set of service primitives:

- `MA-UNITDATA.request`: The LLC sends this primitive to the MAC Layer to request the transfer of a data frame from a local LLC entity to a specific peer LLC entity or group of peer entities on different stations. The data frame could be an information frame containing data from a higher layer or a control frame (for example, a supervisory or unnumbered frame) that the LLC generates internally to communicate with its peer LLC.

- `MA-UNITDATA.indication`: The MAC Layer sends this primitive to the LLC to transfer a data frame from the MAC Layer to the LLC. This occurs only if the

MAC has found that a frame it receives from the Physical Layer is valid, has no errors, and that the destination address indicates the correct MAC address of the station.

- *MA-UNITDATA-STATUS.indication:* The MAC Layer sends this primitive to the LLC Layer to provide status information about the service provided for a previous MA-UNITDATA.request primitive.

Note

The current ANSI/IEEE 802.2 standard (dated May 7, 1998) states that the 802.2 Working Group is developing a single-service specification of primitives that is common to all MAC Layers. IEEE will refer to this change in the 802.2 standard, not the individual MAC Layer standards (for example, 802.3, 802.5, 802.11).

Introduction to the IEEE 802.11 Standard

The initial 802.11 PAR states, "...the scope of the proposed [wireless LAN] standard is to develop a specification for wireless connectivity for fixed, portable, and moving stations within a local area." The PAR further says that the "purpose of the standard is to provide wireless connectivity to automatic machinery and equipment or stations that require rapid deployment, which may be portable, handheld, or which may be mounted on moving vehicles within a local area."

The resulting standard, which is officially called *IEEE Standard for Wireless LAN Medium Access (MAC) and Physical Layer (PHY) Specifications*, defines over-the-air protocols necessary to support networking in a local area. As with other IEEE 802–based standards (for example, 802.3 and 802.5), the primary service of the 802.11 standard is to deliver MSDUs (MAC Service Data Units) between peer LLCs. Typically, a radio card and access point provide functions of the 802.11 standard.

Note

To order a copy of the IEEE 802.11 standard, contact the IEEE 802 Document Order Service at 800-678-4333. You can also order the standard via IEEE's Web site at www.ieee.org.

The 802.11 standard provides MAC and PHY functionality for wireless connectivity of fixed, portable, and moving stations moving at pedestrian and vehicular speeds within a local area. Specific features of the 802.11 standard include the following:

- Support of asynchronous and time-bounded delivery service

- Continuity of service within extended areas via a distribution system, such as ethernet

- Accommodation of transmission rates of 1 and 2 Mbps

- Support of most market applications

- Multicast (including broadcast) services
- Network management services
- Registration and authentication services

Target environments for use of the standard include the following:

- Inside buildings, such as offices, banks, shops, malls, hospitals, manufacturing plants, and residences
- Outdoor areas, such as parking lots, campuses, building complexes, and outdoor plants

The 802.11 standard takes into account the following significant differences between wireless and wired LANs:

- *Power management:* Because most wireless LAN NICs are available in PCM-CIA Type II format, obviously you can outfit portable and mobile handheld computing equipment with wireless LAN connectivity. The problem, however, is these devices must rely on batteries to power the electronics within them. The addition of a wireless LAN NIC to a portable computer can quickly drain batteries.

  The 802.11 Working Group struggled with finding solutions to conserve battery power; however, they found techniques enabling wireless NICs to switch to lower-power standby modes periodically when not transmitting, reducing the drain on the battery. The MAC Layer implements power-management functions by putting the radio to sleep (that is, lowering the power drain) when no transmission activity occurs for some specific or user-definable time period. The problem, however, is that a sleeping station can miss critical data transmissions. 802.11 solves this problem by incorporating buffers to queue messages. The standard calls for sleeping stations to awaken periodically and retrieve any applicable messages.

- *Bandwidth:* The ISM spread spectrum bands do not offer a great deal of bandwidth, keeping data rates lower than desired for some applications. The 802.11 Working Group, however, dealt with methods to compress data, making the best use of available bandwidth. Efforts are also underway to increase the data rate of 802.11 to accommodate the growing need for exchanging larger and larger files (see the section titled "Future of the IEEE 802.11 Standard" at the end of this chapter).

- *Security:* As mentioned in Chapter 1, "Introduction to Wireless Networks," in the "Network Security" section, wireless LANs transmit signals over much larger areas than that of wired media, such as twisted-pair, coaxial, and optical fiber cable. In terms of privacy, therefore, wireless LANs have a much larger area to protect. To employ security, the 802.11 Working Group coordinated their work with the IEEE 802.10 Standards Committee responsible for developing security mechanisms for all 802 series LANs.

- *Addressing:* The topology of a wireless network is dynamic; therefore, the destination address does not always correspond to the destination's location. This raises a problem when routing packets through the network to the intended destination. Therefore, you may need to utilize a TCP/IP-based protocol, such as MobileIP, to accommodate mobile stations. Chapter 6, "Wireless System Integration," provides details on the MobileIP protocol.

To ensure interoperability with existing standards, the 802.11 Working Group developed the standard to be compatible with other existing 802 standards, such as the following:

- *IEEE 802:* Functional Requirements

- *IEEE 802.2:* MAC Service Definition

- *IEEE 802.1-A:* Overview and Architecture

- *IEEE 802.1-B:* LAN/MAN Management

- *IEEE 802.1-D:* Transparent Bridges

- *IEEE 802.1-F:* Guidelines for the Development of Layer Management Standards

- *IEEE 802.10:* Secure Data Exchange

Note

At the time of this writing, key participants of the IEEE 802.11 standard effort included the following:

Victor Hayes, Chair

Stuart Kerry and Chris Zegelin, Vice Chairs

Bob O'Hara and Greg Ennis, Chief Technical Editors

George Fishel and Carolyn Heide, Secretaries

David Bagby, MAC Group Chair

Jan Boer, Direct Sequence Chair

Dean Kawaguchi, PHY Group and Frequency Hopping Chair

C. Thoman Baumgartner, Infrared Chair

HIPERLAN

High Performance Radio Local Area Network (HIPERLAN) is a European family of standards that specify high-speed digital wireless communication in the 5.15–5.3 GHz and the 17.1–17.3 GHz spectrum. These standards specify the Physical and Data Link Layers of network architecture, similar in scope to 802.11. However,

continues

continued

HIPERLAN operates using different proto-cols and is not compatible with other IEEE standards, such as IEEE 802.2 Logical Link Control.

Two stations in a HIPERLAN can exchange data directly, without any interaction from a wired network infrastructure. The simplest HIPERLAN consists of two sta-tions. If two HIPERLAN stations are out of range with each other, a third station can relay the messages. HIPERLAN networks have the following specifications:

- Short range, approximately 150 feet (50 meters)
- Support of asynchronous and isoch-ronous traffic
- Support of audio at 32 Kbps
- Support of video at 2 Mbps
- Support of data at 10 Mbps

HIPERLAN is unlikely to be a serious com-petitor to 802.11-based LANs, especially outside of Europe.

IEEE 802.11 Topology

The IEEE 802.11 topology consists of components, interacting to provide a wireless LAN that enables station mobility transparent to higher protocol layers, such as the LLC. A station is any device that contains functionality of the 802.11 protocol (that is, MAC Layer, PHY Layer, and interface to a wireless medium). The functions of the 802.11 standard reside physically in a radio NIC, the software interface that drives the NIC, and access point. The 802.11 standard supports the following two topologies:

- Independent Basic Service Set (IBSS) networks
- Extended Service Set (ESS) networks

These networks utilize a basic building block the 802.11 standard refers to as a BSS, providing a coverage area whereby stations of the BSS remain fully connected. A station is free to move within the BSS, but it can no longer communicate directly with other stations if it leaves the BSS.

Note

Harris Semiconductor was the first company to offer a complete radio chip set (called PRISM) for direct sequence spread spectrum that is fully compliant with IEEE 802.11. The PRISM chip set includes six inte-grated microcircuits that handle all signal processing requirements of 802.11.

Independent Basic Service Set (IBSS) Networks

An IBSS is a stand-alone BSS that has no backbone infrastructure and consists of at least two wireless stations (see Figure 3.6). This type of network is often referred to as an *ad hoc network* because it can be constructed quickly without much planning.

The ad hoc wireless network will satisfy most needs of users occupying a smaller area, such as a single room, a sales floor, or a hospital wing.

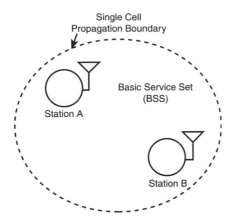

FIGURE 3.6   *An independent BSS (IBSS) is the most basic type of 802.11 wireless LAN.*

Extended Service Set (ESS) Networks

For requirements exceeding the range limitations of an independent BSS, 802.11 defines an Extended Service Set (ESS) LAN, as illustrated in Figure 3.7. This type of configuration satisfies the needs of large-coverage networks of arbitrary size and complexity.

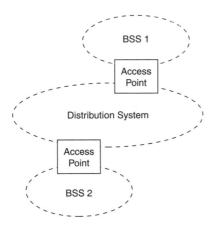

FIGURE 3.7   *An Extended Service Set (ESS) 802.11 wireless LAN consists of multiple cells interconnected by access points and a distribution system, such as ethernet.*

The 802.11 standard recognizes the following mobility types:

- *No-transition:* This type of mobility refers to stations that do not move and those that are moving within a local BSS.

- *BSS-transition:* This type of mobility refers to stations that move from one BSS in one ESS to another BSS within the same ESS.

- *ESS-transition:* This type of mobility refers to stations that move from a BSS in one ESS to a BSS in a different ESS.

The 802.11 standard clearly supports the no-transition and BSS-transition mobility types. The standard, however, does not guarantee that a connection will continue when making an ESS-transition.

The 802.11 standard defines the *distribution system* as an element that interconnects BSSs within the ESS via access points. The distribution system supports the 802.11 mobility types by providing logical services necessary to handle address-to-destination mapping and seamless integration of multiple BSSs. An *access point* is an addressable station, providing an interface to the distribution system for stations located within various BSSs. The independent BSS and ESS networks are transparent to the LLC Layer.

Within the ESS, the 802.11 standard accommodates the following physical configuration of BSSs:

- *BSSs that partially overlap:* This type of configuration provides contiguous coverage within a defined area, which is best if the application cannot tolerate a disruption of network service.

- *BSSs that are physically disjointed:* For this case, the configuration does not provide contiguous coverage. 802.11 does not specify a limit to the distance between BSSs.

- *BSSs that are physically collocated:* This may be necessary to provide a redundant or higher-performing network.

The 802.11 standard does not constrain the composition of the distribution system; therefore, it may be 802-compliant or some nonstandard network. If data frames need transmission to and from a non–IEEE 802.11 LAN, these frames, as defined by the 802.11 standard, enter and exit through a logical point called a *portal*. The portal provides logical integration between existing wired LANs and 802.11 LANs. When the distribution system is constructed with 802-type components, such as 802.3 (ethernet) or 802.5 (token ring), the portal and the access point become one and the same.

IEEE 802.11 Logical Architecture

A topology provides a means of explaining necessary physical components of a network, but the *logical architecture* defines the network's operation. As Figure 3.8 illustrates, the logical architecture of the 802.11 standard that applies to each station consists of a single MAC and one of multiple PHYs.

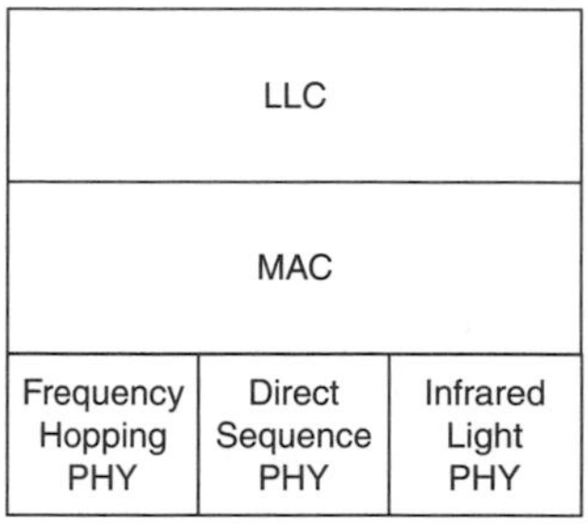

LLC
MAC

Frequency Hopping PHY	Direct Sequence PHY	Infrared Light PHY

FIGURE 3.8   *A single 802.11 MAC Layer supports three separate PHYs: frequency hopping spread spectrum, direct sequence spread spectrum, and infrared light.*

IEEE 802.11 MAC Layer

The goal of the MAC Layer is to provide access control functions (such as addressing, access coordination, frame check sequence generation and checking, and LLC PDU delimiting) for shared-medium PHYs in support of the LLC Layer. The MAC Layer performs the addressing and recognition of frames in support of the LLC. The 802.11 standard uses CSMA/CA (carrier sense multiple access with collision avoidance); whereas, standard ethernet uses CSMA/CD (carrier sense multiple access with collision detection). It is not possible to both transmit and receive on the same channel using radio transceivers; therefore, an 802.11 wireless LAN takes measures only to avoid collisions, not to detect them.

IEEE 802.11 Physical Layers

The working group decided in July 1992 to concentrate its radio frequency studies and standardization efforts on the 2.4 GHz spread spectrum ISM bands for both the direct sequence and frequency hopping PHYs. The final standard specifies 2.4 GHz because this band is available license free in most parts of the world. The FCC Part 15 in the United States governs the radiated RF power in the ISM bands. Part 15 limits antenna gain to 6 dBi maximum and radiated power to one watt within the United States. European and Japanese regulatory groups limit radiated power to 10 milliwatts per 1 MHz. The actual frequencies authorized for use in the United States, Europe, and Japan differ slightly.

In March 1993, the 802.11 committee began receiving proposals for a direct sequence Physical Layer standard. After much discussion and debate, the committee agreed to include a chapter in the standard specifying the use of direct sequence. The direct sequence Physical Layer specifies two data rates:

- 2 Mbps using Differential Quaternary Phase Shift Keying (DQPSK) modulation

- 1 Mbps using Differential Binary Phase Shift Keying (DBPSK)

The standard defines seven direct sequence channels. One channel is exclusively available for Japan. Three channel pairs are defined for the United States and Europe. Channels in a pair can work without interference. In addition, the channels of all three pairs can be used simultaneously for redundancy or higher performance by developing a frequency plan that avoids signal conflicts.

In contrast to direct sequence, the 802.11-based frequency hopping PHY uses radios to send data signals by hopping from one frequency to another, transmitting a few bits on each frequency before shifting to a different one. Frequency hopping systems hop in a pattern that appears to be random, but really has a known sequence. A particular hop sequence is commonly referred to as a *frequency hopping channel*. Frequency hopping systems tend to be less costly to implement and do not consume as much power as their direct sequence counterpart, making them more suitable for portable applications. However, frequency hopping is much less tolerant of multiple-path and other interference sources. The system must retransmit data if it becomes corrupted on one of the hop sequence frequencies.

The 802.11 committee defined the frequency hopping Physical Layer to have a 1 Mbps data rate using 2-level Gaussian frequency shift keying (GFSK). This specification describes 79 channel center frequencies identified for the United States, from which there are three sets of 22 hopping sequences defined.

The infrared Physical Layer describes a modulation type that operates in the 850 to 950 nM band for small equipment and low-speed applications. The basic data rate of this infrared medium is 1 Mbps using 16-PPM (pulse position modulation) and an enhanced rate of 2 Mbps using 4-PPM. Peak power of infrared-based devices are limited to a peak power of 2 watts.

As with the IEEE 802.3 standard, the 802.11 Working Group is considering additional PHYs as applicable technologies become available.

For an inside look of each layer of the 802.11 standard, refer to Chapter 4, "Medium Access Control (MAC) Layer," and Chapter 5, "Physical (PHY) Layer."

IEEE 802.11 Services

The 802.11 standard defines *services* that provide the functions that the LLC Layer requires for sending MSDUs (MAC service data units) between two entities on the network. These services, which the MAC Layer implements, fall into two categories:

- Station services

    Authentication

    Deauthentication

    Privacy

    MSDU delivery

- Distribution system services

    Association

    Disassociation

    Distribution

    Integration

    Reassociation

The following sections define the station and distribution system services.

Station Services

The 802.11 standard defines services for providing functions among stations. A station may be within any wireless element on the network, such as a handheld PC or handheld scanner. In addition, all access points implement station services. To provide necessary functionality, these stations need to send and receive MSDUs and implement adequate levels of security.

Authentication

Because wireless LANs have limited physical security to prevent unauthorized access, 802.11 defines authentication services to control LAN access to a level equal to a wired link. All 802.11 stations, whether they are part of an independent BSS or ESS network, must use the authentication service prior to establishing a connection (referred to as an association in 802.11 terms) with another station with which they will communicate. Stations performing authentication send a unicast management authentication frame to the corresponding station.

The IEEE 802.11 standard defines the following two authentication services:

- *Open system authentication:* This is the 802.11 default authentication method, which is a very simple, two-step process. First the station wanting to authenticate with another station sends an authentication management frame containing the sending station's identity. The receiving station then sends back a frame alerting whether it recognizes the identity of the authenticating station.

- *Shared key authentication:* This type of authentication assumes that each station has received a secret shared key through a secure channel independent from the 802.11 network. Stations authenticate through shared knowledge of the secret key. Use of shared key authentication requires implementation of the Wireless Equivalent Privacy algorithm.

Deauthentication

When a station wishes to *disassociate* with another station, it invokes the *deauthentication* service. Deauthentication is a notification, and cannot be refused. Stations perform deauthentication by sending an authentication management frame (or group of frames to multiple stations) to *advise* the termination of authentication.

Privacy

With a wireless network, all stations and other devices can "hear" data traffic taking place within range on the network, seriously impacting the security level of a wireless link. IEEE 802.11 counters this problem by offering a privacy service option that raises the security level of the 802.11 network to that of a wired network. The privacy service, applying to all data frames and some authentication management frames, is based on the 802.11 *Wired Equivalent Privacy* (*WEP*) algorithm that significantly reduces risks if someone eavesdrops on the network. This algorithm performs encryption of messages, as shown in Figure 3.9. With WEP, all stations initially start "in the clear"—that is, unencrypted. Refer to Chapter 4, in the section titled "Private Frame Transmissions," for a description of how WEP works.

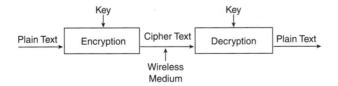

FIGURE 3.9 *The Wired Equivalent Privacy (WEP) algorithm produces ciphertext, keeping eavesdroppers from "listening in" on data transmissions.*

Note

The WEP protects RF data transmissions using a 64-bit seed key and the RC4 encryption algorithm. When enabled, WEC only protects the data packet information. Physical Layer headers are left unencrypted so that all stations can properly receive control information for managing the network.

Distribution System Services

Distribution system services, as defined by 802.11, provide functionality across a distribution system. Access points provide distribution system services. The following sections provide an overview of the services that distribution systems need to provide proper transfer of MSDUs.

Association

Each station must initially invoke the *association service* with an access point before it can send information through a distribution system. The association maps a station to the distribution system via an access point. Each station can associate with only a single access point, but each access point can associate with multiple stations. Association is also a first step to providing the capability for a station to be mobile between BSSs.

Disassociation

A station or access point may invoke the *disassociation service* to terminate an existing association. This service is a notification; therefore, neither party may refuse termination. Stations should disassociate when leaving the network. An access point, for example, may disassociate all its stations if being removed for maintenance.

Distribution

A station uses the *distribution service* every time it sends MAC frames across a distribution system. The 802.11 standard does not specify how the distribution system delivers the data. The distribution service provides the distribution system with only enough information to determine the proper destination BSS.

Integration

The *integration service* enables the delivery of MAC frames through a portal between a distribution system and a non-802.11 LAN. The integration function performs all required media or address space translations. The details of an integration function depends on the distribution system implementation and are beyond the scope of the 802.11 standard.

Reassociation

The *reassociation service* enables a station to change its current state of association. Reassociation provides additional functionality to support BSS-transition mobility for associated stations. The reassociation service enables a station to transition its association from one access point to another. This keeps the distribution system informed of the current mapping between access point and station as the station moves from BSS to BSS within an ESS. Reassociation also enables changing association attributes of an established association while the station remains associated with the same access point. The mobile station always initiates the reassociation service.

Note

IEEE 802.11 allows a client to roam among multiple access points that may be operating on the same or separate channels. To support the roaming function, each access point typically transmits a beacon signal every 100 milliseconds. Roaming stations use the beacon to gauge the strength of their existing access point connection. If the station senses a weak signal, the roaming station can implement the reassociation service to connect to an access point emitting a stronger signal.

Case Study 3.5:
Reassociation Provides Roaming

A grocery store in Gulfport, Mississippi, has a bar code–based shelf inventory system that helps the owners of the store keep track of what to stock, order, and so on. Several of the store clerks use handheld scanners during the store's closed hours to perform inventory functions. The store has a multiple cell 802.11-compliant wireless LAN (that is, ESS) consisting of access points A and B interconnected by an ethernet network. These two access points are sufficient to cover the store's entire floorspace and backroom.

At one end of the store in the frozen meat section, a clerk using a handheld device may associate with access point A. As the person walks with the device to the beer-and-wine section on the other end of the store, the mobile scanner (that is, the 802.11 station within the scanner) will begin sensing a signal from access point B. As the signal from B becomes stronger, the station will then *reassociate* with access point B, offering a much better signal for transmitting MSDUs.

Station States and Corresponding Frame Types

The state existing between a source and destination station (see Figure 3.10) governs which IEEE 802.11 frame types the two stations can exchange.

The following types of functions can occur within each class of frame:

- Class 1 Frames
  - Control Frames

      Request to send (RTS)

      Clear to send (CTS)

      Acknowledgment (ACK)

      Contention-free (CF)
  - Management Frames

      Probe request/response

      Beacon

      Authentication

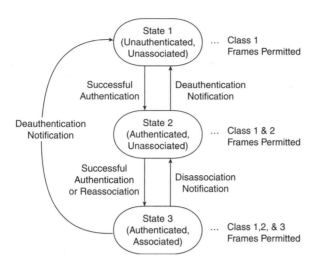

FIGURE 3.10   *The operation of a station depends on its particular state.*

        Deauthentication

        Announcement traffic indication message (ATIM)

- Data Frames

- Class 2 Frames

  - Management Frames

        Association request/response

        Reassociation request/response

        Disassociation

- Class 3 Frames

  - Data Frames

  - Management Frames

        Deauthentication

  - Control Frames

        Power Save Poll

To keep track of station state, each station maintains the following two state variables:

- *Authentication state:* Has values of either unauthenticated and authenticated

- *Association state:* Has values of either unassociated and associated

Implications of the IEEE 802.11 Standard

As with any technologies and standards, one must be aware of the implications sur-
rounding the implementation of wireless networks based on the IEEE 802.11 standard. Chapter 1, in the section "Wireless Network Concerns," discusses the general
issues of implementing wireless networks. In addition to these problems, the following are a couple of implications specifically related to the IEEE 802.11 standard:

- *Relatively low data rates:* As mentioned before, the 802.11 standard currently
  supports data rates up to 2 Mbps. Some end users and vendors claim this data
  rate is too low. In some cases, this is true; but in other cases, it is not true.
  Video transmissions, for example, may require higher data rates if applications
  need frame rates, pixel depth, and resolutions that require greater amounts of
  bandwidth. Large data block transmissions may also require higher data rates
  to keep transmission delays tolerable.

  On the other hand, bar code applications, such as receiving, inventory, and
  price marking, generally work well under the 2 Mbps limitation of the current 802.11 standard.

- *Lack of standard roaming across multiple-vendor access points:* The 802.11 standard
  does not define the protocols necessary to move 802.11 frames within the distribution system because it falls outside the scope of 802-type LANs. The
  Network and Transport Layers are left to address distribution system protocols. As a result, the 802.11 standard does not define communications *between*
  access points.

  Currently, it is up to the access point vendors to define the protocols necessary to support roaming from one access point to another. To be safe, you
  should consider purchasing access points from a single vendor, although you
  can mix-and-match radio cards in the appliances. Chapter 6, "Wireless
  System Integration," discusses industry standards, such as the Inter Access
  Point Protocol (IAPP) specification, that are beginning to define multiple-
  vendor roaming protocols.

IEEE 802.11 Standard Compliance

No standard is worthwhile unless vendors and end users comply with it. The following sections describe activities taking place to ensure compliance with 802.11.

Vendor Compliance

Most wireless LAN vendors (that is, manufacturers of the hardware) are releasing
initial radio cards and access points throughout 1998 and 1999 that comply with the
official 802.11 standard. Before deeming their devices as 802.11 compliant, they
must follow the protocol implementation compliance procedures that the 802.11
standard specifies in its appendix. The procedures state that the vendor shall

complete a Protocol Implementation Conformance Statement (PICS) proforma. The structure of the PICS proforma mainly includes a list of fixed questions that the vendor responds to with yes or no answers, indicating adherence to the standard. The PICS can have the following uses:

- A checklist that helps the vendor reduce the risk of failure to conform to the standard

- For the vendor and system implementor to better understand what 802.11–compliancy means

- As a basis for designing an interface between the 802.11 device and another network or system

- As the basis for developing protocol conformance tests and simulations

To ensure proper compliance, vendors test their products at the InterOperability Laboratory located at the Leavitt Center on the campus of The University of New Hampshire. In March 1997, for example, Aironet Wireless Communications, Inc.; Breezecom Wireless Communications; Netwave Technologies, Inc.; Proxim Inc.; Raytheon Electronics; and Symbol Technologies performed joint interoperability testing to advance customer adoption of wireless technology. In some cases, users can upgrade their existing proprietary radio cards to be 802.11 compliant by just reinstalling NIC interface software on their appliances.

Note

Vendors are easing the transition to 802.11-compliant radio networks by offering relatively simple ways to upgrade existing radio LAN devices. Symbol, Inc., for example, offers a firmware upgrade to your existing Symbol 2.4 GHz (Spectrum 24) networks, avoiding the purchase of new network adapters.

The InterOperability Laboratory, founded in 1988, performs research and development work and is used by more than 100 vendors to verify the interoperability and conformance of their computer communications products. The University of New Hampshire encourages vendors to conduct interoperability testing by providing facilities for a multiple-vendor test environment. The goal of the laboratory is to provide complete testing for all networking products, including ethernet, ADSL, ATM, fast ethernet, FDDI, FDSE, Fibre Channel, gigabit ethernet, IP/Routing, Network Management, and Wireless.

Note

Be aware that in 1997 some vendors released "802.11-compliant" wireless LAN radio cards and access points that were not certified as compliant with the final 802.11 standard. These products may or may not operate within the final official standard.

WLI Forum

The Wireless LAN Interoperability Forum (WLI Forum), a not-for-profit corporation founded in March 1996, promotes the growth of the wireless LAN market by delivering interoperable products and services. The Forum consists primarily of appliance suppliers/vendors (such as Hewlett-Packard, Fujitsu, Monarch Marking Systems, and Handheld Products) having products that operate on the WLI Forum's OpenAir™ wireless network. The Forum provides certification via an independent third-party test lab to ensure proper compliance.

The OpenAir™ specification describes a MAC and radio frequency Physical Layer, similar in scope to the 802.11 specification. The OpenAir™ network is based on Proxim's RangeLAN2 protocol, employing frequency hopping spread spectrum technology in the unlicensed 2.4 GHz ISM band. The OpenAir™ operates at a data rate of 1.6 Mbps per channel, with 15 independent channels (hopping patterns) available. This architecture enables up to 15 wireless LANs to overlap independently in the same physical space,

providing up to 24 Mbps of aggregate network bandwidth.

The WLI Forum wrote the OpenAir™ specification to motivate third-party development of compatible products. At the time, with no official IEEE standard on wireless networking, the Forum decided to base its specification on Proxim's product. Soon after the release of the 802.11 specification in June 1997, the WLI Forum announced its support for the adoption of the IEEE 802.11 standard and urged the supplier community to move toward conformance. As a result, the WLI Forum is likely to establish conformity to the IEEE 802.11 standard as well.

The WLI Forum is a worldwide organization, and is completely self funded through membership dues and fees. Membership is open to all companies that develop, manufacture, or sell wireless LAN products or services. For more information on the WLI Forum, visit their Web site located at http://www.wlif.com.

End-User Compliance

Throughout 1999 and beyond, end users should begin widespread implementations of 802.11-compliant LANs. As an end user, do you need to purchase and use products that comply with the 802.11 standard? Of course the answer is no, but you should carefully consider the advantages and disadvantages of implementing 802.11-compliant networks. Most likely, complying with 802.11 will be favored over the use of proprietary networks unless extenuating circumstances prevail. If the decision is to go with 802.11, you will be starting with one of the following scenarios:

- No existing implementation of wireless LANs

- Existing implementation of proprietary wireless LANs

If you are an end user with no existing installation of wireless networking components, compliance with the 802.11 standard is easy. Right? Actually, it is not as simple as it seems. The 802.11 standard is not as Plug and Play as the 802.3 ethernet standard. With 802.11, you must first decide which version of 802.11 best satisfies your needs. You might consider the following questions:

- *What type of modulation do I need?* Do I have radio interference implications that lean toward using the infrared PHY? Does the application require wider area coverage that may depend on the longer range capability of one of the spread spectrum PHYs? If the choice is spread spectrum, should I use direct sequence or frequency hopping?

- *Will the application require roaming across BSS cells interconnected by access points of different vendors?* If yes, you will need to think about how to provide roaming between access points.

- *Does the network require the optional WEP security?* If the answer is yes, be sure to choose wireless devices having WEP available.

- *Do the appliances I need to comply with have the 802.11 options I have chosen?* If not, you need to choose options that comply with the appliance, or you must choose different appliances.

Answers to the preceding questions define the options you need to consider when planning to purchase radio cards and access points complying with 802.11.

If proprietary wireless LANs already exist, you will need to either upgrade or replace the existing network to make it compliant with 802.11. Many of the vendors offer free upgrades to make your existing wireless LANs (if they are of a recent enough version) compliant with 802.11. BreezeCOM, for example, guarantees software upgrades to the IEEE 802.11 standard for its BreezeNET PRO product line.

If it is not possible or feasible to upgrade your existing wireless LAN, then of course you must perform a complete replacement if benefits outweigh the expenses. The replacement of the network will be difficult to cost-justify; however, it may become necessary as proprietary wireless components become obsolete.

International Electromagnetic Compliance

The 802.11 standard specifies operation in the 2.4 GHz band; however, electromagnetic compatibility requirements vary from one country to another. Operating frequencies, power levels, and spurious levels differ throughout the world.

Regional and national regulatory administrations of each individual country demand certification of wireless equipment. The 802.11 standard, however, identifies the minimum technical requirements for interoperability and compliance based on established regulations for Europe, Japan, and the North America. Therefore, wireless LAN vendors must be aware of all current regulatory requirements prior to releasing a product for sale in a particular country. The following agencies and documents specify the current regulatory requirements for various geographical areas:

Canada
- *Approval standards:* Industry Canada (IC)
- *Documents:* GL36
- *Approval authority:* Industry Canada

Europe
- *Approval standards:* European Telecommunications Standards Institute
- *Documents:* ETS 300-328, ETS 300-339
- *Approval authority:* National Type Approval Authorities

France
- *Approval standards:* La Reglementation en France por les Equipements fonctionnant dans la bande de frequences 2,4 GHz "RLAN-Radio Local Area Network"
- *Documents:* SP/DGPT/ATAS/23, ETS 300-328, ETS 300-339
- *Approval authority:* Direction Generale des Postes et Telecommunications

Japan
- *Approval standards:* Research and Development Center for Radio Communications (RCR)
- *Documents:* RCR STD-33A
- *Approval authority:* Ministry of Telecommunications (MKK)

Spain
- *Approval standards:* Supplemento del Numero 164 del Boletin Oficial del Estado (published 10 July 91; revised 25 June 93)
- *Documents:* ETS 300-328, ETS 300-339
- *Approval authority:* Cuadro Nacional De Atribucion De Frecuesias

The United States of America
- *Approval standards:* Federal Communications Commission (FCC)
- *Documents:* CFR47, Part 15, Sections 15.205, 15.209, 15.247
- *Approval authority:* FCC

Operation in countries within Europe and other areas outside Japan or North America may be subject to additional regulations.

IEEE 802.11 Working Group Operations

The 802.11 Working Group is a part of the IEEE LAN MAN Standards Committee (LMSC), which reports to the Standards Activity Board (SAB) of the IEEE Computer Society. IEEE 802.11 meetings are open to anyone. The only requirement to attend is to pay dues, which offset meeting expenses. Most of the active participants are representatives from companies developing wireless LAN components. The IEEE bylaws explain that to vote on standards activities, however, you must become a member by participating in at least two out of four consecutive plenary meetings. Then, you must continue to attend meetings to maintain voting status. The 802.11 Working Group meets three times a year during the plenary sessions of the IEEE 802 and three times a year between plenary sessions.

The IEEE 802.11 Working Group consists of about 200 members; membership falls into the following categories:

- *Voting members:* Those who have maintained voting status.

- *Nearly members:* Those who have participated in two sessions of meetings, one of which being a plenary session. Nearly members become voting members in the first session they attend following their qualification for nearly membership.

- *Aspirant members:* Those who have participated in one plenary or interim session meeting.

- *Sleeping voting members:* Those who were once voting members, but have chosen to discontinue.

Future of the IEEE 802.11 Standard

What is the future of IEEE 802.11? Will end users eventually fully comply with the standard? Will the 802.11 Working Group solve implications revolving around the standard? Only time will tell for certain. It is known today, however, that all major wireless LAN vendors are releasing 802.11-compliant wireless LANs throughout 1998, and these vendors are making it fairly easy for end users to upgrade their existing systems. This, combined with the advantages of standardization, should proliferate the use of 802.11-compliant networks.

To solve implications of the current release of the standard, the IEEE 802.11 Working Group is actively working on the following projects that will aid the widespread acceptance of the standard:

- *802.11rev: Revision of IEEE Standard 802.11-1997:* This project was charted to rectify a number of errors in the current standard and to accommodate input from the JTC1 review to result in a single JTC1/IEEE standard.

- *802.11a: Extension of the IEEE Standard 802.11-1997 with a higher data rate PHY in the 5 GHz band:* This project was initiated to develop a high speed (about 20 Mbps) wireless PHY suitable for data, voice, and image information services in fixed, moving, or portable wireless local area networks. The project concentrates on improving spectrum efficiency and will review the existing 802.11 MAC to ensure its capability to operate at the higher speeds.

  The IEEE 802.11 Working Group will actively correspond with regulatory bodies worldwide to encourage spectrum allocations that match these frequencies.

- *802.11b: Extension of the IEEE Standard 802.11-1997 with a higher data rate PHY in the 2.4 GHz band:* The purpose of this project is to extend the performance and the range of applications of the existing 802.11 standard. The header of the two existing radio-based PHYs can support data rates up to 4.5 Mbps for frequency hopping and up to 25.5 Mbps for direct sequence. This project will investigate ways to exploit these data rate capabilities and analyze the capability of the existing 802.11 MAC to support higher data rates.

  The actual data rates targeted by this project are at least 3 Mbps for the frequency hopping PHY and at least 8 Mbps for the direct sequence PHY. As with project 802.11a, IEEE 802.11 will correspond with regulatory bodies worldwide to ensure that the proposed extension will be applicable as widely as possible.

In addition to the preceding official projects, the 802.11 Working Group is actively studying the needs for standardization of wireless communications of wearable computing devices. The study is examining the requirements for Wireless Personal Area Networking (WPAN) of devices that are worn or carried by individuals. The objectives of the study group are as follows:

- Review WPAN requirements.

- Determine the need for a standard.

- If a standard is necessary, draft a PAR for submittal.

- Seek appropriate sponsorship within 802.

The study group is soliciting industry input on market requirements and technical solutions for a WPAN with 0-to-30–foot range, data rates of less than 1 Mbps, low power consumption, small size (less than 0.5 cubic inches), and low cost relative to target device.

As mentioned in this chapter, the 802.11 wireless LAN standard certainly has benefits that an organization should consider when selecting components that provide LAN mobility. IEEE 802 is a solid family of standards that will provide much greater multiple-level interoperability than proprietary systems.

Wireless LANs conforming to 802.11 provide interoperability between radio cards and access points. The 802.11 standard has the backing of IEEE, having an excellent track record of developing long-lasting standards, such as IEEE 802.3 (ethernet) and IEEE 802.5 (token ring). When designing a wireless LAN, definitely consider the use of 802.11-compliant products, but ensure that the data rates of 802.11 will support your application and that the chosen components support roaming between access points.

With 802.11, system implementors have several choices. You will need to choose the type of physical medium, for example: frequency hopping spread spectrum, direct sequence spread spectrum, or infrared light. This concept is similar to choosing between twisted-pair, optical-fiber, and coaxial cable in an ethernet LAN. You will also need to determine how to interface wireless devices with server operating systems and applications. In defining these elements, be sure the resulting network supports all requirements.

PART II

Inside IEEE 802.11

CHAPTER 4

Medium Access Control (MAC) Layer

- **MAC Layer operations**
  The 802.11 MAC Layer provides both contention and contention-free access to a shared wireless medium. An explanation of medium sensing and inter-frame timing shows how 802.11 networks provide multiple levels of priority to frame transmissions.

- **MAC frame structure**
  A description of MAC frame structure illustrates the makeup of a MAC frame, providing basic building blocks of different MAC frame types.

- **MAC frame types**
  The 802.11 MAC Layer uses various frame types to implement its functions. An overview of the various MAC management, control, and data frames gives a foundation for understanding MAC functionality.

MAC Layer Operations

Each station and access point on an 802.11 wireless LAN implements the MAC Layer service, which provides the capability for peer LLC entities to exchange MAC service data units (MSDUs) between MAC service access points (SAPs). The MSDUs carry LLC-based frames that facilitate functions of the Logical Link Control Layer (LLC). Overall, MAC services encompass the transmission of MSDUs by sharing a wireless radio wave or infrared light medium.

The MAC Layer provides these primary operations:

- Accessing the wireless medium
- Joining a network
- Providing authentication and privacy

The following sections describe these operations.

Accessing the Wireless Medium

Before transmitting a frame, the MAC coordination must first gain access to the network using one of the following modes:

- *Carrier-sense multiple access with collision avoidance (CSMA/CA):* A contention-based protocol similar to IEEE 802.3 ethernet. The 802.11 specification refers to this mode as the *distributed coordination function* (DCF).

- *Priority-based access:* A contention-free access protocol usable on infrastructure network configurations containing a controller called a point coordinator within the access points. The 802.11 specification refers to this mode as the *point coordination function* (PCF).

Both the distributed and the point coordination function can operate concurrently within the same BSS to provide alternating contention and contention-free periods. The following sections describe each of these MAC operational modes.

Distributed Coordination Function

The distributed coordination function is the primary access protocol for the automatic sharing of the wireless medium between stations and access points having compatible PHYs. Similar to the MAC coordination of the 802.3 ethernet wired line standard, 802.11 networks use a carrier-sense multiple access/collision avoidance (CSMA/CA) protocol for sharing the wireless medium.

Carrier Sense Mechanism

A combination of both physical and virtual carrier sense mechanisms enables the MAC coordination to determine whether the medium is busy or idle (see Figure 4.1). Each of the PHY layers provides a physical means of sensing the channel (as described in Chapter 5, "Physical (PHY) Layer"). The results of the physical channel assessment from the PHY coordination are sent to the MAC coordination as part of the information factored when deciding the status of the channel.

The MAC coordination carries out the virtual carrier sense protocol based on reservation information found in the Duration field of all frames. This information announces (to all other stations) a station's impending use of the medium. The

MAC coordination will monitor the Duration field in all MAC frames and place this information in the station's Network Allocation Vector (NAV) if the value is greater than the current NAV value. The NAV operates like a timer, starting with a value equal to the Duration field value of the last frame transmission sensed on the medium, and counting down to zero. After the NAV reaches zero, the station can transmit if the PHY coordination indicates a clear channel.

The physical channel assessment and NAV contents provide sufficient information for the MAC to decide the status of the channel. As an example, the PHY may determine that no transmissions are taking place on the medium, but the NAV may indicate that a previous frame transmission had a value in the applicable Duration field that disables transmissions for a specific time period. In this case, the MAC would hold off transmission of any frames until the Duration time period expires. If the channel is busy, the MAC protocol implements a backoff algorithm.

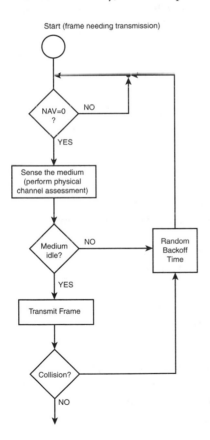

FIGURE 4.1 *This flowchart illustrates the operation of the CSMA/CA contention-based 802.11 distributed coordination function (DCF) medium access protocol.*

The CSMA/CA protocol avoids the probability of collisions among stations sharing the medium by utilizing a random backoff time if the station's physical or logical sensing mechanism indicates a busy medium. The period of time immediately following a busy medium is the highest probability of collisions occurring, especially under high utilization. The reason for this is many stations may be waiting for the medium to become idle and attempt to transmit at the same time. When the medium is idle, a random backoff time defers a station from transmitting a frame, minimizing the chance that stations collide.

The MAC coordination calculates the random backoff time using the following formula:

```
Backoff Time = Random() X aSlotTime
```

`Random()` is a pseudo-random integer drawn from a uniform distribution over the interval `[0,CW]`, in which `CW` (collision window) is an integer within the range of values of the Management Information Base (MIB) attributes `aCWmin` and `aCWmax`. The random number drawn from this interval should be statistically independent among stations. `aSlotTime` equals a constant value found in the station's MIB.

Note

The MAC Layer includes a management information base (MIB) that stores parameters the MAC protocol needs to operate. Refer to the 802.11 standard for a complete description of these parameters. Most access points require you to supply an alphanumeric name if accessing configuration parameters via the network.

The MAC Layer has access to the MIB via the following MAC sublayer management entity (MLME) primitives:

- MLME-GET.request: Requests the value of a specific MIB attribute.
- MLME-GET.confirm: Returns the value of the applicable MIB attribute value that corresponds to an MLME-GET.request.
- MLME-SET.request: Requests the MIB set a specific MIB attribute to a particular value.
- MLME-SET.confirm: Returns the status of the MLME-SET.request.

Figure 4.2 illustrates the value of `CW` as the station goes through successive retransmissions. The reason `CW` increases exponentially is to minimize collisions and maximize throughput for both low and high network utilizations.

Under low utilization, stations are not forced to wait very long before transmitting their frames. On the first or second attempt, a station will make a successful transmission within a short period of time. If the utilization of the network is high, the protocol holds stations back for longer periods of time to avoid the probability of multiple stations transmitting at the same time.

Under high utilization, the value of CW increases to relatively high values after successive retransmissions, providing substantial transmission spacing between stations needing to transmit. This mechanism does a good job of avoiding collisions; however, stations on networks with high utilization will experience substantial delays while waiting to transmit frames.

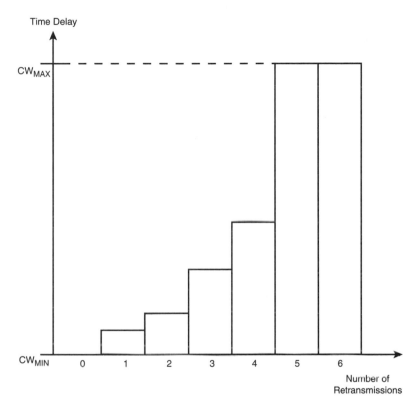

FIGURE 4.2 *The backoff time increases exponentially as between the minimum and maximum values of* CW.

Error Recovery Mechanisms

Because of transmission impairments, such as interference and collisions, bit errors can disrupt the sequencing of frames. Station A may send an RTS (Request to Send) frame and never receive the corresponding CTS (Clear to Send). Or, station A may send a data frame and never receive an acknowledgement. Because of these problems, the MAC coordination performs error recovery mechanisms.

Stations initiating the exchange of frames have the responsibility of error recovery. This generally involves the retransmission of frames after a period of time if no response is heard from the destination station. This process, commonly referred to as automatic repeat-request (ARQ), takes into account that bits errors could have made the ACK frame unrecognizable.

To regulate the number of retransmissions, the MAC coordination differentiates between short and long frames. For short frames (frames with length less than the MIB attribute aRTSThreshold), retransmissions continue until the number of attempts reaches the MIB value aShortRetryLimit. The MAC coordination retransmits long frames similarly based on the MIB value aLongRetrylimit. After exceeding the retry limit, the station discards the frame.

Access Spacing

The 802.11 specification defines several standard spacing intervals (defined in the MIB) that defer a station's access to the medium and provides various levels of priority. Figure 4.3 illustrates these intervals. Each interval defines the time from the end of the last symbol of the previous frame to the beginning of the first symbol of the next frame.

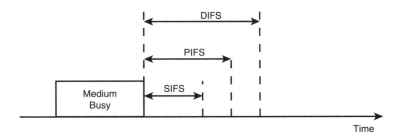

FIGURE 4.3 *The interframe space (IFS) illustrates the spacing between different aspects of the MAC access protocol.*

The following describes each of the interframe space (IFS) intervals:

- *Short IFS (SIFS):* The SIFS is the shortest of the interframe spaces, providing the highest priority level by allowing some frames to access the medium before others. The following frames use the SIFS interval:

  - ACK (Acknowledgement) frame

  - CTS (Clear to Send) frame

  - The second or subsequent MSDU of a fragment burst

  These frames require expedient access to the network to minimize frame retransmissions.

- *PCF IFS (PIFS):* The PIFS is the interval that stations operating under the point coordination function use to gain access to the medium. This provides priority over frames sent by the distributed coordination function. These stations can transmit contention-free traffic if they sense the medium is idle. This interval gives point coordination function-based stations a higher priority of access than DCF-based (CSMA) stations for transmitting frames.

- *DCF IFS (DIFS):* All stations operating according to the distributed coordination function use the DIFS interval for transmitting data frames and management frames. This spacing makes the transmission of these frames lower priority than PCF-based transmissions.

- *Extended IFS (EIFS):* All DCF-based stations use the EIFS interval—which goes beyond the time of a DIFS interval—as a waiting period when a frame transmission results in a bad reception of the frame due to an incorrect FCS value. This interval provides enough time for the receiving station to send an ACK frame.

Point Coordination Function (PCF)

The optional priority-based point coordination function provides contention-free frame transfer. With this operating mode, a point coordinator resides in the access point to control the transmission of frames from stations. All stations obey the point coordinator by setting their NAV value at the beginning of each contention-free period. Stations can optionally respond to a contention-free poll (CF-Poll frame), however.

At the beginning of the contention-free period, the point coordinator has an opportunity to gain control of the medium. The point coordinator follows the PIFS interval as a basis for accessing the medium; therefore, it may be able to maintain control during the contention-free period by waiting a shorter time between transmissions than stations operating under the distributed coordination function.

The point coordinator senses the medium at the beginning of each contention-free period. If the medium is idle after the PIFS interval, the point coordinator sends a Beacon frame that includes the CF Parameter Set element. When stations receive the beacon, they update their NAV with the CFPMaxDuration value found in the CF Parameter Set. This value communicates the length of the contention-free period to all stations and prevents stations from taking control of the medium until the end of the contention-free period.

After sending the Beacon frame, the point coordinator then transmits one of the following frames after waiting at least one SIFS interval:

- *Data frame:* This frame is directed from the access point's point coordinator to a particular station. If the point coordinator does not receive an ACK frame from the recipient, the point coordinator can retransmit the unacknowledged frame during the contention-free period after the PIFS interval. A point coordinator can send individual, broadcast, and multicast frames to all stations, including stations in power save mode that are pollable.

- *CF Poll frame:* The point coordinator sends this frame to a particular station, granting the station permission to transmit a single frame to any destination. If the polled station has no frame to send, it must send a Null data frame. If the sending station does not receive any frame acknowledgement, it cannot retransmit the frame unless the point coordinator polls it again. If the receiving station of the contention-free transmission is not CF pollable, it acknowledges the reception of the frame using distributed coordination function rules.

- *Data+CF Poll frame:* In this case, the point coordinator sends a data frame to a station and polls that same station for sending a contention-free frame. This is a form of piggybacking that reduces overhead on the network.

- *CF End frame:* This frame is sent to identify the end of the contention period, which occurs when one of the following happens:

    - The `CFPDurRemaining` time expires.

    - The point coordinator has no further frames to transmit and no stations to poll.

Stations have an option of being *pollable*. A station can indicate its desire for polling using the CF-Pollable subfield within the Capability Information field of an Association Request frame. A station can change its *pollability* by issuing a Reassociation Request frame. The point coordinator maintains a polling list of eligible stations that may receive a poll during the contention-free period. The point coordinator will send at least one CF-Poll if entries exist in the polling list in order by ascending AID value. When associating with an access point, a station may request to be on the polling list via the Capability Information field.

The point coordination function does not routinely operate using the backoff time of the distributed coordination function; therefore, a risk of collisions exists when overlapping point coordinators are present on the same PHY channel. This may be the case when multiple access points form an infrastructure network. To minimize these collisions, the point coordinator utilizes a random backoff time if the point coordinator experiences a busy medium when attempting to transmit the initial beacon.

Implementing the Wireless Access Method

By default, all 802.11-compliant stations operate using the *distributed coordination function* (*DCF*), which is a carrier sense access mechanism. As an option, you can initialize the stations to also implement the priority-based *point coordination function* (*PCF*).

In most cases, the DCF will suffice; however, consider activation of the PCF if needing to support the transmission of time-bounded information, such as audio and video. The PCF, however, will impose greater overhead on the network because of the transmission of polling frames.

Joining a Network

After a station is turned on, it needs to first determine whether another station or access point is present to join before authenticating and associating with an applicable station or access point. The station accomplishes this discovery phase by operating in a passive or active scanning mode. After joining with a BSS or ESS, the station accepts the Service Set Identifier (SSID), Timing Synchronization Function (TSF), timer value, and PHY setup parameters from the access point.

With passive scanning, a station listens to each channel for a specific period of time, as defined by the `ChannelTime` parameter. The station just waits for the transmission of Beacon frames having the SSID that the station wishes to join with. After the station detects the beacon, the station can negotiate a connection by proceeding with authentication and association processes, respectively.

Note

You can configure a station to passively scan for other stations for a particular amount of time before enabling the station to form its own network. The typical default time for this setting is 10 seconds.

Active scanning involves the transmission of a Probe frame indicating the SSID of the network that the station wishes to join. The station that sent the probe will wait for a Probe Response frame that identifies the presence of the desired network.

Some vendors enable you to set up each radio card so that it associates with a preferred access point even if the signal from that particular access point is lower than the signals from other access points. This may be useful if there is a need to regulate the flow of traffic through particular access points. In most cases, however the station will reassociate with another access point, if it doesn't receive beacons from the preferred access point.

A station can also send Probe frames using a broadcast SSID that causes all networks within reach to respond. An access point will reply to all probe requests in the case of infrastructure-based networks. With independent BSS networks (that is, one access point), the station that generated the last Beacon frame will respond to probe requests. The Probe Response frame indicates the presence of the desired networks, and the station can complete its connection by proceeding with the authentication and association processes.

Station Synchronization

Stations within the BSS must remain in synchronization with the access point to ensure all stations are operating with the same parameters (such as using the correct hopping pattern) and enabling power saving functions to work correctly. To accomplish this, the access point periodically transmits Beacon frames.

A Beacon frame contains information about the particular Physical Layer being used. The Beacon identifies the frequency hopping sequence and dwell time, for example, so the station can implement the applicable demodulation. The Beacon frame also contains the access point's clock value. Each station receiving the Beacon frame will use this information to update its clock accordingly, so the station knows when to wake up (if in sleep mode) to receive beacons.

Providing Authentication and Privacy

Because of the open broadcast nature of wireless LANs, designers need to implement appropriate levels of security. The 802.11 standard describes two following types of authentication services that increase the security of 802.11 networks:

- *Open system authentication:* The default authentication service that just announces the desire to associate with another station or access point

- *Shared key authentication:* Involves a more rigorous exchange of frames, ensuring the requesting station is authentic

The following sections describe the operation of each of these authentication types, as well as the *Wired Equivalent Privacy (WEP)* function.

Choosing Authentication Type

When setting up your wireless LAN, base your consideration of the type of authentication to use on security requirements. Vendors enable you to easily configure a station or access point to operate using either open encryption or shared key, or no security. The default operation is generally open encryption. If you implement the shared key mode, you will need to configure all stations with the same key.

Open System Authentication

An organization may wish to utilize open system authentication if it is not necessary to positively validate the identity of a sending station. A station can authenticate with any other station or access point using open system authentication if the receiving station designates open system authentication via the MIB parameter aAuthenticationType.

Figure 4.4 illustrates the operation of open system authentication. The Status Code located in the body of the second authentication frame identifies success or failure of the authentication.

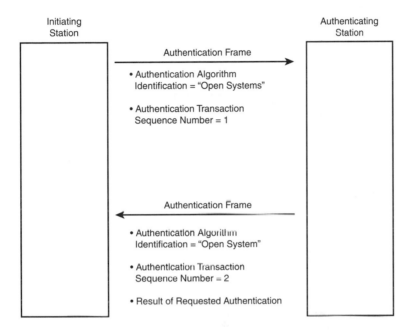

FIGURE 4.4 *The first frame of the open system authentication service requests authentication, and the second frame transmission indicates acceptance or rejection.*

Shared Key Authentication

The shared key authentication approach provides a much higher degree of security than the open system approach. For a station to utilize shared key authentication, it must implement WEP. Figure 4.5 illustrates the operation of shared key authentication. The secret shared key resides in each station's MIB in a write-only form to make it available to only the MAC coordination. The 802.11 standard, however, does not specify the process of installing the key in stations.

The process is as follows:

1. A requesting station sends an Authentication frame to another station.

2. When a station receives an initial Authentication frame, the station will reply with an Authentication frame containing 128 octets of challenge text that the WEP services generate.

3. The requesting station will then copy the challenge text into an Authentication frame, encrypt it with a shared key, and then send the frame to the responding station.

4. The receiving station will decrypt the value of the challenge text using the same shared key and compare it to the challenge text sent earlier. If a match occurs, the responding station will reply with an authentication indicating a successful authentication. If not, the responding station will send a negative authentication.

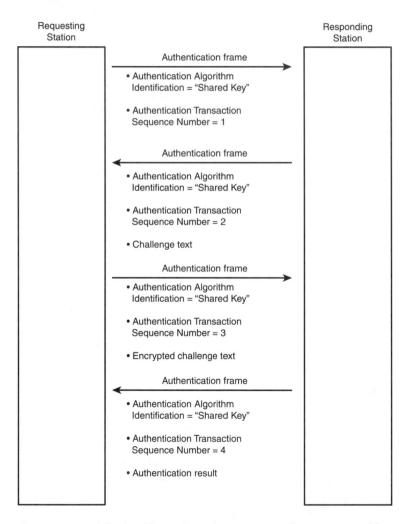

FIGURE 4.5 *The shared key authentication service uses the transmission of frames that (1) request authentication, (2) deliver challenge text, (3) deliver an encrypted frame, including the challenge text, and (4) accept or reject the authentication.*

Private Frame Transmissions

To offer frame transmission privacy similar to a wired network, the 802.11 specification defines optional WEP. The WEP generates secret shared encryption keys that both source and destination stations can use to alter frame bits to avoid disclosure to eavesdroppers. This process is also known as *symmetric encryption*. Stations can utilize WEP alone without authentication services, but they should implement both WEP and authentication together to avoid making the LAN vulnerable to security threats.

Figure 4.6 shows the processing that occurs with the WEP algorithm:

1. At the sending station, the WEP encipherment first runs the unencrypted data located in the Frame Body field of a MAC frame through an integrity algorithm that generates a four-octet integrity check value that is sent with the data and checked at the receiving station to guard against unauthorized data modification.

2. The WEP process inputs the secret shared encryption key into a pseudo-random number generator to create a key sequence with length equal to the `plaintext` and integrity check value.

3. WEP encrypts the data by using `bitwise XOR` on the `plaintext` and integrity check value with the key sequence to create `ciphertext`. The pseudo-random number generator makes key distribution much easier because only the shared key must be made available to each station, not the variable length key sequence.

4. At the receiving station, the WEP process deciphers the `ciphertext` using the shared key that generates the same key sequence used initially to encrypt the frame.

5. The station calculates an integrity check value and ensures it matches the one sent with the frame. If the integrity check fails, the station will not hand the MSDU off to the LLC, and a failure indication is sent to MAC management.

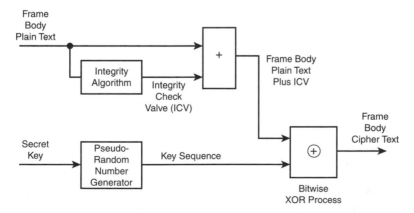

FIGURE 4.6 *The Wired Equivalent Privacy (WEP) safeguards data transmissions by performing a series of operations using a secret shared key.*

MAC Frame Structure

The following sections define each field and subfield of the MAC frame. For a formal description (using the ITU Specification and Description Language) of the MAC Layer operation, refer to Appendix C of the 802.11 standard.

Overall MAC Frame Format

The IEEE 802.11 standard specifies an overall MAC frame format, as shown in Figure 4.7. This frame structure is found in all frames that stations transmit, regardless of frame type. After forming the applicable frame, the MAC coordination passes the frame's bits to the physical layer convergence procedure sublayer (PLCP), starting with the first bit of the Frame Control field and ending with the last bit of the frame check sequence (FCS).

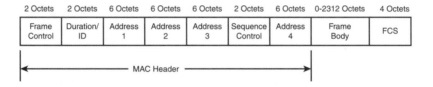

FIGURE 4.7   *The MAC frame consists of a header, variable length frame body, and a 32-bit frame check sequence (FCS), all of which support MAC Layer functionality.*

The following list defines each of the main MAC frame fields:

- *Frame Control:* This field carries control information being sent from station to station. Figure 4.8 illustrates specific subfields within the Frame Control field.

- *Duration/ID:* In most frames, this field contains a duration value, depending on the type of frame sent. (See the section "MAC Frame Types" later in this chapter for possible values.) In general, each frame contains information that identifies the duration of the next frame transmission. As an example, the Duration/ID field in data and acknowlededgment (ACK) frames specifies the total duration of the next fragment and acknowledgement. Stations on the network monitor this field and hold off transmissions based on the duration information.

  In Power Save (PS)-Poll control frames only, the Duration/ID field carries the 14 least significant bits of the association identity of the sending station. The two remaining bits for this field are set to 1. Possible values for this identification are currently in the decimal range 1–2007.

- *Address 1, 2, 3, and 4:* The address fields contain different types of addresses, depending on the type of frame being sent. These address types may include the Basic Service Set Identification (BSSID), source address, destination address, transmitting station address, and receiving station address. IEEE standard 802-1990 defines the structure of the addresses, which are all 48 bits in length.

The addresses can be either individual or group addresses. There are two types of group addresses: *multicast*, which associate with a group of logically related stations; and *broadcast* addresses, which refer to all stations on a given LAN. A broadcast address consists of all 1s.

- *Sequence Control:* The leftmost 4 bits of this field consist of a Fragment Number subfield, indicating the fragment number of a particular MSDU. This number starts with 0 for the first fragment, and then increments by one for each successive transmission. The next 12 bits of this frame are the Sequence Number subfield starting at 0 and incrementing by 1 for each subsequent MSDU transmission. Each fragment of a specific MSDU will have the same sequence number.

  Only one MSDU can be outstanding at a time. On reception of a frame, a station can filter duplicate frames by monitoring the sequence and fragment numbers. The station knows the frame is a duplicate if the sequence number and fragment number are equal to the frame immediately preceding, or if the Retry bit is set to 1.

  Duplicate frames can occur when a station receives a frame without errors, sends an ACK frame back to the sending station, and transmission errors destroy the ACK frame en route. After not receiving the ACK over a specific time period, the sending station retransmits a duplicate frame. The destination station performs an acknowledgement of the retransmitted frame even if the frame is discarded due to duplicate filtering.

- *Frame Body:* This field has a variable length payload and carries information that pertains to the specific frame being sent. In the case of a data frame, this field may contain an LLC data unit (also called an MSDU). MAC management and control frames may include specific parameters in the Frame Body that pertain to the particular service the frame is implementing. If the frame has no need to carry information, this field has a length of zero. The receiving station will determine the frame length from a field within the applicable Physical Layer headers. (See Chapter 5, "Physical (PHY) Layer," for more information.)

- *Frame Check Sequence (FCS):* The MAC Layer at the sending station calculates a 32-bit *frame check sequence (FCS)* using a *Cyclic Redundancy Check (CRC)* and places the result in this field. The MAC Layer uses the following generator polynomial over all fields of the MAC header and Frame Body to calculate the FCS:

$$G(x)=X^{32}+X^{26}+X^{23}+X^{22}+X^{16}+X^{12}+X^{11}+X^{10}+X^{8}+X^{7}+X^{5}+X^{4}+X^{2}+X+1.$$

The result's highest-order coefficient is placed in the field, from the leftmost bit. The receiver implements a CRC to check for transmission errors in the frame.

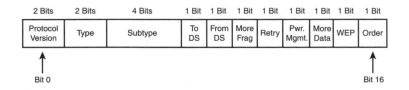

FIGURE 4.8 *The Frame Control field defines the frame as a management, control, or data frame.*

Setting Up a Network ID

The *Basic Service Set Identification (BSSID)*, also known as a network ID, is a 6-byte address that distinguishes a particular access point from others. Most access points will ship with a default BSSID, and you can change the ID through configuration parameters if you are installing a network with multiple access points.

Be sure to avoid conflicts by assigning a different BSSID for each access point. Typically, you can set up the access point via its management utility to automatically choose a BSSID that doesn't conflict with other BSSs operating in the same area.

Frame Control Field

The following defines each of the subfields within the Frame Control field:

- *Protocol Version field:* For the current standard, the protocol version is zero; therefore, the Protocol Version field always contains a 0. IEEE will add additional version numbers in the future if a newer version of the standard is fundamentally incompatible with an earlier version.

- *Type field:* This field defines whether the frame is a management, control, or data frame as indicated by the bits in the following table:

Bit 3, Bit 2	Frame Type
0,0	Management frame
0,1	Control frame
1,0	Data frame
1,1	Reserved

Note

All reserved bits are transmitted as value 0 and are ignored by the receiving station.

- *Subtype field:* This field defines the function of the frame, as shown in the following table:

Frame Type	Subfield (Bits 7, 6, 5, 4)	Frame Function
Management Type (bit 3, bit 2)=00	0000	Association Request
	0001	Association Response
	0010	Reassociation Request
	0011	Reassociation Response
	0100	Probe Request
	0101	Probe Response
	0110–0111	Reserved
	1000	Beacon
	1001	Announcement Traffic Indication Map (ATIM)
	1010	Disassociation
	1011	Authentication
	1100	Deauthentication
	1101–1111	Reserved
Control Type (bit 3, bit 2)=01	0000–1001	Reserved
	1010	Power-Save (PS) Poll
	1011	Request to Send (RTS)
	1100	Clear to Send (CTS)
	1101	Acknowledgement (ACK)
	1110	Contention Free (CF) End
	1111	CF End + CF ACK
Data Type (bit 3, bit 2)=10	0000	Data
	0001	Data + CF ACK
	0010	Data + CF Poll
	0011	Data + CF ACK + CF Poll
	0100	Null (no data)
	0101	CF ACK
	0110	CF Poll
	0111	CF ACK + CF Poll
	1000–1111	Reserved
Reserved Type (bit 3, bit 2)=11	0000–111	

Limiting Multicast Traffic

A *delivery traffic indication message* (*DTIM*) determines how often the MAC Layer forwards multicast traffic. This parameter is necessary to accommodate stations using power save mode. You can set the DTIM value via the access point. If you set the value to 2, the access point will save all multicast frames for the BSS and forward them after every second beacon.

Smaller DTIM intervals deliver multicast frames in a more timely manner, causing stations in power save mode to wake up more often and drain power faster. Higher DTIM values, however, delay the transmission of multicast frames.

- *To DS field:* The MAC coordination sets this single-bit field to 1 in any frame destined to the distribution system. It is 0 for all other transmissions. An example of this bit being set would be the case when a frame's destination is in a radio cell (also called BSS) of a different access point.

- *From DS field:* The MAC coordination sets this single-bit field to 1 in any frame leaving the distribution system. It is 0 for all other transmissions. Both the To DS and From DS fields are set to 1 if the frame is being sent from one access point through the distribution system to another access point.

- *More Frag field:* This single-bit field is set to 1 if another fragment of the same MSDU follows in a subsequent frame.

Implementing Fragmentation

The MAC services provide fragmentation and defragmentation services to support the division of MSDUs into smaller elements for transmission. Fragmentation can increase reliability of transmission because it increases the probability of a successful transmission due to smaller frame size. Each station can support the concurrent reception and defragmentation of fragments for up to three MSDUs. The MAC Layer fragments frames having a unicast receiver address only. It never fragments broadcast and multicast frames because of significant resulting overhead on the network.

If the length of the MSDU needing transmission exceeds the aFragmentationThreshold parameter located in the MAC's management information base (MIB), the MAC protocol will fragment the MSDU. Each fragmented frame consists of a MAC header, FCS, and a fragment number indicating its ordered position in the MSDU. Each of the fragments is sent independently and requires separate ACKs from the receiving station. The More Fragment field in the Frame Control field indicates whether a frame is the last of a series of fragments.

After decryption takes place (if the station is implementing WEP), the destination station will combine all fragments of the same sequence number in the correct order to reconstruct the corresponding MSDU. Based on the fragment numbers, the destination station will discard any duplicate fragments.

If there is significant interference present or if there are collisions resulting from high network utilization, try setting the fragment size to send smaller fragments. This will enable the retransmission of smaller frames much faster. It is more efficient, however, to set the fragment size larger if very little or no interference is present (because it requires overhead to send multiple frames). The fragment size value can typically be set between 256 and 2048 bytes.

- *Retry field:* If the frame is a retransmission of an earlier frame, this single-bit field is set to 1. It is 0 for all other transmissions. The reason for retransmission could be because the errors in the transmission of the first frame resulted in an unsuccessful FCS.

Setting the Transmission Retry Time

You can set the retry time on stations to govern the amount of time a station will wait before attempting to retransmit a frame if no acknowledgement appears from the receiving station. This time value is normally set between 1 and 30 seconds. You can also set the number of retries that will occur before the station gives up. This value can normally be set between 0 and 64.

- *Power Management field:* The bit in this field indicates the power management mode that the sending station will be in after the current frame exchange sequence. The MAC Layer places 1 in this field if the station will be in a sleep mode (802.11 defines this as power-save mode). A 0 indicates the station will be in full active mode. A receiving station can utilize this information to adjust transmissions to avoid waking up sleeping stations. In most cases, battery-operated devices should be kept in power-save mode to conserve battery power.

- *More Data field:* If a station has additional MSDUs to send to a station that is in power-save mode, then the sending station will place 1 in this field. The More Data field is 0 for all other transmissions. The more data feature alerts the receiving station to be ready for additional frames. An example of using this feature is when a station is sending a group of fragments belonging to a single MSDU.

- *WEP field:* A 1 in this field tells the receiving station that the WEP algorithm has processed the Frame Body; that is, the data bits have been encrypted using a secret key. The WEP field bit is 0 for all other types of transmissions. Refer to the section "Private Frame Transmissions" earlier in this chapter to learn how the WEP algorithm works.

- *Order field:* This field is set to 1 in any data frame being sent using the StrictlyOrdered service class, which tells the receiving station that frames must be processed in order.

Note

The IEEE 802.11 standard makes use of the same 48-bit MAC address that is compatible with the entire 802 LAN family. The 802.11 architecture can handle multiple logical media and address spaces, which makes 802.11 independent of the distribution system implementation.

continues

The vendor you purchase the radio card and access points from usually guarantees that the MAC address loaded in the radio is unique from all other radios, even ones from other vendors. You normally have the ability to change the MAC address of the card; however, you should use the factory-set address to avoid the potential of address conflicts.

IEEE 802.11 defines the following address types:

- Destination address (DA): *The final destination of the MSDU located that is in the Frame Body of the MAC frame*
- Source address (SA): *The address of the MAC entity that initiated the MSDU transmission*
- Receiver address (RA): *The address of the access point that is to receive the frame next*
- Transmitter address (TA): *The address of the immediate preceding access point sending the frame*

MAC Frame Types

To carry out the delivery of MSDUs between peer LLCs, the MAC Layer uses a variety of frame types, each having a particular purpose. The IEEE 802.11 specification divides MAC frames into three broad categories that provide management, control, and data exchange functions between stations and access points. The following sections describe the structure of each major frame type.

Management Frames

The purpose of Management frames is to establish initial communications between stations and access points. Thus, Management frames provide such services as association and authentication. Figure 4.9 depicts the common format of all Management frames.

2 Octets	2 Octets	6 Octets	6 Octets	6 Octets	2 Octets	0-2312 Octets	4 Octets
Frame Control	Duration	DA	SA	BSSID	Sequence Control	Frame Body	FCS

F I G U R E 4.9 *The Management frame format includes destination address, source address, and BSSID in Address fields 1, 2, and 3, consecutively.*

The Duration field within all Management frames during the contention-free period (as defined by the point coordination function) is set to decimal 32,768 (hexadecimal value of 8000), giving Management frames plenty of time to establish communications before other stations have the capability to access the medium.

During the contention period (as defined by the CSMA-based distributed coordination function), all Management frames have the Duration field set as follows:

- If the destination address is a group address, the Duration field is set to 0.

- If the More Fragments bit is set to 0 and the destination address is an individual address, the Duration field contains the number of microseconds required to transmit one ACK frame and one short *interframe space*. (The section "Access Spacing" earlier in this chapter defines the interframe space.)

- If the More Fragments bit is set to 1 and the destination address is an individual address, the Duration field contains the number of microseconds required to transmit the next fragment, two ACK frames, and three short interframe spaces.

A station receiving a Management frame performs address matching for receive decisions based on the contents of the Address 1 field of the MAC frame, which is the destination address (DA). If the address matches the station, that station completes the reception of the frame and hands it off to the LLC Layer. If a match does not occur, the station ignores the rest of the frame.

The following defines each of the management frame subtypes:

- *Association Request frame:* A station will send this frame to an access point if it wants to associate with that access point. A station becomes associated with an access point after the access point grants permission.

- *Association Response frame:* After an access point receives an Association Request frame, the access point will send an association response frame to indicate whether it is accepting the association with the sending station.

- *Reassociation Request frame:* A station will send this frame to an access point if it wants to reassociate with that access point. A reassociation may occur if a station moves out of range from one access point and within range of another access point. The station will need to reassociate with the new access point (instead of merely *associate*) so that the new access point knows that it will need to negotiate the forwarding of data frames from the old access point.

- *Reassociation Response frame:* After an access point receives a Reassociation Request frame, the access point will send a Reassociation Response frame to indicate whether it is accepting the reassociation with the sending station.

- *Probe Request frame:* A station sends a Probe Request frame to obtain information from another station or access point. For example, a station may send a Probe Request frame to determine whether a certain access point is available.

- *Probe Response frame:* If a station or access point receives a Probe Request frame, the station will respond to the sending station with a Probe Response frame containing specific parameters about itself (for example, parameter sets for the frequency hopping and direct sequence PHYs).

- *Beacon frame:* In an infrastructure network, an access point periodically sends a Beacon frame (according to the `aBeaconPeriod` parameter in the MIB) that provides synchronization among stations utilizing the same PHY. The Beacon frame includes a timestamp that all stations use to update what 802.11 defines as a timing synchronization function (TSF) timer.

If the access point supports the point coordination function, it uses a Beacon frame to announce the beginning of a contention-free period. If the network is an independent BSS (that is, having no access point), all stations periodically send Beacon frames for synchronization purposes.

- *ATIM frame:* A station with frames buffered for other stations sends an ATIM (announcement traffic indication message) frame to each of these stations during the ATIM window, which immediately follows a Beacon frame transmission. The station then transmits these frames to the applicable recipients. The transmission of the ATIM frame alerts stations in sleep state to stay awake long enough to receive their respective frames.

- *Disassociation frame:* If a station or access point wants to terminate an association, it will send a Disassociation frame to the opposite station. A single Disassociation frame can terminate associations with more than one station through the broadcast address of all 1s.

- *Authentication frame:* A station sends an Authentication frame to a station or access point that it wishes to authenticate with. The authentication sequence consists of the transmission of one or more Authentication frames, depending on the type of authentication being implemented (that is, open system or shared key). Refer to the section "Providing Authentication and Privacy" earlier in this chapter.

- *Deauthentication frame:* A station sends a Deauthentication frame to a station or access point with which it wants to terminate secure communications.

The content of the Frame Body field of management frames depends on the type of management frame being sent. Figure 4.10 identifies the Frame Body contents of each management frame subtype.

Implementing Power Management

The power-management function of an IEEE 802.11 network enables stations to go into sleep mode to conserve power for long periods of time without losing information. The 802.11 power management is supported with the use of access points; therefore, it is not available when implementing ad hoc networks. You should definitely consider implementing this feature if the conservation of batteries powering the radio card and appliance is a concern.

You implement power management on IEEE 802.11 LANs by first setting the access points and radio cards to power save mode via the vendor's parameter initialization routines. The access points and radio cards will then carry out the power-management functions automatically. As part of the power-management routine, the access points will maintain a record of the stations currently working in power save mode by monitoring the single-bit power-management field in the Frame Control field of the MAC header for frames sent on the network. The access points will buffer packets addressed to the stations in power save mode.

The access points will forward the buffered packets to the applicable stations when they return to active state (awake state) or when the stations request them. The access point knows when a station awakens because the station will indicate its active state by toggling the power-management bit in the Frame Control field of the MAC frames.

A station can learn that it has frames buffered at the access point by listening to the beacons sent periodically by the access point. The beacons will have a list (called a *traffic indication map*) of stations having buffered frames at the access point. A station uses a Power-Save Poll frame to notify the access point to send the buffered packets.

Frame Body Contents	Association Request	Association Response	Reassociation Request	Reassociation Response	Probe Response	Probe Request	Beacon	Disassociation	Authentication	Deauthentication
Authentication Algorithm Number									X	
Authentication Transaction Sequence Number									X	
Beacon Interval					X		X			
Current AP Address			X							
Listen Interval	X		X							
Reason Code								X		X
Association ID (AID)		X		X						
Status Code		X		X					X	
Timestamp					X		X			
Service Set Identity (SSID)	X		X		X	X	X			
Supported Rates	X	X	X	X	X	X	X			
FH Parameter Set					X		X			
DS Parameter Set					X		X			
CF Parameter Set					X		X			
Capability Information	X	X	X	X	X		X			
Traffic Indication Map (TIM)							X			
IBSS Parameter Set					X		X			
Challenge Text									X	

FIGURE 4.10 *The Frame Body contents of a management frame depend on the frame subtype.*

The 802.11 standard describes the Frame Body elements of the management frame subtypes. Refer to the standard if you need detailed information, such as field formats. The following, however, summarizes each of the elements:

- *Authentication Algorithm Number:* This field specifies the authentication algorithm that the authenticated stations and access points are to use. The value is either 0 for open system authentication or 1 for shared key authentication.

- *Authentication Transaction Sequence Number:* This field indicates the state of progress of the authentication process.

- *Beacon Interval:* This value is the number of time units between beacon transmission times.

- *Capability Information:* This field announces capability information about a particular station. For example, a station can identify its desire to be polled in this element.

- *Current AP Address:* This field indicates the address of the *access point* that the station is currently associated with.

- *Listen Interval:* This value identifies, in units of Beacon Interval, how often a station will wake to listen to Beacon management frames.

- *Reason Code:* This field indicates the reason (via a numbered code) a station is generating an unsolicited disassociation or deauthentication. Examples of the reasons are as follows:

  - Previous authentication no longer valid

  - Disassociated due to inactivity

  - Station requesting association is not authenticated with responding station

- *Association ID (AID):* This ID, which is assigned by an access point during association, is the 16-bit identification of a station corresponding to a particular association.

- *Status Code:* This code indicates the status of a particular operation. Examples of status are as follows:

  - Successful

  - Unspecified failure

  - Association denied because the access point is unable to handle additional associated stations

  - Authentication rejected due to timeout waiting for next frame in sequence

- *Timestamp:* This field contains the timer value at the sending station when it transmits the frame.

- *Service Set Identify (SSID):* This field contains the identity of the Extended Service Set (ESS).

- *Supported Rates:* This field identifies all data rates a particular station can accept. This value represents the data rate in 500 Kbps increments. The MAC coordination has the capability to change data rates to optimize performance of frame transmissions.

- *FH Parameter Set:* This field indicates the dwell time and hopping pattern needed to synchronize two stations using the *frequency hopping* PHY.

- *DS Parameter Set:* This field identifies the channel number that stations are using with the *direct sequence* PHY.

- *CF Parameter Set:* This field consists of a series of parameters that support the *point coordination function (PCF)*.

- *TIM:* The *traffic indication map (TIM)* element specifies the stations having MSDUs buffered at the access point.

- *IBSS Parameter Set:* This field contains parameters that support the Independent Basic Service Set (IBSS) networks.

- *Challenge Text:* This field contains the challenge text of a shared key authentication sequence.

Note

Some vendors add optional extensions to 802.11 management frames that provide functionality beyond the standard. As an example, additional information of an Association Request frame could set priorities for which access point a station associates with.

If you're using access points from multiple vendors, you should disable the transmission of the extensions.

Control Frames

After establishing association and authentication between stations and access points, control frames provide functionality to assist in the delivery of data frames. Figure 4.11 shows a common flow of control frames.

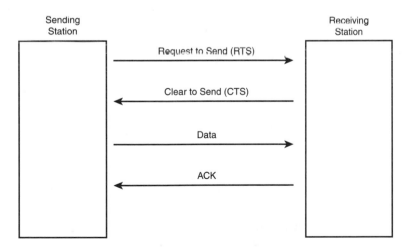

FIGURE 4.11   *Control frames provide synchronization between sending and receiving stations.*

The following defines the structure of each control frame subtype:

- *Request to Send (RTS):* A station sends an RTS frame to a particular receiving station to negotiate the sending of a data frame. Through the aRTSThreshold attribute stored in the MIB, you can configure a station to either always, never, or only on frames longer than a specified length, initiate an RTS frame sequence.

  Figure 4.12 illustrates the format of an RTS frame. The value of the Duration field, in microseconds, is the amount of time the sending station needs to transmit the frame, one CTS frame, one ACK frame, and three *short interframe space (SIFS)* intervals.

2 Octets	2 Octets	6 Octets	6 Octets	4 Octets
Frame Control	Duration	RA	TA	FCS

FIGURE 4.12   *The Request to Send frame format includes the receiver address (RA) and transmitter address (TA).*

- *Clear to Send (CTS):* After receiving an RTS, the station sends a CTS frame to acknowledge the right for the sending station to send data frames. Stations will always pay attention to the duration information and respond to an RTS frame, even if the station was not set up to initiate RTS frame sequences.

  Figure 4.13 illustrates the format of a CTS frame. The value of the Duration field, in microseconds, is the amount of time from the Duration field of the previous RTS frame minus the time required to transmit the CTS frame and its SIFS interval.

2 Octets	2 Octets	6 Octets	4 Octets
Frame Control	Duration	RA	FCS

FIGURE 4.13   *The Clear to Send and Acknowledgement frame formats include the receiver address (RA).*

- *Acknowledgement (ACK):* A station receiving an error-free frame can send an ACK frame to the sending station to acknowledge the successful reception of the frame. Figure 4.13 illustrates the format of an ACK frame.

  The value of the Duration field, in microseconds, is equal to zero if the More Fragment bit in the Frame Control field of the preceding data or management frame is set to 0. If the More Fragment bit of the previous data or management frame is set to 1, the Duration field is the amount of time from the

Duration field of the preceding data or management frame minus the time required to transmit the ACK frame and its SIFS interval.

- *Power-Save Poll (PS Poll):* If a station receives a PS Poll frame, the station updates its *network allocation vector (NAV)*, which is an indication of time periods that a station will not initiate a transmission. The NAV contains a prediction of future traffic on the medium. Figure 4.14 illustrates the format of a PS Poll frame.

2 Octets	2 Octets	6 Octets	6 Octets	4 Octets
Frame Control	AID	BSSID	TA	FCS

FIGURE 4.14   *The Power-Save Poll frame format includes the association identifier (AID), Basic Service Set Identification (BSSID), and the transmitter address (TA).*

- *Contention-Free End (CF End):* The CF End designates the end of a contention period that is part of the point coordination function. Figure 4.15 illustrates the format of a CF End frame. In these frames, the Duration field is always set to 0, and the receiver address (RA) contains the broadcast group address.

2 Octets	2 Octets	6 Octets	6 Octets	4 Octets
Frame Control	Duration	RA	BSSID	FCS

FIGURE 4.15   *The CF End and CF End + CF ACK frame formats include the receiver address (RA) and Basic Service Set Identification (BSSID).*

- *CF End + CF-ACK:* This frame acknowledges the Contention-Free End announcement of a CF End frame. Figure 4.15 illustrates the format of a CF End + CF ACK frame. In these frames, the Duration field is always set to 0, and the receiver address (RA) contains the broadcast group address.

Using RTS/CTS

Because of the possibility of partial network connectivity, wireless LAN protocols must account for potential hidden stations. You can activate the RTS/CTS mode via the setup utility for the access point.

The RTS/CTS operation provides much better performance over basic access when there is a high probability of hidden stations. In addition, the performance of RTS/CTS degrades more slowly than basic access when network utilization increases. The use of RTS/CTS, however, will result in relatively low throughput in a situation where there is very little probability of hidden stations.

In the network depicted in Figure 4.16, station A and station B can both communicate directly with the access point; however, the barrier that represents lack of connectivity, prevents stations A and B from communicating directly with each other. The problem is that a collision will occur when station A attempts to access the medium because it will not be able to detect that station B is already transmitting.

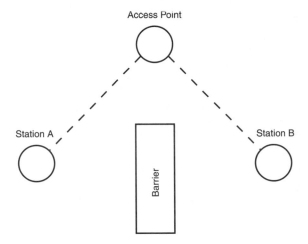

FIGURE 4.16   *The barrier between stations A and B causes an access collision when station A attempts to access the medium while station B is transmitting a frame to the access point.*

To guard against collisions based on hidden nodes and high utilization, the transmitting station B should send an RTS frame to the access point, requesting service for a certain amount of time. If the access point approves, it will broadcast a CTS frame announcing this time to all stations that hear the frame transmission. As a result, all stations, including station A, will not attempt to access the medium for the specified amount of time.

Setting the Packet Size for RTS/CTS Operation

You can set the minimum size packet that the station can use with the RTS/CTS function by accessing the configuration file of an access point or radio card. This value is normally within the range of 100 to 2048 bytes. Be aware that setting the minimum packet size too small may add excessive overhead to the network.

The RTS/CTS exchange also performs both a type of fast collision inference and a transmission path check. If the station originating the RTS does not detect the return CTS, the originating STA may repeat the process (after observing the other medium-use rules) more quickly than if the long data frame had been transmitted and a return ACK frame had not been detected. The RTS/CTS mechanism need not be used for every data frame transmission. Because the additional RTS and CTS frames add overhead inefficiency, the mechanism is not always justified, especially for short data frames.

Data Frames

The main purpose of data frames is to carry information, such as MSDUs, to the destination station for handoff to its applicable LLC Layer (see Figure 4.17). These data frames may carry specific information or supervisory or unnumbered frames from the LLC Layer.

2 Octets	2 Octets	6 Octets	6 Octets	6 Octets	2 Octets	6 Octets	0-2312 Octets	4 Octets
Frame Control	Duration/ ID	Address 1	Address 2	Address 3	Sequence Control	Address 4	Frame Body	FCS

To DS	From DS	Address 1	Address 2	Address 3	Address 4
0	0	DA	SA	BSSID	N/A
0	1	DA	BSSID	SA	N/A
1	0	BSSID	SA	DA	N/A
1	1	RA	TA	DA	SA

FIGURE 4.17   *The To DS and From DS subfields of the Frame Control field define the valid contents of the address fields of a data frame.*

The MAC Layer is only part of the overall operations of the 802.11 protocol. A key to implementing a wireless network that fully satisfies requirements is to choose the appropriate Physical Layer. Chapter 5, "Physical (PHY) Layer," addresses each of the 802.11 Physical Layers.

Physical (PHY) Layer

- **Physical Layer architecture**
  This chapter begins by providing an overview of the IEEE 802.11 Physical Layer architecture, providing a foundation for understanding the operations of the Physical Layer.

- **Physical Layer operations**
  A description of how the physical layer convergence procedure (PLCP) and physical medium dependent (PMD) sublayers interact provides a general understanding of Physical Layer operations. Learn how the PLCP sublayer provides carrier sense, transmit, and receive functions by communicating with the PMD sublayer via primitives.

- **Frequency hopping spread spectrum (FHSS) physical layer**
  Learn when to utilize frequency hopping over direct sequence and infrared physical layers. A description of the specific FHSS PLCP defines Physical Layer frame formats. Learn how the PMD transmits frames of data using FHSS by understanding the frequency hopping function and frequency shift keying modulation techniques the PMD uses to transform binary representations of the data frames into signals suitable for radio wave propagation.

- **Direct sequence spread spectrum (DSSS) physical layer**
  Learn when to utilize direct sequence over frequency hopping and infrared physical layers. A description of the specific DSSS PLCP defines Physical Layer frame formats. A description of the DSSS PMD explains how stations transmit frames using DSSS. You will understand the spreading and modulation techniques this PMD uses to transform binary representations of the data frames into signals suitable for radio wave propagation.

- **Infrared (IR) physical layer**
  You can utilize infrared over frequency hopping and direct sequence physical layers. A description of the PMD explains how stations transmit frames using

the Infrared physical layer. Understand the modulation techniques the PMD uses to transform binary representations of the data frames into signals suitable for infrared light propagation.

Physical Layer Architecture

The architecture of the Physical Layer consists of the following three components for each station (see Figure 5.1):

- *Physical Layer management:* The Physical Layer management works in conjunction with MAC Layer management and performs management functions for the Physical Layer.

- *Physical Layer convergence procedure (PLCP) sublayer:* The MAC Layer communicates with the PLCP via *primitives* through the Physical Layer service access point (SAP). When the MAC Layer instructs, the PLCP prepares MAC protocol data units (MPDUs) for transmission. The PLCP also delivers incoming frames from the wireless medium to the MAC Layer.

  The PLCP appends fields to the MPDU that contain information needed by the Physical Layer transmitters and receivers. The 802.11 standard refers to this composite frame as a PLCP protocol data unit (PPDU). The frame structure of a PPDU provides for asynchronous transfer of MPDUs between stations. As a result, the receiving station's Physical Layer must synchronize its circuitry to each individual incoming frame.

  Refer to the following sections later in this chapter for more detail on each specific PLCP: "FHSS Physical Layer Convergence Procedure," "DSSS Physical Layer Convergence Procedure (PLCP) Sublayer," and "IR Physical Layer Convergence Procedure (PLCP) Sublayer."

- *Physical medium dependent (PMD) sublayer:* Under the direction of the PLCP, the PMD provides actual transmission and reception of Physical Layer entities between two stations via the wireless medium. To provide this service, the PMD interfaces directly with the wireless medium (that is, the air) and provides modulation and demodulation of the frame transmissions. The PLCP and PMD communicate via primitives to govern the transmission and reception functions.

  Refer to the following sections later in this chapter for more detail on each specific PMD: "FHSS Physical Medium Dependent (PMD) Sublayer," "DSSS Physical Medium Dependent (PMD) Sublayer," and "IR Physical Medium Dependent (PMD) Sublayer."

Physical Layer Operations

The general operation of the individual physical layers is very similar. To perform PLCP functions, the 802.11 standard specifies the use of state machines. Each state machine performs one of the following functions:

- *Carrier sense:* To determine the state of the medium
- *Transmit:* To send individual octets of the data frame
- *Receive:* To receive individual octets of the data frame

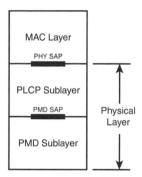

FIGURE 5.1 *The physical layer convergence procedure (PLCP) sublayer minimizes the dependence of the MAC Layer on the physical medium dependent (PMD) sublayer by mapping MAC protocol data units into a frame format suitable for transmission by the PMD.*

The following sections describe each of the PLCP functions in more detail and the primitives used for transferring data between the MAC and Physical Layers.

Physical Layer Service Primitives

The Physical Layer provides its functionality to the MAC Layer via the following service primitives:

- `PHY-DATA.request`: Transfers an octet of data from the MAC Layer to the Physical Layer. This primitive is only possible after the Physical Layer issues a `PHY-TXSTART.confirm`.

- `PHY-DATA.indication`: Transfers an octet of received data from the Physical Layer to the MAC Layer.

- `PHY-DATA.confirm`: A primitive sent from the Physical Layer to the MAC Layer confirming the transfer of data from the MAC Layer to the Physical Layer.

- `PHY-TXSTART.request`: A request from the MAC Layer for the Physical Layer to start transmission of an MPDU.

- `PHY-TXSTART.confirm`: A primitive from the Physical Layer to the MAC Layer confirming the start of transmission of an MPDU.

- `PHY-TXEND.request`: A request from the MAC Layer to the Physical Layer to end the transmission of an MPDU. The MAC Layer issues this primitive after it receives the last `PHY-DATA.confirm` primitive for a particular MPDU.

- `PHY-TXEND.confirm`: A primitive from the Physical Layer to the MAC Layer confirming the end of transmission of a particular MPDU.

- `PHY-CCARESET.request`: A request from the MAC Layer to the Physical Layer to reset the clear channel assessment state machine.

- `PHY-CCARESET.confirm`: A primitive from the Physical Layer to the MAC Layer confirming the resetting of the clear channel assessment state machine.

- `PHY-CCA.indication`: This primitive is sent from the Physical Layer to the MAC Layer to indicate the state of the medium. The status is either *busy* or *idle*. The Physical Layer sends this primitive every time the channel changes state.

- `PHY-RXSTART.indication`: This primitive is sent from the Physical Layer to the MAC Layer to indicate that the PLCP has received a valid start frame delimiter and PLCP header (based on the CRC error checking within the header).

- `PHY-RXEND.indication`: This primitive is sent from the Physical Layer to the MAC Layer to indicate that the receive state machine has completed the reception of an MPDU.

Carrier Sense Function

The Physical Layer implements the carrier sense operation by directing the PMD to check whether the medium is busy or idle. The PLCP performs the following sensing operations if the station is not transmitting or receiving a frame:

- *Detection of incoming signals:* The PLCP within the station will continually sense the medium. When the medium becomes busy, the PLCP will read in the PLCP preamble and header of the frame to attempt synchronization of the receiver to the data rate of the signal.

- *Clear channel assessment:* The clear channel assessment operation determines whether the wireless medium is busy or idle. If the medium is idle, the PLCP will send a `PHY-CCA.indicate` (with its status field indicating *idle*) to the MAC Layer. If the medium is busy, the PLCP will send a `PHY-CCA.indicate` (with its status field indicating *busy*) to the MAC Layer. The MAC Layer can then make a decision whether to send a frame.

Note

With DSSS, the MAC Layer performs the clear channel assessment via one of the subsequent modes:

- Mode 1: *The PMD measures the energy on the medium that exceeds a specific level, which is the energy detection (ED) threshold.*

- Mode 2: *The PMD detects a DSSS signal present on the medium. When this occurs, the PMD sends a* `PMD_CS` *(carrier sense) primitive to the PLCP layer.*

- Mode 3: *The PMD detects a DSSS signal present on the medium that exceeds a specific level (ED threshold). When this occurs, the PMD sends* `PMD_ED` *and* `PMD_CS` *primitives to the PLCP layer.*

After any of these modes occur, the PMD sends a `PMD_ED` *primitive to the PLCP layer, and the PLCP then indicates a clear channel assessment to the MAC Layer.*

Note

IEEE 802.11–compliant stations and access points store the clear channel assessment operating mode in the Physical Layer MIB attribute aCCAModeSuprt. *A user can set this mode through station initialization procedures.*

Transmit Function

The PLCP will switch the PMD to transmit mode after receiving the PHY-TXSTART.request service primitive from the MAC Layer. The MAC Layer sends the number of octets (0–4,095) and the data rate instruction along with this request. The PMD responds by sending the preamble of the frame at the antenna within 20 microseconds.

The transmitter sends the preamble and header at 1 Mbps to provide a specific common data rate for the receiver to always listen. After sending the header, the transmitter changes the data rate of the transmission to what the header specifies. After the transmission takes place, the PLCP sends a PHY-TXSTEND.confirm to the MAC Layer, shuts off the transmitter, and switches the PMD circuitry to receive mode.

Receive Function

If the clear channel assessment discovers a busy medium and valid preamble of an incoming frame, the PLCP will monitor the header of the frame. The PMD will indicate a busy medium when it senses a signal having a power level of at least 85 dBm. If the PLCP determines the header is error-free, the PLCP will send a PHY-RXSTART.indicate primitive to the MAC Layer to provide notification of an incoming frame. The PLCP sends the information it finds in the frame header (for example, number of octets, RSSI, and data rate) along with this primitive.

The PLCP sets an octet counter based on the value in the PSDU Length Word field in the header. This counter will keep track of the number of received frames, enabling the PLCP to know when the end of the frame occurs. As the PLCP receives data, it sends octets of the PSDU to the MAC Layer via PHY-DATA.indicate messages. After receiving the final octet, the PLCP sends a PHY-RXEND.indicate primitive to the MAC Layer to indicate the final octet of the frame.

Note

Most access point products have LED displays that indicate transmit and receive activity. Generally, a light will glow whenever the access point is sending or receiving data via the radio or distribution system connection.

The receive function will operate with single or multiple antenna diversities. You can select the level of *diversity* (that is, the number of antennas) via access point and radio card parameters. The strength of the transmitted signal decreases as it propagates to the destination. Many factors—such as the distance, heat, rain, and fog—cause this signal degradation. *Multiple-path* propagation can also lessen the signal strength at the receiver. *Diversity* is a method of improving reception by receiving the signal on multiple antennas and processing the superior signal.

Frequency Hopping Spread Spectrum (FHSS) Physical Layer

The frequency hopping spread spectrum (FHSS) Physical Layer is one of three Physical Layers that you can choose from when designing an 802.11 wireless LAN. (The following two sections, "Direct Sequence Spread Spectrum (DSSS) Physical Layer" and "Infrared (IR) Physical Layer," cover the other physical layers.) The choice of Physical Layer depends on application requirements. When making a decision on which Physical Layer to use, consider the following characteristics of FHSS:

- Lowest cost

- Lowest power consumption

- Most tolerant to signal interference

- Lowest potential data rates from individual physical layers

- Highest aggregate capacity using multiple physical layers

- Less range than direct sequence, but greater range than infrared

If the benefits, in light of the pitfalls, outweigh using direct sequence and infrared light, frequency hopping should be your choice of Physical Layer.

Case Study 5.1:
Implementing FHSS over DSSS

A car dealership in Boston needing to implement a radio network to support a data-collection application via bar codes within its service department evaluates its requirements to determine whether to use FHSS, DSSS, or infrared light as the Physical Layer of an 802.11-compliant wireless LAN. Rather than keep paper records of the maintenance it performs on cars, significant benefits result from storing the information in a central database and bar coding each car serviced.

The dealer wants to track the status of each car and enter and receive relevant information at all points of the repair cycle. This system enables the car dealer to more effectively satisfy customers because of greater efficiency and accuracy in servicing the cars. The system also makes it much easier to perform trend analysis on parts requirements, when most customers bring their cars in, pick them up, etc.

Most data traversing the wireless network are short 15-character bar code numbers due to operators' scanning the bar codes on the cars. Other, very small data frames go across the network when the user inputs data on the data collector's keypad. As part of the project, the dealership had a wireless network consultant investigate the potential interference of a nearby radio station antenna. The consultant found, using a radio spectrum analyzer, that the narrow-band radio signal from the radio station could offer significant interference.

Also, because of the very large single-floor maintenance facility, the company needs to install 10 individual radio cells. Because of the low bandwidth needs, potential radio interference and a relatively large operating area, the benefits of FHSS outweigh DSSS and infrared light.

The Advent of Frequency Hopping Spread Spectrum

Hedy Lamarr, who was a well-known film actress during the 1940s, originally conceived the idea of frequency hopping spread spectrum during the early part of World War II to keep the Germans from jamming the radios that guided U.S. torpedoes against German warships. (Lamarr was desperate to find a way that she could help win the war against Germany. She was strongly opposed to the Nazis; In fact, she left her first husband for selling munitions to Hitler.)

Lamarr's idea was to utilize a method of transmitting the communications signals by randomly hopping from frequency to frequency to prevent the enemy from knowing what radio signal frequency to send for jamming purposes. It is amazing that she had no technical education, but still thought of this very important communications concept.

Lamarr and film-score composer George Antheil, who had extensive experience in synchronizing the sounds of music scores with motion pictures, set out to perfect the idea. One problem was how the torpedo's receiver was to know the frequency to listen to at specific times, because the idea was to send a random sequence of frequencies. Antheil was able to devise methods to keep a frequency-hopping receiver synchronized with the transmitter. His idea was to send signals to the torpedo using a long pattern of different frequencies that would appear random. The receiver, knowing the secret hopping pattern, would be able to tune to the correct frequency at the right time. This pseudo-random hopping sequence is what 802.11 uses today.

Lamarr and Antheil sent details of their invention to the National Inventors Council. Charles Kettering, the director of the council, encouraged them to patent the idea. They filed the patent in 1941. Lamarr and Antheil then teamed with electrical engineers from MIT to provide the technical design. On August 11, 1942, Lamarr and Antheil received U.S. Patent Number 2,292,387 for their idea.

continues

continued

Because of the newness of the technology and clumsy mechanical nature of the initial design, spread spectrum was never used during World War II. The initial prototype used many moving parts to control the frequency of transmission and reception.

In the 1950s, Sylvania began experimenting with frequency hopping, using newly developed digital components in place of the initial mechanical system. By then, Lamarr and Antheil's patent had expired. Sylvania, under contract with the U.S. Navy, utilized spread spectrum for the first time on ships sent to blockade Cuba in 1962. In the mid-1980s, the U.S. military declassified spread spectrum technology, and commercial companies began to exploit it for consumer electronics. Of

course, today the technology is a key modulation technique that the IEEE 802.11 standard specifies.

Lamarr and Antheil conceived an excellent modulation technique; however, they never received any compensation for their idea. Their main interest, expressed in a high degree of patriotism, was to help win the war against the Nazis. In March 1997, Lamarr and Antheil were honored with the Electronic Frontier Foundation's Pioneer Award at its San Francisco conference, "Computers, Freedom, and Privacy." Because Antheil died in 1959 and Lamarr makes it a habit not to appear in public, her son Anthony Loder accepted the honor on behalf of his mother.

FHSS Physical Layer Convergence Procedure

Figure 5.2 illustrates the format of a FHSS PPDU (also called a PCLP frame). In general, the preamble enables the receiver to prepare clocking functions and antenna diversity before the actual contents of the frame arrives. The header field provides information about the frame, and the whitened PSDU (PLCP service data unit) is the MPDU the station is sending.

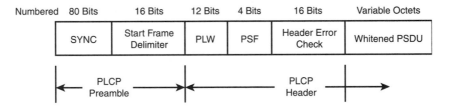

FIGURE 5.2 *FHSS physical layer convergence procedure (PCLP) frames consist of a PLCP preamble, PLCP header, and a PLCP service data unit.*

The following describes each of the FHSS PLCP frame fields:

- *SYNC:* This field consists of alternating 0s and 1s, alerting the receiver that a potentially receivable signal is present. A receiver will begin to synchronize with the incoming signal after detecting the sync.

- *Start Frame Delimiter:* The contents of this field is always the following bit pattern, defining the beginning of a frame: 0000110010111101.

- *PLW (PSDU Length Word):* This field specifies the length of the PSDU in octets. The receiver will use this information to determine the end of the frame.

- *PSF (PLCP Signaling Field):* This field identifies the data rate of the whitened PSDU portion of the frame. The preamble and header of the PPDU is always sent at 1 Mbps, but the remaining portion of the frame can be sent at different data rates as indicated by this field. The PMD, however, must support the data rate.

  The leftmost bit, bit 0, of the PLCP Signaling field is always 0. The following table identifies the data rate based on the value of bits 1, 2, and 3:

Bits 1–3	Data Rate
000	1.0 Mbps
001	1.5 Mbps
010	2.0 Mbps
011	2.5 Mbps
100	3.0 Mbps
101	3.5 Mbps
110	4.0 Mbps
111	4.5 Mbps

Note

The 1997 version of the IEEE 802.11 standard only supports 1 and 2 Mbps operation. The lower data rate will realize longer range transmission because the receiver has greater gain at lower data rates. Future editions of the standard will support other data rates. Most access points enable the setting of a maximum data rate, and the stations will automatically adapt to the highest rate.

- *Header Error Check:* This field contains a 16-bit CRC result based on CCITT's CRC-16 error detection algorithm. The generator polynomial for CRC-16 is $G(x)=x^{16}+x^{12}+x^5+1$. The Physical Layer does not determine whether errors are present within the PSDU. The MAC Layer will check for errors based on the frame check sequence (FCS).

  CRC-16 detects all single- and double-bit errors and ensures detection of 99.998 percent of all possible errors. Most experts believe CRC-16 is sufficient for data transmission blocks of 4 kilobytes or less.

- *Whitened PSDU:* The PSDU can range from 0–4,095 octets in length. Before transmission, the Physical Layer whitens the PSDU by stuffing special symbols every four octets to minimize dc bias of the data signal. The PSDU whitening process involves the use of a length-127 frame-synchronous scrambler and a 32/33 bias-suppression encoding algorithm to randomize the data. Figure 5.3 illustrates the process of whitening the PSDU.

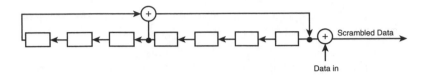

FIGURE 5.3 *PSDU whitening at the transmitting station consists of inputting the PSDU into a scrambler, as shown here. All registers initialize with 1s. This logic circuitry also performs the unscrambling necessary at the receiving station.*

FHSS Physical Medium Dependent (PMD) Sublayer

The PMD performs the actual transmission and reception of PPDUs under the direction of the PLCP. To provide this service, the PMD interfaces directly with the wireless medium (that is, the air) and provides FHSS modulation and demodulation of the frame transmissions.

FHSS PMD Service Primitives

The PLCP and PMD communicate primitives, as shown in Figure 5.4, enabling the PLCP to direct the PMD when to transmit data, change channels, receive data from the PMD, and so on. The following defines each of the PLCP/PMD primitives:

- PMD_DATA.request: This is a request from the PLCP to the PMD to transfer a 1 or 0 data bit. This action tells the PMD to modulate and send the data bit on the medium.

- PMD_DATA.indicate: The PMD implements this primitive to transfer data bits to the PLCP. The value sent is either 1 or 0.

- PMD_TXRX.request: The PLCP uses this request to place the PMD in transmit or receive mode. The value sent is either transmit or receive.

- PMD_PA_RAMP.request: This request from the PLCP to the PMD initiates the ramp-up or ramp-down of the transmitter's power amplifier. The value sent is either on or off.

- PMD_ANTSEL.request: The PLCP sends this primitive to select the antenna that the PMD shall use. The value sent is a number from 1 to N, for which N is the total number of antennas the PMD supports. For transmit, this request selects one antenna. For receive, the PLCP can select multiple antennas for diversity.

- PMD_TXPWRLVL.request: This request from the PLCP defines the transmit power level of the PMD. The value is Level 1, Level 2, and so on, up to Level 8, and corresponds to power levels in the *management information base (MIB)*. Level 1, for example, corresponds to the MIB value TxPowerLevel 1.

- PMD_FREQ.request: The PLCP sends this primitive to the PMD to define the transmit frequency. The value sent is the channel ID.

- PMD_RSSI.indicate: The PMD uses this primitive to return a continual receiver signal strength indication of the medium to the PLCP. The PLCP uses this primitive for clear channel assessment functions. The value can range from 0 (weakest) to 15 (strongest) signal strength.

- PMD_PWRMGMT.request: The PLCP sends this primitive to the PMD to place the radio in sleep or standby mode so that it will drain less power. The value sent is either on for full operational mode, or off for standby or sleep mode.

Physical Sublayer Management Entity (PLME) Primitives

The Physical Layer has access to the management information base (MIB) via the following physical sublayer management entity (PLME) primitives:

- PLME-GET.request: Requests the value of a specific MIB attribute.

- PLME-GET.confirm: Returns the value of the applicable MIB attribute value that corresponds to a PLME-GET.request.

- PLME-SET.request: Requests the MIB set a specific MIB attribute to a particular value.

- MLME-SET.confirm: Returns the status of the PLME-SET.request.

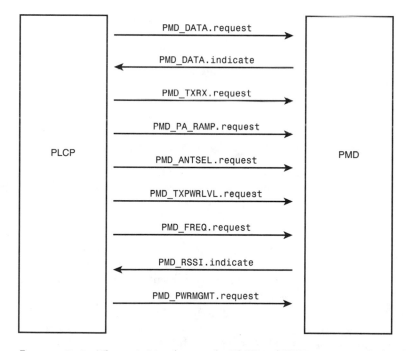

FIGURE 5.4 *These primitives between the PLCP and PMD are commands that the Physical Layer uses to operate the transmission and reception functions of the station.*

FHSS PMD Operation

The operation of the PMD translates the binary representation of the PPDUs into a radio signal suitable for transmission. The FHSS PMD performs these operations via a frequency hopping function and frequency shift keying modulation technique. The subsequent sections explain the FHSS PMD.

Frequency Hopping Function

The 802.11 standard defines a set of channels that are evenly spaced across the 2.4 GHz ISM band. The number of channels depends on geography. As examples, the number of channels for North America and most of Europe is 79, and the number of channels for Japan is 23.

The channels are spread across a band of frequencies, depending on geography. For example, 802.11-compliant stations in North America and most of Europe operate from 2.402 and 2.480 GHz, and stations in Japan operate from 2.473 and 2.495 GHz. Each channel is 1 MHz wide; therefore, the center operating frequency for channel 2 (the first channel) in the United States is 2.402 GHz, channel 3 is 2.403 GHz, and so on.

The FHSS-based PMD transmits PPDUs by hopping from channel to channel according to a particular pseudo-random hopping sequence that uniformly distributes the signal across the operating frequency band. After the hopping sequence is set in an access point, stations automatically synchronize to the correct hopping sequence. The 802.11 standard defines a particular set of hopping sequences. It specifies 78 sequences for North America and most of Europe, for example, and 12 sequences for Japan. The sequences avoid prolonged interference with one another. This enables designers to collocate multiple PMDs to improve performance.

Setting the Hopping Set and Hopping Sequence

When setting up a wireless LAN, you need to select a hopping set and hopping sequence. The 802.11 standard defines three separate hopping sets, called Set 1, Set 2, and Set 3, that contain a variety of hopping sequences designed to have minimal interference with one another within each set.

If setting up a single Basic Service Set (BSS), then the choice of hopping set and hopping sequence is arbitrary. In fact, for this case, you can just utilize default settings supplied by the vendor. If setting up several Basic Service Sets in the same area, though, be sure to choose a different hopping sequence for each access point from a common hopping set to minimize interference among the Basic Service Sets.

After selecting the hopping set, you'll need to choose a hopping sequence that is valid for the chosen set. Product vendors utilize an 802.11-defined number to represent specific hopping sequences; therefore, you'll need to specify which hopping sequence number you want to use for that particular access point and applicable BSS. (Refer to the 802.11 standard for learning the actual hopping frequencies for each of the possible sequences.)

The following identifies valid hopping sequence numbers for each set.

For North America and most of Europe:

Set 1: {0, 3, 6, 9, 12, 15, 18, 21, 24, 27, 30, 33, 36, 39, 42, 45, 48, 51, 54, 57, 60, 63, 66, 69, 72, 75}

Set 2: {1, 4, 7, 10, 13, 16, 19, 22, 25, 28, 31, 34, 37, 40, 43, 46, 49, 52, 55, 58, 61, 64, 67, 70, 73, 76}

Set 3: {2, 5, 8, 11, 14, 17, 20, 23, 26, 29, 32, 35, 38, 41, 44, 47, 50, 53, 56, 59, 62, 65, 68, 72, 74, 77}

For Japan:

Set 1: {6, 9, 12, 15}

Set 2: {7, 10, 13, 16}

Set 3: {8, 11, 14, 17}

For Spain:

Set 1: {0, 3, 6, 9, 12, 15, 18, 21, 24}

Set 2: {1, 4, 7, 10, 13, 16, 19, 22, 25}

Set 3: {2, 5, 8, 11, 14, 17, 20, 23, 26}

For France:

Set 1: {0, 3, 6, 9, 12, 15, 18, 21, 24, 27, 30}

Set 2: {1, 4, 7, 10, 13, 16, 19, 22, 25, 28, 31}

Set 3: {2, 5, 8, 11, 14, 17, 20, 23, 26, 29, 32}

Some vendors enable you to choose hopping sequences that are not defined by the 802.11 standard (for example, having numbers above 77); therefore, be sure to select only those sequences that are 802.11-compliant to ensure interoperability among vendors.

Case Study 5.2:
Implementing Higher-Capacity
Wireless LANs

A manufacturing company has requirements to implement a wireless LAN; however, data rate requirements of their application exceed the 2 Mbps limit of 802.11-compliant radio LAN products. This company, which manufactures automobile engines, frequently reconfigures its plant and wants to enable assembly workers to view assembly diagrams online via portable computers from a central server across a wireless LAN.

The wireless LAN must move these diagrams (contained within large multiple-megabit files) from the server to the portable computers, requiring more network capacity than what a single radio cell can provide. The solution to this problem was to provide an amount of bandwidth capacity by collocating multiple PMDs to increase performance. Therefore, the company decided to install multiple access points in common areas to create concurrent radio cells (BSSs) operating on different non-interfering hopping patterns.

The hop rate is adjustable, but the PMD must hop at a minimum rate that regulatory bodies within the country of operation specify. For the United States, FHSS must operate at a minimum hop rate of 2.5 hops per second. In addition, the minimum hop distance in frequency is 6 MHz in North America and most of Europe and 5 MHz in Japan.

FHSS Frequency Modulation Function

The FHSS PMD transmits the binary data at either 1 or 2 Mbps using a specific modulation type for each, depending on which data rate is chosen. The PMD uses two-level Gaussian frequency shift key (GFSK) modulation, as shown in Figure 5.5, for transmitting data streams at 1 Mbps. The concept of GFSK is to vary the frequency of the carrier frequency to represent different binary symbols. Thus, changes in frequency maintain the information content of the signal. Noise usually affects the amplitude of the signal, not the frequency. As a result, the use of GFSK modulation reduces potential interference.

The input to the GFSK modulator is either a 0 or 1 coming from the PLCP. The modulator transmits the binary data by shifting the transmit frequency slightly above or below the center operating frequency (Fc) for each hop. To perform this operation, the modulator transmits on a frequency using the following rules:

Transmit frequency = Fc + fd for sending a logic 1

Transmit frequency = Fc − fd for sending a logic 0

In the equation, Fc is the operating center frequency for the current hop, and fd is the amount of frequency deviation. The value of fd shall be greater than 110 KHz. The 802.11 specification explains how to calculate exact values for fd, but the nominal value is 160 KHz.

Other Uses of FHSS

Other, non-LAN systems use FHSS to satisfy modulation requirements. Amateur radio operators, for example, chose FHSS as the basis for a new wide area radio network infrastructure. This new wireless network will enable higher-speed access to Web-based applications from mobile platforms, such as automobiles.

They chose frequency hopping because it operates better than direct sequence at ranges beyond typical LANs. In addition, they selected quadrature phase shift keying (QPSK) modulation rather than GFSK (which 802.11 uses) to provide greater gain performance necessary to transmit farther distances. The phase shift keying process varies the phase of a carrier frequency to represent different binary symbols.

Traditionally, amateur radio enthusiasts have only been able to send data via packet radio networks, which are limited to lower data rates (9600 bps). These data rates are not adequate to support access to the Web. The general requirements of this new system are to provide at least 128 Kbps throughput with a range of 20 miles with 1 watt transmit output power in the 902–928 MHz frequency band.

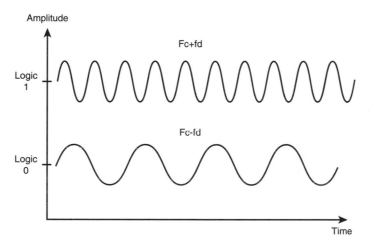

FIGURE 5.5 *Two-level Gaussian frequency shift key (GFSK) modulation uses two possible frequencies at each hop to indicate whether a single data bit is a 1 or a 0.*

The FHSS PMD uses four-level GFSK modulation, as shown in Figure 5.6, for transmitting data streams at 2 Mbps. Stations implementing the 2 Mbps version must also be able to operate at 1 Mbps for the entire MSDU. For 2 Mbps operation, the input to the modulator is combinations of 2 bits (00, 01, 10, or 11) coming from the PLCP. Each of these 2-bit symbols is sent at 1 Mbps, meaning each bit is sent at 2 Mbps. Thus, the four-level modulation technique doubles the data rate while maintaining the same baud rate of a 1 Mbps signal.

Similar to two-level GFSK, the modulator transmits the binary data bits by shifting the transmit frequency slightly above or below the center operating frequency for each hop. In this case, however, the transmitter can transmit at four possible frequencies, one for each 2-bit combination. To perform this operation, the modulator will transmit on the operating center frequency with a frequency deviation equal to fd. Two values of fd move the transmit frequency above Fc, and two values of fd move the transmit frequency below Fc. The 802.11 standard describes how to calculate the exact value of fd.

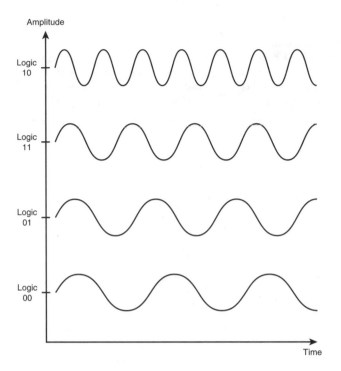

FIGURE 5.6 *Four-level Gaussian frequency shift key (GFSK) modulation uses four possible frequencies at each hop to represent 2 data bits.*

Overall, the transmit power of the FHSS radio shall comply with IEEE standard C95.1-1991. The 802.11 specification also limits the maximum amount of transmitter output power to 100 milliwatts of *isotropically radiated power* (meaning that the measurements are taken with an antenna having no gain). Apparently this limit enables 802.11 radio products to comply with transmit power limits in Europe. The effective power will be higher, however, using antennas that offer higher directivity (that is, gain).

The 802.11 specification also says that all PMDs must support at least 10 milliwatts transmit power. Most access points and radio cards enable you to select multiple transmit power levels via initialization parameters.

Note

The 802.11 standard calls for wireless LAN hardware to be capable of operating in either office or industrial environments. The operating temperature range for office environments (referred to as Type 1) is 0–40 degrees Celsius (32–104 degrees Fahrenheit). The operating temperature range for industrial environments (referred to as Type 2) is −30–−70 degrees Celsius (−22–−158 degrees Fahrenheit).

A FHSS wireless LAN will adequately support most applications requiring mobile stations. It is generally a cost-effective solution for most implementations. Be sure, however, to consider direct sequence spread spectrum and infrared light Physical Layers before deciding which one to implement.

Direct Sequence Spread Spectrum (DSSS) Physical Layer

The direct sequence spread spectrum (DSSS) Physical Layer is one of three physical layers that you can choose from when designing an 802.11 wireless LAN. (The other physical layers are addressed elsewhere in this chapter in the sections "Frequency Hopping Spread Spectrum (FHSS) physical layer" and "Infrared (IR) physical layer.") The choice of physical layer depends on application requirements. When deciding which physical layer to use, consider the following characteristics of DSSS:

- Highest cost

- Highest power consumption

- Highest potential data rates from individual physical layers as compared to frequency hopping. (The current version of 802.11 specifies the same data rates for both frequency hopping and direct sequence; however, future versions of the standard are likely to support higher data rates for direct sequence)

- Lowest aggregate capacity using multiple physical layers than frequency hopping

- Smallest number of geographically separate radio cells due to a limited number of channels

- More range than frequency hopping and Infrared physical layers

If the benefits above, in light of the pitfalls, outweigh using frequency hopping and infrared light, then direct sequence should be your choice of Physical Layer.

Case Study 5.3:
Implementing DSSS over FHSS

A small hospital in Boston found that implementing a wireless LAN was needed to support bedside computing applications that nurses and doctors would use to access patient data and other information, such as medical references. The hospital already had PCs at each ward's nursing station, and these PCs were connected to a central server via a token-ring network.

Along with the porting of paper-based patient records to a database residing on the server, the hospital wanted to make the records available from patient rooms through the use of mobile pen-based computers that each nurse and doctor would receive.

Designers of the network realized the benefits of implementing 802.11-compliant wireless LAN components; however, they had to decide whether to use frequency hopping, direct sequence, or infrared technology. The designers quickly eliminated the idea of using infrared

continues

continued

because of limited availability of products. In addition, infrared would not work because the wireless LAN had to provide mobility as nurses and doctors went from room to room. Designers decided frequency hopping would not support the higher data rate requirements necessary for supporting large amounts of data needing transmission.

The designers chose direct sequence for this implementation, mainly because of long-range requirements (to limit the number of access points) and the need to migrate up to higher data rates that direct sequence should support in the future.

Harris Semiconductor's PRISM

As a move to exploit the higher data rate capability of direct sequence, Harris Semiconductor released a new PRISM chipset for companies to develop 11 Mbps direct sequence spread spectrum radio LAN products in the unlicensed 2.4 GHz ISM band. At this data rate, wireless LAN devices operate at equal or better performance than existing wired ethernet systems.

The PRISM design enables the operation of seven simultaneous channels and offers an in-building range of 100–200 feet. It has the capability of operating at 11 Mbps, and then dropping back to 1 or 2 Mbps data rates; it also interoperates with 802.11-based devices. Users of the older 2Mbps PRISM chipset can upgrade to 11 Mbps relatively easily by replacing a single chip.

Note

The first commercial use of direct sequence spread spectrum was developed by Equitorial Communications in 1980 for multiple access communications over synchronous satellite transponders.

DSSS Physical Layer Convergence Procedure (PLCP) Sublayer

Figure 5.7 illustrates the DSSS PCLP frame format that the 802.11 specification refers to as a PLCP protocol data unit (PPDU). The preamble enables the receiver to properly synchronize to the incoming signal before the actual contents of the frame arrive. The header field provides information about the frame, and the PSDU (PLCP service data unit) is the MPDU the station is sending.

The following describes each of the DSSS PLCP frame fields:

- *SYNC:* This field consists of alternating 0s and 1s, alerting the receiver that a potentially receivable signal is present. A receiver will begin to synchronize with the incoming signal after detecting the sync.

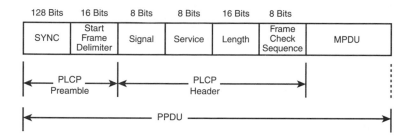

FIGURE 5.7 *DSSS physical layer convergence procedure (PCLP) frames consist of a PLCP preamble, PLCP header, and an MPDU.*

- *Start Frame Delimiter:* The contents of this field defines the beginning of a frame. The bit pattern for this field is always the following bit pattern, which is unique for DSSS PLCPs: 1111001110100000.

- *Signal:* This field identifies the type of modulation that the receiver must use to demodulate the signal. The value of this field is equal to the data rate divided by 100 Kbps. The only two possible values for the June 1997 version of 802.11 are 00001010 for 1 Mbps DSSS and 00010100 for 2 Mbps DSSS. The PLCP preamble and header are both always sent at 1 Mbps.

- *Service:* The 802.11 specification reserves this field for future use; however, a value of 00000000 means 802.11 device compliance.

- *Length:* The value of this field is an unsigned 16-bit integer indicating the number of microseconds to transmit the MPDU. The receiver will use this information to determine the end of the frame.

- *Frame Check Sequence:* Similar to the FHSS physical layer, this field contains a 16-bit CRC result based on CCITT's CRC-16 error-detection algorithm. The generator polynomial for CRC-16 is $G(x)=x^{16}+x^{12}+x^5+1$. The CRC operation is done at the transmitting station before scrambling.

  The Physical Layer does not determine whether errors are present within the PSDU. The MAC Layer will check for errors based on the FCS. CRC-16 detects all single- and double-bit errors and ensures detection of 99.998 percent of all possible errors. Most experts feel CRC-16 is sufficient for data transmission blocks of 4 kilobytes or less.

- *PSDU:* The PSDU, which is actually the MPDU being sent by the MAC Layer, can range from 0 bits to a maximum size that can be set by the aMPDUMaxLength parameter in the MIB.

DSSS Physical Medium Dependent (PMD) Sublayer

As with the FHSS and Infrared physical layers, the DSSS PMD performs the actual transmission and reception of PPDUs under the direction of the PLCP. To provide this service, the PMD interfaces directly with the wireless medium (that is, the air) and provides DSSS modulation and demodulation of the frame transmissions.

DSSS PMD Service Primitives

With direct sequence, the PLCP and PMD communicate via primitives, enabling the PLCP to direct the PMD when to transmit data, change channels, receive data from the PMD, and so on. The following defines each of the PLCP/PMD primitives:

- `PMD_DATA.request`: This is a request from the PLCP to the PMD to transfer a data symbol. The value of the symbol sent with this request is 1 or 0 data bits if transmitting at 1 Mbps, or any combination of 2 data bits if transmitting at 2 Mbps. The `PMD_DATA.request` primitive must be sent to the PMD before beginning the actual transmission of data with the `PMD_TXSTART.request` primitive.

- `PMD_DATA.indicate`: The PMD implements this primitive to transfer of symbols to the PLCP. As with the `PMD_DATA.request` primitive, the value of the symbol sent with this request is 1 or 0 data bits if receiving at 1 Mbps, or any combination of 2 data bits if receiving at 2 Mbps.

- `PMD_TXSTART.request`: The PLCP sends this primitive to the PMD to initiate the actual transmission of a PPDU.

- `PMD_TXEND.request`: The PLCP sends this primitive to the PMD to end the transmission of a PPDU.

- `PMD_ANTSEL.request`: The PLCP sends this primitive to select the antenna that the PMD shall use. The value sent is a number from 1 to N, for which N is the total number of antennas the PMD supports. For transmit, this request selects one antenna. For receive, the PLCP can select multiple antennas for diversity.

- `PMD_ANTSEL.indicate`: This primitive indicates which antenna the Physical Layer used to receive the latest PPDU.

- `PMD_TXPWRLVL.request`: This request from the PLCP defines the transmit power level of the PMD. The value is `Level 1`, `Level 2`, and so on, up to `Level 8`, and corresponds to the corresponding power levels in the MIB. `Level 1`, for example, corresponds to the MIB value `TxPowerLevel 1`.

- `PMD_RATE.request`: The PLCP sends this primitive to the PMD to identify the data rate (either 1 or 2 Mbps) that the MPDU portion of the PPDU should be sent. This data rate applies only to the rate of transmission. The PMD must always be able to receive at all possible data rates.

- `PMD_RATE.indicate`: This primitive, sent from the PMD to the PLCP when the PMD detects the Signaling field within the PLCP preamble, identifies the data rate (either 1 or 2 Mbps) of a received frame.

- `PMD_RSSI.indicate`: The PMD uses this primitive during receive states to return a continual receiver signal strength indication (RSSI) of the medium to the PLCP. The PLCP uses this primitive for clear channel assessment functions. The value of the RSSI is one of 256 levels, represented by an 8-bit data word.

- **PMD_SQ.indicate**: This optional primitive provides a signal quality (SQ) measure of the DSSS PN code correlation. The value of the signal quality is one of 256 levels, represented by an 8-bit data word.

- **PMD_CS.indicate**: The PMD sends this primitive to the PLCP to indicate that demodulation of a data signal is occurring. This signals the reception of a valid 802.11 direct sequence PPDU.

- **PMD_ED.indicate**: This optional primitive indicates that the energy value indicated by a particular **PMD_RSSI.indicate** primitive is above a predefined threshold (stored in the **aED_Threshold** parameter in the MIB). The value of the **PMD_ED.indicate** primitive is either enabled, if the **PMD_RSSI.indicate** value is above the threshold, and disabled, if below the threshold. This primitive provides a means to detect the presence of non–802.11 direct sequence signals, at least those that exceed the threshold value.

- **PMD_ED.request**: The PLCP uses this primitive to set the value of the *energy detect threshold*—which is the minimum signal that the PMD can detect—in the PMD to the value of the **aED_Threshold** parameter in the MIB.

- **PMD_CCA.indicate**: The PMD sends this primitive to the PLCP to indicate the detection of RF energy adhering to the CCA algorithm.

DSSS PMD Operation

The operation of the DSSS PMD translates the binary representation of the PPDUs into a radio signal suitable for transmission. The DSSS physical layer performs this process by multiplying a radio frequency carrier by a pseudo-noise (PN) digital signal. The resulting signal appears as noise if plotted in the frequency domain. The wider bandwidth of the direct sequence signal enables the signal power to drop below the noise threshold without loss of information.

As with FHSS, the DSSS physical layer operates within the 2.4 GHz to 2.4835 GHz frequency ranges, depending on regulatory authorities in different parts of the world. The 802.11 standard specifies operation of DSSS on up to 14 channels of different frequencies (see Table 5.1).

Note

Similar to FHSS, you can set the operating channel of a DSSS station or access point via a user-settable parameter. This enables designers to operate multiple direct sequence networks in the same area. Be sure, however, that you choose frequencies separated by at least 30 MHz to avoid having the channels interfere with each other.

TABLE 5.1   THE SPECIFIC DSSS CHANNELS FOR DIFFERENT PARTS OF THE WORLD

Channel No.	Frequency (GHz)	U.S. and Canada	Europe	Spain	France	Japan
1	2.412	✔	✔			
2	2.417	✔	✔			
3	2.422	✔	✔			
4	2.427	✔	✔			
5	2.432	✔	✔			
6	2.437	✔	✔			
7	2.442	✔	✔			
8	2.447	✔	✔			
9	2.452	✔	✔			
10	2.457	✔	✔	✔	✔	
11	2.462	✔	✔	✔	✔	
12	2.467		✔		✔	
13	2.472		✔		✔	
14	2.484					✔

The subsequent sections explain the spreading sequence and modulation functions of the DSSS PMD.

DSSS Spreading Sequence

The general idea of direct sequence is to first digitally spread the baseband data frame (that is, PPDU), and then to modulate the spread data to a particular frequency. Figure 5.8 illustrates typical components of a DSSS transmitter.

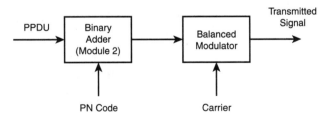

FIGURE 5.8   *A direct sequence transmitter consists of a binary adder, PN code, and a modulator.*

The transmitter spreads the PPDU by combining the PPDU with a *pseudo noise* (PN) code (sometimes referred to as a *chip* or *spreading sequence*) via the binary adder. The PN sequence for direct sequence systems consists of a series of plus and minus

1s. The specific PN code for 802.11 DSSS is the following 11-chip Barker sequence, with the leftmost bit applied first to the PPDU:

+1, −1, +1, +1, −1, +1, +1, +1, −1, −1, −1

The output of the binary adder is a DSSS signal having a higher-rate signal than the original data signal. A 1 Mbps PPDU at the input, for example, will result in an 11 Mbps spread signal at the output of the adder. The modulator translates the base-band signal into an analog signal at the operating transmit frequency of the chosen channel.

DSSS is different from CDMA (code division multiple access). CDMA operates in a similar fashion; however, CDMA uses multiple orthogonal spreading sequences to enable multiple users to operate at the same frequency. The difference is that 802.11 DSSS always uses the same spreading sequence, but enables users to choose from multiple frequencies for concurrent operation.

A figure of merit for DSSS systems is known as *processing gain* (sometimes called *spreading ratio*), which is equal to the data rate of the spread DSSS signal divided by the data rate of the initial PPDU. The minimum allowable processing gain allowed is 10 within the United States and Japan, according to applicable frequency regulatory agencies (that is, the FCC and MKK, respectively). To ensure compliance and to minimize potential signal interference, the IEEE 802.11 standard decided to set their minimum processing gain requirements at 11.

DSSS Frequency Modulation Function

A balanced modulator modulates the spread PPDU by combining the spread PPDU with a carrier set at the transmit frequency. The DSSS PMD transmits the initial PPDU at 1 Mbps or 2 Mbps using different modulation types, depending on which data rate is chosen. For 1 Mbps (basic access rate), the PMD uses *differential binary phase shift keying* (DBPSK) modulation.

The concept of phase shift keying is to vary the phase of the carrier frequency to represent different binary symbols. Thus, changes in phase maintain the information content of the signal. Noise usually affects the amplitude of the signal, not the phase. As a result, the use of phase shift key modulation reduces potential interference.

The input to the DBPSK modulator is either a 0 or 1 coming from the PLCP. The modulator transmits the binary data by shifting the carrier signal's phase, as shown conceptually in Figure 5.9.

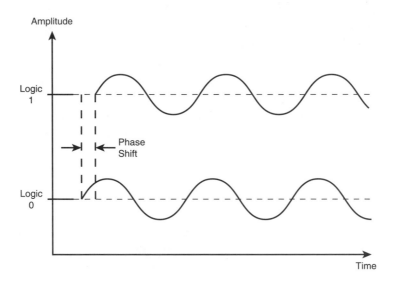

Figure 5.9 *DBPSK (differential binary phase shift keying) modulation operates at a specific center frequency and varies the phase of the signal to represent single-bit symbols.*

For 2 Mbps transmission (enhanced access rate), the PMD uses *differential quadrature phase shift keying* (DQPSK) modulation to send data at 2 Mbps. Figure 5.10 illustrates this concept. In this case, the input to the modulator is combinations of 2 bits (00, 01, 10, or 11) coming from the PLCP. Each of these 2-bit symbols is sent at 1 Mbps, resulting in a binary data rate of 2 Mbps. Thus, the four-level modulation technique doubles the data rate while maintaining the same baud rate of a 1 Mbps signal. This makes effective use of the wireless medium.

The following list shows the transmit power levels for DSSS:

- 1,000 milliwatts for the United States (according to FCC 15.247)

- 100 milliwatts for Europe (according to ETS 300-328)

- 10 milliwatts for Japan (according to MPT ordinance for Regulating Radio Equipment, Article 49-20)

In addition, the radiated emissions of the DSSS radio shall comply with ANSI uncontrolled radiation emission standards (IEEE standard C95.1-1991) for operation within the United States.

The effective power will be higher, however, using antennas that offer higher directivity (that is, gain). Wireless LAN suppliers have optional antennas that provide a variety of radiation patterns. The 802.11 specification also says that all PMDs must support at least 1 milliwatt transmit power. Most access points and radio cards enable you to select multiple transmit power levels via initialization parameters. In fact, the standard calls for the radio to have power-level controls for radio that can transmit greater than 100 milliwatts. Higher power radio must be capable of switching back to 100 milliwatt operation.

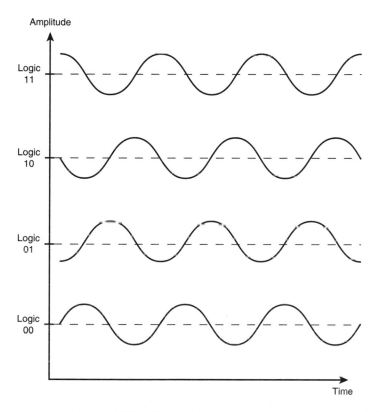

FIGURE 5.10   *DQPSK (differential quadrature phase shift keying) modulation operates at a specific center frequency and varies the phase of the signal to represent double-bit symbols.*

Note

Most DSSS 802.11–compliant devices enable users to set the operating data rate of the network to either 1 or 2 Mbps.

DSSS wireless LAN devices are capable of operating at relatively high data rates, supporting applications that require more range and bandwidth within a single cell. DSSS products, however, costing more than other wireless technologies, may cause the total price of the system to be higher than other alternatives. Therefore, be certain to consider frequency hopping spread spectrum and Infrared physical layers before making a decision on which one to implement.

Infrared (IR) Physical Layer

At the time of this writing, no wireless LAN products comply with the 802.11 Infrared physical layer. As products become available, however, the Infrared physical layer will become one of the three physical layers that you should consider when designing an 802.11 wireless LAN. (The sections "Frequency Hopping Spread Spectrum (FHSS) Physical Layer" and "Direct Sequence Spread Spectrum (DSSS) Physical Layer" elsewhere in this chapter address the other physical layers.) The following are characteristics of infrared that you should consider when deciding which physical layer to use:

- Lowest cost

- Highest tolerance to RF signal interference

- Lowest range compared to spread spectrum radio systems

- Most resistive to eavesdropping because the room contains the infrared light signals

- Must operate in areas where a ceiling is present (primarily indoors) to act as a reflection point for the infrared signals

- Accepted worldwide without frequency regulation

- No 802.11–compliant infrared products available (as of this writing)

If the advantages of infrared-based LANs far outweigh those of spread spectrum radio, consider the use of proprietary infrared–based LAN components.

Case Study 5.4:
Implementing IR over FHSS and DSSS

A large military communications base located in the eastern United States needed to perform renovations to many of the base office facilities, one building at a time, during one year. The improvements included carpeting, painting, and the tearing down of walls to accommodate office cubicles. As a result, office personnel had to move into temporarily constructed facilities for up to four weeks while renovations to their offices were taking place. As the contractors started work on anoth-

er building, they would relocate the temporary offices next to the building under renovation so that the employees would be near fellow personnel.

To continue network access for workers in the temporary offices, the base MIS group considered alternatives in providing LAN and WAN connections. At first, they thought of wiring the temporary offices with twisted-pair wiring to support traditional ethernet connectivity. The problem, however, was they would have to rewire the offices each time they were moved to the location of the next renovation site.

Another alternative was to utilize a wireless solution. MIS thought of using spread spectrum radio, but that would most likely interfere with the many radio frequency communications devices located throughout the base. The MIS group ultimately chose infrared light technology because it would not interfere with existing communications devices, and it would easily support the needs of moving the temporary offices from site to site.

Because an 802.11-compliant radio product was not available, the company decided to utilize proprietary devices from an infrared LAN product company. The infrared light–based products would work only within a single room of an office because of the transmission characteristics of infrared light. As a result, the organization installed a wired ethernet distribution system that linked infrared controllers located in each room. The controllers, acting as local bridges, interface the wireless stations in each room to other rooms and servers located on the distribution system.

IrDA Devices

Many infrared-based wireless LAN devices on the market today utilize the Infrared Data Association (IrDA) standard that specifies short range (up to 3 feet) point-to-point infrared connectivity. The IrDA, formed in 1993, supports a wide range of computing and communications devices.

IrDA devices are relatively low cost. If requirements lead you to the selection of infrared devices, be sure to consider IrDA-based products in lieu of passive reflection devices.

IR Physical Layer Convergence Procedure (PLCP) Sublayer

Figure 5.11 illustrates the infrared PCLP frame format that the 802.11 specification refers to as a PLCP protocol data unit (PPDU). The preamble enables the receiver to properly synchronize to the incoming signal before the actual contents of the frame arrives. The header field provides information about the frame, and the PSDU (PLCP service data unit) is the MPDU the station is sending.

The following describes each of the PLCP frame fields:

- *SYNC:* This field consists of alternating presence of a pulse in consecutive time slots. The 802.11 standard specifies that the Sync field shall have a minimum length of 57 time slots and a maximum length of 73 time slots. A receiver will begin to synchronize with the incoming signal after first detecting the sync.

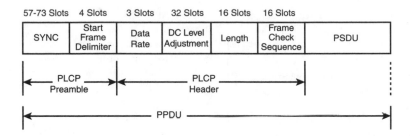

FIGURE 5.11 *Infrared physical layer convergence procedure (PCLP) frames consist of a PLCP preamble, PLCP header, and a PLCP service data unit (PSDU).*

- *Start Frame Delimiter:* The contents of this field defines the beginning of a frame. The bit pattern for this field is always the following bit pattern, which is unique for infrared PLCPs: 1001. A 1 represents the presence of a pulse, whereas a 0 represents no pulse for information conveyed in infrared PPDUs.

- *Data Rate:* This field identifies the data rate at which the PMD shall transmit the frame. The only two possible values, based on the June 1997 version of 802.11, are **000** for 1 Mbps and **001** for 2 Mbps. The PLCP preamble and header are both always sent at 1 Mbps.

- *DC Level Adjustment:* This field consists of a bit pattern that enables the receiving station to stabilize the DC level of the signal. The bit patterns for the two supported rates are as follows:

    1 Mbps: 00000000100000000000000010000000

    2 Mbps: 00100010001000100010001000100010

- *Length:* The value of this field is an unsigned 16-bit integer indicating the number of microseconds to transmit the MPDU. The receiver will use this information to determine the end of the frame.

- *Frame Check Sequence:* Similar to the FHSS physical layer, this field contains a 16-bit CRC result based on CCITT's CRC-16 error-detection algorithm. The generator polynomial for CRC-16 is $G(x)=x^{16}+x^{12}+x^5+1$. The CRC performs the operation on the Length field before transmitting the frame.

    The Physical Layer does not determine whether errors are present within the PSDU. The MAC Layer will check for errors based on the FCS. CRC-16 detects all single- and double-bit errors, and ensures detection of 99.998 percent of all possible errors. Most experts feel CRC-16 is sufficient for data transmission blocks of 4 kilobytes or less.

- *PSDU:* This is actually the MPDU being sent by the MAC Layer, which can range from 0 to a maximum size of 2,500 octets.

IR Physical Medium Dependent (PMD) Sublayer

The operation of the PMD translates the binary representation of the PPDUs into an infrared light signal suitable for transmission. The 802.11 Infrared physical layer operates using non-directed transmission, as shown in Figure 5.12, eliminating the need for line-of-sight operation. Most radio LAN suppliers refer to this type of transmission as *diffused infrared*.

Because of this form of transmission, the Infrared physical layer is intended only for indoor operation where a ceiling is present to reflect the signals. Windows can significantly attenuate the infrared signals, so be sure to test the operation of infrared devices in the facility before installing the entire system. Because of the use of a ceiling as a reflection point, 802.11 infrared devices are limited in transmission range. Typical ranges are 30 to 60 feet (10 to 20 meters), depending on ceiling height.

The Infrared physical layer transmits its signals in the nearly visible 850–950 nanometers range at a maximum transmit power level of 2 watts peak optical power. Because of the relatively high transmission frequency, there are no frequency regulatory restrictions for infrared-based systems. In fact, the only regulatory standards that apply to the 802.11 infrared-based system are safety regulations, namely IEC 60825-1 and ANSI Z136.1.

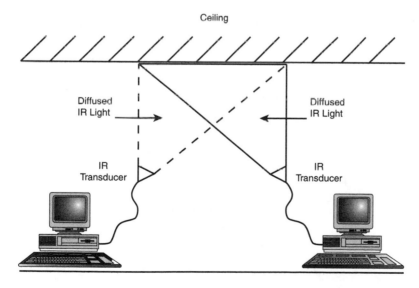

FIGURE 5.12 *An 802.11-based infrared LAN system uses the ceiling as a reflection point for supporting carrier sense access protocols.*

> **Note**
>
> *The 802.11 specifications make it possible for inexpensive development of 802.11-compliant infrared products using LED emitters and PIN diode detectors.*

The infrared PMD transmits the binary data at either 1 Mbps (basic access rate) or 2 Mbps (enhanced access rate) using a specific modulation type for each, depending on which data rate is chosen. For 1 Mbps operation, the infrared PMD uses 16-pulse position modulation (PPM). The concept of *pulse position modulation* is to vary the position of a pulse to represent different binary symbols. Thus, changes in pulse positions maintain the information content of the signal.

Noise usually affects the amplitude of the signal, not the phase. As a result, the use of pulse position modulation reduces potential interference. As shown in Table 5.2, 16-PPM maps each possible group of 4 bits in the PPDU to one of 16 symbols. The 1 bit in the 16-PPM symbol illustrates the position of a pulse representing a particular group of 4 PPDU data bits. The transmission order is from left to right. A 0 represents no pulse.

For 2 Mbps operation, the infrared PMD uses 4-PPM, as shown in Table 5.3. The order of the data fields in both Table 5.2 and Table 5.3 is based on the gray code, which ensures that there is only a single bit error in the data if a pulse of the transmitted signal gets out of position by one time slot. This is why the bits forming the data bits words look out of order. The 1 bit in the 4-PPM symbol illustrates the position of a pulse representing a particular group of two PPDU data bits. The transmission order is from left to right.

TABLE 5.2   16-PULSE POSITION MODULATION

Data Bits	16-PPM Symbol
0000	0000000000000001
0001	0000000000000010
0011	0000000000000100
0010	0000000000001000
0110	0000000000010000
0111	0000000000100000
0101	0000000001000000
0100	0000000010000000
1100	0000000100000000
1101	0000001000000000
1111	0000010000000000
1110	0000100000000000
1010	0001000000000000

Data Bits	16-PPM Symbol
1011	0010000000000000
1001	0100000000000000
1000	1000000000000000

TABLE 5.3   4-PULSE POSITION MODULATION

Data Bits	4-PPM Symbol
00	0001
01	0010
11	0100
10	1000

An infrared wireless LAN offers excellent noise immunity and more security than spread spectrum radio implementations; however, the lack of products forces you to utilize proprietary devices. Therefore, be sure to fully consider 802.11 spread spectrum radio Physical Layers before deciding which one to implement.

PART III

Deploying Wireless LANs

CHAPTER 6

Wireless System Integration

- **Wireless system architecture**
  The scope of the IEEE 802.11 specification is limited to the functionality of a wireless LAN with the radio cards and access points, but other components are necessary to implement a complete wireless system.

- **Network distribution systems**
  As options for implementing the network distribution system, you need to be aware of wired LAN and WAN technologies. Understanding the pros and cons of network protocols, such as ethernet, token ring, frame relay, and ATM, is essential.

- **Roaming protocols**
  If you are implementing a wireless network having multiple access points, be sure a roaming protocol is capable of meeting requirements. Understand the operation of a typical proprietary roaming protocol and an up-and-coming standard roaming protocol called Inter-Access Point Protocol (IAPP).

- **Communications protocols**
  The radio card, access points, and distribution system are not sufficient to communicate with an application or database residing on a server. TCP/IP, Mobile IP, and DHCP can maintain a communications link between the appliances and servers.

- **Connectivity software**
  As options for connecting the appliance to application software, be aware of the different types of connectivity software, such as terminal emulation, direct database connectivity, intranet-based access, and middleware. It is important to understand the pros and cons of each.

Wireless System Architecture

A complete wireless system consists of more than what IEEE 802.11 specifies. Other components are necessary to fully depict an architecture that satisfies application requirements. Figure 6.1 illustrates additional components that may be necessary to complete a wireless system. You need to specify these components when designing the system. Some of these components, such as the distribution system, may already be present. Companies will generally have existing distribution systems, such as ethernet LANs and WAN connectivity.

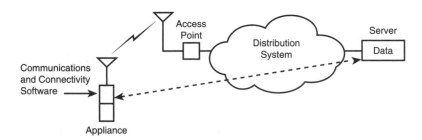

FIGURE 6.1   *In addition to IEEE 802.11 components, a wireless system includes a distribution system, communications protocols (for example, TCP/IP), connectivity software, and network management protocols.*

Many technical issues must be resolved when designing a method of system integration: What works in one context won't necessarily work in another. The remaining sections in this chapter explain the wireless system components that are beyond the scope of 802.11, and explain the problems that must be addressed.

Network Distribution Systems

Designers of the 802.11 standard purposely avoided the definition of a particular distribution system for connecting access points, leaving system architects the freedom to implement 802.11-compliant networks the most effective way. As a result, you need to decide what technologies and products will constitute the distribution system if multiple access points are necessary to extend the range of the complete wireless system. A network distribution system is also necessary if databases and applications reside on systems accessible only from a wired network (see Figure 6.2).

In most cases, you can specify a wired LAN backbone to act as the distribution system. Typically, vendors sell access points capable of connecting to either IEEE-compliant ethernet or token-ring LANs. In addition, wide area network (WAN) components may be necessary to connect LANs separated by longer distances. The following sections explain alternatives you have for LAN and WAN distribution systems.

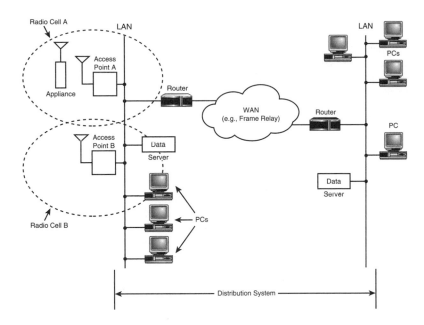

FIGURE 6.2 *The network distribution system may include common LAN and WAN systems to connect access points and access to resources located on other networks.*

IEEE 802.3 Carrier Sense Multiple Access (CSMA)

IEEE 802.3 is based on the ethernet product developed by Xerox Corporation's Palo Alto Research Center (PARC) in the 1970s. In 1980, the IEEE released the IEEE 802.3 carrier sense multiple access (CSMA) LAN standard, often called ethernet, which has now become by far the most preferred wired LAN. Ethernet operates at 10, 100, and 1000 Mbps, depending on the type of Physical Layer chosen. The use of ethernet satisfies most performance requirements, and, because of its high degree of proliferation, applicable products are low cost compared to other networks, such as token ring. Figure 6.3 illustrates the frame header fields of the IEEE 802.3 protocol.

7 Bits	1 Bit	6 Bits	6 Bits	2 Bits	46-1500 Bits	4 Bits
Preamble	Start of Frame	Destination Address	Source Address	Length	Data	Frame Check Sequence

FIGURE 6.3 *IEEE 802.3 specifications describe a MAC frame header common to all 802.3 PHYs.*

The following list describes each of the IEEE 802.3 MAC frame header fields:

- *Preamble:* Both ethernet and IEEE 802.3 frames begin with an alternating pattern of 1s and 0s called the Preamble, which tells receiving stations that a frame is arriving. This provides time for the receiving station to synchronize to the incoming data stream.

- *Start-of-Frame:* The Start-of-Frame delimiter ends with two consecutive 1 bits, which serve to synchronize the frame reception functions of all stations on the LAN.

- *Destination and Source Address:* The Destination and Source Address fields are 6 bytes long and refer to the addresses contained in the ethernet and IEEE 802.3 network interface cards. The first 3 bytes of the addresses are specified by the IEEE on a vendor-dependent basis, and the last 3 bytes are specified by the ethernet or IEEE 802.3 vendor.

  The Source Address is always a unicast (single node) address. The Destination Address can be unicast, multicast, or broadcast.

- *Length:* The Length field in IEEE 802.3 frames indicates the number of bytes of data in the Data field.

- *Data:* The Data field contains the actual data carried by the frame that will eventually be given to an upper-layer protocol at the destination station. With IEEE 802.3, the upper-layer protocol must be defined within the data portion of the frame if necessary.

  The Data field can be up to 1500 bytes long. As a minimum, the field will be at least 46 bytes long because it will contain at least the header of the higher-layer protocol data unit.

- *Frame Check Sequence:* The 4-byte frame check sequence field contains a Cyclic Redundancy Check (CRC) value so the receiving device can check for transmission errors.

The operation of 802.3 ethernet is very similar to what IEEE 802.11 defines. Ethernet stations share a common physical wire medium rather than air. If wishing to transmit a data frame, an ethernet station must first sense the medium to determine whether another station is already transmitting. If the medium is idle, the station may transmit. The station must wait a random amount of time, however, if the medium is busy.

Traditional ethernet operates at a wire speed of 10 Mbps. Fast ethernet, which is part of the 802.3 standard and operates at 100 Mbps, is cost effective in situations requiring higher data rates. The strengths of fast ethernet include multiple-vendor product support, high data rates with a small-price premium over 10 Mbps versions, compatibility with existing 10 Mbps networks, and the capability to use existing UTP cable (Category 3 or higher). Gigabit ethernet, having a PHY based on ANSI

X3T11 FibreChannel technology, is a recent addition to the 802.3 family. Gigabit ethernet, a strong alternative to Asynchronous Transfer Mode (ATM), shares similar advantages as fast ethernet.

Some suppliers offer full-duplex versions of their ethernet products at a higher price than standard half-duplex products. Full duplex can double the data rate between two ethernet network devices by enabling simultaneous transmission in both directions. In most cases, however, applications and servers do not take advantage of the full bandwidth in both directions when communicating with each other. Therefore, be sure you are able to gain the advantages of a full-duplex operation before spending the additional money.

Of course ethernet is not subjected to the perils of wireless communications, such as hidden stations and radio interference, but other factors common to both 802.11 and 802.3 still apply. Ethernet operates at relatively high data rates; however, specified data rates deal with wire speed, not throughput. A 10 Mbps ethernet link enables an ethernet station to transmit a data packet to another ethernet station at 10 Mbps, for example, only when the station is actually transmitting the data. The aggregate data rate (that is, throughput) for a shared ethernet link will at best be 1–2 Mbps. The reason for this is that stations must take turns transmitting and collisions may occur, causing gaps in the delivery of information.

Ethernet products that support a variety of physical mediums and data rates are available. Options for ethernet wiring include the following:

- Unshielded twisted-pair (UTP) wire
- Optical fiber cable
- Coaxial cable

These options are described in the succeeding sections.

Unshielded Twisted-Pair (UTP) Wire
UTP wire uses metallic conductors, providing a path for current flow that represents information. As the name implies, UTP wiring doesn't include shielding found in other forms of twisted-pair wires. The wire is twisted in pairs to minimize the electromagnetic interference resulting from adjacent wire pairs and external noise sources. A greater number of twists per foot increases noise immunity.

UTP is inexpensive and easy to install, and it is currently the industry standard for wiring LANs. Consider the use of twisted pair for all wired connections inside buildings. Figure 6.4 illustrates the topology of a typical UTP-based ethernet LAN.

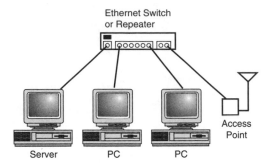

FIGURE 6.4 *IEEE 802.3 ethernet stations that use UTP connect to an ethernet switch or repeater (hub), forming a star topology.*

The Electronic Industry Association (EIA) 568 building wiring standard specifies the following five categories of UTP wiring:

- *Category 1:* Old–style phone wire, which is not suitable for data transmission. This includes most telephone wire installed in the United States before 1983.

- *Category 2:* Certified for use with the 4 Mbps version of IEEE 802.5 token-ring networks.

- *Category 3:* Certified for 10 Mbps (10Base-T) and some 100 Mbps (100Base-T) versions of IEEE 802.3 ethernet networks. Many facilities that have an initial installation of a 10 Mbps ethernet network have an installed base of Category 3 cabling.

- *Category 4:* Certified for use with the 16 Mbps version of IEEE 802.5 token-ring networks.

- *Category 5:* Certified for use with ANSI FDDI token ring, as well as 100 and 1000 Mbps versions of IEEE 802.3 ethernet networks. Category 5 UTP is the most popular form of wiring for wired LANs.

Tip

There is very little difference in price between Category 5 and the other lower-category wiring, and labor costs to install them are the same. Therefore, you should install Category 5 cable for all UTP-based network installations, regardless of whether you need the extra bandwidth. This will avoid the expensive rewiring if you require higher performance in the future.

Understanding Ethernet Repeaters and Switches

An ethernet repeater (commonly called a *shared ethernet hub*) refers to a component that provides ethernet connections among multiple stations sharing a common collision domain (see Figure 6.5). Consider utilizing a hub when connecting local user stations (that is, a workgroup) to a single server having only one connection to the LAN.

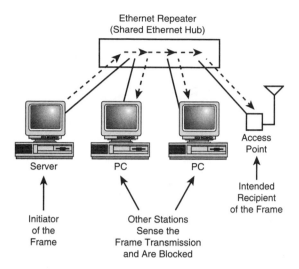

FIGURE 6.5 *When stations connect to a shared ethernet hub, the transmission of a frame from one station blocks all other stations from transmitting.*

A switch is more intelligent than a hub, having the capability to connect the sending station directly to the receiving station (see Figure 6.6). This results in multiple collision domains that significantly increase throughput. A switch is generally more expensive than a hub; however, consider using a switch if needing to connect user stations if multiple server connections exist or high utilization is impacting the performance of a repeater-based LAN.

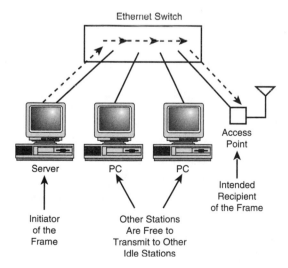

FIGURE 6.6 *When stations connect to a switch, the transmission of a frame from one station doesn't block the other stations from transmitting.*

Optical Fiber Cable

If you need a very high degree of noise immunity or information security, consider the use of optical fiber rather than UTP. Optical fiber is a medium that uses changes in light intensity to carry information from one point to another. An optical fiber system consists of a light source, optical fiber, and a light detector. A light source changes digital electrical signals into light (that is, on for a logic 1 and off for a logic 0), the optical fiber transports the light to the destination, and a light detector transforms the light into an electrical signal.

The main advantages of optical fiber are very high bandwidth (Mbps and Gbps), information security, immunity to electromagnetic interference, lightweight construction, and long-distance operation without signal regeneration. As a result, optical fiber is superior for bandwidth-demanding applications and protocols, operation in classified areas and between buildings, as well as installation in airplanes and ships. IEEE 802.3's 10Base-F and 100Base-F specifications identify the use of optical fiber as the physical medium. Of course, FDDI identifies the use of optical fiber as well.

Tip

Use optical fiber to connect hubs and switches to provide connections between buildings. This will be more expensive than using UTP, but benefits such as higher data rates and less possibility of interference on interbuilding links generally outweigh the higher cost.

Coaxial Cable

The construction of coaxial cable includes a solid metallic core with a shielding as a return path, offering a path for electrical current representing information to flow. The shielding does a good job of reducing electrical noise interference within the core wire. As a result, coaxial cable can extend much farther than UTP. The disadvantage of coaxial cable, however, is its bulky shape, which makes it difficult to install. Also, coaxial cable doesn't lend itself very well to centralized wiring topologies, making it difficult to maintain.

During the 1980s, coaxial cable was very popular for wiring LANs; therefore, you might find some still existing in older implementations. Very few, if any, new implementations will require the use of coaxial cable; however, you should be aware of these types of networks in case you have to interface the wireless users to it.

IEEE 802.3 defines two Physical Layer specifications, 10Base-2 and 10Base-5, based on the use of coaxial cable. 10Base-2 uses RG58 cable, the same used to connect your television to a cable outlet, and will operate over a distance of up to 200 meters (600 feet). 10Base-5 uses a much larger cable than RG58, but is capable of operating up to 500 meters (1,500 feet) without the use of repeaters. Both 10Base-2 and 10Base-5 use a bus topology, as shown in Figure 6.7.

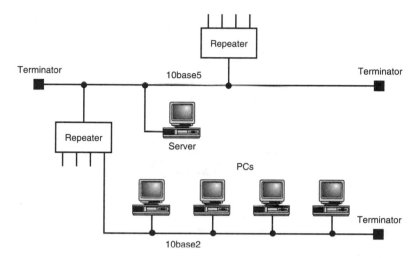

FIGURE 6.7 *10Base-2 and 10Base-5 ethernet network configurations are less reliable than 10Base-T networks because a break at one point in the cable can bring down the network.*

Note

Access points typically have the capability to connect to ethernet networks via 10Base-T, 10Base-2, and 10Base-5 connectors, as shown in Figure 6.8.

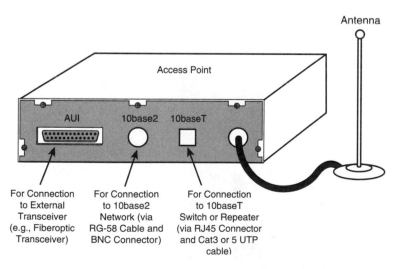

FIGURE 6.8 *Access points generally provide the capability for connecting to multiple ethernet network types.*

IEEE 802.5 Token Ring

The IEEE 802.5 standard specifies a 4 and 16 Mbps token-ring LAN. The first token-ring network was developed by IBM in the 1970s, and then IEEE released the 802.5 specification based on IBM's work. Because of the IBM orientation of token ring, you will find most token-ring networks in facilities deploying IBM mainframes and servers.

Today, IBM Token Ring and IEEE 802.5 networks are compatible, although there are minor differences. IBM's Token-Ring network specifies a star configuration, for example, with all end stations attached to a device called a *multi-station access unit* (*MSAU*). IEEE 802.5 does not specify a topology, but most 802.5 implementations are based on a star configuration similar to the UTP version of ethernet. Also, IEEE 802.5 does not specify a media type, but IBM Token Ring identifies the use of UTP wire (see the section "Unshielded Twisted-Pair (UTP) Wire" earlier in this chapter).

Token-ring protocols ensure that only one station transmits at a time through the use of a token. The token, which is a distinctive group of bits, circulates the ring. If a station wishes to transmit data, it must first wait its turn to receive the token, and then transmit its data. The capturing of the token ensures that no other station will transmit. The data circulates the ring, and the appropriate destination will sense its address and process the data. Once finished, the sending station will forward the token to the next station downline.

Because of the token-passing mechanism, 802.5 operates with more stability under heavier traffic than 802.3 ethernet. The predictable access method of 802.5 enables it to handle synchronous-type information transfers. IEEE 802.5 is the second most popular LAN medium-access technique and is slightly more expensive to implement than ethernet.

Figure 6.9 illustrates the token-ring frame formats, and the following lists explain the purpose of each field.

The following describes the fields of an 802.5 token:

- *Start Delimiter:* The Start Delimiter alerts each station that a token (or data frame) is arriving. This field includes signals that distinguish the byte from the rest of the frame by violating the encoding scheme used elsewhere in the frame.

- *Access Control:* The Access Control byte contains the priority and reservation fields, as well as a token bit that is used to differentiate a token from a data or command frame. The active monitor uses the monitor bit to determine whether a frame is endlessly circling the ring.

- *End Delimiter:* The End Delimiter identifies the end of the token or data/command frame. It also contains bits to indicate a damaged frame, as well as the last frame in a logical sequence.

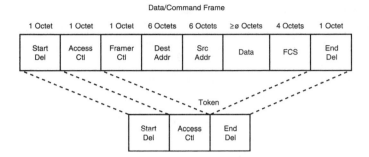

FIGURE 6.9 *Token-ring protocols use a token and standard MAC frame structure to implement token-passing protocols.*

The following describes the fields of an 802.5 MAC frame:

- *Frame Control:* The Frame Control byte indicates whether the frame contains data or control information. In control frames, Frame Control byte specifies the type of control information.

- *Destination and Source Address:* As with IEEE 802.3, the Destination and Source Address are 6 bytes long and designate the source and destination stations.

- *Data:* The Data field contains the data being sent from source to destination. The length of this field is limited by the ring token holding time, which defines the maximum time a station may hold the token.

- *Frame Check Sequence (FCS):* The 4-byte FCS field contains a Cyclic Redundancy Check (CRC) value so that the receiving device can check for errors.

- *End Delimiter:* The End Delimiter identifies the end of the data/command frame. It also contains bits to indicate a damaged frame, as well as the last frame in a logical sequence.

ANSI Fiber Distributed Data Interface (FDDI)

The ANSI X3T9.5 standards committee produced the Fiber Distributed Data Interface (FDDI) standard in the mid-1980s. It specifies a 100 Mbps dual token-ring campus network. FDDI specifies the use of optical fiber medium and will support simultaneous transmission of both synchronous and prioritized asynchronous traffic. The CDDI (Copper Data Distributed Interface) version of FDDI operates over Category 5 twisted-pair wiring. FDDI is an effective solution as a reliable high-speed interface within a LAN or corporate network.

FDDI is an expensive solution, but is effective for supporting high-speed deterministic access to network resources. Some organizations find it necessary to use FDDI for connecting servers in a server pool. It is also beneficial to use FDDI as the backbone for a campus or enterprise network. The synchronous mode of FDDI is used for those applications whose bandwidth and response time limits are predictable in advance, permitting them to be pre-allocated by the FDDI Station Management Protocol. The asynchronous mode is used for those applications whose bandwidth requirements are less predictable or whose response time requirements are less critical. Asynchronous bandwidth is instantaneously allocated from a pool of remaining ring bandwidth that is unallocated, unused, or both.

ANSI is currently developing FDDI II, which is an extension of FDDI. It is unclear when ANSI will release this standard. FDDI II has two modes: the basic mode, which is the existing FDDI; and the hybrid mode, which will incorporate the functionality of basic mode as well as circuit switching. The addition of circuit switching enables the support of *isochronous* traffic. Isochronous transmission is similar to synchronous, but, with isochronous, a node can send data at specific times. This simplifies the transmission of real-time information because of decreased source buffering and signal processing.

Wide Area Networking Concepts

A wide area network may be necessary when deploying a wireless system to provide wired connections between facilities (see Figure 6.10). A department store chain in Texas maintains its pricing information in a centralized database in Dallas, for example. Each of the 100 individual retail stores retrieves pricing information from the central database each night over a frame relay WAN, making their pricing information available to wireless handheld data collectors that clerks use to price items.

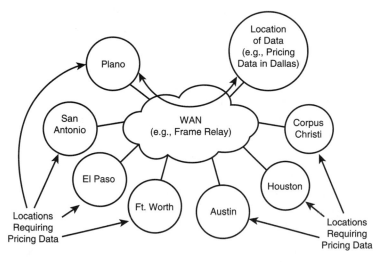

FIGURE 6.10   *The WAN-based distribution system is necessary to connect facilities separated by large distances.*

The components of a wide area network (WAN) consist of routers and links. Routers receive routable data packets, such as Internet Protocol (IP) or Internetwork Packet Exchange (IPX), review the destination address located in the packet header, and decide which direction to send the packet to next to forward the packet closer to the final destination. Routers maintain routing tables that adapt, via a routing protocol, to changes in the network.

Routing Information Protocol (RIP)

The *Routing Information Protocol* (*RIP*) is currently the most common type of routing protocol. RIP bases its routing path on the distance (number of hops) to the destination. In 1982, RIP appeared in the Berkeley Software Distribution (BSD) version of UNIX as part of TCP/IP protocol suite. Today, many other routing protocols, such as AppleTalk's routing protocol, use RIP as a foundation. Other companies, such as Novell and Banyan, have RIP-like routing protocols as well. Also, Microsoft expanded Windows NT's WAN capabilities by adding support for routing packets based on RIP.

A router implements RIP by storing information in its routing table. A destination column indicates all possible destination networks, a next hop field identifies the router port to send the packet next, and the distance field refers to the number of hops it will take to reach the destination network. A RIP routing table contains only the best route to a particular destination. If the router receives new routing information from another node, it will overwrite the entry.

RIP maintains optimum routing paths by sending out routing update messages if the network topology changes. If a router finds that a particular link is faulty, for example, it will update its routing table, and then send a copy of the modified table to each of its neighbors. The neighbors will update their tables with the new information and send updates to their neighbors, and so on. Within a short period, all routers will have the new information.

Open Shortest Path First (OSPF) Protocol

The problem with RIP is that it is not very robust, meaning it lacks the capability to handle larger networks and the capability to effectively determine alternative paths. As a result, the Internet Engineering Task Force developed *Open Shortest Path First* (OSPF) to replace the RIP protocol. The basis of OSPF is the Shortest Path First algorithm developed by Bolt, Beranek, and Newman (BBN) in 1978 for the Advanced Research Project Agency Network (ARPAnet).

OSPF is quickly becoming the industry-standard protocol because of its robustness—it supports the requirements of larger networks, such as special service requests, multiple network layer protocols, and authentication. OSPF is an efficient protocol, supporting speedy recovery from topology changes because OSPF routers can reroute data traffic as necessary. OSPF also minimizes overhead packet traffic when announcing changes by only sending information regarding the change, instead of the entire routing table.

OSPF maintains a topological database that stores information related to the state of links within an autonomous network, and it uses this information to calculate the shortest path. Many companies incorporate OSPF into their routers. Novell's MultiProtocol Router (MPR) Version 3 for NetWare is a NetWare Loadable Module (NLM) software-based router for NetWare 3.x and 4.1 that implements OSPF, for example. In addition, Cisco's routers, such as their 7000 family of routers, support OSPF.

With OSPF, a router announces its presence by sending a Hello message to each of its possible neighbors. Periodically, each neighbor sends a Hello message to show that it is still operational. Therefore, the new router will soon learn of its neighbors as well.

OSPF responds to upper-layer Type of Service (TOS) requests found in the header of an IP packet. Based on the TOS, OSPF calculates the best route. OSPF can respond to all eight combinations of IP's TOS bits, for example, which can represent all combinations of delay, throughput, and reliability. If the TOS bits specify low delay, high throughput, and low reliability, OSPF will calculate a route that best satisfies these requirements.

Private Versus Public WANs

When implementing wide area networking, you need to decide whether to use a private or a public WAN. A private WAN consists of routers and links that the company (containing the system end users) owns and operates. This is the traditional approach to wide area networking. Private WANs often consist of leased T1 and 56 Kbps digital circuits that provide connections between user-owned-and-maintained routers.

With public WANs, the company leases connections to a WAN architecture that supports multiple unrelated companies. Generally, these public networks use frame relay, SMDS, or ATM protocols. Figure 6.11 illustrates conceptual differences between private and public WANs.

In general, there are tradeoffs between the private and public approaches. The benefits and drawbacks of the *private WAN* are as follows:

- More suitable for WANs requiring a low degree of meshing (that is, very few links, such as is in the case of a centralized topology).

- Service fees are economically feasible for metropolitan areas.

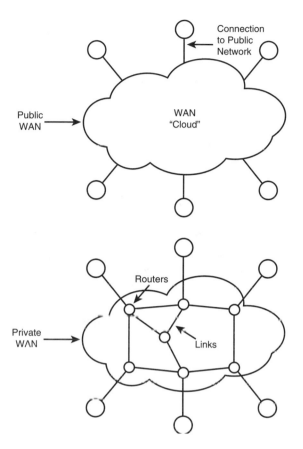

FIGURE 6.11 *An MIS group of a company views a public WAN as a connection to a network "cloud"; whereas, they view a private WAN as a collection of routers and links (communications lines).*

- Higher initial cost because of a greater number of hardware interfaces and circuit installations.

- Lease fees are sensitive to the distance between sites.

- Requires in-house management, therefore potentially higher operating costs.

- Fixed bandwidth.

The benefits of the *public WAN* are as follows:

- More suitable for WAN requiring a high degree of meshing (that is, large number of links, as in the case of a distributed topology).

- Lower initial cost because of a fewer number of hardware interfaces and circuit installations.

- Potentially lower operating cost because of less staffing requirements.

- Lease fees are not sensitive to the distance between sites.

- Offers variable bandwidth (bandwidth on demand).

- The carrier provides management; therefore, potentially lower operating costs.

- Service fees are most economical for long-haul (outside the metropolitan area) distances.

- Very little control, if any, over network restoration in the event of network failure.

Traditionally, organizations have implemented private point-to-point WANs to support communications between remote terminals to centralized mainframe-based applications. T1 is a common communications circuit that companies lease to provide links between routers in a private network. Bell labs originally developed the T1 standard to multiplex multiple phone calls into a composite signal, suitable for transmission through a digital communications circuit. A T1 signal consists of a serial transmission of T1 frames, with each frame carrying 8-bit samples of 24 separate channels. You can lease an entire T1 circuit (1.544 Mbps) or only single fractional T1 channels (64 Kbps each) from a telephone service carrier.

With the development of distributed client/server applications, most organizations now require technologies suitable for highly meshed topologies. There's a greater need to support communications among the remote sites, not just to a centralized data center. Therefore, you should seriously consider leasing the use of a public packet-switching WAN to support today's demand for distributed computing.

You have many technologies to choose from when implementing a WAN. The following sections define the most common technologies for public WANs.

X.25

X.25 was the first public packet-switching technology, developed by the CCITT and offered as a service during the 1970s; it is still available today. X.25 offers connection-oriented (virtual circuit) service and operates at 64 Kbps, which is too slow for some high-speed applications. Designers of this protocol made it very robust to accommodate the potential for transmission errors resulting from the transport over metallic cabling and analog systems used predominately in the 1970s. Therefore, X.25 implements very good error control, which takes considerable overhead.

Some companies have a significant investment in X.25 equipment and are still supporting the technology. You should consider other packet-switching technologies, however, such as frame relay, SMDS, or ATM for new implementations.

Frame Relay

Frame relay is today's most popular and widely available public WAN technology, providing a packet-switching interface operating at data rates of 56 Kbps to 2 Mbps. Actually, frame relay is similar to X.25, minus the transmission error control overhead. Therefore, frame relay assumes a higher-layer, end-to-end protocol that will check for transmission errors. Carriers offer frame relay as permanent connection-oriented (virtual circuit) service. In the future, frame relay will be available as a switched virtual circuit service as well.

To interface with frame relay service, you need to purchase or lease a *frame relay attachment device* (*FRAD*) or router with a frame relay interface. The FRAD or router interfaces a LAN (typically ethernet) to the local frame relay service provider via a T1 circuit. Frame relay is currently overall the most feasible technology you can use for connecting geographically disparate sites, especially if these sites span several metropolitan areas and have distributed applications.

Switched Multimegabit Data Service (SMDS)

SMDS is a packet-switching interface that operates at data rates ranging from 1.5 Mbps to 45 Mbps. SMDS is similar to frame relay, except SMDS provides connectionless (datagram) service. Some companies use SMDS to support highly spontaneous multimedia applications. You can access a local SMDS service provider via T1 or T3 (45 Mbps) circuits. SMDS is not available in all areas.

Asynchronous Transfer Mode (ATM)

Some companies construct private networks using ATM technology and products; however, ATM is now available from most carriers as a public network offering. ATM is a circuit-switching protocol that transmits small data packets called cells passing through devices known as *ATM switches*. An ATM switch analyzes information in the header of the cell to switch the cell to the output interface that connects to the next switch as the cell works its way to its destination. ATM operates at relatively high data rates (up into the Gbps range).

Choosing a Distribution System

The ultimate selection of the distribution system depends on requirements for connecting wireless users to applications and data storage located on wired networks. Be sure to carefully analyze user requirements and existing system designs before making a decision on which wired LAN and WAN technology to implement. In most cases, ethernet will satisfy LAN needs, and frame relay will work best for WAN connections.

Roaming Protocols

A critical function in a multiple-cell wireless LAN (that is, ESS) is *roaming*, which enables wireless users to move from cell to cell seamlessly. Because the 802.11

standard does not provide specifications for roaming, it is up to the radio LAN vendors to define roaming protocols.

Companies that manufacture radio LAN access points have their own flavor of roaming. This often forces 802.11 users to standardize on one particular vendor for access points to ensure seamless roaming. In some cases, wireless LAN companies have established partnerships to standardize on a common roaming protocol to enable interoperabilty between multiple-vendor access points.

Note

Many wireless LAN product vendors enable you to indicate the degree of mobility of each station so that the access point can optimize roaming algorithms. If you set up the station as being mobile, the roaming protocols will allow the station to reassociate as it moves from cell to cell.

Stationary devices may experience a short episode of radio interference and falsely reassociate with a different access point. As a result, the roaming protocols will take this into consideration when dealing with stations you indicate as stationary.

Proprietary Roaming Protocols

In general, companies provide proprietary roaming protocols that operate on the distribution system with interfaces to 802.11. In general, each 802.11 station periodically assesses the signal strength of receivable access points. The station will then reassociate with the access point having the strongest signal. An example of a typical proprietary roaming protocol is Lucent's WaveAROUND, which is part of Lucent's WaveLAN product line. The following paragraphs describe the operation of WaveAROUND as an example of a typical roaming protocol.

All cells in a WaveLAN configuration are linked together in a wireless network group, called a *domain*. Within this domain, a mobile station will automatically switch between different cells to ensure continuous connectivity. The mobile station will monitor the communications quality with the access point of the current cell. If the communications quality drops below a preset value, the station will start searching for another cell. If found, the station will retrieve and adopt the WaveLAN network ID of a new cell to ensure the network connection.

With WaveAROUND, multiple cells do not have to overlap (see Figure 6.12). In situations where cells do overlap, WaveAROUND connects to a new access point before terminating the connection with the predecessor. This provides a constant connection to the network.

Note

WaveAROUND roaming functionality enables a mobile station to detect an out-of-range situation and reestablish a lost connection. The combined characteristics of applications and the NOS, however, may pose problems for network operations because most of today's applications are not designed for use in a wireless mobile environment.

Future developments of applications should allow for temporarily working offline. When a connection is lost, the application must be able to synchronize files as soon as the connection becomes available again.

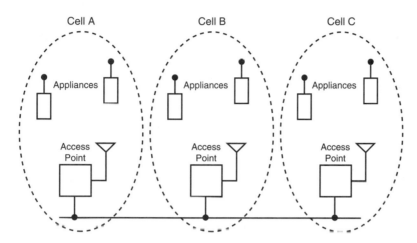

FIGURE 6.12 *If a wireless user moves between two cells that don't overlap, the WaveAROUND roaming protocol automatically reconnects the user to the new cell upon entering the new location.*

The access point broadcasts beacon messages at regular intervals to support roaming mobile stations. Beacon messages contain the domain ID, the WaveLAN network ID of the access point, communications-quality information, and cell-search threshold values. The domain ID identifies the access points and mobile stations that belong to the same WaveLAN roaming network. A mobile station listening for beacons will only interpret beacon messages with the same domain ID. The WaveLAN network ID identifies a specific cell of the WaveLAN network. This is the network ID assigned to each access point. It tells the mobile station which WaveLAN network ID to use to communicate with the network on that location.

You can encode the network ID information by using a *beacon key*. The communications-quality information helps the mobile station to determine the actual link quality with the access point of a particular cell. The cell search thresholds relate to the level of communications quality. They activate the cell search mode when the communications quality drops, such as when the mobile station is moving to another location. In cell search mode, the mobile station will start searching for other access points by listening for beacons. You can change the threshold values by selecting a different level of sensitivity, depending on your environment (see the "Cell Search Thresholds" section).

Responsiveness

A roaming station needs a number of beacons to determine the communications quality with an access point. Responsiveness parameters set beacon interval time and beacon timeout. The beacon interval time enables you to set the frequency of beacon transmissions. This frequency determines how fast a station can decide the actual communications quality. The beacon timeout sets the values of a timer mechanism. This timer activates the cell search mode when the mobile station does not receive a beacon within the specified time limit. Three user-defined presets adjust the level of responsiveness:

- *Relaxed:* If responsiveness is Relaxed, the beacon frequency will be low. This setting avoids unnecessary use of the mobile stations' processing capacity needed to interpret beacon messages. It also limits overhead on the network.

- *Normal:* If responsiveness is Normal, the beacon frequency will be moderate. This setting is a good compromise of station-processing capacity and capability to react to signal-quality changes. It is best for most applications.

- *Fast:* If responsiveness is Fast, the beacon frequency will be high. A mobile station can react faster to a deterioration of communications quality, avoiding communication errors. Faster responsiveness is necessary for interactive mobile applications, whereas stationary operations can function with slow (Relaxed) response. The faster responsiveness, however, will add more overhead on the network.

Cell Search Thresholds

Sensitivity determines the amount of time the mobile station will spend in cell search mode and when the mobile station will switch to another access point. Sensitivity parameters set the values of the *cell search thresholds*, which determine when the mobile station starts or stops looking for another access point. These thresholds are related to the level of communications quality. There are three cell search thresholds:

- *Regular Cell Search:* The Regular Cell Search is the level of communications quality at which the mobile station starts looking for another access point. The station will only switch over to a new access point if the level of communications quality with that access point is higher than the Stop Cell Search threshold.

- *Fast Cell Search:* The Fast Cell Search is the level of communications quality at which the mobile station starts looking for an access point with any acceptable level of communications quality. In this case, the station will immediately switch over to an access point that provides better communications quality.

- *Stop Cell Search:* The Stop Cell Search is the level of communications quality at which the mobile station stops looking for an access point. There are three user-defined sensitivity presets:

- *Low:* If sensitivity is Low, a roaming station will stay connected to an access point as long as possible. It will start searching for another access point later than with the Normal setting and stop searching earlier. The Low sensitivity settings are best when coverage areas are not adjacent to one another. They will avoid a station looking for access points when there is no access point within range.

- *Normal:* The Normal sensitivity setting is designed to work best in most environments. Start with this setting, and then adjust the sensitivity to either Low or High as needed.

- *High:* If sensitivity is High, a roaming station will try to switch to another access point as soon as possible. It will start searching for another access point earlier and stop searching later than with the Normal setting. If Sensitivity is High, for example, a roaming station is likely to spend more time in cell search mode.

In cell search mode, a mobile station has to interpret beacons and network broadcast messages transmitted by different access points. If sensitivity is too high, a station is likely to spend more time in cell search mode than needed. This causes unnecessary use of the processing capacity from the mobile station. A mobile station requires network overhead to switch between two access points.

Inter-Access Point Protocol (IAPP)

Through the collaboration of companies led by Lucent, the Inter-Access Point Protocol (IAPP) specification provides a common roaming protocol enabling wireless users to move throughout a facility while maintaining a connection to the network via multiple-vendor access points. Today, interoperability tests and demonstrations show IAPP works with a variety of access points. As a result, IAPP could become the industry standard if other vendors and users embrace the protocol.

The IAPP specification builds upon the capabilities of the IEEE 802.11 standard, using the distribution system interfaces of the access point that 802.11 provides. IAPP operates between access points, using User Datagram Protocol (UDP) and Internet Protocol (IP) as a basis for communications. UDP is a Transport Layer protocol that provides connectionless and unacknowledged end-to-end data transfers. See the section "Internet Protocol (IP)" later in this chapter for an explanation of IP.

IAPP defines the following two basic protocols: the Announce Protocol and the Handover Protocol. The Announce Protocol provides coordination between access points by performing the following functions:

- It informs other access points about a new active access point.

- It informs the access points of network-wide configuration information.

The Handover Protocol performs the following procedure:

1. It informs an access point that one of its stations has reassociated with a different access point.

2. The old access point forwards buffered frames for the station to the new access point.

3. The new access point updates filter tables to ensure MAC-level filtering (that is, *bridging*), and forwards frames appropriately.

Implementing Roaming

Normally, you won't have the luxury to choose a type of roaming protocol for the wireless system you are implementing. Vendors generally implement a proprietary roaming protocol that works only with their products. When making a selection of which access points to use, be sure to include the presence of multiple-vendor roaming protocols (for example, IAPP) as a factor when comparing access points.

As with other product procurements, however, it is most effective to plan on purchasing components, such as access points and radio cards, from a common vendor. Similar to implementing an ethernet network with common hubs and switches, this will make the resulting wireless system easier to manage.

Communications Protocols

The wireless and wired networking technologies provide lower-level connections among the network interface cards located in end-user appliances, access points, servers, and printers. A communications protocol operates at a higher level (typically Transport and Network Layers) and establishes end-to-end connections between the application software within devices on the network. This is necessary to provide a common path for entities to communicate.

The most common protocol for providing communications among network devices and applications are the Transmission Control Protocol (TCP) and Internet Protocol (IP). These protocols are the basis of standards for connecting to the Internet and providing open systems connectivity in other systems. The IETF has many RFCs (Request for Comments) that explain the operation of TCP/IP protocols. You can purchase TCP/IP software from a variety of vendors for different platforms. In fact, UNIX includes TCP/IP as part of the operating system.

Transmission Control Protocol (TCP)

Transmission Control Protocol (TCP) operates at the OSI Transport Layer and is commonly used for establishing and maintaining communications between applications on different computers. TCP provides highly reliable, full-duplex, connection-oriented, acknowledged, and flow-control services to upper-layer protocols and applications. A mainframe computer, for example, employing TCP software enables a user, having TCP software as well, to log on to the mainframe and run the application using Telnet. Connection-oriented services, such as Telnet, FTP, rlogin, X Windows, and SMTP, require a high degree of reliability and therefore use TCP. Figure 6.13 illustrates the header of the TCP protocol.

16 Bits	16 Bits	32 Bits	32 Bits	16 Bits	16 Bits	16 Bits	16 Bits	Variable Length	Variable Length
Source Port	Destination Port	Sequence Number	Acknowledgement Number	Header Information	Window	Checksum	Urgent Pointer	Options	Data

FIGURE 6.13 *The fields of a TCP datagram provide necessary functionality for reliable communications between a source and destination network device.*

The following list describes the fields of TCP datagram:

- *Source Port and Destination Port:* Identifies the service access points at which upper-layer source and destination processes and applications receive TCP services. Most server processes associate with a fixed port number (for example, 23 for Telnet and 161 SNMP) to provide application developers a standard port to point to when communicating with a server.

  Most client processes, however, request a port number from the server's operating system at the beginning of execution. This enables the server processes to differentiate which client process it is communicating with.

- *Sequence Number:* Specifies the sequence number of the datagram being sent.

- *Acknowledgement Number:* Contains the sequence number of the next datagram the sender of the immediate packet expects to receive.

- *Header Information:* Carries information about the TCP header, such as the length and control flags.

- *Window:* Specifies the size of the sender's receive window (that is, buffer space available for incoming data).

- *Checksum:* Used to determine whether the header contains errors.

- *Urgent Pointer:* Points to the first data in the packet byte that the sender wanted to mark as urgent.

- *Options:* Specifies various TCP options.

- *Data:* Contains upper-layer information and control data.

Tip

Firewalls can filter incoming datagrams based on the port addresses found in the TCP header. This enables system designers to restrict access to specific applications on a network residing behind the firewall. Be sure to incorporate a firewall with appropriate TCP filters to block access to specific applications.

The operation of the TCP protocol is fairly straightforward:

1. Entity A, wishing to establish a connection with Entity B, initiates a three-way handshake protocol starting with a connection request datagram sent to Entity B.

2. Entity B responds to Entity A with an acknowledgement containing control information (for example, window size).

3. Entity A finishes the TCP connection by sending an acknowledgement containing control information back to Entity B.

4. The two entities send TCP datagrams back and forth to each other associated to a particular port address.

Internet Protocol (IP)

The Internet Protocol (IP) operates at the OSI Network Layer. Routers commonly use IP to route TCP datagrams from source to destination. Figure 6.14 illustrates the fields of an IP packet. The following list describes these fields:

- *Version:* The version number of the IP protocol. For example, a value of 4 represents IPv4, and a value of 6 represents IPv6.

- *Internet Header Length:* The length of the IP header in 32-bit words.

- *Type of Service:* The level of service (for example, precedence, delay, throughput, and reliability) the IP datagram should be given as it traverses the network.

- *Total Length:* The length of the datagram in bytes.

- *Identification:* The identification number of the datagram for purposes of combining datagram fragments.

- *Flags:* Data bits for controlling whether fragmentation should take place.

- *Fragment Offset:* The location of a datagram (if it is a fragment) within the complete datagram. The receiving entity uses this to combine fragments.

- *Time-to-Live:* The maximum amount of time the datagram can exist as the datagram traverses the network.

- *Protocol:* The protocol that associates with the data in the Data field of the datagram. A value of 6 indicates that the Data field contains a TCP datagram, for example, and a value of 17 indicates that the Data field contains a UDP datagram.

- *Header Checksum:* 16-bit checksum of the datagram header (up to and including the Protocol field).

- *Source IP Address:* The IP address of the sender of the datagram.

- *Destination IP Address:* The IP address of the destination of the datagram.

- *Options:* A set of fields that describe specific processing that must take place on the packet. Options are generally used for debugging and testing.

- *Padding:* Additional data bits to ensure the packet is a complete set of 32-bit words.

4 Bits	4 Bits	8 Bits	16 Bits	16 Bits	3 Bits	13 Bits	8 Bits	8 Bits	16 Bits	32 Bits	32 Bits	Variable Length	Variable Length
Version	Internet Header Length	Type of Service	Total Length	Identification	Flags	Fragment Offset	Time-to-Live	Protocol	Header Checksum	Source IP Address	Destination IP Address	Options	Padding

FIGURE 6.14 *The fields of an IPv4 packet provide necessary functionality for routing across dissimilar networks.*

If you plan to use applications requiring TCP/IP interfaces or if users will need access to the Internet, you will have to assign a unique IP address to each device connected to the network (handheld appliance, access point, workstation, printer, server, and so on). Actually, the IP address corresponds to a network connection; therefore, a server having two network interface cards requires two IP addresses, one for each card.

The IP packet header contains the source and destination IP address that routers will use, along with a routing table, to determine where to send the packet next. The IP address is 32 bits long; therefore, there are 4,294,967,296 unique IP addresses.

IP Address Classes

The developers of the Internet decided to base IP addressing on the hierarchical format shown in Figure 6.15, distinguishing the address into three classes: Class A, Class B, and Class C. If your organization never plans to interface with the Internet, then you are free to use the IP address space in any way. Otherwise, you must obtain official IP addresses (ones that are unique from others assigned) to operate over the Internet.

You can obtain an official IP address through an Internet service provider (ISP) in your nearest metropolitan area. For an official IP address, you will be given a unique network number, and you are free to assign addresses within the domain. If you are assigned a Class C address, for example, you are free to assign up to 255 addresses.

Troubleshooting Tip

Because of the vast number of organizations deploying Web servers and gaining access to the Internet, IP addresses are quickly running out. In fact, it is impossible to obtain a Class A address and very difficult if not impossible to obtain a Class B address. Therefore, you will probably be issued multiple Class C addresses.

The problem, however, is that it is difficult to manage multiple Class C addresses if they are not contiguous. Therefore, you must predict the number of addresses you will need for the long term to maintain a contiguous series of addresses.

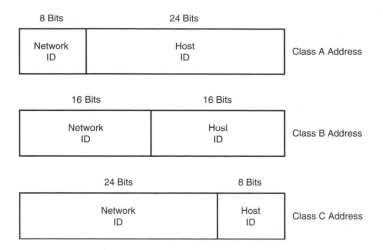

8 Bits 24 Bits

| Network ID | Host ID |

Class A Address

16 Bits 16 Bits

| Network ID | Host ID |

Class B Address

24 Bits 8 Bits

| Network ID | Host ID |

Class C Address

FIGURE 6.15 *A router forwards packets on to a particular network segment based on the network ID portion of the IP address. When the packet arrives at the correct network, the network will deliver the packet to the final destination based on the host ID.*

When planning the allocation of address, ensure that you obtain enough official unique IP addresses for each network connection. An organization having 350 users, 10 access points, and 4 servers, for example, would require at least 364 addresses. You could satisfy this requirement by obtaining one Class B address or two Class C addresses.

Note

Most systems currently use IPv4, having been in use since the early 1980s. Some companies, however, are beginning to migrate their systems to a newer version, IPv6. The main differences are that IPv6 offers much larger IP addresses—128 bits each—providing a solution to the small number of IPv4 IP addresses, and IPv6 includes extensions to support authentication, data integrity, and data confidentiality.

Implementing IP Address Assignment with a Limited Number of Official IP Addresses

If your network implementation requires a large number of IP addresses, or if it is difficult to predict the number of addresses needed in the future, consider private addressing techniques. The Network Information Center has set aside a single Class A address (10.X.X.X) that you can use within your network, giving you a large number of addresses to assign to network devices. You have to agree, however, to not use these addresses on the Internet.

If you need Internet access, you can deploy a proxy server that translates your private addresses into legal Internet addresses. This means that you need to obtain at least one Class C address to support the connections to the Internet. As a result, the outside world sees only a few IP addresses, not the many used within the company.

Static Versus Dynamic IP Addresses

For smaller wireless LANs (fewer than 50 users), it may be feasible to install static IP addresses within the configuration files for each appliance. The problem with installing static IP addresses in larger LANs is that you will more than likely make a mistake and accidentally use a duplicate address or an IP address that doesn't correspond to the immediate network. The wrong IP address will cause problems that are difficult to troubleshoot. In addition, it is tedious and time consuming to change the IP address on all network devices if you must alter the address plan in the future.

For larger LANs, consider the use of a dynamic address assignment protocol, such as Dynamic Host Configuration Protocol (DHCP). DHCP issues IP addresses automatically within a specified range to devices, such as PCs when they are first powered on. The device retains the use of the IP address for a specific license period that the system administrator can define. DHCP is available as part of the Microsoft Windows NT Server NOS and UNIX operating systems, and offers the following advantages over manual installation:

- *Efficient implementation of address assignments:* With DHCP, there is no need to manually install or change IP addresses at every client workstation during initial installation or when a workstation is moved from one location to another. This saves time during installation and avoids mistakes in allocating addresses (such as duplicate addresses or addresses having the wrong subnet number). It is very difficult to track down address-related problems that may occur when using permanently assigned addresses.

- *Central point of address management:* With DHCP, there is no need to update the IP address at each client workstation if making a change to the network's configuration or address plan. With DHCP, you can make these changes from a single point in the network. If you move the Domain Name Service software to a different platform (for example, from a Sun to an NT platform), for example, you would need to incorporate that change for each client workstation if using permanently assigned addresses. With DHCP, you just update the configuration screen from a single point at the Windows NT Server or remote location. Again, this advantage is strongest for larger networks.

TCP/IP: Wireless LAN Issues

TCP/IP provide an excellent platform for high-speed wired LANs with constant connections; however, the use of TCP/IP over wireless LANs offers significant problems. The following explains issues that may affect the performance of the wireless LAN when using standard TCP/IP:

- *High overhead:* Because TCP is connection oriented, it often sends packets that only perform negotiations or acknowledgements and do not contain real data.

This additional overhead consumes a relatively large amount of the limited wireless bandwidth, deteriorating the performance over the wireless LAN.

- *Inability to adjust under marginal conditions:* TCP is fairly rigid when posed with changes in wireless coverage. With TCP, a marginal connection between the wireless appliance and an access point can cause the TCP/IP protocol to terminate the connection, requiring the application or user to reestablish a connection.

- *Difficulty in dealing with mobile node addresses:* Traditional IP addressing assumes the network device will always permanently connect to the network from within the same network domain (that is, the same router port). Problems arise when an appliance associated with an IP address roams to an access point located within a different network domain, separated from the original network domain by a router.

    In most cases, this will confuse the router and possibly other devices located within the new network domain. The result is a network that cannot route the packets to the destination of the mobile station, unless you physically change the IP address in the appliance when being operated within a different domain. This is not feasible in most cases, however.

If the wireless system will consist of a larger number of appliances (usually more than 10) per access point, contemplate the use of wireless *middleware* to deal with the limited bandwidth and need to operate in marginal conditions. Middleware products provide communications over the wireless network by using a lightweight non-TCP/IP protocol between the appliances and middleware software residing on a server or separate PC. The gateway then communicates to the devices on the higher-speed wired network using standard TCP/IP-based protocols. For more information on the advantages of middleware, see the "Middleware" section later in this chapter.

Mobile IP

Consider the use of Mobile IP if users need to roam to parts of the network associated with a different IP address than what is loaded in the appliance. IETF's RFC 2002 defines Mobile IP, an enhancement to the standard IP protocol. The main goal of Mobile IP is to enable mobile stations to roam transparently throughout networks, automatically maintaining proper IP-based connections to their home networks. This avoids the impracticality of changing the IP address in the appliance when operating in a different area of the network.

The need for Mobile IP arises most often in wireless WAN systems. A user, for example, may need to roam temporarily with a wireless appliance into a foreign network having a completely different IP network address than the home network. This situation can also occur in a LAN when users roam from an access point located on one subnet (that is, router port) of a network to an access point on another subnet. In these cases, be sure to consider the use of Mobile IP.

Mobile IP uses an address forwarding mechanism to continue the delivery of packets to a mobile station as it moves from network to network. This operation is similar to the postal mail delivery service. Imagine that you are moving temporarily from Dayton, Ohio, to Washington D.C. for a six-month consulting assignment. After you arrive in D.C. and obtain a new mailing address, you drop off a change of address card at your new post office, which notifies the Dayton post office of your new address. Now when the Dayton post office receives mail for you, it knows to forward the mail to you at your new address in Washington D.C.

The operation of Mobile IP is very similar to the preceding analogy. Imagine, for example, that you are a doctor working in a hospital and you need to wander from your office to the Emergency Room to assist a new patient:

1. You carry your mobile station (a wireless pen-based computer), having an IP address associated with the part of the network where your office is located, toward the Emergency Room. (The wireless access points in the Emergency Room reside on a different subnet of the hospital's network.)

2. As you walk closer to your destination, your pen-based computer associates with the Emergency Room's network.

3. The Mobile IP protocol notifies your home network of a care-of-address (IP address located within the Emergency Room subnet) to which your home network should send packets relevant to your mobile station.

4. Your home network forwards all packets destined to you to the Emergency Room's network (via the care-of-address), which will deliver them to your mobile station.

A positive attribute of Mobile IP is that its implementation does not require changes to routers or the Domain Name Service (DNS). To implement Mobile IP, you have to include only a few software elements, as the following list describes (see Figure 6.16):

- *Mobile node:* The mobile node is an entity contained within a particular wireless mobile station (for example, handheld PC or data collector) that communicates with other Mobile IP components. A mobile node is built in to a TCP/IP protocol stack or can exist as a "shim" under a TCP/IP stack.

- *Home agent:* The home agent resides within the mobile station's home subnet, intercepts packets addressed to the mobile station, and forwards applicable packets to the applicable foreign agent.

- *Foreign agent:* The foreign agent receives packets from home agents and delivers the packets to the mobile node. The foreign agent resides somewhere within the foreign network. In some modes, the foreign agent is not necessary.

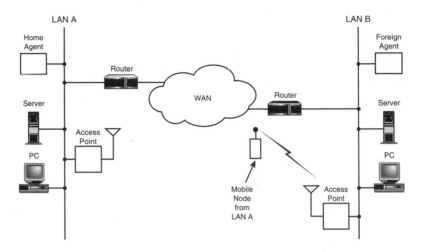

FIGURE 6.16 *Mobile IP enables mobile stations to roam from network to network without you needing to manually reassign an IP address to the mobile station.*

The Mobile IP protocol performs several functions, as detailed in the following sections.

Mobile IP Implementation Issues

Don't expect Mobile IP to work everywhere. You must carefully plan the use of Mobile IP to ensure that the external networks will support wireless mobile stations—as a minimum, with the correct type of access point (that is, direct sequence or frequency hopping)—and that the external networks will implement TCP/IP protocols.

If the external network doesn't support a foreign agent, the network will have to have a dynamic address assignment mechanism, such as DHCP, to issue a temporary IP address to the mobile visiting appliance. Also, you will need to ensure the TCP/IP software product you are using supports Mobile IP. If not, most wireless product vendors can supply you with the appropriate shim for your existing TCP/IP protocol stack.

IPv6 incorporates the Mobile IP protocols, making it much easier to implement support for mobile nodes. So, as you migrate to IPv6-based TCP/IP software and routers, Mobile IP services will already be available.

With Mobile IP, you must also properly configure firewalls, protecting both the home and foreign networks, to enable Mobile IP traffic to flow. Some firewalls are set up to prevent internal users from sending packets destined to external networks having source addresses that do not correspond with the internal network (for example, when a user is trying to spoof another external network). These firewalls will block the transmission of packets from the mobile node because its source address will not correspond to the internal (that is, foreign) network. For this case, you will need to set up the firewall to allow the Mobile IP traffic to pass.

In addition, mobile nodes and foreign agents use Internet Control Message Protocol (ICMP) to register care-of-addresses with the home agent. Therefore, you may need to configure the firewall protecting the home network to enable ICMP datagrams to pass through to the home agent.

Agent Discovery

The agent discovery process is necessary to bind the mobile node to a foreign agent or in some cases directly to the home agent. Foreign and home agents periodically advertise their availability to mobile nodes via broadcast messages. A mobile node can also broadcast a message indicating its presence and discover whether a foreign agent is available.

After receiving communication from a foreign or home agent, the mobile node determines whether it is located on the home network or a foreign network. If the mobile node is within the home network, the mobile station will not use the mobility functions. A mobile node returning to its home network, however, will *deregister* with the applicable foreign agent. If the mobile node finds that it is on a foreign network, it will obtain a care-of-address from the foreign network.

Assignment of Care-of-Address

Before the home network can forward packets to the remote network, it must know the appropriate care-of-address. With Mobile IP, there are two methods to assign a care-of-address:

- With the first method, a foreign agent maintains a single care-of-address for all mobile nodes that may fall within its domain. This makes best use of the limited number of addresses available with IPv4 because all mobile nodes share the same care-of-address. When the foreign agent advertises its presence, the broadcast message contains the care-of-address of the foreign agent.

- With the second method, the mobile node acquires the care-of-address through some external means. The mobile node may obtain the address dynamically through a protocol such as DHCP, for example. The advantage of this method of address assignment is that it enables a mobile node to function without a foreign agent; however, you need to specify a pool of addresses that can be available to the visiting nodes.

Registration

After receiving its new care-of-address, the mobile node (or foreign agent) registers it with the home agent. This establishes a link (also referred to as a tunnel) between the foreign and home networks.

For security purposes, the mobile node and home agent encrypt messages sent back and forth to each other. In addition, the home and foreign agents may reject the registration requests to guard against attacks such as packet forgery and modification.

Tunneling and Encapsulation

Mobile IP transports packets back and forth between the home and foreign networks via a tunnel. The tunnel has two end points: one at the home agent IP address, and the other located at the care-of-address (either of the foreign agent or mobile node). The home agent intercepts datagrams sent to the mobile node's home address, and then encapsulates and transmits the datagrams (generally as the payload of an IP packet) to the care-of-address entity.

After reception at the foreign network, the foreign agent decapsulates the datagram and sends it to the mobile node. Datagrams sent by the mobile node are generally handled using standard IP routing without passing through the home agent.

Connectivity Software

The radio card, access point, and communications software provide lower mid-level connections, but another higher level of functionality is necessary to map the application software, keyboard, display, and peripherals of the appliance to the application software or database residing on the network. This other system component is often referred to as *connectivity software*, which mostly deals with Presentation Layer functions.

Connectivity software comes in many forms, such as terminal emulation, direct database connectivity, Web browsers, and middleware. These are very different approaches to interfacing with applications and databases, and their implementation depends on many factors.

Choosing Connectivity Software

Choosing a form of connectivity software depends on several factors, including the following:

- The existing system (application software, database, and operating system)

- Plans for system migration

- The number of appliances

- The presence of multiple-vendor appliances

If there are very few appliances (less than five) associated with a particular terminal/host system, terminal emulation is the most economical solution for connectivity software. For client/server systems having very few appliances, a direct database solution is probably most effective. If larger numbers of appliances are present, especially if there's a mix of vendor types, then investigate the use of middleware. (The following sections address these options.)

Terminal Emulation

The idea behind terminal emulation is to make the appliance appear as a terminal to the application software running on a host-based operating system, such as UNIX and AS/400. You need VT (Virtual Terminal) emulation running on the appliance, for example, to interface with an application running on a UNIX host. Likewise, 5250 emulation software will interface with an application running on an IBM AS/400. This form of connectivity is common in the traditional terminal/host system. Figure 6.17 illustrates the concept of terminal emulation.

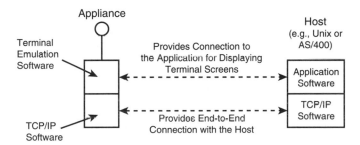

FIGURE 6.17 *Terminal emulation software on the appliance interfaces the keyboard and display of the appliance to the application software on the host via a terminal session.*

Terminal emulation software on wireless appliances generally communicates with the host using Telnet over TCP/IP protocols. The appliance appears to the host as a terminal session. After a connection is made with the host, the application software residing on the host can send display information (such as log on prompts, menus, and data) to the appliance, and keyboard strokes will be sent to the application. Thus, the software on the host provides all application functionality.

Troubleshooting Tip

If a wireless appliance running terminal emulation software does not connect to the host, be sure the host is running TCP/IP protocols. It is common to not implement TCP/IP software for host computers (especially mainframes) if the original implementation did not interface with a network. In these cases, you will have to install the TCP/IP software to establish communication between the appliance and the host.

The following are attributes of terminal emulation:

- *Very little programming, if any, needed to interface with existing host-based applications:* The implementation of appliances that use terminal emulation to interface with the host does not require any software programming on the appliance. You can often purchase appliances with terminal emulation factory loaded, and the only setup needed on the appliance is to load the IP address and some configuration parameters.

In most cases, you can establish a terminal session with an existing host-based application without even making any changes to the application software. Many smaller appliances, however, have small displays, requiring users to scroll around the larger displays that programmers may have developed for desktop-based computer monitors. In this case, many companies rewrite their applications to fit the smaller displays of portable appliances.

If printing is necessary from the appliance, you will probably need to embed the print streams of the particular appliance in the application on the host. If programming is needed on the host, you can leverage existing knowledge in the host application development environment.

- *Central application software control:* With terminal emulation, all application software is updated only at the host, not the individual appliances. All users will automatically take advantage of changes to the application without needing updates to the software on the appliance. This makes configuration management much easier, especially when there are hundreds of appliances.

- *Low cost:* Terminal emulation is generally less expensive than implementing a middleware approach. Most companies charge a couple hundred dollars per appliance for terminal emulation.

- *Limited availability of terminal emulation software for DOS-based appliances:* Terminal emulation software is widely available for Microsoft Windows operating systems; however, it is very difficult to find DOS-based appliance operating systems. The reason for this is that the DOS-based versions of TCP/IP software do not have standard interface-to-appliance software. Many companies, though, have ported their specific appliances to DOS-based terminal emulation software.

- *Inflexible programming environment:* When developing or modifying the application on the host, the terminal emulation specification limits the control of the appliance from the host-based application.

- *Limited support for migration to client/server systems:* Terminal emulation software does not interface directly to databases, making it unsuitable for client/server implementations; thus, terminal emulation enables users to access only the screens that the application provides.

- *Difficulty in supporting the appliances:* With standard terminal emulation, there is no effective way to monitor the performance of the wireless appliances, making it difficult to troubleshoot network problems.

- *Significant effect on wireless networks:* With terminal emulation, all screens and print streams must traverse the wireless network, affecting the performance of the overall system. In addition, terminal emulation uses TCP to maintain a connection with the host, but TCP does not operate efficiently over wireless networks. (See the section "TCP/IP: Wireless LAN Issues" earlier in this chapter.)

Case Study 6.1:

Using Terminal Emulation for System Integration

A police station in Florida was losing track of evidence they acquired through the investigation of crimes. This had become a big problem because police officials couldn't find the evidence in a timely manner when the court needed it, often delaying trial proceedings. As a result, the police chief decided to implement an asset tracking system to manage the items and their specific locations.

The system, based on the use of bar codes and handheld scanning equipment, needed a wireless network to support mobility when performing asset management functions (such as picking and inventory) in the large room that housed the evidence.

Because no IS staff were available to do the project, the police chief outsourced the complete system implementation to a reliable system integrator. After careful analysis of functionality requirements and the existing system, the integrator developed a design that specified the use of the following components:

- Off-the-shelf asset management software
- Two 802.11-compliant handheld scanners
- An 802.11 access point
- Connectivity software

The asset management software was hosted on the existing UNIX server that supported the police station's jail-management software. The access point interfaced the wireless handheld scanners to an existing ethernet network, providing a network connection to the UNIX server.

When dealing with the connectivity software, the integrator narrowed the choices down to either terminal emulation or middleware. Direct database connectivity was not an option because there was not any way to interface directly with the database. All interaction with the database was through the application software only.

The integrator decided to use terminal emulation (VT220) for several reasons:

- There would have been no significant gain in performance by using middleware with only two wireless appliances sending data over the wireless network.
- The relatively small amount of data sent between appliances and the UNIX application offered very little impact to the 2 Mbps wireless network.
- The price for two terminal emulation licenses for the appliances was much less expensive than purchasing middleware software.
- The police station had no plans to move to a client/server system.

All in all, terminal emulation was the least costly form of connectivity software based on the police station's requirements.

Direct Database Connectivity

Direct database connectivity encompasses application software on the appliance (that is, client) that interfaces directly with a database located on a server. With this configuration, the software on the appliance provides all application functionality. Figure 6.18 illustrates the concept of direct database connectivity.

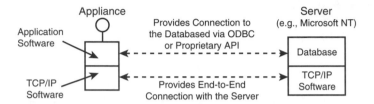

FIGURE 6.18   *Direct database connectivity fits the very popular client/server system model.*

The appliance generally uses TCP/IP software as a basis for communicating with the server for direct database connectivity. After a connection is made with the server, the application software residing on the appliance communicates with the database using vendor specific database protocols (that is, Application Program Interface) or a common protocol such as ODBC (Open Database Connectivity).

The following are attributes of direct database connectivity:

- *Flexible programming environment:* Direct database connectivity enables the programmer to interact directly with database records, rather than be limited to what the application software on the host provides (as is the case with terminal emulation). Direct database connectivity provides the most flexible programming environment as compared to other connectivity approaches.

- *A moderate amount of programming needed to interface new appliances with existing applications:* With direct database connectivity, you must often develop a program that runs on the appliance to interface with the existing database, especially if you are incorporating new appliances into an existing database. This requires the developer to understand how to write software that interfaces with the appliance's specific display, keyboard, scanner, and peripherals.

- *Distributed application software control:* New releases of application software must be installed on each of the appliances when using the direct database connectivity approach. This offers challenges with distributing new application software releases. One method that helps overcome this problem is to store the current version of the appliance application software on a server and have the application software running on the appliance compare its current version with the one located on the server. If the one on the server is a newer release, the application software on the appliance can automatically download and install the newer version of software.

In addition, modifications to the central database structure may require changes to the application software on the appliance. Care must be taken to ensure that these application changes are made so that the application works properly.

- *Low cost:* Direct database connectivity is generally less expensive than implementing a middleware approach.

- *Good support for client/server systems:* Direct database connectivity fits well into the client/server system model, enabling programmers to develop front-end applications that run on the appliance.

- *Application size limited to the amount of appliance memory:* With direct database connectivity, the appliance must have sufficient storage for the application software.

- *Wireless network impacts:* With direct database connectivity, only the database inquiries and data records must traverse the wireless network, making efficient use of the wireless network performance in terms of data transfers. All print streams and screen interfaces are handled within the appliance.

Most direct database implementations use TCP to maintain a connection with the host, however; but TCP does not operate efficiently over wireless networks. (See the section "TCP/IP: Wireless LAN Issues" earlier in this chapter.)

Implementing Client/Server Systems with ODBC

The advantage of writing the appliance software to interface with ODBC is that it provides an open interface to the many databases that are ODBC-compliant, enabling you to write one application that can interface with databases from different vendors. With direct database connectivity, a programmer can interface directly with the database using the database's proprietary language or use the common industry standard Open Database Connectivity (ODBC) interface.

ODBC, Microsoft's implementation of the X/Open and SQL Access Group (SAG) Call Level Interface (CLI) specification, provides interactive database functions, such as adding, modifying, and deleting data. ODBC provides a generic, vendor-neutral interface to relational and nonrelational databases, alleviating the need for developers to learn multiple Application Programming Interfaces (APIs).

The architecture of ODBC encompasses the following components:

- *Host application:* The application software located on the appliance that is responsible for calling ODBC functions to execute statements, retrieve results, and gather statistics.

- *Driver manager:* Loads the specific database drivers, depending on the data source in use.

continues

- *DBMS-specific drivers:* Translates the database function call, submits a request to a data source, and produces results.

- *Data sources:* The specific database that stores data relevant to the application.

If you plan to interface with multiple database types, you should certainly consider using an ODBC interface.

Intranet-Based Connectivity Software

If your wireless system needs to interface with an application on a Web server, the connectivity software can consist of just a Web browser that runs on the appliance (see Figure 6.19) and communicates with the Web server using the HTTP (Hypertext Transfer Protocol). This works fine for appliances that run Microsoft Windows appliances that have larger screens, because a variety of browsers are available that run on Windows and most existing intranet applications are written to fill a full-size monitor.

It is more difficult to integrate a DOS-based appliance (for example, a data collector) with a smaller display with an existing intranet application. Browsers are difficult to find for specific DOS-based appliances. And, the intranet application must be written to fill a much smaller area of the screen to work effectively with the smaller screens of some appliances.

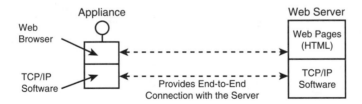

Figure 6.19 *With intranet-based connectivity, a Web browser runs on the appliance and interfaces with an application on the Web server, fitting in well with existing Web applications.*

The following are attributes of intranet-based connectivity. (Many of these are similar to the use of terminal emulation.)

- *Very little if no programming needed to interface with existing host-based applications:* A wireless system implementation using intranet-based connectivity with a Web server does not require any software programming on the appliance. This enables companies to leverage their knowledge of Web-based programming for the development of the application.

- *Central application software control:* With intranet-based connectivity, all application software is updated only on the Web server, not the individual appliances. All users will automatically take advantage of changes to the application without needing updates to the software on the appliance. This makes configuration management much easier, especially when there are hundreds of appliances.

- *Low cost:* Intranet-based connectivity is generally less expensive than implementing a middleware approach. You can purchase Web browsers for the appliances for a relatively small fee.

- *Strong support for client/server systems:* Intranet-based connectivity software (that is, Web browsers) offers a thin client front end to an application residing on the server.

- *Potential impact on wireless network performance:* Intranet-based connectivity can consume large amounts of the limited wireless bandwidth, depending on the type of application. The browser on the appliance may point to a Web page containing large graphic files that must be sent from the server to the appliance, for example.

Most intranet-based implementations may also use TCP to maintain a connection with the host. Unfortunately, as explained in the section "TCP/IP: Wireless LAN Issues" earlier in this chapter, TCP does not operate efficiently over wireless networks.

Middleware

Wireless network middleware is an intermediate software component generally located on the wired network between the wireless appliance and the application or data residing on the wired network (see Figure 6.20). The overall goal of middleware is to increase performance of applications running across a wireless network. To accomplish this, middleware attempts to counter wireless network impairments, such as limited bandwidth and disruptions in network connections.

The following are common features found in middleware products that go beyond the basic functionality of connecting appliances to applications and databases located on the wired network:

- *Optimization techniques:* Many middleware products include data compression at the Transport Layer to help minimize the number of bits sent over the wireless link. Vendors use a variety of compression algorithms to perform the compression, including V.42bis, Hoffman encoding, run-length encoding, and proprietary compression techniques. Some implementations of middleware use header compression, where mechanisms replace traditional packet headers with a much shorter bit sequence before transmission.

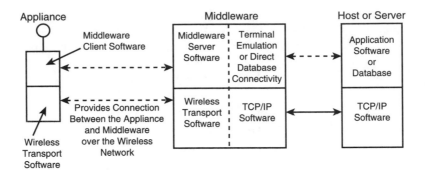

F IGURE 6.20 *With middleware, the appliance communicates with middleware software using a protocol optimized for wireless networks. The middleware then communicates with the actual application or database by using an applicable connectivity software.*

- *Intelligent restarts:* With wireless networks, a transmission may be cut at midstream due to interference or operation in fringe areas. An intelligent restart is a recovery mechanism that detects when a transmission has been cut, and, when the connection is reestablished, the middleware resumes transmission from the break point instead of at the beginning of the transmission.

- *Data bundling:* Some middleware can combine (bundle) smaller data packets into a single large packet for transmission over the wireless network. This is especially beneficial to help lower transmission service costs of wireless WANs. Because most wireless data services charge users by the packet, data bundling results in a lower aggregate cost.

- *Embedded acknowledgements:* Rather than send acknowledgements as separate small packets, middleware products tend to embed acknowledgements in the header of larger information carrying packets to reduce the number of packets traversing the wireless network. Many network protocols (for example, Novell's IPX) require stations to send acknowledgements to each other to continue data flows.

- *Store-and-forward messaging:* Middleware performs message queuing to ensure message delivery to users who may become disconnected from the network for a period of time. After the station comes back online, the middleware will send the stored messages to the station.

- *Screen scraping and reshaping:* The development environment of some middleware products enables the developer to use visual tools to "scrape" and "reshape" portions of existing application screens to more effectively fit within the smaller display of data collectors.

- *Support for Mobile IP:* Some middleware products offer home and foreign agent functions to support the use of Mobile IP protocols.

- *Operational support mechanisms:* Some middleware products offer utilities and tools to monitor the performance of wireless appliances, enabling MIS personnel to better troubleshoot problems.

Note

A wireless gateway consists of the wireless middleware, operating system, and hardware platform.

The following are attributes of middleware connectivity:

- *Highly efficient operation over wireless networks:* Middleware reduces the load on the wireless network through the use of optimization techniques, such as data compression and screen scraping.

- *No programming required on the appliance or host/server:* Most middleware products offer a development environment that shields the developer from understanding appliance and host-based development environments.

- *Supports migration from terminal/host to client/server systems:* Many companies are migrating from terminal/host (that is, mainframes) to client/server systems. Middleware is a cost-effective solution for supporting these migrations, enabling connections to both terminal-based systems and client/server databases, simultaneously.

- *Support of multiple-vendor appliances:* Middleware products interface with a wide variety of appliances.

- *Long-term cost savings:* Because of easier support of operational wireless applications, middleware provides considerable long-term cost savings.

- *Higher initial costs for implementations having smaller numbers of appliances:* The cost for middleware is $5,000 to $10,000 per site, making it relatively expensive for implementing wireless systems having fewer than 10 appliances. Be sure, however, to consider all the advantages of middleware before finalizing a business case.

Case Study 6.2:

Using Middleware for System Integration

A boat-building company in Maine decided to implement a quality assurance system to improve the efficiency of performing periodic inspections. Several times throughout the manufacturing process of each boat, inspectors need to walk throughout the plant and record flaws as the boats are being assembled.

The company's corporate information system consists of the following components:

- An IBM mainframe that supports most of the company's application software

- Servers that host databases

- 3270 terminals that interface with the mainframe applications

- PCs that run client application software that interface with the databases

continues

continued

- An ethernet network that ties everything together

The new system includes a handheld PC with an 802.11-compliant radio card that communicates back to the corporate information system.

For each boat, the inspector enters the boat's serial number; then, the system prompts the inspector through a series of questions that pertain to the quality of specific items of that particular boat. As the inspector answers the questions, the wireless network transports the data back to the corporate information system for viewing by construction managers.

The information that the new quality assurance system would use is located on both the mainframe and database servers. As a result, the corporate IS group had to pay close attention to the type of connectivity software to use to satisfy the requirements of both operating environments.

As alternatives for connectivity software, the IS group evaluated the use of terminal emulation, direct database connectivity, and middleware. 3270 terminal emulation for the handheld PCs would interface easily with the mainframe system, but it would not provide an interface to the database servers. Likewise, direct database connectivity would interface with the database servers, but not the mainframes.

For this project, middleware was clearly the best alternative. The need to seamlessly interface with both the mainframe and database server systems was imperative.

Tip

Maximize caching of data on the appliance to minimize transmissions across the wireless network.

As shown in this chapter, it is evident that there is much more to implementing wireless networks than what the 802.11 standard covers. Therefore, be sure to plan ahead and properly design the entire system before purchasing components.

CHAPTER 7

Planning a Wireless LAN

- Managing a wireless LAN implementation
  Before embarking on a wireless system project, you should understand the concepts of organizing a team, planning the activities, and handling risks and contingencies.

- Defining the requirements for a wireless LAN
  Requirements are crucial in all development projects. Be sure to follow the steps described in this chapter to ensure that you fully understand the basis for your wireless LAN system.

- Analyzing the feasibility of a wireless LAN
  Ensure that you understand the return on investment before implementing a wireless LAN. A feasibility study helps organizations decide whether to proceed with the project based on the costs associated with performing a site survey and purchasing and installing wireless adapters, access points, and other components.

Managing a Wireless LAN Implementation

In most cases, organizations accomplish work in functional groups, which perform parts of an operation that are continuous and repetitive. As the system administrator for a client/server system, for example, you might perform daily backups of databases. This task, as well as others, is part of the operation of a system management function. Projects are similar to functional operations: They are performed by people, constrained by limited resources, and should be planned, executed, and controlled.

Projects, however, are temporary endeavors that people undertake to develop a new service or product. Due to the complexities of wireless networks, most end-user companies will outsource the implementation of the wireless LAN to a system integrator. Therefore, you should classify network implementations as projects because they have a definite beginning and end.

> **Note**
>
> *An important feature of this and the next chapter is a single, comprehensive case study that runs through both chapters, illustrating real-world implementation. The case study is divided into small segments to isolate key steps of planning and installing a wireless LAN.*

Establishing Project Management Principles

The Project Management Institute (PMI) defines project management as *the art of directing and coordinating human and material resources throughout the life of a project.* Project management primarily consists of planning, monitoring, and controlling the execution of the project. Planning involves identifying project goals and objectives, developing work plans, budgeting, and allocating resources. Project monitoring and control ensure that the execution of the project conforms to the plan by periodically measuring progress and making corrections to the project plan if necessary.

> **Note**
>
> *PMI offers a certification titled Project Management Professional (PMP) that you can earn through work experience, education, and successful completion of the PMP examination. The PMP certification ensures that you have mastered the skills necessary to manage a project of any type. Many corporations are beginning to recognize the importance of PMP-certified professionals. You should consider completing the PMP certification process as part of your continuing professional education.*

The use of sound project management principles results in many benefits, such as the following:

- Clarification of project goals and activities
- Better communication among project team members, executives, and the customer
- Accurate projections of resource requirements
- Identification and reduction of risks
- More effective resolution of contingencies

Such benefits help an organization complete a quality wireless system implementation on time and within budget.

Planning a Project

Planning is an important part of any activity. It provides a time at the beginning of a project to think about what could go wrong and visualize solutions that will keep the project on the right track. Specifically, project planning is a process consisting of analysis and decisions for the following purposes:

- Directing the intent of the project
- Identifying actions, risks, and responsibilities within the project
- Guiding the ongoing activities of the project
- Preparing for potential changes

Project planning enables the project to take the most direct path in reaching project goals.

In the planning stage of a wireless system project, visualize the goals you have for implementing the network and actions necessary to maximize a successful outcome. In some cases, you will need to determine the requirements and any necessary products before you can complete the project plan.

You should produce a project plan by performing the following steps:

1. Define the project scope.
2. Develop a work plan.
3. Create a schedule.
4. Identify resources.
5. Develop a budget.
6. Define project operations.
7. Evaluate risks.

After evaluating risks, you might need to refine some of the other elements of the plan. The project, for example, might require the team to interface a handheld wireless data terminal to an existing IBM mainframe computer containing a centralized application or database. If the team's design engineer has no experience working with mainframe databases, you should consider the project at risk and attempt to mitigate the problem. Most likely, you would modify the resource plan by either assigning another employee to the project or utilizing a consultant to assist when necessary.

In fact, you should treat the project plan as a *living document*—one that you should update as more information, such as detailed requirements and design, becomes available.

Identifying Project Scope

Before determining project tasks, staffing, a schedule, and the budget, you must first define the project's scope, which provides a basis for future project decisions. The project scope gives a project team high-level direction, allowing an accurate development of remaining planning elements and execution of the project. For each project, you should prepare a project scope having at least the following items:

- *Project charter:* The project charter formally recognizes the existence of the project, identifies the business need that the project is addressing, and gives a general description of the resulting solution. This description should show the relationship between the solution and the business needs of the organization.

  The requirements phase of the project will define more details of the solution. A manager external to the project should issue the charter and name the person who will be the project manager. The project charter should provide the project manager with the authority to apply people and material resources to project activities.

- *Assumptions:* The project team should state assumptions for unknown or questionable key factors that could affect the project. A product vendor, for example, might tell you that a new wireless device will be available on a specific date. If the success of the project depends on this product, you should identify its availability as an assumption. This will assist you when evaluating project risks. (See the section "Managing Project Risks" later in this chapter.)

- *Constraints:* Constraints limit the project team's options in completing the project. Common constraints are funding limits, technical requirements, availability of resources, type and location of project staff, and schedules. Be sure to fully define constraints to keep the visualized outcome of the project within an acceptable scope.

Case Study 7.1:
Developing a Project Scope for
WarehouseTrack

A manufacturer of auto parts based in Atlanta, Georgia, has nine distribution centers located throughout the United States. As the manufacturing company produces the parts, it ships them to the distribution centers for temporary storage. When resellers and retail stores order more parts, the company can react quickly by shipping them to the requester from the nearest distribution center. Profits for this $800 million-per-year company had been high the preceding year; therefore, the company was looking seriously at investing some of the profits to improve its stance with customers and take on more market share.

The president of the company, Bob, had met with one of his friends who operates a manufacturing company that makes and distributes hydraulic pumps. Bob's friend had mentioned that he implemented a wireless system that supports automation with his distribution centers. The automated system, which included receiving and inventory functions, was saving him over $1 million per year in labor savings. This prompted Bob to immediately notify his warehouse operations manager, Linda, and the head of information systems, Ron, to consider a similar system for parts distribution centers.

Because they had never implemented wireless systems and had limited resources within their information systems group, Ron and Linda decided to contract a system integration company to manage the entire project—from project planning through the implementation. After a couple meetings with the system integrator, Ron decided to contract Debra, an employee of the system integrator and a certified project manager, to develop a project plan and feasibility study so that Bob could decide on funding.

The project plan—which consists of a work plan, resource identification, preliminary budget, and risk identification—will provide a basis for the costs shown within the feasibility study. A business process analysis will provide information regarding the benefits of implementing the system.

As the first step for planning the project, Debra developed a project scope that would ensure everyone would be focusing on the same basic requirements throughout the project, and provide a basis for determining the following:

- Project tasks
- Staffing
- Scheduling
- Budgeting

Debra met with Bob to clearly understand his perspective of the project. She asked questions that probed the business problem and addressed the constraints that will limit the project. Debra also met with both Linda and Ron to gain a basic understanding of the issues and needs of the warehouse staff and information systems group concerning the proposed project.

After gathering this information, Debra prepared a project scope. The following are the main points of the document:

- *Project charter:* The purpose of this project, dubbed WarehouseTrack, is to develop a wireless bar code system to automate functions that result in a significant return on investment within the distribution center warehouses. The warehouse staff currently utilizes paper-based methods to manage all aspects of the warehouse, resulting in inefficient use of labor and higher delays than competitors when processing orders for customers. A wireless automatic identification and data capture (AIDC) system is a solution that will decrease delays in getting parts to customers by enabling the warehouses to keep more accurate records of parts in stock, shorten order picking time, and speed up the shipping preparation process.

The AIDC system will consist of a wireless LAN, applicable application software, and database. The AIDC will need to interface with the company's existing corporate information system to feed management and reporting systems already in place.

This project will consist of a requirements analysis and feasibility study phase that the president (Bob) and his financial officers will use to decide whether the expense for the system is in the best interest of the

continues

continued

company. If the feasibility of implementing the system is positive, the
project will also include steps for
designing, installing, and supporting
the system.

• *Constraints:* The manufacturing company will fund the analysis and feasibility study and spend up to
$500,000 during the next year to
implement the system. There are no
restrictions to the selection of hardware and software for this project.

Developing a Work Breakdown Structure

To reach the goals of the project, plan a series of activities that produce the end
product with a minimum amount of time and money. The development of a *work
breakdown structure (WBS)* is a good way of planning the tasks, as well as tracking the
progress of the project. A WBS has a tree-like structure and identifies the tasks that
the team will need to perform and the products they must deliver. The first level of
the WBS should indicate major phases, followed by lower layers that identify primary and secondary tasks. The WBS also provides a basis for other planning elements,
such as resource allocations and schedules.

A common question is what level of detail should the WBS include? As a minimum, you should specify enough detail so that it is possible to determine the length
of time to complete and estimate the cost of each phase and task. This will make it
possible to more accurately plan the project.

Case Study 7.2:
Developing a Work Breakdown
Structure (WBS) for
WarehouseTrack

Debra, the project manager developing
the project plan and feasibility study for
WarehouseTrack, had received acceptance of the project scope from upper
management of the manufacturing company. She was now ready to develop a
WBS identifying the necessary actions
the project needs to accomplish.

The following list gives an overview of
each phase of WarehouseTrack:

• *Requirements phase:* Defines the
needs of the eventual users of
WarehouseTrack and existing systems (if any). This phase provides the
basis for the solution.

• *Design phase:* Consists of selecting
a set of technologies, standards,
and products that satisfy the
requirements.

- *Development phase:* Consists of developing application and connectivity software that resides on the appliances and server.
- *Operational support preparation phase:* Consists of the planning necessary to effectively support the system after it is installed. Preparations include training development and delivery, and plans for support elements, such as maintenance, system administration, and security.
- *Installation and testing phase:* Consists of physically installing the system components and running tests to verify proper operation.

The following represents a WBS for the implementation of the WarehouseTrack system:

1. Requirements phase

    1.1 Elicit end-user information

    1.2 Elicit system information

    1.3 Define the requirements

    1.4 Update the project plan

2. Design phase

    2.1 Perform a site survey

    2.2 Define system elements

    2.3 Select products

    2.4 Identify the location of access points

    2.5 Verify the design

    2.6 Document the design

    2.7 Update the project plan

    2.8 Obtain approvals for the design

    2.9 Procure components

3. Development phase

    3.1 Develop appliance software

    3.2 Develop database

    3.3 Develop PC application software

    3.4 Develop connectivity software

    3.5 Perform system testing

    3.6 Perform pilot testing

4. Operational support preparation phase

    4.1 Prepare training courses

    4.2 Define system administration staffing and procedures

    4.3 Establish help desk support

    4.4 Define network management methods and procedures

    4.5 Establish a maintenance process

    4.6 Define configuration control procedures

5. Installation and testing phase

    5.1 Plan the installation

    5.2 Stage system components

    5.3 Install the components

    5.4 Test the installation

    5.5 Perform acceptance testing

    5.6 Transfer the network to operational support

Creating a Schedule

The schedule indicates the element of timing in a project, making it possible for the project manager to coordinate work activities. The schedule and WBS are the basis for selecting and coordinating resources, as well as the primary tools for tracking project performance. A schedule should contain the following information:

- Names of the phases and tasks listed on the WBS

- Starting date, duration, and due date of each task

- Relationships between phases and tasks

The project manager should create the schedule by first recording the phase names listed in the WBS and assigning someone to be responsible for each. The next step, working with the responsible team members, is to determine the starting date, duration, and due date for each task. If you cannot determine these characteristics for each task, consider further division of the task into subtasks to accommodate a more accurate assessment. You should also indicate the relationships between tasks using precedence relationships. In other words, show conditions that must be met (such as the completion of a particular task) before starting each task.

A project team must often deal with unrealistic schedules; therefore, there might not be enough time to complete a quality implementation. In this case, you might want to consider decreasing the scope of the project.

Case Study 7.3:
Developing a Schedule for
WarehouseTrack

The next step for Debra, the project manager developing the project plan and feasibility study for WarehouseTrack, is to create a schedule. After reviewing the project scope and WBS, Debra created the schedule shown in Figure 7.1.

Identifying Resources

Resources are the people and materials that you need to perform the activities identified in the work plan. The goal of resource allocation, like most other planning activities, is to assign people and materials that maximize the success of the project, while minimizing the cost and time to complete the project. As you identify the resources, confirm their availability and schedule them to ensure that they are ready when needed.

To properly plan resources, you need to

1. Establish a project team.

2. Identify necessary materials.

Figure 7.2 illustrates recommended members of a wireless system implementation project team and the potential customers whom the team is designed to serve.

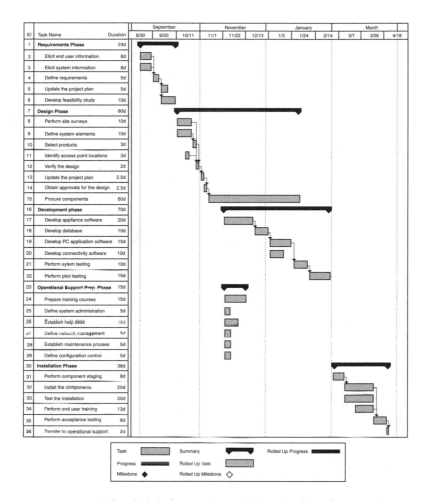

ID	Task Name	Duration
1	**Requirements Phase**	23d
2	Elicit end user information	8d
3	Elicit system information	8d
4	Define requirements	5d
5	Update the project plan	5d
6	Develop feasibility study	10d
7	**Design Phase**	80d
8	Perform site surveys	10d
9	Define system elements	10d
10	Select products	3d
11	Identify access point locations	3d
12	Verify the design	2d
13	Update the project plan	2.5d
14	Obtain approvals for the design	2.5d
15	Procure components	60d
16	**Development phase**	70d
17	Develop appliance software	20d
18	Develop database	10d
19	Develop PC application software	15d
20	Develop connectivity software	10d
21	Perform sytem testing	10d
22	Perform pilot testing	15d
23	**Operational Support Prep. Phase**	15d
24	Prepare training courses	15d
25	Define system administration	5d
26	Establish help desk	10d
27	Define network management	5d
28	Establish maintenance process	5d
29	Define configuration control	5d
30	**Installation Phase**	38d
31	Perform component staging	8d
32	Install the components	20d
33	Test the installation	20d
34	Perform end user training	13d
35	Perform acceptance testing	8d
36	Transfer to operational support	2d

FIGURE 7.1 *The schedule for WarehouseTrack, in the form of a Gantt chart, is an invaluable tool for managing the project.*

The following describes the team members of a wireless system implementation project:

- *Project manager:* The team should have one project manager who manages, directs, and is ultimately responsible for the entire project. This person coordinates the people and resources, ensuring that all objectives of the project are met on time and within budget. The project manager should have experience and education in managing projects, have excellent communication skills, be familiar with wireless networking concepts, and be familiar with the customer's environment.

Customer   Project
                                              Team

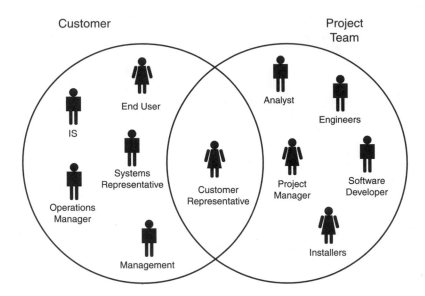

FIGURE 7.2 *A project team should include members capable of completing the project tasks. The customer representative binds the two "worlds."*

- *Customer representative:* The team should have a customer representative who portrays the interests of the users of the network and aims the project team in the right direction when determining requirements. The customer focal point should be very familiar with the user population and be able to honestly speak for the users.

- *Analysts:* Analysts gather information and define the needs of the users and the organization. The analyst should have good interviewing skills and be able to translate user and organizational needs into system requirements. It is also beneficial that at least one analyst on the team fully understands the customer's business area.

- *Engineers:* Engineers provide the technical expertise necessary to fulfill the objectives of the project. Engineers should be part of analyzing needs, but primarily they work on designing solutions that satisfy requirements. Therefore, engineers should be very familiar with wireless technologies and should understand how to interface wireless products to existing networks and systems. In addition, engineers can assist with installing the network components.

- *Implementors:* The implementors are the software engineers and technicians who develop application software and install and test the network. *Installers* set up and interface network hardware, software, and wiring; therefore, they should be familiar with reliable installation practices. *Testers* should be independent from the design and development of the system. They ensure that the installation meets user expectations, system requirements, and quality standards.

- *Operations representative:* The project team should have one operations representative to coordinate the project with existing network support organizations, ensuring that the implementation integrates well into the existing network infrastructure and support mechanisms. Therefore, the operations representative should have a good knowledge of the existing network and understand current network support mechanisms.

How many analysts, engineers, and implementors should you have on the team? There are no accurate rules because the level of staffing depends on the complexity of the customer organization, the scope of the project, schedule constraints, and the experience of the people you have available to perform the work. For smaller projects, very few people may fill the role of all project team members. In other cases, several team members may be needed to complete the project activities.

If you are planning to deploy a wireless data entry system for a business having 50 employees, for example, you can probably get by with one or two team members. A deployment of this system to a company with 5,000 users, however, will require several analysts and engineers to define requirements and design the system, as well as a cadre of installers. The most important thing, however, is to make certain that the team is composed of people having the ability to complete the project on time.

Case Study 7.4:
Developing a Resource Plan for WarehouseTrack

The next step for Debra, the project manager developing the project plan and feasibility study for WarehouseTrack, is to assign resources for the project. To accomplish this, she had to look over the project scope, WBS, and schedule to determine the type of resources necessary and when they would be needed.

Ron, the head of information systems at the manufacturing company, had decided to outsource the entire project; therefore, the system integration company will plan on providing all the resources, except the customer and operations representatives. Debra proceeded by coordinating the availability of resources with the manufacturing company and her

functional manager. The following is a list of resources that Debra assigned to the project and their primary responsibilities:

- *Project manager:* Debra, to manage the entire project.

- *Customer representative:* Linda, to be the primary focal point for the manufacturing company. Ron is the warehouse manager at the manufacturing company.

- *Business analyst:* Brian, to define the needs of the end users and the organization to support the development of functional requirements and benefits for the feasibility study.

continues

continued

- *System analyst:* Evan, to define the existing system as part of the requirements analysis.
- *Engineer:* Jared, to provide the technical expertise necessary to design the system.
- *Software developer:* Eric, to develop the software for the system.
- *Software developer:* Pete, to perform independent system testing.

- *Operations representative:* Sophie, the system operations manager at the manufacturing company, to assist with preparing for operational support of the AIDC system.

In addition to human resources, Debra identified other resources, such as PCs and application development tools, necessary for completing the project.

Developing a Budget

As part of the decision to begin a project, managers might have performed an economic analysis and allocated a specific amount of funding for the project. Therefore, the project team might need only to validate and refine the budget, given the knowledge of the work plan and staff availability. If no previous budgeting has been done, the team will need to start from scratch. For this case, estimate hardware and software costs by performing some requirement assessment and preliminary design. Most system integrator and value added reseller (VAR) companies refer to these as *presale activities*, providing a basis for a preliminary budget.

The WBS, schedule, and resource plan provide the basis for determining the cost of a wireless project. Before estimating the cost, you will need to assign resources to each WBS task. The next step is to calculate labor, material, travel, and shipping costs for each task and phase of the entire project. Again, you might need to perform at least a preliminary requirements assessment and design before you can determine costs associated with the hardware and software of the system being implemented. Be sure to include sufficient travel costs for site surveys, on-site installations, and periodic on-site post installation support.

During the execution of the project, you will need to track whether the project is being completed within budget. To facilitate budget control, assign unique account codes to project phases and subcodes to each WBS task. During the planning stages of the project, the initial budget is likely to be merely an estimate. After completing the requirements and design stages, the team might need to adjust the budget to reflect more precise information. The following are the major items of a project budget:

- Labor costs
- Hardware and software costs

- Travel costs
- Meeting costs

Tip

To minimize budget overruns, ensure that the contract with the customer states a process for handling changes and enhancements the customer voices after the project is underway. As a minimum, the process should include provisions for assessing the impacts on the project resources, schedule, and cost.

Defining Project Operations

The scope, work plan, schedule, resources, and budget of the project are its physical makeup. To ensure that a project runs smoothly, however, you should also define project operations by developing an operations plan. This plan covers the rules and practices people should follow during the project.

What aspects of the project should the operations plan cover? Generally, you should specify procedures for project actions that need to be followed each time the action is required. You should include at least the following items in the operations plan:

- Roles and responsibilities of team members
- Methods for coordinating with other organizations
- Staffing procedures
- Travel policies
- Engineering drawing standards
- Document sign off procedures

To develop a project operations plan, review existing corporate and local policies and regulations, and then define procedures for items that team members must accomplish in a unique manner. Also, be sure to identify any restrictions that corporate policies and other regulations place on the project.

Managing Project Risks

The success of a project is often jeopardized by unforeseen elements that crop up at inopportune times. The nasty truth is that many projects are not completed on time, within schedule, or as expected. A project team might successfully complete the design stage of the project and be ready to purchase the components, for example, when they discover the customer's upper management has lost interest in the project and has withheld further funding. Or, you do a thorough job of defining user needs and then the team is not successful at determining a set of technologies and products that will fulfill the requirements.

To maximize the success of a project, the project team must not only develop a WBS, project schedule, and resource plan, but also continually identify and manage risks. Risk management should begin early in the project, even during the planning stage, and then continue throughout the project. A risk factor usually has more impact if you don't attempt counter measures until later in the project. To avoid negative consequences, the team can manage risks by identifying risk factors and determining methods to reduce them. A risk factor is anything that might have adverse effects on the outcome of the project.

You can control risks by following these steps:

1. Review the project's WBS, schedule, resource plan, and budget, and assess the status of the preceding potential risk factors.

2. Define the potential impact each risk has on the successful completion of the project.

3. Pinpoint the causes of the risks.

4. Refine the work plans to reflect the risk reduction strategy.

5. Periodically reevaluate the potential risk factors, especially those found earlier in the project, and take necessary counteractive measures.

Case Study 7.5:
Identifying Risks for
WarehouseTrack

Before finalizing a project plan, Debra, the project manager for WarehouseTrack, thought that she needed to identify and resolve any risks that might affect the project before finalizing a project plan. She decided to hold a meeting with the entire team and go through a list of potential risks. The following is a list of risks she and the team discussed:

- Project Factors

    - *Clarity of project objectives:* The objectives of the project seem clear enough as stated in the project scope. The requirements analysis would provide much greater detail.

- *Project team size:* The project team size, as indicated in the resource plan, seems adequate based on the size of the project.

- *Team geographical disbursement:* The project team is located within the same city, making the project easy to manage.

- *Project duration:* The duration of the project seems adequate to meet all requirements.

- *Project manager's prior experience:* Debra, the project manager for WarehouseTrack, has experience managing similar projects of this scope. She also has a project management certification from the Project Management Institute.

- Resource Factors

  - *Experience of project team members:* All project team members have adequate experience to fulfill their roles, except possibly the operations representative, Sophie. She was new to the manufacturing company and didn't have a complete understanding of the existing systems; therefore, she may not be able to fully determine the impact of the new AIDC system on the existing corporate information system. As a result, Debra will need to ensure that Sophie utilizes others knowledgeable about the systems within the manufacturing company to consider all operational elements of the new AIDC system.

  - *Working relationships among project team members:* All the team members from the system integration company had worked on projects together before. In fact, they had been through a series of team building exercises in the past. The system integration company, however, had not implemented a system for this manufacturing company before. Therefore, Debra decided to set up a few team-building exercises with the entire team as they began the project.

  - *Use of contractors:* This would be an issue with this project. It will take the system integration company some time to become familiar with this manufacturing

company. The team building and analysis phase of the project, however, will provide time for "ramping up" the project.

  - *Potential loss of team members to other projects:* This may be a problem with this project, especially with the resources supplied by the system integration company. The availability of the software developer, Eric, and the system tester, Pete, is at risk because their active part of the project doesn't occur until later in the schedule, providing time for them to become unavailable due to other projects lasting longer than expected. Debra will have to periodically remind Eric's and Pete's functional manager about their future work on the WarehouseTrack project.

- Organizational Risk Factors

  - *Level of management and customer commitment:* The company president, Bob, is fully backing this project.

  - *Funding constraints:* The funding of $1,200,000 will limit the amount of the system that can be deployed during the first year.

  - *Level of user involvement and support during the project:* The operations manager, Linda, will be available throughout the project, but she has stated that only one warehouse clerk per distribution center will be available to answer questions concerning the project to ensure productivity levels remain high enough to reach

continues

---

continued

operational goals. This will be acceptable assuming Linda chooses clerks that have a good understanding of the operations of their individual warehouses.

- *Firmness of benefits:* The benefits of implementing this AIDC system are unclear, making this a high-risk item.

- *Length of time necessary to receive a return on investment:* The return on investment for implementing this AIDC system is unclear, making this a high-risk item.

- Technical Factors

  - *Range of technologies available to satisfy requirements:* The technologies that provide the basis for implementing an AIDC system within a warehouse are mature.

  - *Availability of crucial hardware and software:* Hardware and software is available.

  - *Complexity of the interfaces to existing systems.* This is unknown at this point in the project; therefore, it is a high-risk item.

Executing the Project

After completing the planning stage of the project, the project manager can begin work activities with a kick-off meeting and guide the project through the activities identified in the WBS. The project team should periodically hold status meetings to assess the progress to date and make changes to the plan if necessary to keep the project on course. These project management actions include the following:

- Kick-off meeting
- Status checks
- Technical interchange meetings
- Progress reporting

The Kick-Off Meeting

The entire project team should have a kick-off meeting to review the project plan and officially start the project. This starts the team off together and avoids having people stray away from the primary objectives. At the kick-off meeting, discuss and agree on the following items:

- Project scope
- Task descriptions
- Schedule
- Staffing
- Budget

- Policies and procedures

- Risks

The key to an effective kick-off meeting (or any meeting for that matter) is to stay focused by keeping discussions within scope of the specific agenda items. Spend a few minutes at the beginning of the meeting to review the agenda, to ensure that everyone agrees that the topics are applicable, and to see whether anything is missing. It is not too late at this time to make alterations to the agenda if necessary.

Note

To keep everyone focused, some organizations institute the three knock rule (TKR)*: If someone starts to stray away from the matter at hand, or the discussion is going nowhere without accomplishing anything, anyone can just rap his knuckles on the table three times as an indication that the meeting is off track. Discussion stops, and the leader refocuses the group.*

Periodic Activities

Periodically, the team should check the status of the project, perform technical interchange meetings, and report progress to upper management. The following list explains each of these activities:

- *Status checks:* For most projects, a weekly or biweekly status check is often enough to review project progress. You can normally accomplish this at a project staff meeting. The project manager should at least review completed tasks and check whether the project is on time and within budget. It is also a good idea to review risk factors and take action to minimize their impact.

- *Technical interchange meetings (TIMs):* TIMs address technical issues needing attention by project team members and customer representatives. A TIM is effective if a single team member cannot adequately provide the solution to a technical requirement or problem. In this case, schedule a TIM and invite the people needed to solve the problem.

- *Progress reports:* Progress reports summarize the technical, schedule, and cost status of the project. The main idea is to show a comparison between planned and actual elements. Project managers should periodically send progress reports to upper management to keep them abreast of the status of the network development.

  It is normally best to alert management of conditions that might affect the project as early as possible. This allows enough time for upper management to assist in countering the problems. Also, be sure to include tasks the project team still needs to complete, especially the ones that are planned to take place up until the next progress report.

  Management reports should focus on current accumulative costs and the schedule status, past and present resource utilization, negative impacts on the project schedule, identification of successful and unsuccessful tasks, as well as major changes made to the project plan. Any major changes should also be thoroughly explained. The progress report also should explain how the project team will counter all deficiencies.

Enhancing Communication

During the execution of the project, take steps to maximize the flow of information among team members when determining requirements, designing the system, and performing installations. The problem with many project organizations is that they operate in a serial communication form, as shown in Figure 7.3. As a result, they depend heavily on documentation to convey requirements, solutions, and ideas. In this case, the customer represents the needs of potential end-users of the system or product under development.

In companies that develop software products, sales and marketing staff typically expresses customer needs in terms of requests and requirements. Otherwise, requirements generally flow directly from the customer. Project managers are often responsible for managing the overall development, installation, and support of the product or system. Typically they produce the first specification the development group uses to design, code, and install the system.

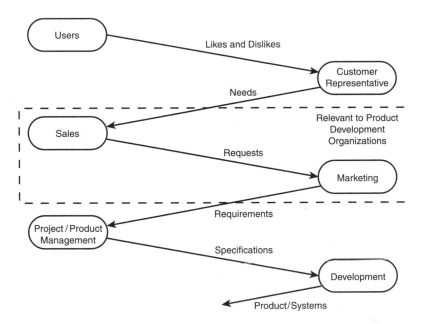

FIGURE 7.3 *Serial communication significantly limits the effective flow of information.*

There are several problems with this process, which lead to systems and products that don't adequately meet the users' needs. The series of hand–offs between the different players in the process, for example, can take a long time, delaying the creation of a prototype for validation purposes. In addition, the process doesn't engage the customer continually throughout the process, forcing developers to guess at missing or incomplete requirements. The process also dilutes the clarity of requirements as they flow via documentation and the spoken word from one element to the next.

The solution to this serial communication problem is to utilize team meetings that incorporate representatives from all organizational groups, especially when defining requirements. Sometimes this is referred to as *joint application design (JAD)*. See the section "Conducting a Joint Application Design Meeting" later in this chapter for a detailed description of this process.

Case Study 7.6:

Developing a Project Plan for WarehouseTrack

At this point in the WarehouseTrack project, Debra, the project manager, assembled a project plan consisting of the following elements:

- *Project scope* (refer to Case Study 7.1)

- *Work breakdown structure* (refer to Case Study 7.2)

- *Schedule (*refer to Case Study 7.3*)*

- *Resource plan* (refer to Case Study 7.4)

- *Preliminary budget:* Provides costs of all elements of the project. At this point, the budget is accurate for the requirements analysis and design phases, but not the development and installation phases. Debra feels comfortable in showing precise labor costs for Brian, the business analyst, Evan, the systems analysis, and Jared, the design engineer, because the amount of time they need to perform the analysis and design is well known (based on other projects of similar size).

The exact amount of time and associated labor costs for Eric, the software developer, will not be known until after the design phase of the project. In addition, the cost of hardware and software will be unclear as well. A rough order of magnitude was given for the development and installation phases so that the decision makers would have some idea of the cost for the entire system.

The cost of the requirements analysis phase is $30,000, and the cost of the design phase is $20,000. A rough order of magnitude for the development and installation, including hardware and software, for all nine distribution centers is $2,500,000. This amount was based on a preliminary design defining the use of handheld scanner/printers, radio LAN access points, database, and application software. The system would also cost approximately $400,000 per year to maintain.

continues

continued

> • *Risk assessment* (refer to Case Study 7.5)
>
> Debra presented the project plan to Linda, the warehouse manager, and Ron, the information systems manager, to obtain their feedback before presenting the plan to Bob, the company president. Bob approved the project plan and provided enough funding to complete the analysis phase of the project.

Defining the Requirements for a Wireless LAN

Incomplete or missing requirements are the major reasons for unsuccessful projects, resulting in 60–80 percent of system defects that eventually surface late in the development phase or after delivery to the users. These system defects are very time-consuming and expensive to correct. Shabby up-front requirements also lead to the continual stream of "new" requirements that fill in for inadequacies throughout the project. New requirements cause a great deal of rework, extending development time and costs.

Requirements that are ambiguous, untestable, and most of all, not able to fully satisfy needs of potential users contribute to high development costs, lagging time-to-market, and unhappy users and customers. Therefore, organizations must emphasize the definition of requirements to keep their heads above water. Figure 7.4 illustrates the concept of requirements for wireless system projects.

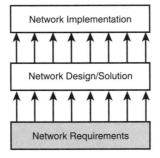

FIGURE 7.4 *Requirements are the foundation of design, implementation, and support of a wireless system project.*

A large part of planning the requirements phase is to calculate how much work it will take to determine what the requirements are. For all projects, thoroughly assess requirements for security and interfacing to existing systems; keep in mind, however, that the amount of time spent analyzing the user's requirements differs depending on whether you are developing software applications or just using off-the-shelf products. You should spend more time defining user functional requirements for an application development than you would for the deployment of just the network infrastructure. The reason for this is that users spend more time interfacing directly with applications rather than the network components.

A project meant to create a specific graphical user interface (GUI) for nurses to access healthcare records from a centralized database, for example, would require a detailed analysis of the business processes the nurses' work involves. A project that creates a wireless network infrastructure for off-the-shelf applications, however, would not need such detail. In that case, you only need to examine high-level business processes and product requirements in order to select the correct wireless components. If you are going to develop an application, be sure to illustrate all functional elements, such as user screens and menus, using diagrams that can aid the programmer.

Although the system analyst is generally responsible for specifying requirements, the rest of the project team should be involved as well. This chapter describes the types of requirements you need to define and discusses the following steps that the project team should take when defining requirements:

- Elicit information
- Define the requirements
- Update the project plan

Types of Requirements

Before eliciting information, you should have an understanding of the type of requirements you are attempting to define to help you focus on gathering the best information related to user needs and system requirements. The following are common requirement types related to wireless system implementations (which are described in the succeeding sections):

- User profile and interface
- Functional
- Application
- Information flow
- Mobility
- Performance
- Security
- System interface
- Environmental

- Departmental support
- Regulations
- Budget
- Schedule

User-Profile and Interface Requirements

The user-profile requirement identifies the attributes of each person who will be utilizing the system, providing human factors that designers can use to better select or develop applications. A person's in-depth experience with Windows-based applications, for example, would prompt the design team to procure or develop standard Windows applications. In addition, the profile assists the installation team when assigning user names.

The user profile should identify the person's name, job title and description, level of networking experience, and knowledge of applications. Users will require some form of interface to the system's databases and other resources. Most interfaces today are graphical client/server-based applications that run on Microsoft Windows. The user interface requirement should indicate screen layouts and leveling of menus.

Functional Requirements

Functional requirements describe what the users and the organization expect the system to do. Therefore, functional requirements run parallel to the tasks and actions users perform. The need to enter packing slip information from all received shipments into a database is a functional requirement, for example. In most cases, application software implements functional requirements.

Application Requirements

Application requirements specify that the system can utilize specific applications. An organization that uses Microsoft Office for word processing and spreadsheets should indicate that standard as an application requirement, for example. An organization moving from paper-based inventory control to a centralized computer system, however, would probably delay the selection of the actual application until the beginning of the design phase (after all other requirements are known).

Information Flow Requirements

Business processes within companies depend heavily on communication. To complete their tasks, people need to communicate with other people and systems. Because the network's primary role is the support of communication, it is imperative that you fully define information flow requirements. For this requirement, specify the information path flow between people and systems, types and formats of information sent, frequency of information transmission, and maximum allowable error rates. These requirements will provide a basis for the selection of network components, such as the network interface card and medium.

Mobility Requirements

Mobility requirements describe the movement of the users when performing their tasks, distinguishing whether the degree of movement is continuous or periodic.

When the user or network component must have the capability to utilize network resources while physically moving, they are said to be in *continuous movement*. Examples of users requiring access to network resources while continuously moving include emergency vehicles, military personnel on a battleground, delivery services, and healthcare professionals.

Periodic mobility—often referred to as *portability*—implies the utilization of network resources from temporary locations, but not necessarily while the user is in transit between locations. Portability implies a temporary connection to the network from a stationary point, but the interface associated with a portable connection should be easy to move, set up, and dismantle. Examples of users requiring portable interfaces include cashiers, conference organizers, and employees working from a temporary office facility. When specifying mobility requirements, be sure to identify the users needing mobility and the range of movement each user or component needs.

Performance Requirements

Performance indicates how well a network provides applications and services. You never hear people complain that performance is too high. Low performance, however, creates disgruntlement because users cannot do their work as quickly as they want or are accustomed to. For performance requirements, identify expected values for reliability, availability, and delay, as follows:

- *Reliability:* The length of time a system or component will operate without disruption. Most product vendors refer to this as *mean time before failure (MTBF)*.

- *Availability:* The length of time the system must be operational. As an example, the availability could indicate that a network should be operational 12 hours a day from 6:00 a.m. until 6:00 p.m.

- *Delay:* The length of time users or systems can wait for the delivery of a particular service.

Security Requirements

Security requirements identify the information and systems that require protection from particular threats. The degree of security depends on the severity of the consequences the organization would face if the system were damaged or if data were lost. Of course, military and law-enforcement agencies require high-level security.

Security requirements should address the sensitivity of information processed on the network, the organization's security regulations, and probability of disasters such as equipment failure, power failure, viruses, and fire.

System Interface Requirements

Most likely, the system being developed will have to interface and interoperate with existing systems such as networks, applications, and databases. Therefore, the system interface requirements describe the architectures of these systems and the hardware, software, and protocols necessary for proper interfacing. If the interfacing method is not known, you will need to determine a solution during the design phase.

Environmental Requirements

Environmental requirements state conditions such as weather, pollution, presence and intensity of electromagnetic waves, building construction, and floor space that could affect the operation of the system.

Operational Support Requirements

Operational support requirements define the elements needed to integrate the system into the existing operational support infrastructure. You should require the inclusion of Simple Network Management Protocol (SNMP), for example, if current network monitoring stations require SNMP.

Regulation Requirements

Some organizations might have to conform to certain local, state, or federal regulations; therefore, be certain to specify these conditions as requirements. Regulations imposing safety and environmental procedures place definite requirements on network implementations. The operation of a wireless radio wave adapter, for example, must conform to Federal Communication Commission regulations.

Another example is the use of radio-based wireless products on military installations within the United States. The military's use of these devices is regulated by a special frequency management organization, not the FCC. Therefore, radio-based implementations on military bases must conform to the military's frequency management policies. In addition, the company itself might have policies and procedures, such as strategic plans and cabling standards, that the implementation should follow.

Budget Requirements

An organization might have a certain amount of money to spend on the system implementation. Budget constraints can affect the choice of solution because some technologies cost more than others to implement. The budget requirements should consider the funding plan for the installation project—that is, the availability of funds at specific times. The reason for this is for planning the procurement of components and scheduling of resources.

Schedule Requirements

Schedule requirements should include any definite schedule demands that will affect the project. By their nature, organizations impose scheduling conditions on projects, such as availability of project funds, urgency to begin a return on investment, availability of project team members, and interdependency between this project and other projects. Define schedule requirements so that the team knows the timeframes it can work within. The design team might have a choice of using a current wireless adapter, for example, or waiting eight months for the next, faster release. If the organization must have the system operational within three months, the team would have to choose the existing product.

Eliciting Information

The objective of eliciting information is to gather as many facts as you can relating to each of the requirements types. This information will enable you to define each of the requirements during a later step. The following is a checklist of items you should consider performing when eliciting requirements:

- Review user needs
- Review existing systems
- Review the environment

The following sections explain each of these steps.

Reviewing User Needs

It's imperative that you determine users' needs before deploying a system. These needs will lead you to the definition of these types of requirements: user profile and interface, applications, information flow, mobility, performance, security, regulations, budget, and schedule.

The most effective method in reviewing needs of potential users is to interview them. It is generally not practical to interview every user—just a cross section will do. Talk with managers to obtain a high-level overview of what the people do and how they interact with other organizations. During the interview, ask questions that enable you to define specific requirements. The following sections give samples of good questions and describe the requirements that you need to define.

Note

In some cases, reviewing needs of users will identify weaknesses in the current business processes, motivating business process reengineering, which is a realignment of the way a company operates. In fact, the introduction of wireless networking makes it possible to redesign the current paper-intensive methods to a more mobile and electronic form.

Interviewing Techniques

The interviews should determine the organization's structure, departmental missions, work flow, user profiles, and existing system attributes. Before conducting an interview with a particular set of users, be sure to get permission from their manager. Having the bosses "buy in" to the project can result in a better response from the interviewees.

Ask managers the questions relating to the mission and major functions of their staffs. Questions you ask the staff should be more specific, relating mainly to the individual. Be certain, however, that you interview a truly representative group of users and don't miss any unique needs.

A day or two before the interview, draft a set of questions and distribute them to allow the users to prepare answers. The following is a sample set of questions for managers:

- What are the functions and major activities of your staff?
- How does your organization interface with other organizations within your company?
- What is your current staffing level? What is the projected level?
- Is your staff's work environment under constant construction?
- Does your organization rearrange desks frequently?
- What are your staff's needs for a new system (applications and network)?
- What security policies does your organization follow?
- What funds are available for this implementation?
- What schedule constraints exist for this project?
- What local, state, and federal regulations exist that might influence the project?
- What types of applications can benefit from a wireless network?
- What types of handheld appliances do you plan to use?

Also, ask potential end-users of the system the following questions:

- What tasks do you perform? How do you accomplish these tasks? How do your tasks interface with tasks that other people perform?
- What mobility and portability do you require when performing your day-to-day activities?
- What types of handheld appliances do you use?
- Do you travel? If yes, how often do you travel and where do you travel?

- What internal and external systems to your organization do you need to access?

- With which internal and external people do you need to communicate?

- Which types (data, voice, imagery, video), formats (DOC, PIF, GIF, JPEG), and methods (FTP, email, postal mail) do you use to exchange information?

- What type of computer do you use? Desktop or portable? CPU type, amount of RAM, size of hard drive?

- What applications are you currently utilizing? Where do these applications reside (desktop, server, mainframe)?

- What is your experience using client/server applications?

- What systems (hardware and software) are currently supporting the applications you utilize?

- What system availability do you require to perform your tasks?

- What are your needs for information security?

- What are your needs for a new system (applications or network)?

- What schedule constraints exist for this project?

You will certainly need to tailor these lists of questions to the type of system you are deploying.

Tip

If possible, have two interviewers during the interview: one to ask questions and the other to take notes. This ensures the capturing of all comments. A recording device, such as an audio tape recorder, can prove beneficial; however, it can intimidate some interviewees.

Written Surveys

A written survey is another method for gathering user needs: Write a series of questions that probe the potential user for information that will enable you to assess specific needs, distribute the survey via mail, and insist that people complete and return the survey. Unfortunately, this process often doesn't work as expected. It is extremely difficult and time-consuming to write questions that elicit usable responses. Also, many people will not complete the survey; the typical return rate on written surveys is 10–15 percent. As a result, you should stick with personal interviews, especially for projects where you have access to the eventual users of the system.

Defining the Business Processes

After you gather information from the managers and users, you should define and document the business processes:

- The function of each organization

- The tasks each user or group of users perform

- The types of information people and groups exchange

This assists you when defining the information-flow requirements. The level of detail of gathering information depends on whether the project is developing an application or using strictly off-the-shelf products.

Reviewing Existing Systems

User needs are only part of the requirements—existing systems also portray important requirements. Reviewing existing systems helps you to define the system interface and operational support. To review existing systems, begin by interviewing the Information System (IS) managers and review system documentation, as discussed in the following sections.

Interviewing Information Systems Managers

Information Systems managers, including people in charge of applications development, system implementation, and the mainframe data center, are the best sources of information about the existing systems. Again, interviewing is the best method to use. You should follow the same recommendations described for interviewing users, but your questions should focus more on the technical information.

Following are sample questions for interviewing IS managers:

- Which networks and systems (hardware and software) does IS currently support?

- What is the current telecommunications/WAN topology? (That is, where are the facility locations and are they interconnected via telecommunications or WAN services?)

- What are the internal and external communication links of the corporation?

- Which documents describe your existing networks and systems?

- What networks and system links are planned for the future?

- Which tools are currently used for systems and network management?

- What are the company's requirements for information security?

- What functionality do you envision the company's information system providing in the future? How does this differ from the vision of users and executive management?

- What are the company's business plans that might affect the network architecture? (That is, future staffing, geographical coverage, and so forth.)

- What is the company's budget to deploy this system?

- Are any documents that describe user and organization requirements for information systems available for review?

- What policies does IS have for deploying networks and systems?

Also, if the manager will be a user of the system, be sure to ask the questions for users in the earlier section "Interviewing Techniques."

Reviewing System Documentation

When determining requirements, the project team should review current documentation that provides an accurate description of existing systems. Review the concept of operations, for example, to examine system-level functionality, operational environment, and implementation priorities for an organization's information system.

Also, review the strategic information system plan, which provides a long-term vision and the general procedures necessary to manage the efficient evolution of the corporate information system. This provides policies and standards the design team might need to follow. In addition, the organization may have other plans, such as business and employee projections, that the team can consider. Business plans describe the future markets and strategies the company wishes to pursue, which is useful in determining the types of applications and services the users might require.

To determine environmental requirements, look at the conditions in which the network will operate. Gather information by interviewing the company's facility manager and visually inspecting the area.

Here are questions you will need to answer for wireless network implementations:

- What is the physical building made of?

- What devices in the area might cause interference?

- Are there any trees that might block the transmission of line-of-sight radio waves?

- Does the area occasionally experience severe snow, rain, fog, or smog?

- Where is it possible to install access points within the building?

- Where is it possible to install directional antennas on top the building?

The obvious unseen hindrance to a radio-based wireless network is interference. Therefore, in addition to talking with the facility manager or frequency manager about potential interference, consider using a radio-based site survey tool to evaluate the radio wave activity within the part of the radio spectrum your components will operate. Most wireless LAN vendors include these site survey tools with their products. You can use a spectrum analyzer to measure the amplitude of signals at various frequencies.

If your wireless system project includes wired network components (for example, ethernet) for backbone cabling, perform the following activities to determine environmental requirements:

- *Investigate the capability to run cables throughout the facility.* Be sure to check above the ceilings to determine whether there is enough room to run the cabling, as well as locate and assess all vertical cabling conduits.

- *Evaluate the electrical system.* An electrical evaluation provides information on whether the building's electrical system will support the network components. Check to see whether there is adequate building power for the new components and whether the building has experienced power outages. If there are problems with the electrical system, recommend appropriate corrective action.

- *Investigate server and communication room locations.* If applicable, determine locations for the system servers and network hubs. Be certain the rooms have adequate power, air conditioning, and space for future expansion.

Defining Requirements

After gathering information, you are ready to define the requirements that will provide the basis for the design. To define the requirements, perform these steps:

1. Determine potential requirements.

2. Validate and verify the requirements.

3. Baseline the requirements.

Determining Potential Requirements

The first step in defining requirements is to identify potential requirements by specifying each requirement using the information gathered during interviews, review of documents, and inspections. You can accomplish this by doing the following:

- Conducting a joint application design meeting

- Assessing constraints

- Documenting requirements

Conducting a Joint Application Design Meeting

An effective method for drafting requirements is to conduct a series of team meetings using *joint application design (JAD)* techniques. With JAD, all the active participants work together in the creation of requirements. Figure 7.5 illustrates the concept of JAD that utilizes a team approach for defining requirements.

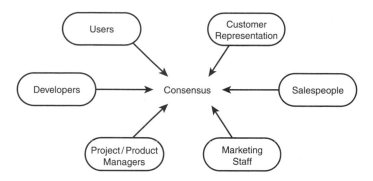

FIGURE 7.5 *JAD is a parallel process, simultaneously defining requirements in the eyes of the customer, users, sales, marketing, project managers, analysts, and engineers.*

The goal of JAD is to reach consensus on requirements among all team members, especially the customer and developers. JAD ensures the early definition of accurate requirements, minimizing later rework.

JAD is extremely effective for defining requirements because the customer and users become partners in the development project, allowing an effective customer–developer team, which breaks down communication barriers and increases levels of trust and confidence. Because JAD helps you to determine requirements quickly, developers can start prototyping earlier. This is important because it provides a vision of the system for the users, fueling the refinement of requirements. JAD also keeps the customer accurately informed on what can and can't be done because engineers can validate the requirements as the customer states them.

In addition to the active participants, JAD consists of a facilitator, scribe, and optional observers, as follows:

- *Facilitator:* The facilitator manages the overall meeting, acting as a mediator and guide to guarantee the group stays focused on objectives and follows all JAD meeting rules. The facilitator should have good communication skills, be impartial to the project, have team-building experience and leadership skills, be flexible, and be an active listener.

- *Scribe:* The scribe records the proceedings of the JAD and should have good recording skills and some knowledge of the subject matter.

- *Observers:* It might be beneficial to have impartial observers monitor the JAD sessions and provide feedback to the facilitator and project manager. In addition, managers as observers can spot and take action on problems that go beyond the scope of the facilitator's and project manager's domain. However, to ensure appropriate interaction among the customer and developers, observers must not actively participate during the JAD meeting.

The following are some tips in preparing for a JAD:

- *Obtain the appropriate level of coordination and commitment to using JAD.* In many cases, participation in a JAD will stretch across organizational boundaries. Engineers are often from the Information Systems (IS) group, and the customer might represent users spanning several functional groups. Without concurrence of all group managers, the JAD meetings will appear biased to those not buying into the idea, causing some people to not participate or accept the outcomes. Therefore, to receive commitment to the method, the initiators of the JAD should discuss the benefits and purpose of the JAD with applicable managers of each group.

- *Ensure that there are clear objectives for the JAD meeting.* If not, the JAD proceedings will flounder and lead to unnecessary outcomes.

- *Consider using an independent consultant as a facilitator.* This ensures neutrality and avoids siding with one particular group. Be certain, however, to avert the selection of a consultant closely allied with the department responsible for development. A close alliance here could tempt the facilitator to favor the engineers, letting them dominate the meeting and hamper ideas from the customer. It doesn't hurt to have internal people in mind to groom as facilitators; however, be sure they have proper training and are not connected to the project they're facilitating.

- *Talk to all participants before the JAD.* Discuss the issues involved with the particular project, such as potential conflicts. Give all new participants an orientation to JAD if it is their first time attending one. In some cases, it might be the first time business people and engineers work together. Therefore, minimize communication problems by preparing participants to speak the same language. Avoid using computer jargon. Otherwise, communication could be difficult and the customer participation will decline.

- *Establish rules.* This is absolutely necessary because the different agendas of the customer, users, and developers can often derail the JAD and raise conflicts. Rules should state that all members will conform to an agenda, all participants are equal, observers will remain silent, and the bottom line is to reach consensus on requirements. Be sure to have the participants contribute to the formation of rules.

- *Don't let developers dominate the meeting.* Many JADs tend to have too many developers and not enough representation of the potential end-users. This usually blocks users from expressing their ideas. In addition, there is a tendency of IS departments using JAD to "rubber stamp" the requirements—that is, to have the customer merely review and approve them. You should limit the developers to architects and engineers because programmers might push the team toward a design too soon. The facilitator must ensure that everyone has fair time to voice his or her ideas.

Assessing Constraints

As part of the requirements definition, you should identify which of the requirements are constraints: the firm requirements that limit the choice of solution alternatives. *Constraints* usually deal with money, regulations, environment, existing systems, and culture. Any requirement could be a constraint, however, if that requirement is absolutely necessary and not subject to change.

Regulations are constraints because they often carry a mandate directing a particular form of conformance. The environment, such as building size and construction, establishes constraints because the facility might be too expensive to change to accommodate certain solutions. Existing systems are not always easy to change; therefore, solutions will have to conform to particular platform constraints, memory, and so on.

Documenting Requirements

To adequately support the remaining phases of the project, be sure to clearly document the requirements. Without good documentation, requirements can become unclear as time passes and memories lapse. Good documentation is necessary also because the handover of project information from person to person can dilute original intentions. To make matters worse, the analysts responsible for defining the requirements could leave and not be available during the design phase. Undocumented requirements also make it too easy for changes to occur in an uncoordinated fashion during later stages of the project, making it difficult to find the correct solution.

Therefore, the team should develop a requirements document containing, as a minimum, an illustration of the organization's high-level business processes (that is, how the company or applicable organizations operate) and a definition of each requirement type. The following are the major elements of a requirements document:

- Requirement overview
- Specific requirements
- Constraints
- Assumptions
- Information elicitation methods
- Issues

Case Study 7.7:
Performing a Requirements
Analysis for WarehouseTrack

At this point in the WarehouseTrack project, Debra, the project manager, held a kick-off meeting for the project and directed Brian, the business analyst, and Evan, the system analyst, to begin the requirements phase of the project.

Brian scheduled interviews with Linda, the warehouse manager, and a clerk within each of the nine warehouses. The main goal of these interviews was to gain a good understanding of each of the functions within the warehouse worked.

Brian found that the operations within the warehouses were very similar. The staff performed receiving, put-away, picking, inventory, and shipping functions manually (using pencil and paper), and then entered the applicable data into the corporate information system via terminals located at certain points within the warehouse. A clerk at the unloading dock performs the following steps, for example:

1. Writes down a tracking number from a box

2. Goes to a terminal located near the dock, types the number into the system

3. Retrieves a printed label from a nearby printer

4. Walks back to the box and affixes the label to it

At one of the warehouses, Brian performed time studies to determine the length of time the staff took to perform various functions, such as receiving items from the shipping dock and picking items from the warehouse. This will provide a basis for determining benefits when developing the feasibility study.

Evan set up an interview with Ron, the Information Systems manager, to better understand the existing system. Evan found that the manufacturing company had a mainframe located at the headquarters facility in Atlanta. This mainframe hosted accounting software for managing the company. Each of the nine warehouses had 10 desktop terminals that clerks used to enter information applicable to each warehouse function. 56 Kbps telecommunications lines connected each of the terminals to the mainframe system at headquarters. Evan discovered that the company was planning a migration to a client/server-based system over the next two years.

After eliciting the information, Debra, Brian, and Evan wrote a requirements document having the following elements:

• *User profile:* Each of the users is warehouse staff having no experience using data collection equipment, such as handheld scanners and printers.

• *Functional:* Warehouse clerks need automated methods for performing receiving, put-away, picking, inventory, and shipping functions within a warehouse.

• *Application:* The project will need to develop application software that interfaces with the existing corporate information system.

• *Information flow:* Each warehouse will have a database for handling information dealing with the AIDC system. Information flow will take place between these databases and the corporate information system at midnight each day. Information flow will also take place between the handheld appliances and databases over a radio network located in each warehouse.

- *Mobility:* The system will need to provide mobility for warehouse clerk to perform functions while carrying handheld appliances.

- *Performance:* The system must be able to provide end-user transactions in less than three seconds.

- *Security:* The information that flows through the system must not be available to unauthorized people. All systems and information must be accessible only by user ID and password.

- *System interface:* The AIDC system must interface with the existing mainframe-based information system.

- *Environmental:* All hardware must be cable of operating in temperatures between 40–110 degrees Fahrenheit.

- *Budget:* A $1,200,000 budget is available during the first year.

- *Schedule:* The system must be implemented within the next year.

The completion of the requirements phase of the project didn't require any changes to the project plan.

Substantiating Requirements

The importance of requirements can't be overstated: Inaccurate requirements lead to solutions that don't adequately support the needs of the users. Therefore, the project team should *verify* and *validate* the requirements:

- *Validation* determines whether the requirements fully represent the needs of the users and conform to the company's business processes. It asks the question, Are we building the right product?

- *Verification* checks whether the requirements are accurate based on the needs. It asks the question, Are we building the product right?

Validating Requirements

The best method to validate requirements is to build a prototype as a model that represents the requirements. This approach will provide effective feedback from potential users by eliciting missed functions and features. For application development, you can build a software prototype using a fourth-generation language—such as Powersoft's Powerbuilder or Microsoft's Visual Basic—that contains the screens and some functionality that implement the requirements.

For off-the-shelf applications and hardware, of course, vendors will normally allow enough evaluation time, such as one or two months, to test the application. For either case, you can have the users exercise the prototype and observe whether their needs will be met.

Verifying Requirements

The most important verification point is to be sure that the requirements are complete and unambiguous. Complete requirements describe all aspects of the needs of the users and organization. For example, incomplete requirements might state needs for users and existing systems, for example, but not identify anything about the environment, such as the presence of potential electromagnetic interference. For wireline systems, this might not be critical, but it could have serious impact on the operation of radio-based products.

Requirements should be unambiguous to avoid needing clarification later. Ambiguous requirements force the designer to seek the finer details. To save time, most designers will guess the values of the remaining details, causing the designer to choose inappropriate characteristics.

For most projects, you can verify the requirements by referring to the requirements document and answering the following questions:

- Do the requirements address all user and organizational needs?

- Do the requirements clearly state the needs?

- Do the requirements avoid describing solutions to the requirements?

Baselining Requirements

The *baselining* (or in other words, *standardizing*) of requirements involves final documenting and approval of the requirements. This process makes the requirements *official*, and you should only change them by following an agreed-upon process.

Who approves the requirements? Ultimately, the customer representative should give the final sign-off; however, an analyst should endorse the requirements in terms of their accuracy and efficacy. If you are deploying the system under a contract, other people such as the project manager and contract official might also need to offer approvals. Be certain to indicate that both the organization and modification teams will consider the set of requirements as a firm baseline from which to design the network.

Updating the Project Plan

After defining the requirements, it is time to revisit the planning elements you prepared earlier in the project. At first, you probably based the project WBS, schedule, and budget on incomplete and assumed requirements. The actual requirements, however, might cast the project in a different light. Maybe you found during the user interviews that information security was more important than you had expected, for example. This might create a need to modify the WBS—and possibly the schedule and budget—to research security technologies and products. Or, you might have planned to spend three weeks during installation setting up 150 computers, but during the interviews, you found there will only be 75. This could enable you to cut back the schedule, or reallocate the time to a task that might take longer than expected.

With an updated project plan and final requirements, the project team is ready to move into analyzing the feasibility of the wireless system.

Case Study 7.8:
Conducting a Joint Application Design Meeting for WarehouseTrack

Before finalizing the requirements, Brian and Evan both agreed to conduct JAD sessions to ensure consensus. For the JAD meeting, they contracted an independent JAD facilitator to manage the overall meeting and act as a mediator and guide to guarantee the group stays focused on objectives. The active participants of the JAD session included the following:

Debra, project manager

Brian, business analyst

Evan, system analyst

Ron, Information Systems manager

Linda, warehouse manager and customer representative

Sophie, operations representative

A warehouse clerk from three of the nine warehouses

In addition to the active participants, the JAD meeting included a scribe and some observers. Jared the design engineer and Eric the software developer were invited to the meeting as observers. They were not required to attend because Evan could handle any technical issues that might arise. Three days prior to the JAD meeting, Debra sent each of the participants a copy of the requirements document.

At the meeting, Debra went through each requirement, allowing time for questions and discussions. There was some disagreement among the group over the performance requirement "to provide end-user transactions in less than three seconds." All three of the warehouse clerks thought that was too long to wait for a transaction to occur. They thought most end-users would think there was something wrong with the device if nothing happened for that long. After some debate, the team decided to lower the maximum transaction time to less than two seconds.

Sophie indicated that the requirements needed to specify general operational support elements such as system administration and maintenance. The team had included these elements in the budget; however, they hadn't specified them in the requirements document. The group decided to mention the need for system administration and maintenance in the requirements document, and then provide more details after designing the system.

At times, the meeting got out of control, but the facilitator was able to bring everyone back in line. The completion of the requirements phase of the project didn't require any changes to the project plan. (Refer to the section "Conducting a Joint Application Design Meeting" earlier in this chapter to learn how to facilitate a JAD session.)

Analyzing the Feasibility of a Wireless LAN

Implementing a wireless system is generally a costly event. You need to perform a thorough site survey, purchase and install wireless adapters and access points, and possibly procure and install other elements such as portable computers, handheld terminals, cabling, and servers.

A feasibility study helps organizations decide whether to proceed with the project based on the costs associated with these components and the expected benefits of deploying the system. Before an organization will allocate funding for a project, the executives will want to know what return on investment (ROI) to expect within a particular amount of time. Most companies will not invest a large amount of money, such as $50,000 or more, to deploy a wireless system without the assurance that gains in productivity will pay for the system. Executives should consider the following key factors when making this decision:

- Costs

- Savings

- Impacts on users (for example, training, lower initial productivity)

- Effects on existing systems

Humans are notorious for adapting to change very slowly—or not at all. For instance, there are many benefits in replacing paper-based record systems such as those used in hospitals and warehouses with handheld wireless devices that provide an electronic means (via bar codes) of storing and retrieving information from a centralized database. Most people can't make this type of change very quickly. Therefore, executives will need to understand how much time and training the current staff might need before realizing the benefits of the wireless system.

Furthermore, some people also resist change when the key concepts of the solution are not their own or it conflicts with another solution they had in mind. If these people have an impact on the success of the project, be sure to get their buy-in as early as possible.

Systems managers should be concerned with how the new system will affect the operations and cost of the existing systems. They will ask questions such as: Will there need to be additional system administrators? Will there be any additional hardware or software maintenance costs? Will we need to interact with new vendors?

This section addresses the following steps necessary to analyze the feasibility of a wireless network:

- Performing a preliminary design

- Developing a business case
- Deciding whether to implement

Performing a Preliminary Design

To figure costs for a project, you need to perform a preliminary design to identify the major system components. The preliminary design provides a high-level description of the network, at least enough detail to approximate the cost of implementing and supporting the system.

For radio LANs, it is very important to perform a site survey to determine the effects of the facility on the propagation of radio waves. This will help you calculate the number of access points if multiple cells are necessary. The preliminary design should indicate enough of the solution as a basis for a cost estimate. Later stages of the design phase will further define the components and configurations necessary to implement the system.

In some cases, the customer may not want to pay for a site survey because he doesn't want to fund the project until he knows all project costs. As a result, it is important to clearly state the benefits of a site survey to the customer. Without the site survey, there's a risk that the number of access points quoted in the preliminary design may be inaccurate, and interference may be present at some locations that may make the wireless network inoperable.

If the customer still demands a total system proposal without paying for a site survey, you can estimate the number of access points. Be certain, however, to clearly state in the contract with the customer that the costs associated with the wireless network may escalate, and unforeseen interference may cause network performance problems.

Developing a Business Case

A business case involves conducting a feasibility study to document the costs and savings of implementing a particular system, as well as offer a recommendation on which direction to proceed. To define costs and savings, you will have to create a boundary for the business case—that is, base it on a specific operating time period. Generally, this operating period is the life expectancy of the system. Most organizations are satisfied with a two-to-three–year recovery of benefits on network purchases. Predicting costs and benefits beyond three years can lead to significant margins of error because technologies rapidly change, and most business plans are fairly unstable beyond two years.

The business case contains the following elements:

- *Executive overview:* Provides a concise overview of the business case.

- *Project scope:* Defines the resulting wireless system, assumptions, and constraints.

- *Costs:* Details all costs necessary to implement and support the new system.

- *Savings:* Identifies the savings resulting from the deployment and operation of the new system.

- *Return on investment (ROI):* Describes the difference between the costs and savings of deploying the new system. The ROI is the main factor for basing the decision to proceed with the project.

- *Risks:* Identifies the issues that may cause the project to be unsuccessful.

In summary, when developing a business case, you should perform the following activities:

- Recognize applicable feasibility elements

- Identify costs

- Identify savings

- Decide whether to proceed with the project

Recognizing Applicable Feasibility Elements

The goal of developing a business case is to decide which elements apply to the implementation you are undergoing and then to assign costs and savings for each element. Some elements are tangible and some are not. Modification costs, such as the purchase of hardware and software, result in real dollars spent. In addition, increases in productivity result in labor savings or increases in revenue.

The computerized image a wireless system brings to a company, however, offers intangible benefits. In the eyes of the customers, for example, a company having a state-of-the-art wireless order-entry system might appear to be superior over other companies with older systems. This does not relate to tangible savings; however, in addition to other factors, it might increase the company's level of business.

Identifying Costs

When identifying costs, be sure to include everything that the project will require for the implementation and operational support of the system. Do not forget that sustaining the system after it becomes operational will require continual funding. Organizations commonly do not include all costs for operational support, such as training and periodic maintenance.

The best format for identifying costs is to utilize a spreadsheet and layout of all cost categories and the prices of each. For the cost elements that apply to your project, determine their associated costs, as shown in the following sections.

Hardware and Software Costs

The cost of hardware and software components is one of the highest expenses when implementing a system. These costs include wireless adapters, access points, ethernet boards, network operating systems, application software, cabling, and other components. Other costs associated with hardware and software costs include maintenance plans and warranties.

Project Costs

Project costs constitute another large percentage of total expenses. Project costs include the labor and materials necessary to complete each phase of the project. These expenses fall into the following categories:

- *Planning:* Costs for scheduling the modification, establishing an implementation team, and periodically revising plans.

- *Requirements analysis:* Labor costs for the analysts and travel to the customer site.

- *Network design:* Labor costs of the engineers and the purchase of any design tools, such as network simulators.

- *Software development:* The cost of programmers and possibly the purchase of compilers or software development kits.

- *Operational support preparations:* Labor of the engineers and operational support staff necessary to analyze support requirements and write a support plan.

- *Installation and testing:* Primarily the cost of technicians and testers, but the team might also need to purchase special tools such as spectrum analyzers and cable testers to complete their jobs.

- *Documentation:* Documentation is part of every stage of the modification process; therefore, include the price of creating requirement documents, design specifications, schematics, user manuals, and so on.

- *Training:* Includes the labor costs associated with developing the training materials and teaching the courses.

- *User inactivity:* Costs applying the decrease in efficiency while the users learn how to use the system effectively. If users are disrupted during the installation of the system, be sure to factor in the cost of their inactivity.

Operational Costs

After the system is operational, it will cost money to keep it running properly; therefore, include operational expenses over the time period you are basing the business case on. The following describes the costs associated with operating the system:

- *Electricity costs:* The electronic devices within the system—such as computers, access points, network interface cards, servers, and specialized cooling equipment—of course all require electricity; therefore, include a projected cost for the electricity over the applicable time period.

- *System administration costs:* The operational support of the system might require one or more system administrators. These people are needed to maintain usernames and passwords, as well as configure printers and back up the files on the server.

- *Maintenance costs:* An effective system maintenance organization consists of an adequate set of spare components, documentation, employees, and a facility for the maintenance staff.

- *Training costs:* The system might require both initial and recurring training for users and support staff. This results in tuition and (possibly) travel expenses.

- *Ramp-up costs:* In addition to direct training costs, include other costs associated with migrating to the new system. Initially, user productivity might be low because users normally experience a learning curve when first using the new system.

A staff of accountants, for example, might be accustomed to keeping figures on paper and in spreadsheets. A wireless system may utilize a centralized database, allowing the accountants to input and output data directly from a PC. This changes the way that they manage their information, causing a loss in productivity as they get used to the new system.

Over time, employees will become more productive using the database than they were with pencil and paper, but be sure to include the time lost as a cost.

Identifying System Benefits (Savings)

The objective of identifying system benefits is to show how the new system will reduce or avoid costs and increase revenue. Base the benefits of the system on the following factors:

- Increases in productivity

- Faster service

- Accuracy

- Lower maintenance costs

- Improved corporate image

- Employee job satisfaction

Some of these benefits result from lower costs in operating the system, an increase in productivity, faster service, lower maintenance costs, fewer changes to network cabling, improved corporate image, and employee morale. Other elements deal with the implementation itself, such as less-expensive installation in areas that are difficult to wire and reduced installation time.

Chapter 1, "Introduction to Wireless Networks," describes several benefits of wireless networks, such as mobility, the ability to install in difficult-to-wire areas, reduced installation times, and fewer changes to network cabling. These benefits convert to cost savings when comparing wireless solutions with ethernet or other wireline approaches. Review these benefits in Chapter 1, and use them as a basis for comparison.

The following list further describes general networking benefits and associated cost savings that you can also use in justifying a wireless system:

- *Increased productivity:* Applications such as file transfer, email, printer sharing, electronic calendaring, networked fax machines, and mobile access to centralized databases and network services enable users to get their tasks done faster, resulting in lower labor costs and higher profits. Increases in productivity equate to lower task-completion times, resulting in cost savings based on lower labor hours needed to complete the tasks.

  You can easily calculate the cost savings based on an increase in user productivity. Start by determining the amount of time an individual can save by using the new system and multiply this time by the person's pay rate. This equals the cost savings for that individual. An aggregate cost savings can be calculated by adding the savings from all users.

- *Lower software upgrade costs:* With a network, software upgrades become much faster and less expensive because of the centralized storage of applications. Imagine having 300 standalone PCs, for example. Now assume someone decides to upgrade an application from one version to another. You could have the users install their own software. Some would not waste their time, others would perform the installation and have trouble, and a few would perform the installation flawlessly.

  In this case, the best method would be for the system administrator to install the new version of software on all 300 PCs. Assuming an average time of 15 minutes to install the software on each computer, it would probably take this person a couple of weeks to install the upgrade.

  Upgrading software via networked computers is less expensive and less time consuming. In a network, the installer just installs the new version of software on the server, giving everyone immediate access to the new upgrade. This takes only 15 minutes (enabling the installer to spend his time working on "more important" items).

  To calculate this type of savings, estimate the number of software upgrades that might occur over the applicable period of time and figure the amount of time and dollar savings based on the rate you pay people to install software.

- *Qualitative benefits:* Qualitative benefits are based on elements that cannot be assigned specific dollar values. These types of benefits are very important— they often provide an extra incentive to implement a system. A company that develops software, for example, would want to maintain a good corporate image and retain employees by implementing a state-of-the-art network. Otherwise, clients might not consider the company to be a credible software developer. Also, customers of a retail store seeing store staff use wireless terminals to update prices leaves the customer with a good impression of accuracy.

Note

Be sure to run a time study before finalizing the feasibility study. Time actual users performing existing manual functions that the wireless system will affect. Also time them using a prototype of the wireless system. This will indicate the savings in terms of efficiency gain you should expect to receive. In addition, you can use the results to verify and validate the wireless system after completing the project.

Documenting the Business Case

Be sure to document all elements of the business case in a form that makes the ROI readily apparent. Before submitting the business case to the executives for review, assess it according to the following criteria:

- Describes realistic and achievable savings

- Describes complete and accurate costs

- Compares costs and savings

- Clearly explains return on investment

- Describes issues and risks associated with realizing benefits

- Is based on a plausible time frame

- Provides a recommendation on whether to implement the system

Making the Decision to Proceed

The final step is to decide whether to proceed with the implementation. Distribute the feasibility study to the appropriate managers, and schedule a meeting to discuss the project. Assuming the study convinces management that a strong ROI exists, the decision on how to proceed will be based on the availability of money to fund the project and the presence of implementation issues. Funding constraints and implementation issues, such as weak requirements and solutions, can affect the project schedule.

In some cases, managers might want to divide the project into phases and stagger the implementation over a longer period of time to accommodate the following scenarios:

- *Limited funding and no implementation issues:* If there are no implementation issues and complete funding is not possible, the company could agree to the entire project and spread the deployment out over a time period that accommodates the future availability of money.

A company may have 100 sales people located throughout the United States needing mobile access to the company's proposal and contract databases located at the company's headquarters, for example. The proposed wireless system may consist of 100 mobile portable computers, linked to the headquarters' building via CDPD. Managers may feel strong benefits in providing wireless access to their sales people; however, the existing budget may only be able to fund 50 of the connections (CDPD modems and corresponding service) during the current year. The company may decide to deploy the remaining half of the system the following year.

- *Implementation issues, but no funding issues:* If plenty of money is available, but there is concern whether the requirements or design is solid, the company should consider funding only the requirements and design phases of the project to better clarify the needs and the solution. This will increase the accuracy of the cost estimate associated with hardware, software, and support. It also ensures the purchase of the right components.

The business case may do a good job of identifying the benefits and savings a company will receive by deploying the system, for example, but it may not have been possible to define a solution that would provide assurance of component costs or whether a solution even exists. In this case, the company should fund enough of the project to accurately define components necessary to satisfy the requirements. This would enable the company to make a better decision later to allocate money for component procurement and the installation phase of the project.

- *Limited funding and implementation issues:* If funding is limited and there are issues with implementing the system, the company should not continue with the project (or should proceed with extreme caution).

There may be marvelous benefits in deploying a wireless patient record system in a hospital, for example, but limited funding and the presence of implementation issues, such as potential interference with medical instruments and the task of migrating existing paper-based records into a database, should cause the organization to think twice before funding the project. In this case, however, the company could fund smaller projects to resolve the issues, and then reconsider the implementation of the system at a later date.

Case Study 7.9:
Developing a Feasibility Study
for WarehouseTrack

Before continuing with the design phase of the project, Debra, the project manager for the WarehouseTrack project, needed to develop a feasibility study for the project for Bob, the company president.

Debra and Brian, the business analyst, spent some time defining the cost saving benefits that the manufacturing company would realize if they implemented the system.

continues

continued

Based on the time studies that Brian had completed during the requirements phase, they were able to estimate the amount of time warehouse clerks would save by using an AIDC-based solution for each warehouse function. This provides a basis for determining labor savings and efficiency gains.

Brian found that the time it takes a clerk to receive each item is approximately 30 seconds. The use of an AIDC system will cut the time to 10 seconds. This is a savings of 20 seconds per item. Each warehouse receives an average of 5,000 items per day, resulting in a time savings of 27.7 man-hours per day.

Based on similar analysis techniques, the total time savings per day for all the functions using the AIDC system is 100 hours per day, resulting in 36,500 hours per year. Based on an average pay for warehouse staff of $10 per hour, the annual labor savings for using the AIDC system is $365,000 per warehouse per year. The total labor savings per year for all nine

warehouses is then $3,285,000.

Of course the company will realize this savings only if they reduce the warehouse staff, and the savings will begin after the system becomes operational. Other benefits of the AIDC system will include faster deliver times to customers and better accuracy of inventories. The return on investment for this project is positive. The company will need to invest a sizable amount of money, but the resulting labor savings are substantial. The first year of operation of the system will recover the initial investment and still provide some additional savings.

Based on the feasibility study results, Bob decided to go ahead and implement the system, but break the project into phases to fit the $1,200,000 funding available during the first year. Therefore, the project team decided to focus the first phase of the project on deploying the radio LAN throughout all nine warehouses and implement receiving and inventory functions only.

As this chapter explains, a great deal of work is necessary to properly plan a project, specify requirements, and determine the feasibility of implementing a wireless system. The actual implementation of the system uses these preparatory elements as a basis for the design, installation, and operational support activities. It is essential that you spend adequate time with these elements to ensure that the project will be successful—that is, completed on time, within budget, and in a cost-effective manner.

Chapter 8, "Implementing a Wireless LAN," continues with the next series of steps that completes the installation of the wireless network.

Implementing a Wireless LAN

- **Designing a wireless LAN**
  The design of a system determines the components that are necessary. You must define network elements, select products, identify the location of access points, document the design, and procure components.

- **Preparing for operational support of a wireless LAN**
  The main goal of support planning is to make certain the system continues to operate effectively. Proper support includes training, system administration, help desk, network monitoring, maintenance, system development, and configuration control.

- **Installing a wireless LAN**
  The installation of a wireless system involves several steps: planning the installation, staging the components, installing the components, and testing the installation. You will learn the steps that are crucial for a successful installation and testing of a wireless LAN.

Designing a Wireless LAN

Chapter 7, "Planning a Wireless LAN," addressed defining the requirements and determining the feasibility for a wireless system. The next step is to perform the design. The design phase determines the technologies, products, and configurations providing a solution. As with any engineering activity, the goal of network design is to find a solution that meets requirements providing the greatest return on investment.

> **Note**
>
> *A comprehensive case study for a project called WarehouseTrack recurs throughout this chapter to provide real-world examples of key steps for implementing a wireless LAN. This case study is a continuation of the one begun in Chapter 7, "Planning a Wireless LAN."*

In some cases, you may have performed a preliminary design as a basis for initial cost estimating and work planning. But, the design phase of the project defines all aspects of the solution, supporting the product procurement, installation, testing, and operational support of the system.

Note

If a company or organization has a large internal information system group, it may implement the wireless network itself. Many companies and organizations, however, don't have the necessary resources to perform the implementation. As a result, many outsource the implementation to system integrators or consultants both to implement the wireless network and even to manage the project. Refer to Appendix B, "Products, Companies, and Organizations," for a list of system integrators and consultants.

The design phase of the project produces items, such as schematics, building layout drawings, bill of materials (parts list), and configuration drawings. These items are necessary to fully define the design. For most projects, you can complete the design by accomplishing the following general steps:

1. Define network elements.
2. Select products.
3. Identify the location of access points.
4. Verify the design.
5. Document the design.
6. Procure components.

The succeeding sections explain how to accomplish each of these steps.

Defining Network Elements

The definition of network elements includes deciding which technologies, standards, and products to utilize as a solution to requirements. For example, you may decide to use an ethernet network to provide connectivity between access points. In some cases, the selection of a product will define the network element. This is mostly applicable with the network operating system and off-the-shelf applications.

The general process of defining network elements is as follows:

• Identify which network elements apply.
• Determine requirements for each network element.

In other words, identify what part of the network architecture you need to concentrate on to find a solution, and then determine the technologies, standards, and, if necessary, the products for each element.

Identifying Which Network Elements Apply

The total solution consists of many elements that support the dissemination of information among applications, databases, and systems. The following list identifies the elements constituting a network, from the Application to the Physical Layer:

- Application software
- Network operating system
- Desktop operating system
- Hardware appliances
- Communications software
- LAN medium access
- Physical connectivity
- LAN backbone
- Building-to-building connections
- Wide area network
- Addressing
- Network management protocols

Some of these elements, such as access points and network operating system, constitute actual hardware and software, respectively; however, the address plan indicates a procedure. The goal of this step is to identify the network elements applying to your specific implementation. To accomplish this, review the network requirements and develop the list of elements that you will need to consider. To accomplish this, first determine the geographical area the wireless system needs to cover. This will help you decide which elements are necessary.

Determining Requirements for Network Elements

The next step in defining the network elements is to determine values for each element. As with most engineering efforts, it is a good idea to maximize the use of standards when selecting technologies and to use a top-down approach.

Ideally, the design team should select technologies and standards having the highest level of maturity. This leads to longer lasting solutions that are easier to maintain. When assessing maturity levels, utilize the following evaluation criteria:

- Low Maturity
    - No standard and low product proliferation
    - De facto standard and low product proliferation

- Emerging official standard and low product proliferation
- Stable official standard, but reaching obsolescence; low or high product proliferation, with vendors and end-users switching to other technologies
- Moderate Maturity
  - No standard and high product proliferation
  - Emerging official standard and high product proliferation
- High Maturity
  - Stable official standard and high product proliferation
  - De facto standard and high product proliferation

A top-down design approach first defines high-level specifications directly satisfying network requirements, and then defines the remaining elements in an order that mostly satisfies specifications already determined. Designers should first define applications, for instance, because this will set a basis for the remaining design. Then, designers should choose the best platform for these applications, which would consist of the network operating system and hardware/software platforms. Designers would then continue with specifying network elements—such as medium access, medium, bridges, and so on—that support the network operating system and platforms. If you are charged with implementing the wireless network only, be sure that someone has properly addressed all other system elements.

Application Software

Application software provides the functionality users require, such as database access, bar code scanning, and electronic mail. Therefore, application software directly satisfies network requirements, particularly user requirements. There are many types of applications, ranging from simple utilities to full-feature office automation.

Most traditional applications are hosted centrally on mainframe computers, and users access these applications via terminals or PCs running terminal emulation software. In this case, the application runs entirely on the mainframe computer. The user interfaces tend to be character oriented versus graphical, making them somewhat unfriendly to the user.

Another problem with such applications is that they are costly and time-consuming to change. A programmer normally must alter the program to accommodate simple changes to a report format, for example. Yet another problem is that mainframe applications tend to be full-screen oriented (25 lines by 80 columns). This is an issue when using handheld appliances having smaller screens because the user is forced to scroll up and down and left and right to see the entire screen.

Today, many companies are beginning to deploy client/server applications based on the model shown in Figure 8.1. There are several benefits of developing applications based on client/server principles. For one, the interfaces are graphical (generally based on Microsoft Windows) and are very simple to use and relatively easy to develop and modify. Powersoft's Powerbuilder and Microsoft's Visual Basic, for example, are common tools for developing client server applications that interface with various databases.

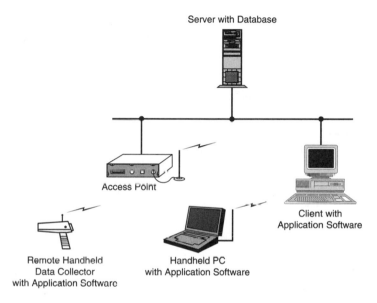

FIGURE 8.1 *The user interfaces with the application located on the server via a client program that performs some of the processing. The server software is generally a database, such as Sybase or SQL Server.*

Many applications are available off-the-shelf, especially common office software. In some cases, however, it may be necessary to develop custom software for a specific application. Custom development may be cost-effective if an organization cannot feasibly change its processes to match the functionality of off-the-shelf software.

The process of developing custom software is beyond the scope of this book, but would include a software engineering process similar to deploying a wireless network—that is, analyze requirements, design the software, implement the code, and install. The main difference of the analysis phase is the level of detail. Generally, you must determine much more specific requirements for applications than for networks that support them.

Wireless Connections

The design for the wireless elements of a wireless system implementation will require the selection of options that pertain to the wireless NICs, access points, and connectivity software. As a result, you will need to choose from the following options:

- *Proprietary or IEEE 802.11 standard products:* In most cases, unless you already have a significant installed base of wireless products, you should utilize IEEE 802.11–compliant products. But, keep in mind, however, the availability of proprietary networks may not receive adequate levels of vendor support as standard 802.11 LANs proliferate.

- *Data rate (1 or 2 Mbps for IEEE 802.11):* Be sure to analyze your data rate requirements, and select a data rate that will meet your needs. Some wireless network products that are 802.11 compliant also support higher data rates. You can utilize these higher data rates but only if all radio cards and access points are from the same vendor. In addition, the IEEE 802.11 committee is working on a higher data rate standard to offer data rates higher than 2 Mbps.

- *Physical Layer (radio waves or infrared):* Refer to Chapter 2, "Wireless Network Configurations," for an overview of radio wave and infrared transmission. For most applications, radio waves will be the best alternative, especially if your requirements call for mobility. For portable applications requiring greater immunity to noise and better security, infrared may be a better choice.

  If you utilize radio wave-based products, you will also need to decide which spread spectrum modulation to utilize: frequency hopping or direct sequence. Refer to the section "Spread Spectrum Modulation" in Chapter 2 for a comparison of modulation types, and then choose one that best meets requirements. Chapter 5, "Physical (PHY) Layer," also provides attributes for each modulation type.

- *Connectivity software (terminal emulation, gateway, or direct ODBC connectivity):* Refer to Chapter 6, "Wireless System Integration," for a comparison of connectivity software, and then choose one that best meets requirements.

For providing wireless links among buildings, consider the use of radio waves for the following situations:

- When buildings are far apart (up to 30 miles, 49 kilometers, apart)
- When the lowest cost solution is desirable

Consider the use of infrared light for the following situations:

- When high bandwidth is required
- When the potential for radio frequency interference is high
- When buildings are separated by less than 1 mile
- When information security is important

Selecting Products

After you have defined the technologies necessary to support network requirements, you need to identify appropriate products. In some cases, such as the NOS and applications, you may have already selected the product as part of the network element definition phase. Regardless, select all products and materials necessary for implementing the network, and create a bill of materials.

In general, select products based on the following criteria:

- Capability to provide necessary degree of functionality

- Product Availability

- Level of vendor support after the purchase

- Price

Note

Not all 802.11-compliant products provide all 802.11 functions. An 802.11-compliant access point may not include power management and the point coordination function (PCF) modes of operation, for example. In addition, some 802.11-compliant products may have non-802.11-defined features. For example, an 802.11-compliant access point may implement bit rates higher than 2 Mbps and provide load balancing.

Also, these criteria are important when selecting wireless products:

- For wireless LANs, compliance with the IEEE 802.11 standard

- Availability of tools that assist with installation (site survey tools, field strength meters, and so on)

- Availability of encryption for higher security

- Availability of power management when using battery-operated devices

- Capability to fit the form factors of your computers (that is, ISA, PCMCIA, and so forth)

- Capability to interoperate with the selected network operating system

---

Migrating to 802.11-Compliant Networks

Many companies and organizations have an installed base of proprietary wireless LAN networks and corresponding wireless appliances. To accommodate newer 802.11-compliant appliances while still maintaining wireless LAN connectivity for existing proprietary-based appliances, consider installing access points that have dual radio card slots.

Several of the wireless LAN manufacturers provide these types of access points. One slot will accommodate the proprietary version of the radio network card, and the other slot can house an 802.11-compliant radio card. The resulting access point will then enable both proprietary and 802.11-compliant appliances to share the same access point, which is less expensive than having separate access points for both wireless LANs.

Identifying the Location of Access Points

Many environments, such as hospitals, factories, and warehouses, will cover an area exceeding the range of wireless LAN devices. Part of the design is to identify the location of these access points to provide an interface to network resources located on wired networks and adequate coverage for roaming users throughout the facility.

It would be easy if you were deploying a wireless network in a completely open area, free from obstacles like walls, desks, and window blinds. This would enable radio waves from the wireless devices to maintain an omnidirectional radiation pattern, making it simpler to predict the maximum operating range among all devices and the location of the access points. The presence of items and construction of the facility offers attenuation to radio wave signals that distorts the radio propagation pattern, however, making it difficult if not impossible to predict.

The penetration of radio waves through flooring, for example, depends on the building materials present between the floors. Range is greatest if passing through plywood, fair if passing through concrete, and very poor if going through metal. Table 8.1 gives you an idea of the degree of attenuation of various types of RF barriers.

TABLE 8.1   RELATIVE ATTENUATION OF RF BARRIERS

RF Barrier	Relative Degree of Attenuation	Example
Wood	Low	Office partitions
Plaster	Low	Inner walls
Synthetic material	Low	Office partitions
Asbestos	Low	Ceilings
Glass	Low	Windows
Water	Medium	Damp wood, aquariums
Bricks	Medium	Inner and outer walls
Marble	Medium	Inner walls
Paper	High	Paper rolls
Concrete	High	Floors and outer walls
Bullet-proof glass	High	Security booths
Metal	Very High	Desks, office partitions, reinforced concrete, elevator shafts

When establishing requirements for the network, you should have reviewed the environment, giving you enough information to select the type of wireless medium. To identify the location of access points, you need to evaluate the environment to a much lower level of detail, concentrating on the effects of the environment on propagation of radio waves.

The best method of identifying the location of access points is to perform an RF site survey. System integrators who specialize in wireless system integration and consulting offer site survey services for a fee (see Appendix B, "Products, Companies, and Organizations"). If you are going to do the work yourself, however, start by obtaining the following items:

- Blueprints of the facility

- At least one access point from the selected vendor

- An appliance that will be used by the users of the system

Employing Site Survey Tools

Many companies supply tools for performing site surveys. With the appropriate tool loaded, walk with the portable computer and record the signal quality at all applicable locations. If the signal quality falls below suggested values supplied by the vendor, consider relocating the access point.

Proxim, for example, ships a site survey tool with its RangeLAN products that loads on the appliance and broadcasts messages to all other units with the specified domain. Each unit responds to these broadcasts, and the survey tool, after 10 broadcasts, displays a Link Quality number that represents the percentage of packets to which the tool received a response.

The tool displays a Link Quality of 5 for 100-percent packet acknowledgment. A Link Quality of 4 represents 80 percent, a Link Quality of 3 represents 60 percent, and so on. Of course a Link Quality of 5 is optimum, but operation is still possible at lower-quality levels. (Users will experience some delay, however.)

Perform the following steps to conduct the site survey:

1. Verify the accuracy of the facility blueprints.

   An architect draws initial blueprints before the building is constructed. Changes are not always made to the drawings as the building is modified, especially the relocation of walls and office partitions. You should walk through the facility before running tests to be sure walls are where they are supposed to be—if not, update the drawings.

2. Mark permanent user locations.

   On the blueprints, mark the locations of users who will be operating from a fixed location.

3. Mark potential user roaming areas.

   In addition to the permanent user locations, outline potential user roaming areas within the building. In some cases, the roaming areas may be the entire facility. However, there may be some areas where users will never roam.

4. Identify obstacles that may offer significant attenuation to the radio waves.

   Observe the construction of the facility, and mark the location of obstacles that may cause a hindrance to radio wave propagation.

5. Identify potential sources of interference.

   You should have done this when reviewing the environment as part of the definition of requirements. If not, determine what other RF devices are present, and assess their effect on the wireless LAN. You can do this by talking to someone at the facility who manages existing RF devices, or you can utilize a spectrum analyzer to record RF transmissions that fall within the frequency band your wireless LAN will operate.

   Outline the areas on the blueprints that the sources of interference will affect. Keep in mind that this step is important! One company in Washington D.C. purchased 200 wireless LAN cards, installed them, and later discovered radio interference from a nearby military base blocked the operation of half the users. A proper verification of coverage or even the use of a spectrum analyzer would have saved this company a great deal of money and frustration.

6. Identify the preliminary location of access points.

   Based on the wireless LAN vendor's range specifications and information gained from steps 4 and 5, identify preliminary location(s) of access points and wireless servers. The goal here is to ensure that all permanent and roaming users can maintain access to applicable network resources via access points. For small areas (less than 1,000 feet diameter), no access points may be necessary. But larger areas will require access points to produce a multiple-cell system. Mark the presumed locations on the blueprints.

7. Verify the location of access points.

   This is best done by installing an access point or master station at each of the locations identified in step 6, and testing the signal strengths at each of the permanent and potential user locations. You will need to configure an appliance with the applicable wireless LAN adapter and site survey software supplied by the vendor.

   If possible, be sure to utilize an appliance and wireless LAN components that will actually be part of the eventual system. This provides the most accurate results because it exhibits the same propagation patterns as the future system.

**Case Study 8.1:
Selecting Wireless LAN
Components for WarehouseTrack**

Debra, the project manager for the WarehouseTrack system, began the design phase of the project by having a site survey done at each of the nine warehouses of the parts manufacturing company. (Refer to the case studies throughout Chapter 7, "Planning a Wireless LAN," to review planning elements of the WarehouseTrack project.) The site survey results showed that each warehouse would require eight access points located throughout the facility to provide enough radio LAN coverage to enable warehouse clerks to work at any point within the facility and around the loading and unloading docks.

Next, Debra directed Jared, the design engineer for the project, to begin defining the system elements related specifically to the wireless LAN. A preliminary design used for budgeting purposes earlier in the project depicted a system architecture composed of 10 wireless handheld scanners and printers, a radio LAN, and a database and PC application software residing on a server within each warehouse. Jared still needed to define the radio network modulation type and other required radio network features, such as power management and security, as well as connectivity software.

Jared decided to utilize wireless LAN products that comply with the IEEE 802.11 frequency hopping physical layer because the AIDC system would not need the higher data rate potential of direct

sequence. The use of frequency hopping at 2 Mbps in conjunction with the other system components would meet the two-second-transaction performance requirement. (See Case Study 7.8, "Conducting a Joint Application Design Meeting for WarehouseTrack," for a discussion of transaction time.) Infrared was not considered because it would not provide the mobility requirements.

In addition to the choice of modulation type, Jared specified the use of 802.11-compliant wireless network components that implement power management to conserve battery power of the handheld appliances. Jared recommended a single vendor for obtaining the 802.11 wireless components, which would minimize the possibility of incompatibilities and enable them to utilize additional add-on features, such as load balancing.

Wired Equivalent Privacy (WEP) was not necessary because security requirements indicate the need for the users to input only a username and password to utilize the system. This feature would be part of the appliance application software and database, not the wireless LAN. To connect the access points to the server, Jared specified a 10Base-T ethernet network using shared ethernet repeaters.

Verifying the Design

Design verification ensures the solution you have chosen will support requirements. Actually, the verification of access points covered in the preceding section was a form of design verification that tested the wireless network portion of a network architecture: the Physical and Data Link Layers. But, you may also need to verify higher-layer architectural elements, such as applications, communications protocols, and system interfaces. This will avoid the purchase of inappropriate network components and hours of time working out bugs at the last minute before the system needs to be operational.

The following are methods you can utilize to verify the design:

- Physical prototyping
- Simulation
- Design review

Verifying the Design Through Physical Prototyping

A physical prototype is the construction and testing of the part of the system you wish to verify. It consists of the actual hardware and software you may eventually deploy. In some cases, you could include the prototype as part of the initial implementation, such as a system pilot. Or, the prototyping can take place in a laboratory setting or testbed.

The main attributes of physical prototyping are as follows:

- Yields very accurate (real) results because you are using the actual hardware and software
- Relatively inexpensive because you can obtain components under evaluation from vendors
- Takes time to reconfigure the prototype to reflect changes in requirements
- Requires access to network components, which can be a problem if you don't have easy access to vendors (for example, from remote areas such as ships at sea, the South Pole, and so on)
- Requires space to lay out the hardware

Typically, you don't need to physically prototype the entire system, especially those parts that other organizations have implemented without encountering problems. Consider prototyping any solutions that have not been tested before. The following list offers some examples:

- Interfaces between wireless users and network resources located on a wireline network such as ethernet
- Access from users to mainframe applications
- Operation of newly developed applications
- Operation of the system in areas where there is a high potential for inward and outward interference

Verifying the Design Through Simulation

Simulation is using software that artificially represents the network's hardware, software, traffic flows, and utilization as a software model. A simulation model consists of a software program written in a simulation language. You can run the simulations and check results quickly, greatly compressing time by representing days of network activity in minutes of simulation runtime.

The main attributes of using simulation for verifying the design are the following:

- Results are only as accurate as the model—in many cases, you will need to estimate traffic flows and utilization.

- After building the initial model, you can easily make changes and rerun tests.

- Does not require access to network hardware and software.

- Does not require much geographical space, just the space for the hardware running the simulation software.

- Simulation software is fairly expensive, making simulation not economically feasible for most one-time designs.

- The people working with the simulation program will probably need training.

For most implementations, you won't need to run simulations. However, consider using simulation for the following situations:

- When needing a better understanding of the bandwidth requirements (system sizing) based on predicted user activity (it is not practical to do this with physical prototyping)

- If you are in an area where it is difficult to obtain hardware and software for testing purposes

Simulation Tools: OPNET and NetGuru Simulator

Simulation tools on the market can assist designers in developing a simulation model. Most simulation tools represent the network using a combination of processing elements, transfer devices, and storage devices. Mil 3's OPNET and American Hytech's NetGuru Simulator are two prominent ones.

Mil 3's OPNET simulator has evolved as a response to the problems resulting from network complexity. Structured around a top-down, graphical hierarchy of representation that uses the latest software technology, nodes are represented as objects that communicate through data-flow networks and can be quickly customized to specific details.

The entire system, including statistical analysis of network traffic, is portrayed through an X Window graphical user interface. As a result, the designer can think in terms of basic architectures and explore the consequences without having to code a design from the bottom up.

OPNET is structured as a series of hierarchical graphical editors that address each

continues

continued

level of network design, consisting of three levels:

- The highest tier is based on connectivity or a network editor that targets topology, operating as a schematic-capture function. Graphical representations of a network can be superimposed on backgrounds representing floor plans or geographic areas.

- The second level, the node editor, captures node activity in terms of data-flow analysis of hardware and software subsystems.

- The third level contains a process editor that defines the control flow such as a protocol or algorithm.

American Hytech's NetGuru Simulator is a fully functional network simulation module that is integrated with NetGuru Designer. The Simulator uses object-oriented programming techniques with graphical icons that enables even non-technical users to perform design and simulation activities.

The NetGuru family of tools has plug-and-play, Windows-based modules that represent generic physical and logical network elements. The product addresses the needs of professionals dealing with LANs with hundreds of workstations, or larger networks that can be further segmented.

NetGuru provides the capability to design the network from scratch or document an existing design and conduct *what-if* analysis. This helps the designer understand whether the networks are performing efficiently, identify potential bottlenecks, and predict the effect of new hardware, software, users, network configurations, or network tools as they relate to overall performance.

Verifying the Design Through Design Reviews

Whether you have performed simulation and physical prototyping or not, you should conduct a design review as a final verification process. This review ensures that there are no design defects or issues before pressing on with component procurements. It is best to have the entire team, especially analysts and engineers, review the design to ensure it will adequately support all requirements. Analysts should raise questions related to the capability of the design to satisfy requirements, and engineers should be able to fully explain how the design will meet requirements.

For first-time complex implementations, consider hiring a consultant to verify the design. This could eliminate a lot of problems when you install and test the system.

During the design review, participants should do the following:

1. Review all design documentation.

2. Identify defects in the design.

3. Describe potential technical problems.

4. Recommend further prototyping or simulation of unclear design specifications.

Be sure to utilize lessons learned from other projects to spot problems in the inability of the specifications to meet requirements.

Documenting the Final Design

As with requirements, you need to document the details of the design to support further implementation activities, such as component procurements, installation, and so on. The final design documentation should include the following:

- A description of each network element
- The location of access points
- Standards
- The products necessary for satisfying specific requirements

Be certain to update any documentation prepared throughout the design with any changes made after verifying the design. Also, update the project documentation, such as the budget, schedule, and resources required to complete the project.

The last step before procuring the components is to obtain approvals for the design. This ensures applicable managers agree to fund the implementation shown in the design. This normally involves network configuration management, the customer representative, and people with funding authority. For approvals, you can have these people sign a letter having at least the following elements:

- Design document number
- Change control procedures
- Signatures of technical manager, project manager, customer representative, and funding authority

After the approval, consider the design as a baseline that can be changed only by following the stated change control procedures.

Case Study 8.2:
Completing the Design for
WarehouseTrack

In addition to selecting the wireless LAN components for WarehouseTrack, the design team needed to specify the connectivity software and the design of the software, verify and document the design, obtain approvals, and procure the components before developing the system.

The choice of connectivity software was the most difficult decision to make concerning the system design. Eric, the

continues

continued

software developer, identified three valid alternatives that included terminal emulation, direct database connectivity, and middleware. (Refer to Chapter 6, "Wireless System Integration," for understanding the tradeoffs of each of these connectivity software types.)

Eric decided to utilize middleware, mainly to enable the AIDC system to interface with both the client/server database that is part of the AIDC system and the existing corporate mainframe system. Additional factors in favor of middleware are the following:

- It will ensure a smooth migration from the existing corporate mainframe system to the future corporate client/server system.

- It will provide optimum performance.

- It will make system management easier.

The use of middleware is more expensive than using terminal emulation or direct database connectivity; therefore, the project team had to show that the savings in support costs would outweigh the higher cost of middleware.

Because this project was implementing a complete system (that is, application software and a wireless LAN), Eric also needed to design the software for handheld appliances, PC software, and database. The manufacturing company, however, was not going to implement all system functions during the first year. Instead, they would only deploy receiving and inventory functions. They did agree, however, to design the entire system.

Eric drew flowcharts that describe the appliance software and PC application software. For software development tools, he specified the use of C for the appliance software and Microsoft's Visual Basic for the PC application software. Eric developed a design for the relational database by defining the structure of each table. He also specified the use of Microsoft's Windows NT for the server operating system and Microsoft's SQL Server for the database.

The project team felt confident that the system would work as designed. They were using 802.11-compliant wireless LAN devices from a reputable vendor, and Jared, the engineer, and Eric had experience in utilizing the chosen middleware to connect appliance software to both databases and mainframes.

In addition, this AIDC system wasn't stretching the capabilities of the radio LAN or other system components. Therefore, the team didn't think that they needed to verify the design through simulation or prototyping. If requirements stated more appliances or performance requirements were stringent, the team would have performed simulation to ensure that the system would operate as expected.

Jared and Eric developed a design specification that described and illustrated all the design elements, including a list of all components the company would need to purchase. Then, Debra scheduled a design review meeting consisting of the entire project team, as well as Ron, the information system manager. At the meeting, Jared and Eric described the system design, and Ron approved the design specification.

The outcome of the design phase didn't require any updates to the budget or project plan. At this point, Debra, working with the purchasing department at the manufacturing company, placed orders for all the components to have them delivered to the company headquarters in Atlanta.

Procuring Components

Obviously, before installing components, you need to purchase them and have them delivered to either the staging or installation site. Before doing this, be sure to confirm the amount of time it takes for the vendor or supplier to ship the components. In some cases, the provider may have components in stock that can be shipped within a few days. But, it may take several months if the components must first be manufactured by the vendor. This may be the case for larger orders. So, be sure to include this lead-time in the schedule when planning the installation dates.

Warranties

When procuring components, you need to understand warranties and maintenance agreements the vendors offer. Most vendors offer excellent warranties and also have maintenance agreements at an additional charge.

Here are some questions you should ask vendors:

- How long is the product covered by the warranty?
- When does the warranty begin?
- What are the limitations of the coverage?
- How should the product be returned if it becomes defective?
- Does the vendor provide on- or off-site maintenance?

Spare Components

Be certain to include an adequate level of spare components when purchasing for the network. Even though vendors will provide warranties on the hardware, they will not typically be able to respond fast enough with a replacement component if one fails. Spares should be kept near the operational site to provide fast replacement of faulty network components. Of course, extra components will add additional cost to the project, but this must be weighed against potential downtime if a unit should fail.

Note

Because most component warranties begin at the time of delivery, be certain that each component works properly before putting it in storage. It is difficult to prove the component was bad when shipped from the vendor if you find that the component is defective six months later.

Component Storage

Before actually ordering the components, you should plan where the components will be stored after delivery. For small implementations, this may not be significant; but for larger implementations, it is crucial. Imagine ordering 75 PCs, 150 radio cards, and 5 printers, for example. Do you know where you would put all the boxes when they arrive? Because implementations of this size or larger require a great deal of component storage space (before they are needed for installation), plan the following items:

- The delivery location for the components

- Storage locations while waiting for installation

- Mechanisms for moving components from the delivery point to the storage area

- Mechanisms for moving the components from the storage area to the point of installation

---

Case Study 8.3:
Developing a Wireless System for
WarehouseTrack

The next phase of the WarehouseTrack project entails developing the system that the team would install at the warehouses. Eric, software developer, wrote the software for the handheld scanners and printers that implements the receiving and inventory functions. He then had Pete, another software developer, perform unit testing of each software module. While Pete was testing the software, Eric developed the database and PC application software.

After Pete was done testing the appliance software, database, and PC application software as individual components, Eric constructed the entire system, including appliances, radio LAN, server, database, and PC application software in a lab at the system integration company. Then,

Pete performed system testing to ensure that all components would operate together correctly.

The next step was to perform pilot testing of the system at one warehouse to ensure that the system operated properly (to minimize the amount of rework needed if bugs had been found). Eric and Jared installed a couple access points, the server, database, PC application software, connectivity software, and two appliances at one of the warehouses. They gave some operational training to a couple of the warehouse clerks and asked them to utilize the WarehouseTrack system in parallel with their existing manual processes for a period of three weeks. Some bugs were found, and Eric corrected them.

Preparing for Operational Support of a Wireless LAN

As part of the wireless system project, be sure to plan all aspects of operational support. It is advisable to perform this planning in parallel with the design phase of the project. The main goal of support planning is to make certain that the system continues to operate effectively during its operational phase. Be sure to prepare the support elements, as described in the following sections, before allowing users to utilize the system.

Training

Training provides users, system administrators, and maintenance staff the know-how to effectively operate and support the new system. Training is crucial to the success of a wireless system project. Users will need to know how to use application software, and the system administrator and support staff will need to understand how to manage the network operating system and diagnose system problems.

The implementation of proper training will significantly increase the effectiveness of a new system because users will have less of a learning curve, minimizing the drop in productivity normally encountered with new systems. Also, the users will require less support from system administrators and the help desk.

System Administration

System administration is the liaison between the system and its users. With a network, a system administrator manages the network operating system. Be sure the system administrator understands the configuration of the network (such as IP address assignments of all access points and appliances).

Help Desk

The help desk is a central point of contact for users needing assistance with utilizing the network and its resources. The help desk should concentrate on user satisfaction by providing first-level support via a single phone number. This is an effective method of support because the centralized help desk will not have to revisit answers to problems when common questions arise. The following are suggestions in establishing or upgrading a help desk:

- Establish a single phone number (with multiple call handling) for the help desk, and ensure that all users know the phone number.

- Plan for increased call volume as the network grows.

- Incorporate a method to effectively track problems.

- Fully train the help desk team in network operations principles, particularly in user applications.

- Use surveys to determine user satisfaction with the help desk.

- Review help-desk usage statistics to determine optimum staffing.

- Periodically rotate network implementation and system administration people into the help desk.

Network Monitoring

Network monitoring seeks to find problems in the network before issues arise. Access points and radio cards maintain a *management information base (MIB)* that stores statistics on the parameters relevant to the radio network, such as the number of duplicate frames, CRC errors, transmit retries, and collisions.

Appendix D of the IEEE 802.11 standard describes the MIBs associated with the 802.11 MAC and Physical Layers in the ISO/IEC Abstract Syntax Notation (ASN.1). Most access points enable you to monitor these statistics via a network monitoring station conforming to Simple Network Management Protocol (SNMP).

Maintenance and System Development

Set up a procedure to perform preventive maintenance on the network, and troubleshoot and repair the network if it becomes inoperable. Be sure maintenance technicians are familiar with the wireless network access points and appliances so that they can diagnose problems when they arise. An effective method for repairing hardware, for example, is to replace the defective component with a spare, and then to send the defective component back to the vendor for repair or replacement.

Engineering and system development groups perform enhancements to the system and assist system administrators, help desk, and maintenance staff in troubleshooting difficult network problems. Be sure engineering and system development staff receive adequate training on the wireless system hardware and application development tools.

Configuration Control

Configuration control procedures make certain proper control procedures exist for making future network and application changes. Changes to a wireless system, however, especially those not managed, can cause a great deal of headaches. The lack of proper control over changes to the network can result in systems and applications that are not interoperable. It then becomes difficult and expensive (and maybe impossible) to provide interfaces that allow the systems and users at these dissimilar sites to share information.

Additionally, the lack of control over network implementation makes it difficult and costly to support the systems. You may end up with three different types of network operating systems and four different types of wireless LAN adapters to support, for example. Centralized support would need to keep abreast of all these product types, resulting in higher training costs.

Implementing a Configuration Management Process

As you prepare for the operational support of a company-wide system, be sure to establish a configuration control process, as shown in Figure 8.2. The design and installation of the system consists of hardware, software, documentation, procedures, and people. It is paramount to consider the system implementation as a baseline, to be changed only when the person initiating the change follows the process. To implement this process, however, you need to identify those elements (configuration items) that are important to control.

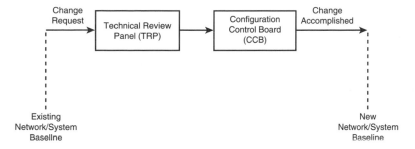

FIGURE 8.2   *A configuration control process will help you to better manage your wireless system.*

The following identifies examples of configuration items that you should consider incorporating as a basis for the configuration control process:

- Network interface adapter vendor and type
- Access point vendor and type
- Network operating system release
- Cabling standard
- Switch vendor and type
- Support plans

The description of these elements should be stored in a library accessible by the entire organization.

To make a change to the configuration items, the person wanting to make the change must submit a change request to the technical review panel (TRP) who will assess the technical nature of the change. This includes an evaluation of whether the change complies with the company's technical standards.

If the TRP thinks that the change is technically feasible, it forwards the request to the configuration control board (CCB) for final approval. The CCB mainly evaluates whether the project team has prepared for adequate levels of support for the implementation and that the change has been coordinated with the proper organizations. With approval of the change, the project team then must ensure the preparation of support documentation.

Documenting Plans for Operational Support

As with all phases of a project, documentation is important to convey the ideas of the operational support phase to other phases of the project. A plan is necessary to effectively carry out the support. An operational support plan describes how the organization will support the operational network. This plan should indicate which network elements require support and which organizations are going to support them. More specifically, the operational support plan should describe how the organization will support the following items:

- Network monitoring
- Network troubleshooting

- Hardware maintenance
- Software maintenance

Preparing for the Transfer to Operational Mode

The transfer of the system from a project status to operational mode should be very well defined; otherwise, it won't be clear who is supporting the network, and "finger pointing" will arise if any problems occur.

The main task of preparing for the transfer to operational mode is to develop a turnover agreement that will be put into effect after completing the installation and testing phase. At the beginning of the project, the project charter gives the project manager responsibility for implementing the network. The turnover agreement transfers this responsibility to the supporting organizations handling system administration, network management, and so on.

Case Study 8.4:
Preparing Operational Support for WarehouseTrack

Before installing the operational system, Sophie, the operations representative for the WarehouseTrack project, needed to further define all operational support elements by developing an operational support plan. As stated in the requirements, none of the potential end users had any experience utilizing an AIDC system; therefore, they would require extensive training on how to operate the appliances and utilize system functions.

Brian, the business analyst on the project, developed a training course for the end-users. The classes would be given to the end-users immediately before the system became operational. The class would consist of two half days of hands-on training. Evan, the system analyst on the project, developed the training for the operational support staff, which would run for three full days.

For system administration, Sophie decided to broaden the role of the system administrators located at the headquarter facility in Atlanta to include the new AIDC system. The new system, however, required the company to hire an additional system administrator. The system administrator would be able to remotely manage the server, access points, and connectivity software; therefore, they wouldn't need to deploy an administrator to each of the warehouses. Someone at each warehouse, however, would be designated to assist the system administrator if needed.

The manufacturing company already had a help desk accessible by a single phone number for users to call if problems arose; however, the help desk staff would need to become very familiar with the WarehouseTrack functionality to help users understand how to perform certain functions if they had forgotten them since training.

The help desk personnel would also need to know whether they should refer a call to a system administrator or to an organization to perform maintenance. If maintenance—such as troubleshooting, hardware replacement, or bug fixes—was required, the help desk would hand off the call to the contracted system integrator deploying the system.

Sophie received agreement from Ron, the Information Systems manager at the manufacturing company, that any change to the WarehouseTrack would have to be authorized by her. This would ensure that they could provide proper operational support for the enhancements. Over the next couple of years, there will be many changes to WarehouseTrack as the company develops and installs additional AIDC functions. Sophie decided to appoint Liza, one of her staff, to manage the changes through the company's configuration management process.

Installing a Wireless LAN

Wireless networks are advantageous because there is less cable to install than with wired networks, such as ethernet. Theoretically, then, a wireless network installation should take less time. Actually, installation time depends on how well you have evaluated the environment before embarking on the installation. If you did not perform a site survey, unseen radio frequency interference might wreak havoc on the operation of a newly installed wireless system, causing significant delays in making the system operate effectively. Therefore, if you have not performed a site survey at this point in the project, do it now before pressing forward!

The installation of a wireless network requires the following steps:

1. Develop an installation plan.
2. Coordinate the installation.
3. Stage the components.
4. Install the components.
5. Test the installation.

This chapter covers each of these steps and explains the actions necessary to finalize the project.

Developing an Installation Plan

Before taking components out of the boxes, installing network interface cards, and setting up antennas, spend some time planning the installation. This will significantly reduce the number of problems that might arise.

Overall, an installation plan explains how to install the network. Developing an installation plan helps you focus on what needs to be installed. It also provides instructions for installers who might not have been involved with the design of the network and, therefore, do not have first-hand knowledge of the network's configuration.

The project team should assign someone as installation manager who will develop the plan and be responsible for the installation.

The following identifies the major components of a network installation plan:

- *Points of contact:* The plan should indicate someone as the central point of contact for each installation site if issues arise. This person could be the customer representative or someone who works in the facility where the installation will take place. Be sure this person can provide access to restricted areas and locked rooms. Also, indicate which person on the project team can answer questions regarding the installation procedures, network configuration, and frequency usage concerns.

- *Safety tips:* When installing network components, accidents are less likely to happen if you incorporate good safety practices and remind people about them. The following are a few safety tips that you should list in your installation plan and stress at your pre-installation meeting:

  - Insist that no installers work alone—use the buddy system. If a severe accident occurs, the other person can obtain help.

  - Recommend that installers remove rings and necklaces while installing hardware components. A metal necklace can dangle into a live electrical circuit (or one that is not connected to a power source, but is still energized by charged capacitors) and provide the basis for electrical shock. Rings also conduct electricity or can catch on something and keep you from removing your hand from a computer or component.

  - Use proper ladders and safety harnesses if placing antennas on towers or rooftops. There is no reason to take high elevation risks.

  - Wear eye and ear protection when using saws and drills.

- *Installation procedures:* The plan should clearly describe the procedures for installing components. In some cases, you can just refer installers to the manufacturer's instructions. Otherwise, write at least the major steps involved in installing each component. You can use the procedures for installing and testing the network outlined in the next sections as a basis.

Tip

The less cluttered the work environment, the greater the range will be for the wireless LAN. A cluttered office can decrease range as much as 50 percent.

- *Tools:* Be sure to identify the tools necessary to complete the job. If you have ever constructed a Barbie house, built a patio cover, or worked on a car engine, you certainly realize the need for having the right tools. Not having the proper tools results in time delays—time looking for the tools and time spent repairing inferior work (this time with the right tools, hopefully). The following is a list of tools the installers might require:

  - Wireless installation tools and utilities assist in planning the location of access points and testing wireless connections. They are generally available from the applicable wireless product vendor.

  - Two-way radios provide communications among the installation team, especially when spread over a large geographical area.

  - Specific test equipment verifies the network installation.

  - Standard tools, such as flashlights, ladders, and crimping tools, should be readily available for the installation team.

- *Reference to design documentation:* The installation will probably require use of design documentation to better understand the overall network configuration. Be sure to indicate the existence of the documentation and how to obtain it.

- *Schedule:* Create a schedule that identifies when to perform each of the installation activities. This helps keep the installation process on schedule. Unfortunately, the best time to install network components is during downtime, such as evening hours and weekends. This minimizes disturbances. Hospitals and warehouses never close, but you should plan the installation activities for when the organization is least active.

- *Resources:* Make certain the plan identifies resources needed to perform the installation procedures. Generally, you will not have a staff of technicians with the experience of installing wireless networks. If you plan to perform wireless installations as a service to other companies, you may want to train existing staff to actually do the implementations. In cases where it is a one-time installation, however, it is best to outsource the work to a company specializing in network installations.

- *Budget:* Create a budget to track expenses related to the installation. The project team has already prepared a budget during the project planning stages. At this time, it may only be necessary to refine the budget to reflect the installation plan.

- *Risks:* Identify any risks associated with the activities and explain how these risks can be minimized. You might be required, for example, to install 200 wireless LAN connections within a two-day time period. With only two installers, you run the risk of not completing the installation on time. Therefore, you will need to look for additional help to keep on schedule. If someone needs to pre-approve your plan, it is best to identify risks and solutions before starting any work.

Coordinating the Installation

Most everyday events require you to coordinate activities. Before you, your spouse, your four kids, and pet dog leave on a five-day automobile trip from Dayton to Sacramento to stay a week with relatives, for example, you would certainly want to communicate with someone at your destination to coordinate items such as sleeping accommodations and eating preferences.

Before leaving on the trip, you should let your relatives know that you are on the way. In addition, you would certainly want to hold a pre-departure meeting with the family, particularly the kids, and talk about proper behavior while traveling. The installation of a network is probably much easier to pull off than the car trip, but the coordination of activities is similar. The coordination of installation activities includes the following:

- *Communicating with the facility managers:* The person designated as the manager for each facility should have a chance to review the installation plan. In fact, he should have been active in developing the schedule to minimize any negative impacts on the organization.

- *Giving the organization's employees a "heads up":* If you have to install components of the network when the organization's staff is present, announce when, where, and for how long installers will be working within the area. Make sure that it is clear to the employees when any existing system resources will not be available. People need time to rearrange their schedules if necessary to accommodate the installation. Have the organization send out a memo or email message to announce the installation.

- *Holding a pre-installation meeting:* The pre-installation meeting enables everyone involved in the installation to come together to review procedures. Be sure everyone knows whom to contact if problems occur. This meeting is also the best time to remind people about good safety practices.

With an installation plan in hand and coordination behind you, it is time to begin the installation.

Staging the Components

If you are implementing a wireless system at multiple sites, be certain to utilize a staging function to ensure the most effective pre-testing and distribution of components to the intended operating locations. The *staging* process essentially puts the system together in a single non-user location to verify that it works as expected. It is best to do this testing before rolling it out to many sites because it significantly reduces the amount of rework necessary if a defect is found in the design or in one or more of the components.

Staging involves the following functions:

- Warehousing of bulk components, such as boxes of radio cards and access points

- Unpacking of bulk components

- Sorting of components for each installation site

- Installation and testing of software on appliances

- Packing and shipping of components destined for specific installation sites

Staging results in reduced installation time at the users' sites, the availability of all necessary components at the installation site, and the knowledge that all subcomponents are properly installed and tested.

Installing the Components

The installation of network components should follow a bottom-up approach. When installing, first construct and configure individual components, such as servers, user workstations, and cabling, and then connect the components together, implement communications software, and install and link the applications. Consider installing the network from the ground up as follows:

1. Install NICs in the computers.

2. Install cabling from ethernet repeaters/switches to the access point installation locations.

3. Install access points using applicable mounting brackets.

4. Establish wide area network connections, if necessary.

5. Assemble server hardware.

6. Install and configure the network operating system.

7. Install client software on the user appliances.

> **Note**
>
> Be sure to follow installation procedures supplied by the vendor when installing network components.

In most cases, the team can install some components in parallel to decrease installation time. There is nothing wrong, for example, with installing network interface cards, cabling, and access points at the same time. Just be sure to properly test each component, as described later in this chapter in the section "Performing Unit Testing," before connecting the pieces together. The point is that you can't fully access or operate the network operating system and applications until after low-level

components, such as cabling, network installation cards, and access points, have
been installed.

Installing Wireless NICs

If you are installing wireless NICs, follow these recommendations:

- Be sure to acquire the correct NIC driver software before attempting to bind
  the appliance's application software to the NIC.

- Some appliances require the vendor's service staff to install wireless NICs to
  ensure that the antenna is properly connected. Be sure to follow these policies
  so that the appliance will operate correctly and be covered under warranties.

- Perform the installation of wireless NICs as part of a centralized staging
  process of the system.

Note

*You can set parameters within the wireless NIC by writing specific instructions in a configuration file that
is part of the wireless NIC installation process.*

Installing Access Points

Most access points have a variety of interfaces, such as RS-485 and RS-232, for
connecting a console (terminal or PC running terminal emulation software) to the
access point for configuration purposes. Some access points even enable you to
change configuration parameters via a Web browser or Telnet session if wired network connectivity exists between the access point and the PC running the Web
browser software or Telnet software. Be sure to set passwords on the access points to
enable access to only those who need to manage the access points.

If you are installing access points within a facility, follow these recommendations:

- Mount the access points as high as possible to increase transmission range;
  however, ensure that there is some way of reaching the device to provide periodic servicing of the unit.

- Follow vendor instructions on configuring the access point with an applicable
  IP address and protocol settings.

- Clearly mark the cables connecting the access points to the corresponding
  ethernet repeater or switch. Ensure that these cable markings are present on
  network diagrams.

Setting the Dwell Time

For each *hop* in the hopping sequence, the transmitter transmits at a specific center operating frequency for a particular amount of time, which is the *dwell time*. You can select
the dwell time via configuration parameters on the access point that all stations will use:

- If there is not much chance of interference, select the longest dwell time possible.

- If significant interference is present, select a shorter dwell time to reduce the amount of time that interference can occur.

Tip

For best performance, observe the following guidelines when installing access points:

  • *Place antennas as high as you can to increase range between the access point and wireless stations.*

  • *Position the units above office partitions and away from metal objects, such as furniture, fans, and doors.*

  • *Install the unit in a central location, such as the center of a large room or corridor.*

Installing Laser Links Between Buildings

If you are installing laser links between buildings, consider the following recommendations and observations:

- *The beam should not be directed near or through electrical power lines or tree branches.* Consider tree growth, wind load on trees, and power lines. Power lines also sag during warm weather and tighten up during cold weather. Make provisions to discourage nest building (by birds and insects) in the optical path.

- *Make sure the transmission path is at least 10 feet above pedestrian or vehicular traffic.* This both prevents accidental viewing of the laser beam and keeps the signal from being interrupted. Make allowances for any unusual effects that traffic may cause, such as dust clouds.

- *Make sure the transmission path is not shooting through or near exhaust vents that can cause steam to be blown into the path.* This has the same effect as fog on the laser beam.

- *Most outdoor point-to-point components are fully weatherproofed.* These units may also be mounted inside buildings and the signal passed through glass windows. When light particles hit a glass surface, some of the light is reflected. With a clear glass window, approximately four percent of the light is reflected per glass surface. If the glass is tinted, the amount of light reflected and absorbed increases. In the case of reflective coatings, the laser light will reflect off of the coating and the light will never be detected at the receiver.

  Another problem when shooting through glass occurs when it rains. Water droplets on the glass in front of the transmit lens act as additional lenses and can cause the beam to diffuse. Mounting the laser near the top of the window will reduce this problem somewhat, especially if there is an awning over the window. Figure 8.3 illustrates the proper critical angle when operating through glass. As the angle of the beam with the glass increases, more and more light is reflected until the critical angle is reached (approximately 42 degrees). Above the critical angle, all the light is absorbed into the glass and no transmission occurs.

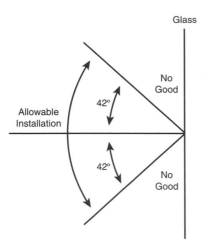

FIGURE 8.3   *When passing signals through glass, it is advisable to keep the beam as close to perpendicular to the glass as possible to minimize reflection losses, which can reduce signal strength.*

- *Avoid east-west orientations.* Although LCI uses optical filters in the receiver and has a small angle of acceptance, direct sunlight can overload the units for several minutes a day for a few days per year.

- *Heat from rooftops, air duct vents, air conditioners, glass-faced buildings, and so on can cause a condition known as shimmer.* Shimmer causes the light beam to bend and appear to dance around the receiver. If sufficient heat is present, the beam deflects enough to miss the receiver altogether, usually for a few milliseconds at a time, and burst error will occur. When mounting on rooftop locations, the preferred location is at the leading edge of the roof, with the front of the laser at least 6 inches over the edge. This minimizes the effect of roof heating, heat rising up the side of the building, and snow accumulation in front of the unit. This also provides access to the rear of the unit for easier setup and alignment.

- *The movement of laser units caused by a strong mechanical vibration could cause the system to intermittently go in and out of alignment.* It is advisable to avoid mounting laser equipment near vibrating machinery such as air conditioning units, compressors, motors, and so on.

- *The laser beam produced by laser units is not subject to the interference produced by EMI sources.* If laser units are placed within proximity of such sources, however, the unit's electronics may "pick-up" this interference which would then be impressed on the signals to and from the equipment. It is advised that laser units be mounted away from large microwave dishes, antennas, radio stations, or any unusual electronic equipment that may be radiating electromagnetic signals.

- *Laser units are normally designed to project a two-meter diameter beam at the receiver.* This provides some latitude for beam movement. It is essential, however, that unit movement should be kept to an absolute minimum to ensure peak performance. A movement of only 1 mm at the transmitter can divert the beam off of the receiver if the units are installed 1 kilometer apart.

- *Under ideal conditions, laser units would be mounted on the corner of the building to which they will be attached and preferably to masonry construction.* This will provide the most stable arrangement. When transmitting signals over 300 meters, it is not advisable to mount LACE units anywhere except at the corner of the structure. On buildings where a thin metal skin is covering the building, the base for the mounts must be made to the supporting structure or to the metal substructure.

- *Do not mount laser units on structures that can sway, such as trees, fences, towers, poles or buildings exceeding 40 stories in height.* Always avoid moveable camera mounts.

- *Do not mount laser units to wooden structures.* The expansion/contraction properties of these materials through precipitation and temperature make them good sources for movement and should be avoided. High humidity will cause the units to go out of alignment due to the wood expanding, for example.

- *Make sure that when the laser is mounted there are no ledges in front of the laser that could be used by roosting birds.* Ledges can also cause a problem in rain and snow. Water bouncing up from the ledge onto the optics or snow buildup in front of the optics will diminish performance.

Testing the Installation

In the software world, testing is extremely important—countless problems have resulted from defects in software. You might have heard, for example, about the farmer in a remote area of Nebraska who one day received thousands of the same copy of Time magazine? Apparently, the publisher's label-printing software had a defect that made it spend hours printing the same address. Defects in networks might not cause similar incidents, but improper configurations and unforeseen propagation impairments can easily discontinue the network's operation. This is especially serious in hospitals where a doctor's or rescue person's access to information can create a life-or-death situation.

There are several definitions for testing. Some people say that testing is for checking whether the system offers proper functionality; others say the reason for testing is to find conditions that make the system fail. Actually, testing is a combination of the two: It ensures that the network behaves as expected and that no serious defects exist.

Test Cases

A test case represents an action you perform and its expected result. One test case might determine whether access to a database meets performance requirements, for example. The action would be to run a particular query, and the expected result would be the maximum time it takes for the query to return the corresponding data.

How do you write test cases? First, be sure to review the later sections on performing unit, integration, system, and acceptance testing before writing test cases. Then, referring to the network requirements and design defined earlier in the project, describe the tests necessary to ensure that a network behaves adequately. The following are attributes of a good test case:

- Has a good chance of uncovering a defect.
- Can be performed with attainable test equipment.
- The expected result is verifiable.

Implementing Wireless Link and Carrier Tests

Most radio cards and access points provide wireless link and carrier test functions. Be sure to perform these tests when installing a wireless LAN. It will save a lot of grief when testing the actual application software.

The wireless link test function determines the quality of transmissions between the station (radio card in the appliance) and the access point. This test sends special control packets to a particular destination, which echoes another packet back to the sending station. Based on the sequence numbers of the packets being sent back and forth, the station running the link test knows whether the link corrupts packets on the forward or return leg of the link.

Link test software generally enables you to set test parameters, such as the type of frames sent (that is, multicast or unicast), target station address, frame size, and number of frames to send. The link test produces the following results:

- Percent of frames sent successfully on both forward and return paths
- Time (average, maximum, and minimum) it takes to receive a response from the destination
- Received signal strengths (average, maximum, and minimum) at both ends of the link
- Number (average, maximum, and minimum) of retries the source accomplishes before sending the test frame

Most link testers enable you to run a separate signal strength test from a station by sending out a unicast frame (typically one every second) to each individual station within the BSS. The receiving stations send back a response frame that includes received signal strength information. The link test software will display the signal strength at both ends of the link for monitoring purposes.

To test the worst case scenario of a wireless LAN, transmit frames at the highest bit rate possible and send a large number (typically up to 1,000 frames for most link testers) of full-size frames. Keep in mind, however, that performing worst case tests will take considerably longer to complete than using a smaller number of minimum size frames. These parameters will result in worst-case results.

A carrier test checks for interference within a wireless LAN. The test works by continuously polling the station's carrier sense functions and displaying the percent of time the station senses a busy medium. Be sure to run this test, however, when there is no data traffic on the wireless medium. If the test results in activity, you know that there is an interfering source nearby. If this occurs, utilize a spectrum analyzer to assist in pinpointing the frequency of the interfering source.

Test Execution

With a complete set of test cases, you are ready to run the tests. As you will see later, testing takes place throughout the installation phase. You might have noticed that building contractors must carefully inspect the foundation before building the structure on top; otherwise, the building itself could hide support structure defects that could later cause a disaster. Network testing is similar; you should fully test the radio connectivity and cabling before installing and testing their interaction with the network operating system and application.

Test Results

The outcome of performing test cases is test results. Of course, you hope everything checks out okay. Poor results indicate the need for rework, meaning a design modification is necessary and components need to be reinstalled or reconfigured. This will take time to complete, possibly extending the project. It is a good idea to record test results for observation later when supporting the network. Test results offer baseline measurements that support staff can use when troubleshooting future problems.

Troubleshooting Tip

A wireless link test that results in a relatively large number of retries at a particular station indicates a problem. The cause of the problem could be interference from a nearby source or collisions resulting from excessive network utilization.

Evaluation and Corrective Actions

After obtaining the test results related to the portion of the network under testing, compare them to the expected values identified in the test case. The evaluation comments should explain any differences and, if necessary, recommend corrective action.

Corrective actions provide baseline information for later testing. When problems arise during the network's operational life, you can run tests again and compare them to the ones run during installation. This can help pinpoint problems.

> **Troubleshooting Tip**
>
> *If a wireless station fails to establish a connection with the access point, consider the following corrective actions:*
>
> - *Ensure that the antennas are securely attached to the radio card and access point.*
> - *Try moving the antenna several feet.*
> - *Ensure that the radio card is firmly seated in the PC Card or ISA slot.*
> - *Check for properly set parameters at the station and access point.*

Performing Testing

The best method of testing the network installation is to follow a bottom-up approach by performing the following types of tests:

1. Unit testing
2. Integration testing
3. System testing
4. Acceptance testing

Performing Unit Testing

Unit testing verifies the proper internal operation or configuration of individual network components, such as network interface cards, access points, servers, cables, printers, and so forth. You should unit test each component—before trying to make them work with other parts of the system—to ensure they themselves are not defective. Knowing that individual parts work makes it easier to troubleshoot problems later.

Ideally, you would want to fully test all possible functions and configurations of each unit; however, that is usually not feasible. The following sections offer examples of unit tests you should perform.

Testing Individual Components

Be sure to test the operation of each component, such as printers, servers, and access points, before integrating them with other components. Most components have built-in self-tests that run whenever you turn the device on, or they have test utilities that you can run manually; therefore, you usually won't need to develop specialized test cases for most individual units. Proxim's wireless LAN products, for example, come with a utility that verifies whether you have chosen an I/O address, IRQ, or memory window that conflicts with other hardware.

Testing Category 5 Cable Installations

Cable problems within the backbone of a wireless system rank high as causes of net-working troubles. Mechanical elements, such as cabling, connectors, and wall plates, tend to fail more often than active electronic devices, such as network adapters and switches. Approximately 85 percent of cable problems arise from the installation; therefore, be sure to fully test cable installations. Cable faults result from improper splices, improper connector attachments, lack of termination, and corrosion.

The good news is that cable problems are relatively easy to find, especially if you utilize an effective cable tester conforming to TIA's Technical Service Bulletin (TSB) 67, published by the Link Performance Task Group of the Telecommuni-cations Industry Association (TIA). This TSB is not a standard; however, it describes how to test Category 5 twisted-pair cable. You should definitely consider TSB-67 when selecting a cable tester.

TSB 67 addresses two link configuration models: Channel Link and Basic Link. The *channel link* consists of the patch cords that connect the access points to the hor-izontal wiring, the horizontal wiring itself can span a total of 100 meters. Channel Link testing covers a range that verifies wiring connections up to the user's inter-face. The *basic link* includes only the wiring horizontal to the building ceiling and two two-meter tester equipment cords, and can be 90 meters long. Installation crews commonly perform Basic Link testing after laying the cabling.

The authors of TSB 67 chose two levels of accuracy for testing links: Level I for low accuracy, and Level II for high accuracy. These two accuracy levels take into consid-eration the test configurations you implement for testing the Basic and Channel Links. Channel Link testing almost always requires the use of an RJ45 interface attached directly to your tester, for example. The problem is that the RJ45 interface offers unpredictable crosstalk and affects the accuracy of crosstalk measurements. This type of test, therefore, would only need Level I testing. On the other hand, Basic Link testing enables you to interface the tester to the cable via a connector having much lower crosstalk, such as a DB-9 or DB-25 connector. Therefore, with Basic Link testing, it is possible to run the more accurate Level II tests.

After installing Category 5 cabling, test the installation by performing the following tests that TSB-67 recommends:

- *Wiremap:* The wiremap test ensures that a link has proper connectivity by test-ing for continuity and other installation mistakes, such as the connection of wires to the wrong connector pin. If you don't wire a RJ45 connector exactly according to a standard, such as EIA/TIA 568A's T568A or T568B wiring scheme, for example, you might produce split pairs.

A *split pair* occurs when you attach the connector in a way that a wire pair consists of one lead from one twisted pair and another lead from a different twisted pair, creating a pair of wires that are untwisted. The split pair might result in an excessive amount of external noise interference and crosstalk, which will cause transmission errors. Most cable testers perform wiremap tests to detect this type of cable problem.

- *Link length:* Link length measurements identify whether a cable meets the length limitations. Cable testers utilize a Time-Division Reflectometer (TDR), which measures the length of a cable. The operation of a TDR is shown in Figure 8.4. Several products on the market run TDR tests on metallic or optical-fiber cable. Tektronix TS100 Option 01 Metallic TDR, for example, tests LocalTalk; Type 1 and 3; Category 3, 4, and 5; and thin and thick coax cables. This test set finds shorts, opens, and breaks in the cable. The Tektronix TFP2A Fibermaster OTDR tests single-mode and multiple-mode fiber-optic cables.

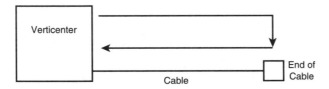

FIGURE 8.4 *The TDR emits a pulse at one end of the cable, which travels to the opposite end of the cable and then reflects back to the TDR. The TDR measures the propagation time and calculates the cable length based on an average wave propagation rate.*

- *Attenuation:* Attenuation tests ensure that the cabling will offer acceptable attenuation over the entire operating frequency range. If too much attenuation is present, digital signals sent throughout the cable will experience rounding, resulting in transmission errors. Cable testers examine attenuation by measuring the effects of sending a series of signals that step through the cable's operating frequency bandwidth.

  For Category 5 testing, most cable testers cover bandwidth of 1 MHz to 100 MHz by taking readings in 1 MHz increments, and this certifies whether the cable meets specifications in the part of the frequency spectrum where the signal mostly resides. The Microtest Pentascanner is an example of a cable tester that measures attenuation on Category 3, 4, and 5 cable.

- *Near-End Crosstalk (NEXT):* Crosstalk is the crossing of current from one wire to a nearby wire, causing transmission errors. Near-end Crosstalk (NEXT) is a specific case in which signals at one end of the link interfere with weaker signals coming back from the recipient. The amount of NEXT varies erratically as you sweep through the operating bandwidth of a cable. For an accurate measurement, cable testers record NEXT by stepping through the cable's operating frequency range at very small increments.

For Category 5 cable, TSB-67 recommends a maximum step size of 0.15 MHz for lower frequencies and 0.25 MHz for higher frequencies within the 1 through 100 MHz frequency range. This requires a fast instrument to take the hundreds of samples necessary. Fluke's DSP-100 handheld cable tester is an example of an incredibly fast NEXT tester. The DSP-100 utilizes digital signal processing to increase its speed and allow samples to be taken at close 100 KHz intervals. The DSP-100 performs all tests required by TSB-67 for a 4-pair cable in less than 20 seconds. The DSP-100 not only identifies the presence of crosstalk, it also locates its source.

If any defects are found through unit testing, correct the problems of each unit before integrating them together with other components.

Performing Integration Testing

The concept of integration testing is shown in Figure 8.5. Although unit testing guarantees the proper functioning of individual components, that is not enough to certify a network. Integration testing goes a step further and ensures that these components operate together. You may have unit tested a PC containing a wireless network interface card, an associated access point, and a server located on the wired network, for example, and found all of them operating sufficiently.

An integration test, such as attempting to log on to the server from the PC via the access point, may fail. The reason could be because the network interface card and access point were set to different channels, not allowing a connection.

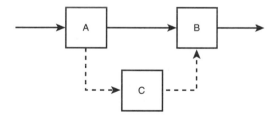

FIGURE 8.5 *Integration testing would verify that components A and B work together okay. Then, after component C is installed, integration testing would verify that all three components work together acceptably.*

Troubleshooting Tip

It is important that you perform integration testing constantly as you add components to the network. You can then find problems soon before they become buried. If you were to finish the entire implementation first, and then run tests, it would be more difficult to find the problems.

If the final configuration of the preceding example includes TCP/IP access to an application residing on the server via a WAN as well, troubleshooting would be much more complex because of the additional components. Therefore, be sure to include integration testing as you build the network.

As with unit testing, the ideal is to verify all possible functions across the set of components you are testing; however, that is not feasible in most cases. To help you narrow possibilities to a workable set, here are some examples of integration tests you should consider performing:

- Capability to roam from one radio cell to another

- Capability to roam throughout the designated coverage area

- Capability of a remote host at the end of a TCP/IP connection to respond to a continuity test, such as a Ping

As with unit testing, correct any defective installations before pressing on with further integration or system testing.

Performing System Testing

System testing determines whether the completed network installation is capable of satisfying the requirements specified at the beginning of the project. Therefore, system testing requires you to first install all components (and perform appropriate unit and integration tests). System testing is the final testing done before handing the system over to the users for acceptance. After installing all network components, such as the clients' terminals, access points, ethernet networks, WAN, servers, and applications, you should check whether the software on the client workstation communicates correctly with the application on the server.

The scope of system testing depends on the potential for disaster if the network fails. If you are building a network to support an information system onboard a manned spacecraft destined for Mars, for example, then you would want to perform exhaustive testing to discover and fix any defects so that unfixable problems don't arise en route. The main reason for the thoroughness is because human lives are at stake if the system fails. Most Earth-based systems without human lives on the line will not require this extreme testing. Be sure, however, to develop test cases that exercise the system from one extreme to another. The goal is to develop and execute system tests that verify, at the minimum, the following system attributes:

- Capability of users to access appropriate applications from terminals and PCs

- Capability to support all security requirements

- Capability to meet performance requirements

- Capability to interface with all external systems

If the testing of these attributes provides unfavorable results, take corrective actions, and then retest the portions of the system that required modification.

Performing Acceptance Testing

After the project team fully tests the system, it is time for the customer to perform acceptance testing, which involves actual users running tests to determine whether the implementation is acceptable. These tests should focus on verifying whether the system functions as specified in the requirements. This does not require the same level of detail as system tests do. Acceptance testing is done at a much higher level to ensure that users can run the appropriate applications while performing their jobs. Mary will be using a wireless terminal tied to a central database to access inventory records as she stocks the shelves, for example. Acceptance testing will determine whether she can actually enter and retrieve data from the database while handling the stock.

It is best not to deploy the network or system to the entire population until a cross section of users performs the acceptance tests. Most people refer to this as a *system pilot*. It is advisable to perform acceptance testing as a pilot of the implementation if any of the following conditions are true:

- The implementation spans multiple geographic locations.
- The network supports mission-critical applications.

In these cases, there is great risk in losing productivity and valuable information if there are defects in the system. If you deploy a wireless inventory system at six warehouses and find that other existing devices interfere, for example, all warehouses stand to lose some productivity until the problem can be resolved. A pilot system at one of the warehouses would have identified the problem, and you could have fixed it before deploying the system to the remaining sites.

The drawback of pilot testing, however, is that it delays the deployment of the system to the users not participating in the pilot. This could make it impossible to meet schedule deadlines. If these preceding conditions exist, however, running a pilot test will be worth the wait.

Finalizing the Project

After the user organization accepts the system, the project might seem to be over. Right? Actually, some tasks are still left, including the following:

- Updating documentation
- Training the users
- Transferring the system to operational support
- Evaluating the outcome of the project

Updating Documentation

During the installation and testing phase, the team may have made changes to the design or layout of the network as a result of corrective actions to failed tests. Therefore, the team might need to update documentation, such as design specifications. In some extreme cases, requirements might need updating if it is found that the installed system can't support desired requirements as expected.

Most companies refer to updated documents as *installed* or *red-lined* drawings. These provide an accurate set of documentation for support staff to use when troubleshooting or modifying the system.

Training Users

The training of users and support staff is extremely important. Training strengthens the interface between the system and the users. If possible, offer the training before or during the system installation. This prepares specific users for performing the acceptance testing and ensures that all users are ready to start using the system when it is operational. You can install a small implementation of the system in a classroom and teach people how to use the system before it is actually deployed to the rest of the company.

In many cases, the implementation team can develop training in the form of a train-the-trainer course. The idea of this form of training is to teach other instructors how to teach the material to the end-users. This case is common when system integrators implement a system for another company.

Transferring the Network to Operational Support

While implementing the network, the project team provides support for the network, such as the creation of user accounts, and troubleshooting and repair actions. In fact, during the requirements phase and acceptance testing, potential users generally assume that members of the project team will always be providing support. In some cases, this will be true. But, regardless of whether the team will be providing operational support, be sure to clearly transfer support of the operational network from the project team to applicable people and organizations.

This clearly marks the end of the project and ensures that users having problems with the system will call on the right people for assistance. Be certain as part of the transfer that the operational support staff have copies of network documentation, such as designs and support plans. Figure 8.6 illustrates the concept of transferring the network to operational support.

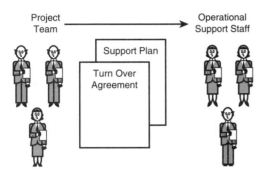

FIGURE 8.6 *Transferring the network to operational support is crucial for properly supporting the installed system.*

This transfer should mark the completion of a successful wireless network implementation. Soon, the numerous benefits of wireless networking will be apparent and your efforts will be justified.

Evaluating the Outcome of the Project

After finishing the project, the project manager should congratulate the team and review the lessons learned throughout the implementation. Gather one last time as a project team and discuss the activities that took place from the beginning of the project and on through the requirements, design, operational support preparation, and installation phases. What did the team learn as a result of completing the project? You can answer this by thinking of what the successes were and why they occurred. Also identify any problems that happened that would be beneficial to solve before undertaking another project.

Here are some questions the team should consider for analyzing the lessons learned:

- Did upper management continue to support the project to the end?

- Did the requirements phase go smoothly?

- Did all members of the team communicate effectively within the team and with other individuals and groups?

- Were there any problems associated with the mechanics of product procurement?

- Was operational support in place before users began using the system?

- Did the training properly prepare users to operate the system?

- Was the project completed on schedule and within budget?

- Do the users think that the system will enhance their performance?

- Does the implemented system perform as expected by the project team and the users?

For the *yes* responses, identify why that particular aspect of the project went well. If any answers to these questions are *no*, determine what went wrong and why. If you treat problems and successes as lessons, your future projects will go much more smoothly.

Case Study 8.5:
Installing a Wireless LAN
for WarehouseTrack

Debra, the project manager for the WarehouseTrack deployment, was ready to install the operational system at each of the nine warehouses. Debra called in Lindsey, the installation manager from her company, to plan the installation based on the design. Debra introduced Lindsey to Morris, the company's facility manager of all the warehouses. Morris would be the point of contact for Lindsey when needing to schedule the installations and gain access to certain parts of the facilities. Lindsey would need to plan around events, such as active periods and construction.

Before sending all the components out to each warehouse, Lindsey set up a staging area at the manufacturing company's headquarters facility, which is where the components had been delivered. During the staging process, the installation crew configured the components for each warehouse to ensure that all components were available and that they worked together properly. After testing each system, the installation crew packed the components destined for each warehouse in individual sets of boxes for shipment to their respective warehouses.

Three installers then traveled to each warehouse sequentially over a 10-week period to install the systems. Pete, the system tester on the project, went with them to perform quality assurance inspections after the installation took place at each warehouse. Brian, the business analyst on the project, also traveled to each location to provide training to the end-users. Meanwhile Evan, the system analyst on the project, delivered the operational support training to each of the support staff back in Atlanta.

The final two steps of the WarehouseTrack project are acceptance testing and transfer of the system to operational status. Debra and Linda, the warehouse manager, visited each site to observe the completion of acceptance testing by warehouse staff. After they completed this testing, Linda officially accepted the completion of this phase of the project for deploying the wireless system with receiving and inventory functions. Sophie, the project operations representative, then announced to all support staff that the WarehouseTrack system was operational, and the users began utilizing the system.

Appendices

A   Automatic Identification and Data Capture (AIDC)

B   Products, Companies, and Organizations

APPENDIX **A**

Automatic Identification and Data Capture (AIDC)

- The benefits of using bar codes
  A bar code system, a primary automatic identification and data capture (AIDC) implementation, is the leading application that uses wireless LANs. Learn about the architecture of a bar code system and how wireless bar code systems significantly increase the efficiency and accuracy within a company.

- Bar code applications
  Bar code applications add significant benefits to a wide variety of tasks within an organization. Such functions as receiving, inventory, shipping, and pricing benefit from wireless bar code systems.

- The concepts of bar code technology
  The main component of a bar code system is the bar code itself. A bar code system comprises different types of bar code symbologies, printers, and readers.

- Radio frequency identification (RF/ID)
  RF/ID, an alternative to using the traditional bar code, uses an electronic tag rather than a printed bar code. Learn how passive and active RF/ID tags operate and about the applications where RF/ID excels.

The Benefits of Using Bar Codes

Many companies and organizations within retail, transportation, manufacturing, government, and other markets are using bar code systems to increase and update records within the bar code system database.

Figure A.1 illustrates the architecture of a wireless bar code system. In most cases, the bar code system is an extension of a much larger corporate software package that the companies use to manage purchases, inventories, accounting, and so forth. The bar code system server houses a database that stores all information relevant to the bar code system. Periodically, new records from the corporate system are downloaded to the bar code system database, and updated records within the bar code system database are uploaded to the corporate system. This movement of data is normally accomplished once each day, generally during slack hours.

Each item has a bar code containing enough information about the item to distinguish it from others. Typically, the bar code represents a unique number (often referred to as a *license plate*) that is keyed to records in the database. In the case of a warehouse bar code system, this license plate is the *stock keeping unit* (SKU) number of an item.

As a minimum, the wireless bar code reader will have a bar code scanning function and radio network connectivity. In addition, the bar code reader may have other elements, such as display, keyboard, and printer, enabling the application to have a wider degree of functionality. Of course, as Chapter 6, "Wireless System Integration," explains, the wireless network and middleware interface the bar code reader to the system server and application software.

Note

For a complete case study that describes the planning, analysis, design, and installation of a wireless network that supports an automatic identification and data capture system, see Chapter 7, "Planning a Wireless LAN," and Chapter 8, "Implementing a Wireless LAN."

General Benefits of Bar Code Systems

Bar code systems provide significant increases in operational efficiency and accuracy. The following sections describe the general benefits derived from employing bar code systems.

Improved Operational Efficiency

Bar codes provide faster recording of information, enabling work to continue at a much faster rate than using manual tracking methods. The scanning of a bar code within a warehouse while performing an inventory will accurately record information about an item directly into a database within 1–2 seconds.

The alternative is to have a clerk spending 30 seconds on each item using manual methods, which generally includes reading the item identification located somewhere on the item, recording the information on a clipboard, and then later entering the data into a database. All in all, it is much faster to scan items on the spot and be done with it, rather than record the information on paper for later processing. The much higher efficiency of using bar codes will provide tremendous labor cost savings.

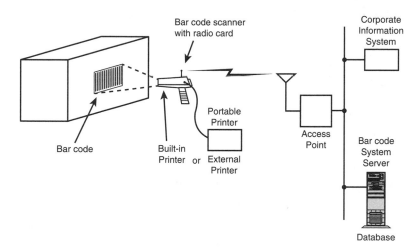

FIGURE A.1 *A wireless bar code system consists of bar-coded items, wireless bar code readers and printers, a wireless network, and an intermediate bar code system server that optionally interfaces with a larger accounting system.*

Accuracy

Bar codes are accurate because they eliminate manual data entry errors. Clerical and data entry errors are very common with manual data collection and identification methods. The data entry error rate for humans is approximately one error for every 300 characters entered.

Bar code scanners are much more accurate. The error rate for bar code scanning is much more tolerable—typically one error in 36 trillion characters, depending on the type of bar code. In some applications, such as those related to healthcare, errors cannot be tolerated. Inaccurate identification of a blood specimen, for example, can have disastrous effects. In most cases, however, inaccuracies lead to significant unpredictable costs that are related to problems, such as unhappy customers and overhead time spent tracking down problem-causing errors.

Compliance with Regulatory Requirements

Some regulatory agencies, and in some cases your customers, may impose requirements for labeling of items that you plan to distribute to them. Many large retailers demand that items you sell them must have a particular label, for example, containing a bar code and human-readable characters on the item's box for identification.

The benefit with compliance with these requirements is that you will be able to do business with the company.

Benefits of Wireless Systems

As discussed in Chapter 1, "Introduction to Wireless Networks," a wireless network has the following benefits over wired networks:

- Increased mobility
- Capability to install in areas that are difficult to wire
- Improved reliability
- Reduced installation time
- Long-term cost savings

Consider these benefits when implementing a bar code system to ensure that you receive the highest return on investment.

Most existing bar code systems incorporate appliances (for example, handheld bar code scanners) that are wired to a system (point-of-sale terminal, for example) or operate in a batch mode. Of course, the wired appliances limit the mobility of the system, and batch appliances require the user to periodically (typically each day) upload and download data between the appliance and a server containing data. In addition, batch appliances have limited capacity for storing application software and data. As a result, many companies are incorporating wireless bar code appliances and software into their systems to better serve applications that benefit from mobility and real-time transaction processing.

Bar Code Applications

The typical bar code system interfaces with larger corporate information systems that provide companywide functions such as receiving, warehouse management, inventory, accounting, and so on. The following sections define how bar code systems provide benefits of greater efficiency and accuracy throughout a company.

Receiving

Most companies, no matter what they do, have some sort of receiving function. As examples, manufacturers have a never-ending flow of incoming raw materials and components that will become parts of finished products; hospitals receive daily shipments of drugs for patients; and retail stores periodically obtain products to replenish empty shelves. A company must monitor incoming goods to update inventory databases and accounting records, alert the person ordering the item that the item has arrived, and initiate the payment for the received items.

A bar code system provides significant advantages over paper-based systems when performing receiving functions (see Figure A.2). As an item is taken off a truck, for example, receiving is performed as follows:

1. A warehouse clerk scans the item's bar code, containing information that identifies that item (for example, part number).

2. The bar code data is sent over the wireless network to a database, which marks the item as received and updates other applicable databases.

3. When the item is ready for put-away, a warehouse clerk scans the item's bar code.

4. The user inputs the dimensions of the item via the handheld appliance's keypad so that the warehouse management system can determine an optimum storage location based on the size of the item (a feature usually found on such systems).

5. After the system finds a location for the item, the appliance prints a label (through a handheld scanner/printer) that can be affixed to the item, indicating the location number and any other pertinent information.

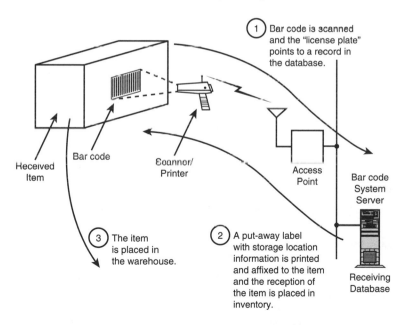

FIGURE A.2 *A wireless bar code system enables clerks to mark an item as received by simply scanning the bar code on the item.*

The use of a wireless appliance for this function, similar to other applications, increases the mobility of the users and enables them to perform the receiving and storage actions immediately when unloading the truck.

Cross Docking

Some organizations must transport, receive, store, and ship a large volume of items. Companies often set up distribution centers in geographical regions. A company will forecast the number of items to meet customer needs, manufacture the items, and then ship the items to distribution centers for stocking. If a retail store places an order, the distribution center will ship the items to the store. This process requires the distribution centers to maintain large warehouses for storing the items temporarily.

Managers of these companies highly value systems that reduce the need to store items in the warehouse, enabling them instead to ship the items directly to the customer. Cross docking is a wireless bar code system that pays off significantly (see Figure A.3). It works as follows:

1. As the warehouse receives an item from the manufacturer, a warehouse clerk scans the bar code on the item.

2. The bar code traverses the wireless network back to the warehouse management system, and determines whether a customer has placed an order for that item.

3. If yes, the warehouse management system responds with customer destination information (customer name, address, and so on).

4. The scanner/printer prints an applicable shipping label that is applied directly to the received item at the loading dock.

Cost savings with cross docking occur because a warehouse clerk loads the item on an outgoing truck instead of storing the item in the warehouse. This reduces warehouse costs and enables the customer to receive the item sooner.

Inventory Management

Periodically, companies must perform the laborious task of inventorying items they have in warehouses, equipment rooms, and store shelves. The timesavings and accuracy of using bar codes for inventory management is significant. Consider, for example, performing the task of inventorying items in a large department store containing hundreds of thousands of items. The use of paper and clipboard for this function is extremely inefficient.

Figure A.4 depicts an inventory application using bar codes. The inventory is much easier to perform if a store clerk can scan each item's bar code to record the identity and presence of the item. This makes the generation of inventory reports that indicate the number of items on hand and discrepancies much easier.

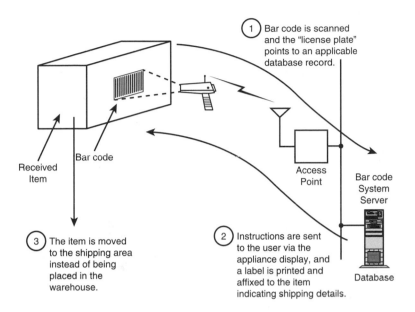

1 Bar code is scanned and the "license plate" points to an applicable database record.

Received Item

Bar code

Access Point

Bar code System Server

3 The item is moved to the shipping area instead of being placed in the warehouse.

2 Instructions are sent to the user via the appliance display, and a label is printed and affixed to the item indicating shipping details.

Database

FIGURE A.3 *With cross docking, a clerk scans the received item with a handheld scanner and printer and is informed to route the item to shipping rather than put the item away in the warehouse.*

If the bar code system didn't exist, the clerk would have to read the part number or stock number of the item and mark the item's presence on a clipboard. The manual process of using a clipboard is much more time-consuming and prone to errors than using a bar code system. Many companies can realize 200–300 percent timesavings when using bar code-based systems over manual paper-based systems when performing inventories.

Picking

Before shipping items from a warehouse to a customer, a warehouse clerk must locate and collect the item. This process is known as *picking*.

The use of a bar code system for picking considerably enhances the efficiency and accuracy of the picking operation (see Figure A.5). These benefits are evident because the wireless handheld data collector can guide the clerk (through instructions on the display) to the item's correct storage location, and enable the clerk to account for actually picking the item after scanning the bar code. This is much more effective than using paper and clipboard to record the information and later enter the data into the warehouse management system.

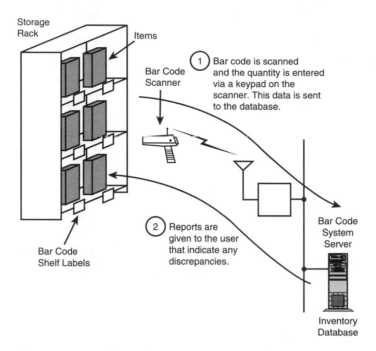

FIGURE A.4 *When performing an inventory, a clerk scans an item's bin bar code or shelf label, and then either scans each item within the bin or counts the items by hand to record the number of items present.*

Note

Some systems determine a pick list automatically based on electronic orders. Other systems require the user to enter the items to be picked via a keyboard or item scan sheet.

Shipping

Companies must account for items they ship from their facilities. Consider a retail distributor that ships 20,000 items each day to hundreds of customers located in all parts of the world, for example. This volume of shipments would be very difficult to perform if using paper-and-pencil–based processes, requiring clerks to write down product codes and serial numbers as the items are packed in trucks. The use of a bar code scanner, as shown in Figure A.6, makes the job much easier, enabling the clerk to record the shipment of the item by scanning the item's bar code.

After the clerk scans the bar code on the item, the system can generate and print a shipping label that complies with the requirements of the customer (specific locations and fonts for the shipping address, order number, and so on). The system can also identify route information for the carrier to use when loading specific delivery trucks.

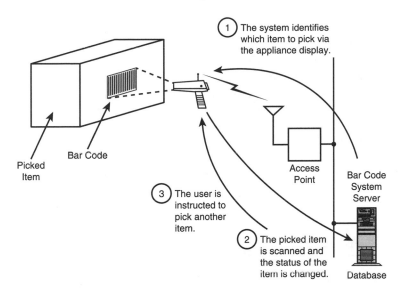

FIGURE A.5   *With picking, a pick list is prepared and the handheld scanner identifies which item to pick and its location in the warehouse.*

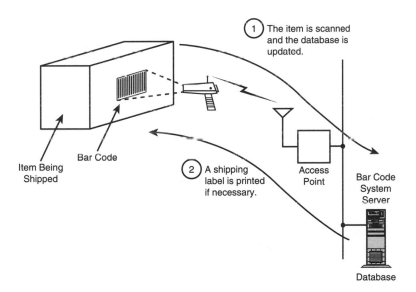

FIGURE A.6   *With shipping, the data the bar code represents is then sent to the database to indicate that the item has been shipped.*

Purchasing

As part of an inventory, a company generally determines the number of items to order to replenish stock. A car dealership, for example, as they count the items left in the parts warehouse, may find that some parts are below the ordering threshold. As a result, the person performing the inventory needs to indicate the number of items needed and process a purchase order.

The purchasing function is very efficient using a bar code system that is interfaced to accounting software because it can either automatically place an order if the inventory is too low or accept the number to order from the clerk via the handheld data collector (see Figure A.7).

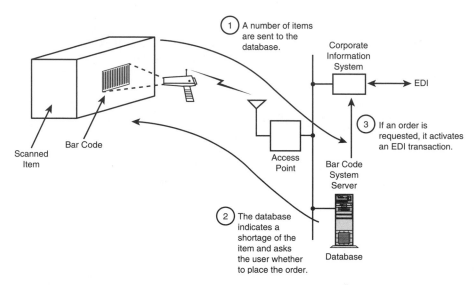

FIGURE A.7 *With purchasing, the clerk scans the item's bar code, and then enters the number of items to order. The accounting software can then either print out a paper purchase order or electronically order the item through Electronic Data Interchange (EDI).*

Electronic Data Interchange (EDI)

EDI is a series of standards providing electronic communication of business transactions, such as purchase orders, shipping documents, invoices, invoice payments, and confirmations between companies and organizations. The communication occurs between a company and its trading partner, which is typically a supplier or customer.

Special EDI software performs the transactions by translating flat files from corporate information systems into a standard format. A value-added network then transports the EDI transactions from company to company.

You can gain tremendous benefits by integrating a bar code system with EDI functions that a company supports. If the company receives all purchase orders via EDI, for example, the bar code system can have access to the purchase order data when verifying receipt of the item at the unloading dock. Or, the bar code system can initiate a purchase order to a specific company when inventory of an item falls below a threshold.

Asset Management

Assets within a company are nonexpendable physical items that have relatively high value. A company may want to maintain a specific record of the existence and location of certain assets, such as computers, test equipment, and portable x-ray machines.

Bar codes are a very effective method for tracking these types of assets. Figure A.8 characterizes an asset management system that uses bar codes.

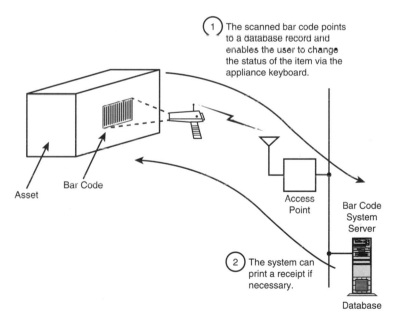

FIGURE A.8 *With asset management, the user scans an item requiring a change in status (for example, owner and location).*

Point-of-Sale (POS) Systems

Everyone is familiar with bar code-based point-of-sale systems. When you purchase something from a store, the cashier often uses a scanner to read the bar code on the item to locate the price in a database and add the price to the total bill. Most POS terminals use scanners that physically attach to the cash register via a cable.

Some POS applications, such as car rental returns and temporary terminals found in sidewalk sales and seasonal shops, utilize wireless networks to link the bar code scanner to the register. Figure A.9 illustrates a bar code-based POS system.

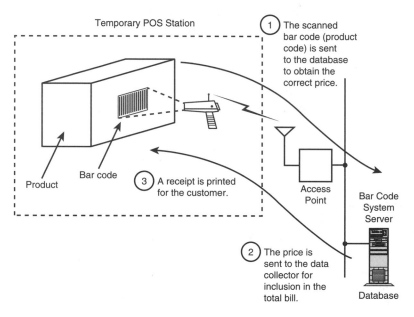

FIGURE A.9 *At the point of sale, the data represented by the bar code traverses the network to a database containing price data that the register uses to total the bill.*

Price Marking and Verification

As prices change, retail stores must print new price labels that are placed on each item and/or the shelf edge directly below the item. When the stock clerk scans the item's bar code, an attached printer immediately prints the new price label if the item has a new price. If the price hasn't changed, the handheld unit can provide some type of appropriate indication, such as a beep sound or a notice in the display. Figure A.10 shows the functions that take place when using a bar code system for pricing items.

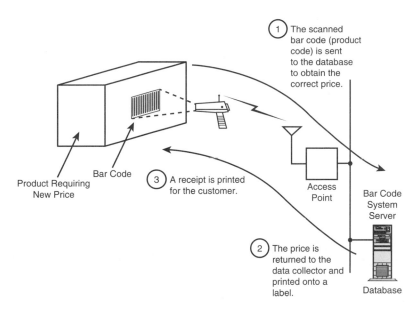

1. The scanned bar code (product code) is sent to the database to obtain the correct price.

2. The price is returned to the data collector and printed onto a label.

3. A receipt is printed for the customer.

Product Requiring New Price

Bar Code

Access Point

Bar Code System Server

Database

FIGURE A.10 *With price marking, a stock clerk scans an item's bar code, and the data represented by the bar code is used to determine the correct price from a database.*

Compliance Labeling

Many of the larger companies and organizations demand that their suppliers comply with a particular labeling format that enables standard layout for price information, bar code symbology and location, logos, and so on. The need to comply pushes suppliers to become familiar with the unique compliance format that each of their customers requires. A shoe manufacturer, for example, may have to label the shoebox with one format when selling to a particular sporting goods store, but use a different format when selling to a specific department store.

The scanning of the bar code enables the server database to point the printer to the correct printing format for the customer the item is intended for. Figure A.11 illustrates the operations of a bar code-based compliance system.

Analyzing the Need for a Bar Code System

Before implementing a bar code system, be sure to answer the following questions:

- *What business problem needs addressing?* Many companies overlook this question and move quickly with implementing a solution. These companies, however, end up with a solution that (at most) partially solves the problems. Be sure to spend some time and clearly understand the inefficiencies and inaccuracies you are facing before applying a particular solution. Time studies of your processes will provide a good basis to work from when developing a business case for implementing the solution.

continues

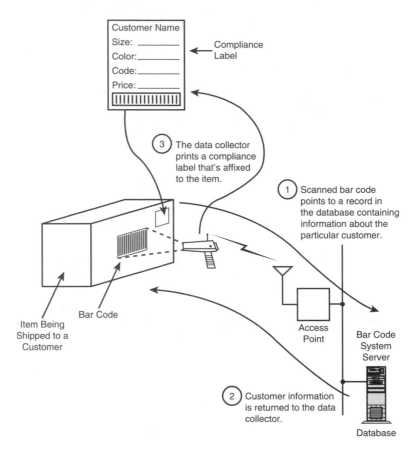

FIGURE A.11 *With compliance labeling, a bar code system enables suppliers to print the correct format for a particular customer by scanning the bar code of an item.*

- *How much money is the business problem costing you?* This will help you understand the payback you will need to realize from the solution.

- *What alternative solutions related to the business problem will improve efficiency?* Can you increase the accuracy of the data entry process, for example? If alternatives exist, be certain to compare them with a bar code solution.

- *Will the higher speed of data collection based on bar code scanners provide efficiencies that lead to significant cost savings?* Will the higher accuracy of data collection based on bar code scanners provide efficiencies that lead to significant cost savings? In other words, will a bar code-based system provide enough savings to make an implementation worthwhile?

- *Is the business problem spread over a large volume of transactions?* Include the magnitude of transactions when calculating cost savings and designing the system. Generally, the higher the transaction volume, the greater the cost savings will be.

- *Do bar codes exist on the items you currently process?* If the items already have bar codes, it will be much easier to implement a bar code system. If not, you will need to apply bar code labels to the items. The printing and application of bar codes will require additional labor, hardware, and printing supplies to the project; therefore, be sure to consider these expenses when preparing the business case.

- *Will a real-time transfer of information of the scanned item into a database provide significant benefits?* If yes, you should certainly consider the use of wireless scanners rather than batch devices. Of course, the use of wireless scanners will add costs associated with the wireless components, such as radio cards, access points, and installation labor.

The Concepts of Bar Code Technology

The bar code is the most popular method for identifying people, places, and things. In general, bar codes have a pattern of bars and spaces of varying widths representing information—such as numbers, letters, and punctuation—that convey information (for example, part number and name) about a particular item.

Many bar code *symbologies* define particular arrangements of bars and spaces to represent different information. A bar code reader scans the bars and translates the patterns into data that is sent to a database. Bar codes have the following common elements (as illustrated in Figure A.12):

- *Start code and stop code:* Special start and stop characters enable the reader to determine the length of the bar code and read it forward or backward.

- *Checksum:* Some bar codes include a checksum character prior to the stop character. The checksum increases accuracy by enabling the reader to verify that the scanned bar code is valid.

- *Encoded data:* This is the main data the bar code represents. The characters of data depend on the type of bar code symbology.

- *Human readable text:* In most cases, bar code label formats include a human-readable form of the encoded data directly below the bar code, along with other human-readable elements (for example, price, quantity, and shipping address) that may or may not have anything to do with the bar code itself. This enables humans to identify information about the item without using a bar code reader.

- *Quiet zone:* All bar codes have quiet zones:clear areas free of marks before and after the series of bars and spaces. Scanners use the quiet zones to establish color and reflectance values as a basis for reading the bars and spaces.

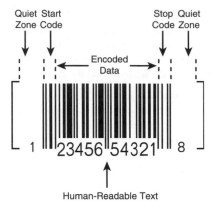

Quiet Start
Zone Code

Stop Quiet
Code Zone

Encoded
Data

1 23456 54321 8

Human-Readable Text

FIGURE A.12 *A bar code is a structured pattern of bars and spaces that represents a character string. This bar code is based on the UPC symbology.*

One-Dimensional Symbologies

A one-dimensional bar code (also referred to as a *linear bar code*) is the most common type of bar code. The main concept of a linear bar code is to store just enough information about the bar coded item to differentiate it from other items. A one-dimensional symbology is read across the x-axis of the printed bar code (refer to Figure A.12). As mentioned earlier, the contents of a linear bar code are often referred to as a *license plate*.

The following explains many of the popular one-dimensional bar codes:

- *Codabar:* The Codabar symbology, developed in 1972, is used in air parcel express, libraries, and blood bank applications. Codabar enables the encoding of strings of up to 16 digits having any combination of numeric digits (0 through 9) and special nonalphabetic characters ("+," "-," "$," "/," ":," and "."). Codabar has four possible start/stop code choices, which are the letters *A*, *B*, *C*, and *D*. The chosen start/stop code must be present at the beginning and ending of each Codabar string.

- *Code 128:* Code 128 can encode all 128 ASCII characters, making it a preferred symbology for many bar code applications.

- *Code 3 of 9:* Code 3 of 9, referred to as *Code 39* (pronounced *thirty-nine*), is one of the most widely used symbologies, used mainly by the Department of Defense and by the automotive industry. Code 39 can encode messages using capitalized letters, numbers *0* through *9*, and seven special characters. The main drawback of Code 39 is that it takes up a lot of label space, causing problems if encoding a great deal of information. An extended version of Code 39 can encode the full 128-code ASCII character set.

- *Code 93:* Code 93, like Code 128, encodes the full set of ASCII characters and is used in data collection processes. The overhead characters in Code 93, like

Code 128, include the start, the stop, and the check characters. Code 93 also includes the optional shifting characters.

- *EAN 13:* EAN 13 is a superset international version of the UPC symbology. It contains one digit more than the UPC, requiring a total of 13 printed characters. The format of EAN-13 includes a country code, manufacturer ID, manufacturer-assigned item code, check digit, and European article numbering code.

Tip

Bar code readers programmed to read the EAN symbology can normally read the UPC symbology automatically.

- *EAN 8:* EAN 8 is a shortened version of EAN-13 and consists of eight characters. EAN 8 has a country code, abbreviated manufacturer ID and item code, and check digit.

- *Interleaved 2 of 5:* Interleaved 2 of 5 (commonly called *I2of5*) is mainly used in distribution applications, and is a numeric symbology, creating a highly compressed string of digits for applications with limited space for bar code placement. It must contain an even number of digits. Each character is constructed with five bars. There can be an optional check character.

- *Postal:* The Postal symbology (also referred to as POSTNET) is used for postal service processing. Postal encodes strings of numbers (for example, zip codes) into a bar code that is usually placed on the bottom right of letters and mailing labels.

- *UPC A:* The *Universal Product Code* (UPC) symbology is very common in point-of-sale systems for consumer goods throughout the grocery industry. The UPC-A format encodes a 12-digit (numeric only) string. Typically, the Uniform Code Council (UCC) assigns a portion of the string for the particular item, and the user (for example, the product vendor) assigns the remaining portion.

- *UPC E:* The UPC E symbology, encoding only six numeric digits, is a shortened version of UPC. Many retailers use UPC E for items too small for regular UPC A bar codes.

Assigning UPC Numbers

If you have a new product requiring a UPC number that you plan to distribute, you must assign a UPC number to the product. You need to first obtain a manufacturer's ID number that uniquely identifies your company. The Uniform Code Council (UCC) in Dayton, Ohio, manages the issuance of these numbers.

The manufacturer's ID number accounts for five digits of the UPC code, leaving five digits to assign in any way. As you distribute the product, you need to provide the retail outlets with a list of the UPC codes for your products so that they can enter them into their cash register systems.

Two-Dimensional Symbologies

A two-dimensional symbology (also called a *matrix code*) can store considerably more information than a standard, one-dimensional symbology. Figure A.13 illustrates an example of a two-dimensional bar code. A bar code based on a two-dimensional symbology acts like a mini-database that is printed and affixed to the item.

A two-dimensional bar code symbology requires special readers that use sophisticated laser scanning or CCD camera technologies, costing more than a standard linear bar code scanner. The storage capacity of a two-dimensional bar code symbology depends on a number of factors, but they can generally store approximately 2,000 to 3,000 characters at a density of up to 2,300 characters per square inch.

FIGURE A.13 *A two-dimensional symbology is read across both the x- and y-axis of the printed bar code. This bar code is based on the PDF 417 symbology.*

Two-dimensional symbologies benefit applications for which data must travel with the bar-coded item and for which a host or server database is not available for quick lookup of information related to the item. Consider cargo that must be sent via trucks and airplanes to reach its final destination, for example. Instead of affixing a printed manifest to the items, a two-dimensional bar code can contain the information and be accessible electronically from a bar code reader. The PDF-417 two-dimensional symbology, for instance, is used for labeling hazardous materials, storing technical specifications, and encoding fingerprints and photographs on the backs of drivers' licenses.

The following explains the popular two-dimensional bar codes:

- *PDF-417:* The PDF-417 symbology can store up to approximately 3,000 printable ASCII characters. The shape of the symbol is rectangular, and the height can expand to hold larger amounts of data. PDF-417 also enables the linking of multiple symbols to theoretically store an unlimited amount of data.

- *DataMatrix:* DataMatrix can store up to 2,000 characters. The symbol is square and can range from 0.001 inch per side up to 14 inches per side. DataMatrix is used to encode product and serial number information on electrical rating plates, eyeglass lenses, medical instruments, circuit boards, and other items during manufacturing. Like PDF-417, DataMatrix requires a two-dimensional scanner for reading the bar code.

Selecting a Bar Code Symbology

If implementing a bar code system, you need to decide which bar code symbology to use. One of the first questions to ask is whether your codes must conform to any industry standards. If you are implementing a bar code system for a grocery store, for example, the system must be compatible with UPC bar codes. If your organization is shipping containers to the U.S. Government, then you will probably need to utilize Code 39.

For strictly internal operations, you can choose any one of the bar code symbologies. If this is the case, you should consider whether you just need to provide a *license plate* for each item (if so, use a one-dimensional bar code) or store a lot of data within the bar code on the item (if so, use a two-dimensional bar code).

For one-dimensional bar code implementations, also question whether you need to encode numeric data only (if so, consider Interleaved 2 of 5) or alphanumeric characters (if so, consider Code 39 or Code 128). Before making a decision for use of a particular bar code, be certain to first review the full specification of the bar codes under consideration.

Troubleshooting Tip

In some situations, if you send an item to a customer, and he can't read the bar code, that customer may return the item to you and ask for a credit. Under the wear and tear of a warehouse, the bar codes may become damaged. Therefore, you should use a bar code verifier to be certain that the bar codes you use meet specific standards. Verifiers grade the bar code so that you have an opportunity to replace the bar code before shipping the item to a customer.

Bar Code Printing

Most coding of items is done by printing the bar code on a label and affixing it to the item. In some cases, such as consumer goods, the manufacturer prints the bar code as part of the design of the container. Look at the bar code on a box of cereal, for example; you will see that the bar code is printed directly on the box.

If the bar code system you are implementing requires the printing of bar codes to mark the items, you can either purchase the printers and create the bar code labels yourself, or you can contract with a company to print the bar codes for you. It is often cost-effective to use contract printing services when printing sequentially numbered bar codes for items. If the item's information changes frequently or requires the inclusion of item-specific information (for example, pricing), however, you should consider printing the labels yourself.

Selecting a Bar Code Printer

Several types of bar code printers, from high-speed tabletop units to handheld printers that print smaller labels, are available from a multitude of vendors. Most of the tabletop printers use replaceable ink ribbons; whereas, the handheld ones use ribbonless thermal printing technologies.

continues

Tabletop printers are suitable for high-volume, large-format labeling (which are often necessary for shipping applications). If needing to label items on the spot (for example, price marking), you should certainly consider a handheld bar code printer.

Be aware, however, that the labels of handheld printers, which are generally printed using thermal transfer, will not last as long as those printed from the tabletop or portable printer using printing ribbons. Sunlight can shorten the life of thermally printed labels to just a few months.

With a wireless bar code system, a great deal of the printing (if necessary) can be done during mobile operations. There are two viable approaches for printing bar codes in a mobile wireless network. The following sections describe these approaches.

Two-Piece Scanning and Printing System

One approach involves a separate scanner and printer. With a two-piece mobile scanning and printing system, the scanner communicates with an external portable printer via a cable or short-range wireless interface.

The following defines the implications of using the two-piece scanning/printing approach:

- Does not support scan, print, and apply applications.

- The external printer must be worn by the user or set within the cable's reach of the scanner. This may hamper the mobility of the user in some situations.

- Need to support the charging of two potentially different batteries (one for the scanner and one for the printer).

- The cable between the scanner and the printer is prone to breakage, increasing support costs and downtime. This assumes the connection between the scanner and the printer doesn't use a wireless IrDA or short-range radio frequency interface.

  The cost associated with cable breakage with these units is significant. The industry average for cable replacement is two cables per scanner per year.

- Only need to purchase the wearable printer assuming existing bar code scanners are available to interface with the printers.

One-Piece Scanning and Printing System

The other approach to printing bar codes in a wireless bar code system involves the use of an appliance that integrates both scanning and printing. With a one-piece mobile scanning and printing appliance, there is no need to communicate with an external printer.

The following defines the implications of using the one-piece scanning/printing approach:

- Strongly supports scan, print, and apply applications

- Less expensive than purchasing a separate scanner and printer for the two-piece mobile printing approach

- Only need to support a single battery for both scanning and printing

- No cable to support, eliminating costs related to replacing broken cables

- May not be cost-effective for situations that don't require printing

Bar Code Readers

Many types of bar code readers come in various sizes, shapes, and levels of functionality. In most cases, bar code readers are just scanners having the capability to only read and interpret bar codes. Scanners that also incorporate keypads, displays, and printing functions are normally referred to as *data collectors*.

The majority of bar code readers on the market utilize infrared light to scan the bar code. The scanner emits pulses of light that hit the bar code and reflect back into the scanner. The bar code bars (dark areas) absorb the light, which the scanner interprets as a logic 1. The spacing between the bars (lighter areas) reflect the light, which the scanner interprets as a logic 0. Thus, scanning the bar code generates a string of 1s and 0s, representing the encoded characters.

To operate correctly, the scanner must shoot a straight line across the bars and spaces; therefore, the taller the bars, the easier it is to aim and scan the bar code (providing a better chance of obtaining a good reading). The scanner's software or firmware translates or decodes the encoded string into characters that the system application software and database will understand.

The light source of a scanner is one way of differentiating between scanner types. Most light sources are *light emitting diodes* (LEDs) or laser. The light from an LED diffuses quickly as it moves away from the LED source. Some scanners use helium-neon lasers or solid-state laser diodes to produce light that maintains a sharp shape over longer distances.

A small fraction of scanners utilize *charge-couple devices* (CCD), operating as a video camera that photographically "sees" the whole bar code symbol simultaneously. Neither the LED nor laser operates very well in bright sunlight. The CCD scanner is generally used to read two-dimensional bar codes and works well even in brightly lit areas.

The following list describes the different types of scanners:

- *Wand laser scanner:* Wand scanners (sometimes referred to as light pens) are very low-cost scanners (list prices from $100 to $200). With these devices, the user touches the tip of the wand to the bar code and manually swipes the wand across the bar code. Wand scanners utilize very little power, enabling them to be small and compact.

A disadvantage, however, is that it often requires several bar code swipes to obtain a successful scan. This can be very inefficient if needing to scan many items. Be sure to utilize wands only with high-quality bar codes on flat surfaces.

- *Handheld laser scanner:* The near-contact handheld laser scanner, seen often in retail stores, provides an efficient method of reading bar codes on a variety of items. Most of these scanners offer an aiming beam, making it easy to scan the bar code in most lighting. Near-contact laser handhelds are moderately priced (list prices from $500 to $750) and can operate up to a few inches from the bar code, making them ideal for point-of-sale applications.

  Non-contact laser scanners can read bar codes from near contact to up to three feet away. These devices are more expensive (list prices from $700 to $1,300), but they are more efficient for some applications, such as in-store inventory management. The non-contact laser scanners (in comparison to wand scanners) are more effective at reading bar codes on curved and irregular surfaces.

- *Long-range handheld laser scanners:* Long-range laser scanners can read bar codes of lower density from 6 to 35 feet away. They use special aiming mechanisms for pointing the scanner at the bar code. Most long-range scanners are found in warehouse applications, and are used for reading shelf and item tags on high racks. These specialty scanners have list prices from $1,200 to $1,700.

- *Pass-through omnidirectional scanners:* Pass-through scanners, often found in supermarkets, enable the user to pass items quickly through a scan field with little or no orientation. Items must be small enough to fit within the scan field. These scanners are the most expensive of the laser scanners, with list prices from $1,400 to $2,500.

- *CCD scanners:* CCD scanners offer a solution to scanning two-dimensional bar codes. Near-contact CCD (charge-couple device) scanners have a row of LEDs providing a light source. The CCD is similar to a camera that photographs the bar code. The LEDs light up the bar code, and the light reflects off the bar code and back into the scanner, hitting an array of photo sensors. CCD scanners are relatively low-cost devices (list prices from $400 to $600).

  Some CCD scanners have difficulty with scanning bar codes on highly curved or irregular surfaces. Non-contact CCD scanners have typical ranges that span from contact to about six inches, with prices slightly higher than the near-contact models (list prices from $600 to $800).

- *Unattended scanners:* Unattended scanners are very effective in automated or conveyor applications in manufacturing and warehouse centers. There are a variety of these types of scanners, ranging widely in throughput, bar code orientation, and cost. Prices range from as low as $800 to many thousands of dollars for the highest-performance scanners.

- *Wearable scanners:* Some vendors offer a form of bar code reader (typically laser scanners) that is worn on the body to keep your hands free for other tasks. Some of these devices embed the scanner into a ring-like device and others enable the scanner to be worn on the back of the hand. The prices for these devices range widely.

Choosing the Right Bar Code Scanner for Your Application

Before choosing a bar code scanner, be sure to fully understand the application you are implementing and the system the scanner needs to interface with. The following are some questions that will help you to gather data required when making a decision on which scanner to choose:

- *Does the item already have a bar code?* If not, you should consider using an integrated scanner/printing device to enable printing of labels as part of the application.

- *What type of item will be scanned?* If the item is flat and the scanning frequency will be low, a wand scanner may be best. If the item is irregular in shape, you should consider using a non-contact handheld scanner.

- *What is the bar code symbology?* For most one-dimensional bar codes, utilize an LED or laser scanner. If the bar code is two-dimensional, use a CCD scanner.

- *What is the distance between the scanner and the bar code?* Carefully consider this question because the answer will directly impact the price of the scanners. If you really need to scan from great distances (for example, in warehouses), then you will need a relatively expensive long-range laser scanner.

- *How often within a given time period will items need scanning?* The answer to this question will help determine the performance requirements of the scanner and number of scanners.

- *What are the ergonomic considerations?* Will users have both hands free for operating the scanner and printing functions (if necessary)? How much space is available to operate the scanner? Answers to questions such as these will help when selecting the form factor of the scanner.

- *Will scanning be done unattended?* If yes, you need to investigate the many types of unattended scanners. As part of this, first determine how the bar code will be oriented, where it will be placed, and how quickly the bar-coded items will automatically pass by the scanner?

- *What are the environmental factors where the scanner will be operated?* What is the minimum, average, and maximum temperature and humidity in the operating area? Does the scanner require any special ruggedness? How bright is the ambient light in the operating area? These questions point to special performance requirements.

Radio Frequency Identification (RF/ID)

As an alternative to using bar codes, the use of radio frequency identification (RF/ID) may better satisfy requirements, especially when there is a need for storing larger amounts of data on the item or when the data needing storage at the item changes frequently. Figure A.14 illustrates the architecture of an RF/ID-based system. The main difference between RF/ID and bar code systems involves the method in which data is stored on the item: Instead of a printed bar code, data is stored electronically inside the RF/ID tag's memory cell.

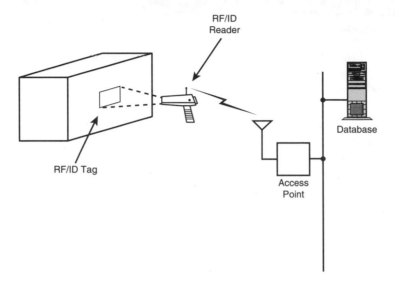

FIGURE A.14 *RF/ID technology uses low-power radio signals to read data stored in a small radio transponder (often called an RF/ID tag) that is affixed to the item being tracked.*

RF/ID Benefits

RF/ID–based systems provide the same efficiency and accuracy benefits of traditional bar code systems; however, RF/ID offers the following additional benefits in addition to larger storage capacity:

- *RF/ID is not limited to contact or line-of-sight operations.* RF/ID tags can be read through nonmetallic materials and do not have to be in direct contact with the tag, making RF/ID ideal for dirty, wet, or harsh environments. Unlike bar codes, RF/ID readers will read tags through mud, dirt, paint, grease, wood, cement, plastic, water, and steam. The RF/ID reader can distinguish among items based on a unique identification number for each item.

- *RF/ID tags are secure.* This is true because RF/ID tags are virtually impossible to counterfeit. An unalterable permanent serial code prevents tampering.

- *RF/ID tags are read at a faster speed.* The time it takes for an RF/ID reader to activate the tag and receive the associated information stored in the tag is approximately 40 percent faster than with traditional printed bar codes.

- *Tags can be hidden (embedded) in most materials.* This improves the aesthetics of the item being marked.

RF/ID will not fit every application, however, mainly because tags cost considerably more than printed bar codes. Consider the previously discussed benefits, and compare an RF/ID system versus a bar code system as part of the system design.

RF/ID Components

The key component of an RF/ID system is the RF/ID tag, consisting of a coil antenna, an integrated circuit, and possibly a battery. The following list describes the two main types of tags:

- *Passive RF/ID tag*: Passive tags don't use any batteries, are low cost, and have long lifetimes; however, they operate over short ranges (less than three feet). Passive tags can be attached to or embedded in almost anything, such as clothing, animals, and railroad cars.

  A passive tag includes an electronic circuit (transponder) and tuned antenna-capacitor circuit, enabling the tag to operate as a very small radio transceiver. In a passive RF/ID system, the reader will emit a radio frequency magnetic field that powers up the RF/ID tag when the user triggers the RF/ID reader to scan. The tag then responds by transmitting the contents of the tag to the reader, which then converts the received signal into a digital signal that can be recognized by a computer.

- *Active RF/ID tag:* Active tags operate similarly to a passive tag, except active tags include a battery. The tag's local power source enables the RF/ID reader to operate using less power over longer ranges, but the active tags are more expensive and have a limited life expectancy.

Both passive and active RF/ID tags are available in the following forms:

- *Read-write tags:* These tags can store data that can be modified during normal operation.

- *Write-once, read-many (WORM) tags:* These tags can store data that can't be modified.

- *Read-only tags:* These tags contain data programmed permanently using a special factory process.

The read-write tags are the most expensive ones. The read-only tags are least expensive and offer excellent security because someone can't alter the data stored in the tag. These tags also come in a wide range of available memories, from simple 1-bit storage tags (mainly used with security systems) to tags that can store up to 128 kilobits of information.

RF/ID Transmission Parameters

RF/ID systems utilize frequencies and modulation that are much different than IEEE 802.11 wireless networks. As a result, RF/ID systems and 802.11-compliant networks are not compatible. These two types of wireless networks, however, serve different purposes. RF/ID is meant to read the tag from a relatively short distance, and an 802.11 LAN provides a wireless delivery system that interfaces RF/ID readers to servers that contain application software and databases.

Most RF/ID systems for data collection operate at low frequencies, typically 125KHz and 13.56MHz. These low-frequency systems generally utilize passive tags, making them suitable for applications such as animal identification, inventory control, and asset tracking. The reading range of low-frequency systems is generally less than 15 feet.

Because of the lower frequencies, only one channel is available. Therefore, a disadvantage of the low-frequency RF/ID systems is the readers must be spaced well apart from each other and noise sources to avoid interference. In addition, low-frequency tags cannot be placed directly on metal objects because metal disturbs the operation of the tag.

Higher-frequency RF/ID systems operate in the following frequency ranges: 850 to 950MHz and 2.4 to 5GHz. This enables operation over longer range and higher scan rates, enabling their use in applications such as railroad car monitoring and toll road meters. The higher-frequency systems operate in line-of-site mode and cost more than lower-frequency ones.

Note

There are no globally accepted standards for how RF/ID systems should operate; therefore, be careful to choose compatible components when implementing an RF/ID system. In most cases, you will need to purchase the RF/ID reader and tags from the same component vendor.

RF/ID Applications

Because of the special benefits of utilizing RF/ID-based components, RF/ID lends itself well to applications that require relatively large amounts of storage that can be changed easily. The following describes applications that realize strong benefits through the use of RF/ID:

- *Railcar container identification:* Rail companies benefit from the use of RF/ID by placing RF/ID tags on railroad cars for identification. This enables RF/ID readers, located at train stations and other strategic points along the track, to monitor the location of the items on the car as the train moves past sensors at full speed. RF/ID also enables train stations to read the identity of railcars for sorting the cars for reconstitution into different trains at marshalling yards.

- *Animal identification:* Some farmers utilize RF/ID to identify and track their animals, such as cattle. The RF/ID tag can be embedded under the animal's skin or attached to its ear. Such information as owner, birth date, and medical records can be stored in the tag and used to verify status of the animal.

- *Toll road control:* The use of RF/ID can electronically identify vehicles passing through a toll station and debit the driver's account automatically. A read-write RF/ID tag is placed in the automobile and stores the number of tolls that the driver has paid for. As the driver passes the tollbooth, an RF/ID reader activates the tag and decrements the number stored in the tag.

The use of bar codes increases efficiency and accuracy of many organizational functions. Wireless networks enhance these benefits by providing a greater degree of mobility and real-time access to data. Be sure, however, to thoroughly analyze your business problems, requirements, and alternatives to bar code technology before implementing a system.

APPENDIX B

Products, Companies, and Organizations

- **Wireless network product suppliers and system integrators**
  As part of a wireless network implementation, you will certainly need to decide which products to use and possibly outsource the implementation. This listing of suppliers of wireless networking products is a handy reference for companies to contact for information about their latest products. The listing also includes system integrators you can consider for bidding on your wireless system project.

- **Organizations and industry groups**
  A list of standards organizations, working groups, and forums provides a means to learn more about wireless networks and to become active in industry events.

Wireless Network Product Suppliers and System Integrators

The following table identifies companies you can contact when evaluating wireless network components or searching for a system integrator that specializes in wireless network implementations. It is followed by an alphabetic list of the companies and their contact information.

Product/Service	Company
Wireless LANs	AeroComm Wireless
	Aironet, Inc.
	Breezecom, Inc.
	Digital Wireless Corp.
	Fourene Systems
	IBM Wireless
	Intermec Corp.

continues

continued

Product/Service	Company
Wireless LANs (cont.)	Lucent Technologies
	Monarch Marking Systems
	Norand Corp.
	Proxim, Inc.
	Raytheon Wireless Solutions
	Solectek Corp.
	Spectrix Corporation
	Symbol Technologies, Inc.
	Telxon Corporation
	Windata Corp.
	Wireless Inc.
	XIRCOM
Wireless point-to-point networks	Cylink
	Direct Network Services
	Laser Communications, Inc.
	MCOM Network Systems
	Multipoint Networks
	Persoft Inc.
	Southwest Microwave Inc.
	Wave Wireless Networking
Wireless WANs	Ameritech Cellular Services
	ARDIS
	AT&T Wireless Services
	Ericsson
	GTE Mobilenet
	Meteor Communications Corporation
	Metricom Inc.
Connectivity software	CIM Concepts
	Connect, Inc.
	Nettech Systems Inc.
Wireless system integration	Compsee
	General Data Corporation
	Intermec Corp.
	Monarch Marking Systems
	Netcom International
	Sidney Mircrosystems
	Sierra Wireless
	Softechnics
	Symbol Technologies, Inc.
	Telxon Corporation
	Wireless Network Consulting

AeroComm Wireless
13228 W. 99th St.
Lenexa, KS 66215

Tel: 800-492-2320, 913-492-2320
FAX: 913-492-1243

Aironet, Inc.
3875 Embassy Parkway
P.O. Box 5292
Akron, OH 44334

Tel: 800-3-WIRELESS, 330-664-7929
FAX: 330-664-7990

Ameritech Cellular Services
2000 W. Ameritech Center Dr.
Hoffman Estates, IL 60195

Tel: 800-MOBILE-1
Wireless data questions: 800-669-4730
FAX: 847-765-9292

ARDIS
300 Knightsbridge Parkway
Lincolnshire, IL 60069

Tel: 847-478-4200
FAX: 847-478-4810

AT&T Wireless Services
Wireless Data Division
10230 NE Points Dr.
Kirkland, WA 98004

Tel: 800-IMAGINE

Breezecom, Inc.
2195 Faraday Ave., Suite A
Carlsbad, CA 92008

Tel: 760-431-9880
FAX: 760-431-2595
Internet: http://www.breezecom.com

CIM Concepts
2 South University Drive, Suite 260
Plantation, FL 33324

Tel: 954-472-7009
FAX: 954-424-9060

Compsee
2500 Port Malabar Blvd, N.E.
Palm Bay, FL 32905

Tel: 407-724-4321
FAX: 407-723-2895

Connect, Inc.
5400 Patton Drive, Suite 300
Lisle, IL 60532

Tel: 630-963-8800
FAX: 630-963-8919

Cylink
P.O. Box 3759
Sunnyvale, CA 94086-3759

Tel: 800-533-3958, 408-735-5800
FAX: 408-735-6643
FAX on demand: 408-735-6614

Digital Wireless Corp.
One Meca Way
Norcross, GA 30093

Tel: 770-564-5540
FAX: 770-564-5541

Direct Network Services
20 Central Ave.
Ayer, MA 01432

Tel: 978-772-9978
FAX: 978-772-9984

Ericsson
1 Triangle Dr.
P.O. Box 13969
Research Triangle Park, NC 27709

Tel: 919-472-7000
FAX: 919-472-6102

Fourene Systems
3375 Scott Blvd. Suite 102
Santa Clara, CA 95054

Tel: 408-565-9100
FAX: 408-565-9130

General Data Corporation
4354 Ferguson Drive
Cincinnati, OH 45245

Tel: 800-733-5252, 513-752-7978
FAX: 513-752-6947

GTE Mobilenet
245 Perimeter Center Parkway
Atlanta, GA 30346

Tel: 770-391-8000
FAX: 770-391-8182

IBM Wireless
700 Park Office Rd., Hwy. 54
Building 662
Research Triangle Park, NC 27709

Tel: 919-543-7708, 919-543-5221 (IBM information)
FAX: 919-543-5568

Intermec Corp.
6001 36th Ave. West
Everett, WA 98203

Tel: 800-347-2636, 425-348-2600
FAX: 425-348-2833

Intermec Technologies Corp.
550 Second St. SE
Cedar Rapids, IA 52401

Tel: 800-553-5971, 319-369-3100
FAX: 319-369-3453

Laser Communications, Inc.
1848 Charter Lane, Suite F
P.O. Box 10066
Lancaster, PA 17605-0066

Tel: 800-527-3740, 717-394-8634
FAX: 717-396-9831

Lucent Technologies
111 Madison Ave.
Morristown, NJ 07960

Tel: 800-ATT-WAVE, 800-242-2121 (Lucent information)

MCFCannon
15 Essex St.
Paramus, NJ 07652

Tel: 800-368-5383

Meteor Communications Corporation
8631 S. 212th St.
Kent, WA 98031-1910

Tel: 253-872-2521
FAX: 253-872-7662

Metricom Inc.
980 University Avenue
Los Gatos, CA 95032-2375

Tel: 800-556-6123, 408-399-8200
FAX: 408-399-8321

Monarch Marking Systems
170 Monarch Lane
Miamisburg, OH 45342

Tel: 800-543-6650
FAX: 937-865-6605

Netcom International
3675 Kennesaw North Industrial Parkway
Kennesaw, GA 30144

Tel: 770-919-0048
FAX: 770-919-0277

Nettech Systems Inc.
600 Alexander Rd.
Princeton, NJ 08540

Tel: 609-734-0300
FAX: 609-734-0346

Persoft Inc.
465 Science Drive
Madison, WI 53711

Tel: 800-368-5283, 608-273-6000
FAX: 608-273-8227

Proxim, Inc.
295 North Bernardo Ave.
Mountain View, CA 94043

Tel: 800-229-1630, 650-960-1630
FAX: 650-960-1984

Raytheon Wireless Solutions
362 Lowell St.
Andover, MA 01810

Tel: 978-470-9011
FAX: 978-470-9452

Sidney Microsystems
1089 Fairington Drive
Sidney, OH 45365

Tel: 937-498-7080
FAX: 937-498-2180

Sierra Wireless
Street 150, 13575
Commerce Parkway
Richmond, BC CANADA V6V2Z1

Tel: 604-231-1100
FAX: 604-231-1109

Softechnics
Commonwealth Square
308 N. Cleveland-Massillon Rd.
Akron, OH 44333

Tel: 330-665-1698
FAX: 330-665-2915

Solectek Corp.
6370 Nancy Ridge Drive, 109
San Diego, CA 92121

Tel: 800-437-1518, 619-450-1220
FAX: 619-457-2681

Southwest Microwave Inc.
2922 S. Roosevelt Street
Tempe, AZ 85282

Tel: 602-968-5995
FAX: 602-894-1731

Spectrix Corporation
106 Wilmot Rd., Suite 250
Deerfield, IL 60015-5150

Tel: 847-317-1770
FAX: 847-317-1517

Symbol Technologies, Inc.
One Symbol Plaza
Holtsville, NY 11742-1300

Tel: 800-SCAN-234, 516-738-2400
FAX: 516-738-5990

Telxon Corporation
3330 W. Market St.
P.O. Box 5582
Akron, OH 44334-0582

Tel: 800-800-8008, 330-867-3700
FAX: 330-873-2099

Wave Wireless Networking
1748 Independence Blvd. E-1
Sarasota, FL 34234-2152

Tel: 941-358-9283
FAX: 941-355-0219

Wireless Inc.
19 Davis Dr.
Belmont, CA 94002-3001

Tel: 650-595-3300
FAX: 650-595-4907

Wireless Network Consulting
685 North Enon Road
Yellow Springs, OH 45387

Tel: 937-767-2180

XIRCOM

2300 Corporate Center Dr.
Thousand Oaks, CA 91320-1420

Sales: 800-438-4526
Tel: 805-376-9300
FAX: 805-376-9311

Organizations and Industry Groups

American National Standards Institute (ANSI)

The American National Standards Institute (ANSI) is a privately funded federation of leaders representing both the private and public sectors with the job of coordinating the U.S. voluntary consensus standards system. ANSI was organized in 1918 and is made up of manufacturing and service businesses, professional societies and trade associations, standards developers, academic institutions, government agencies, and consumer and labor interests, all working together to develop voluntary national consensus standards.

ANSI provides U.S. participation in the international standards community as the sole U.S. representative to the two major nontreaty international standards organizations: The International Organization for Standardization (ISO) and, through the U.S. National Committee, the International Electrotechnical Commission (IEC).

Contact Information:

American National Standards Institute
11 West 42nd Street
New York, NY 10036

Tel: 212-642-4948
FAX: 212-398-0023

Automatic Identification Manufacturers (AIM)

AIM is an industry association representing interests that drive the automatic identification and data capture (AIDC) industry. The primary mission of AIM is to educate end users on integrated technology solutions using bar codes, RF/ID, RF data communications, and so on. AIM is recognized as the industry catalyst for market growth and the center for standards development.

Contact Information:
Automatic Identification Manufacturers
634 Alpha Drive
Pittsburgh, PA 15238

Tel: 412-963-8009
FAX: 412-963-8753

Internet: http://www.aim-europe.org/index.html

Infrared Data Association (IrDA)

The Infrared Data Association (IrDA) was established in 1993 to set and support
hardware and software standards for creating infrared communications links. The
association's charter is to create an interoperable, low-cost, low-power, half-duplex,
serial data interconnection standard that supports a walk-up, point-to-point user
model that is adaptable to a wide range of applications and devices. IrDA standards
support a broad range of computing, communications, and consumer devices.

Contact Information:
Infrared Data Association
P.O. Box 3883
Walnut Creek, CA 94598

Tel: 925-943-6546
FAX: 925-943-5600

Email: daphne@irda.org

Instititute for Electrical and Electronic Engineers (IEEE)

The IEEE is a non-profit professional organization founded by a handful of
engineers in 1884 for the purpose of consolidating ideas dealing with electro-
technology. In the past 100 plus years, IEEE has maintained a steady growth. Today,
the IEEE, which is based in the United States, has more than 320,000 members
located in 150 countries. The IEEE consists of 35 individual societies, including the
Communications Society, Computer Society, and Antennas and Propagation
Society, to name just a few. The Computer Society is the official sponsor of the
IEEE 802.11 Working Group.

The IEEE plays a significant role in publishing technical works, sponsoring conferences and seminars, accreditation, and standards development. IEEE has published
nearly 700 active standards publications, half of which relate to power engineering;
most others deal with computers. The IEEE standards development process consists
of 30,000 volunteers (who are mostly IEEE members) and a Standards Board of 32
people.

Regarding LANs, IEEE has produced some popular and widely used standards. The majority of LANs in the world utilize network interface cards based on the IEEE 802.3 (ethernet), IEEE 802.5 (token ring), and the IEEE 802.11 (wireless LAN) standards, for example.

Contact Information:

Institute for Electrical and Electronic Engineers
445 Hoes Lane
Piscataway, NJ 08855-0459

Tel: 800-678-IEEE

Internet: `http://www.ieee.org/index.html`

International Organization for Standardization

The International Organization for Standardization (ISO) is a worldwide federation of national standards bodies. ISO is a nongovernmental organization established in 1947. The mission of ISO is to promote the development of standardization and related activities in the world with a view to facilitating the international exchange of goods and services, and to developing cooperation in the spheres of intellectual, scientific, technological, and economic activity. ISO's work results in international agreements, which are published as international standards.

Contact Information:

International Organization for Standardization
1, rue de Varembé
Case postale 56
CH-1211 Geneva 20
Switzerland

Tel: 41 22 749-0111

Email: `central@isocs.iso.ch`

International Telecommunication Union (ITU)

The International Telecommunications Union (ITU) is an intergovernmental organization founded in Paris in 1865 as the International Telegraph Union. The International Telecommunication Union took its present name in 1934 and became a specialized agency of the United Nations in 1947.

The ITU adopts international regulations and treaties governing all terrestrial and space uses of the frequency spectrum. It also develops standards to facilitate the interconnection of telecommunication systems on a worldwide scale regardless of the type of technology used.

Contact Information:
International Telecommunication Union
Place des Nations
1211 Geneva 20
Switzerland

Tel: 41 22 730-6666
FAX: 41 22 730-5337

Email: helpdesk@itu.ch

Internet Engineering Task Force (IETF)

The Internet Engineering Task Force (IETF) provides a forum for working groups to coordinate technical developments of new protocols. Its most important function is the development and selection of standards within the Internet protocol suite. The IETF began in January 1986 as a forum for technical coordination by contractors for the then U.S. Defense Advanced Projects Agency (DARPA), working on the ARPAnet, U.S. Defense Data Network (DDN), and the Internet core gateway system. Since that time, the IETF has grown into a large open international community of network designers, operators, vendors, and researchers concerned with the evolution of the Internet architecture and the smooth operation of the Internet.

Contact Information:
Internet: http://www.ietf.cnri.reston.va.us/home.html

Mobile and Portable Radio Research Group

The mission of the Mobile and Portable Radio Research Group (MPRG) is to establish a national resource for research and education in the field of wireless communications. MPRG's mission is to provide design and analysis tools and techniques for U.S. manufacturers, government and consumer service providers, and regulatory agencies, while at the same time providing a high-caliber educational experience for graduate and undergraduate engineering.

Contact Information:
Internet: http://www.mprg.ee.vt.edu

Mobile Management Task Force (MMTF)

The Mobile Management Task Force (MMTF) is an industry group that promotes new management standards that specifically address the concerns of network administrators who must manage mobile computer users. The MMTF was first formed and spearheaded by Epilogue Technology Corporation and Xircom, Inc. Current MMTF member companies include IBM Networking Division, Lannair, Motorola, National Semiconductor Corp., and Zenith Data Systems.

The joint aim of the group is to define and address the needs of mobile computer users, which are inherently different from those of desktop computer users. As defined by the MMTF charter, the group's aim is to "...identify the administrative needs of laptop workstation users, mobile computer users, palmtop users, and others who need reliable access to computer networks on a sporadic basis. The concerns of the MMTF will include managing on-demand access to local area networks, dial-up network access, wireless LAN communications, and related administration issues unique to the needs of mobile computer users."

Contact Information:
Mobile Management Task Force
MMTF c/o Epilogue Technology Corporation
201 Moffett Park Drive
Sunnyvale, CA 94089

Internet: mmtf-request@epilogue.com

Portable Computer and Communications Association (PCCA)

The Portable Computer and Communications Association (PCCA) was established in 1992 to advance the portable computing industry.

Contact Information:
PCCA
P.O. Box 2460
Broulder Creek, CA 95007

Tel: 831-338-0924

Email: pcca@mcimail.com

Wireless LAN Group

At the University of Massachusetts, Amherst, the Wireless LAN Group researches, develops, and introduces efficient wireless LAN architectures that can support the Quality of Service requirements of multimedia applications. Such architectures include point-to-point, single-cell, multiple-cell, and combinations with various wired backbones and connections to other different wireless communication networks.

Contact Information:
Email: wireless@vision.ecs.umass.edu
Internet: http://www.ecs.umass.edu/ece/wireless

Wireless LAN Interoperability Forum (WLIF)

The Wireless LAN Interoperability Forum was formed to promote the use of wireless LANs through the delivery of interoperable products and services at all levels of the value chain. Members of the WLI Forum believe that open competition between compatible products will benefit customers by assuring them that their wireless LAN will support the best products on the market today and will furthermore offer unparalleled flexibility and adaptability for the future.

Contact Information:

Internet: http://www.wlif.com

Wireless Opportunities Coalition (WOC)

The Wireless Opportunities Coalition (WOC) is a diverse group of organizations and companies dedicated to preserving and expanding the opportunities for growth in the wireless industry. The coalition's primary focus is to support the development, manufacturing, and use of wireless communications and related devices that are not licensed by the Federal Communications Commission but are regulated under Part 15 of the FCC's rules.

The Wireless Opportunities Coalition is working to communicate—to the FCC, Congress, and the public—the importance of preserving access to the use of these low-cost, unlicensed devices on the public airwaves.

Contact Information:

Internet: http://ftp.mc.hik.se/pub/doc/eff/Activism/
Groups_organizations/WOC/

Wireless Research Group

At Cornell University, the Wireless Research Group develops systems for future wireless networks. Its activities cover primarily the design, fabrication, and testing of digital millimeter and microwave transmitters and receivers.

Contact Information:

Wireless Research Group
Cornell University
Ithaca, NY 14853

Internet: http://wrg.ee.cornell.edu

Glossary

This glossary is a handy reference to the technical terminology of wireless networking. To make it easy to use, the glossary contains entries for acronyms and abbreviations as well as their respective terms; cross-references are set in *italics*.

Symbols

10Base-2 The *IEEE* standard (known as *thin ethernet*) for 10 Mbps *baseband ethernet* over *coaxial cable* at a maximum distance of 185 meters.

10Base-5 The *IEEE* standard (known as thick *ethernet*) for 10 Mbps *baseband ethernet* over *coaxial cable* at a maximum distance of 500 meters.

10Base-F The *IEEE* standard for 10 Mbps *baseband ethernet* over optical fiber.

10Base-T The *IEEE* standard for 10 Mbps *baseband ethernet* over *twisted-pair wire*.

10Broad-36 The *IEEE* standard for 10 Mbps broadband *ethernet* over *broadband* cable at a maximum distance of 3,600 meters.

100Base-T The *IEEE* standard for 100 Mbps *baseband ethernet* over *twisted-pair wire*.

802.2 The *IEEE* standard that specifies the *Logical Link Control (LLC)* that is common to all 802 series LANs.

802.3 The *IEEE* standard that specifies a carrier sense *medium access* control and *Physical Layer* specifications for wired LANs.

802.4 The *IEEE* standard that specifies a token-passing bus access method and *Physical Layer* specifications for wired LANs.

802.5   The *IEEE* standard that specifies a token-passing ring access method and *Physical Layer* specifications for wired LANs.

802.10   The *IEEE* standard that specifies security and privacy access methods for both wired and wireless LANs.

802.11   The *IEEE* standard that specifies medium access and *Physical Layer* specifications for 1 Mbps and 2 Mbps wireless connectivity between fixed, portable, and moving stations within a local area.

A

acceptance testing   Type of testing that determines whether the network is acceptable to the actual users. The users of the network should participate in developing acceptance criteria and running the tests.

access point (AP)   An interface between the wireless network and a wired network. Access points combined with a distribution system (for example, *ethernet*) support the creation of multiple radio cells (*BSSs*) that enable roaming throughout a facility.

acknowledged connectionless service   A datagram-style service that includes error-control and flow-control mechanisms.

ad hoc network   A wireless network composed only of stations (no *access point*).

adaptive routing   A form of network routing whereby the path data packets traverse from a source to a destination *node* that depends on the current state of the network. Normally with adaptive routing, routing information stored at each *node* changes according to some algorithm that calculates the best paths through the network.

Address Resolution Protocol (ARP)   A TCP/IP protocol that binds logical (IP) addresses to physical addresses.

analog cellular   A telephone system that uses radio cells to provide connectivity among cellular phones. The analog cellular telephone system uses FM (Frequency Modulation) radio waves to transmit voice-grade signals. To accommodate *mobility*, this cellular system will switch your radio connection from one cell to another as you move among areas. Every cell within the network has a transmission tower that links mobile callers to a Mobile Telephone Switching Office (MTSO).

analog signal   An electrical signal with an amplitude that varies continuously as time progresses.

appliance   Runs applications and is a visual interface between the user and the network. There are several classes of user appliances: the desktop workstation, laptop, palmtop, pen-based computer, personal digital assistant (PDA), and pager.

Application Layer   Establishes communications with other users and provides such services as file transfer and electronic mail to the end users of the network. See *Open System Interconnection.*

application process   An entity, either human or software, that uses the services offered by the *Application Layer* of the *OSI* reference model.

application software   Software that accomplishes the functions users require, such as database access, electronic mail, and menu prompts. Therefore, application software directly satisfies network requirements, particularly user requirements.

ARP   See *Address Resolution Protocol.*

ARQ   See *automatic repeat-request.*

association service   An IEEE 802.11 service that enables the mapping of a wireless station to the distribution system via an access point.

Asynchronous Transfer Mode (ATM)   A cell-based, connection-oriented data service offering high-speed (up to 2.488 Gbps) data transfer. ATM integrates circuit and packet switching to handle both constant and burst information. Frequently called *cell relay.*

asynchronous transmission   Type of synchronization without a defined time relationship between transmission of frames.

ATM   See *Asynchronous Transfer Mode.*

attachment unit interface (AUI)   A 15-pin interface between an *ethernet network interface card* and *transceiver.*

AUI   See *attachment unit interface.*

authentication   The process a station uses to announce its identity to another station. IEEE 802.11 specifies two forms of authentication: *open system* and *shared key.*

automatic repeat-request (ARQ)   A method of error correction where the receiving *node* detects errors and uses a feedback path to the sender for requesting the retransmission of incorrect frames.

B

bandwidth   Specifies the amount of the frequency spectrum that is usable for data transfer. In other words, it identifies the maximum data rate that a signal can attain on the medium without encountering significant attenuation (loss of power).

baseband   A signal that has not undergone any shift in frequency. Normally with LANs, a baseband signal is purely digital.

Basic Service Set (BSS)   A set of 802.11-compliant stations that operates as a fully connected, wireless network.

Basic Service Set Identification (BSSID)   A 6-byte address that distinguishes a particular *access point* from others. Also known as a *network ID*.

baud rate   The number of pulses of a signal that occur in one second. Thus, it is the speed at which digital signal pulses travel.

bit rate   The transmission rate of binary symbols (0 and 1). Bit rate equals the total number of bits transmitted in one second.

bridge   A network component that provides internetworking functionality at the *Data Link Layer* or *Medium Access Layer* of a network's architecture. Bridges can provide segmentation of data frames.

broadband   A signal that has undergone a shift in frequency. Normally with LANs, a broadband signal is analog.

BSS   See *Basic Service Set*.

BSSID   See *Basic Service Set Identification*.

bus topology   A type of *topology* in which all *nodes* are connected to a single length of cabling with a terminator at each end.

C

carrier current LAN   A LAN that uses power lines within the facility as a medium for the transport of data.

category 1 twisted-pair wire   Old-style phone wire, which is not suitable for most data transmission. This includes most telephone wire installed before 1983, in addition to most current residential telephone wiring.

category 2 twisted-pair wire   Certified for data rates up to 4 Mbps, which facilitates IEEE 802.5 *token-ring* networks (4 Mbps version).

category 3 twisted-pair wire   Certified for data rates up to 10 Mbps, which facilitates IEEE 802.3 *10Base-T* (*ethernet*) networks.

category 4 twisted-pair wire   Certified for data rates up to 16 Mbps, which facilitates IEEE 802.5 *token-ring* networks (16 Mbps version).

category 5 twisted-pair wire   Certified for data rates up to 100 Mbps, which facilitates ANSI FDDI *token-ring* networks.

CCITT   Abbreviation for Comité Consultatif International Téléphonique et Télégraphique, which translates as *International Telephone and Telegraph Consultative Committee*. (See the main entry.)

CDDI   See *Copper Data Distributed Interface.*

CDPD   See *Cellular Digital Packet Data.*

CDRH   See *Center for Devices and Radiological Health.*

cell relay   See *Asynchronous Transfer Mode.*

Cellular Digital Packet Data (CDPD)   Overlays the conventional analog cellular telephone system, using a channel-hopping technique to transmit data in short bursts during idle times in cellular channels. CDPD operates full duplex in the 800 and 900 MHz frequency bands, offering data rates up to 19.2 Kbps

Center for Devices and Radiological Health (CDRH)   The part of the U.S. Food and Drug Administration that evaluates and certifies laser products for public use.

centronics   A de facto standard 36-pin parallel 200 Kbps asynchronous interface for connecting printers and other devices to a computer.

chip sequence   See *direct sequence spread spectrum.*

clear channel assessment   A function that determines the state of the wireless medium in an IEEE 802.11 network.

coaxial cable   Type of medium having a solid metallic core with a shielding as a return path for current flow. The shielding within the coaxial cable reduces the amount of electrical noise interference within the core wire; therefore, coaxial cable can extend to much greater lengths than *twisted-pair wiring*. Commonly called coax and used in older *ethernet* (*10Base-2*) networks.

connection-oriented service   Establishes a logical connection that provides flow control and error control between two stations needing to exchange data.

connectivity   A path for communications signals to flow through. Connectivity exists between a pair of *nodes* if the destination *node* can correctly receive data from the source *node* at a specified minimum data rate.

connectivity software   A wireless system component that provides an interface between the user's appliance and the database or application software located on the network.

Copper Data Distributed Interface (CDDI)   A version of FDDI specifying the use of unshielded *twisted-pair wiring* (category 5).

CRC   See *Cyclic Redundancy Check*.

Cyclic Redundancy Check (CRC)   An error-detection process that (at the transmitting station) divides the data being sent by a particular polynomial and appends the resulting remainder to the transmitted data. Then (at the receiving station) the process divides the received data by the same polynomial and compares the resulting remainder to the remainder appended to the data at the transmitting station. If the remainders are equal, there is very high probability that no errors are present in the data. If they do not match, errors are present.

D

Data Encryption Standard (DES)   A cryptographic algorithm that protects unclassified computer data. DES is a National Institute of Standards and Technology (NIST) standard and is available for both public and government use.

Data Link Layer   Transforms the packets of the *Network Layer* so that they can be physically conveyed by the *Physical Layer*. Provides synchronization and transmission error control to packets. In IEEE 802.11–compliant LANs, the Data Link Layer encompasses the *Logical Link Control (LLC)* and *Medium Access Control (MAC)* Layers. See *Open System Interconnection*.

data service unit/channel service unit (DSU/CSU)   A set of network components that reshape data signals into a form that can be effectively transmitted over a digital transmission medium, typically a leased 56 Kbps or *T1* line.

datagram service   A connectionless form of packet switching whereby the source does not need to establish a connection with the destination before sending data packets.

DB-9   A standard 9-pin connector commonly used with *RS-232* serial interfaces on portable computers. The DB-9 connector will not support all RS-232 functions.

DB-15   A standard 15-pin connector commonly used with *RS-232* serial interfaces, *ethernet* transceivers, and computer monitors.

DB-25   A standard 25-pin connector commonly used with *RS-232* serial interfaces. The DB-25 connector will support all *RS-232* functions.

DES   See *Data Encryption Standard*.

DHCP   See *Dynamic Host Configuration Protocol*.

differential quadrature phase shift keying (DQPSK)   DQPSK is a modulation process that the IEEE 802.11 direct sequence physical layer uses to transmit data at 2 Mbps. DQPSK modulation operates at a specific center frequency and varies the phase of the signal to represent double-bit symbols.

diffused laser light   Type of laser transmission where the light is reflected off a wall or ceiling.

direct sequence spread spectrum (DSSS)   Combines a data signal at the sending station with a higher data rate bit sequence, which many refer to as a chip sequence (also known as processing gain). A high processing gain increases the signal's resistance to interference. The minimum processing gain that the FCC allows is 10, and most products operate under 20.

disassociation service   An IEEE-802.11 term that defines the process a station or access point uses to notify that it is terminating an existing association.

Distributed Queue Dual Bus (DQDB)   A technology that provides full duplex 155 Mbps operation between *nodes* of a metropolitan area network. The IEEE 802.6 standard is based on DQDB.

distributed routing   A form of routing where each *node* (*router*) in the network periodically identifies neighboring *nodes*, updates its routing table, and, with this information, then sends its routing table to all of its neighbors. Because each *node* follows the same process, complete network *topology* information propagates through the network and eventually reaches each *node*.

distribution service   Used by an *IEEE* 802.11 station to send MAC frames across a *distribution system*.

distribution system   An element of a wireless system that interconnects *Basic Service Sets* via *access points* to form an *Extended Service Set*.

DQDB   See *Distributed Queue Dual Bus*.

DQPSK   See *differential quadrature phase shift keying*.

DSSS   See *direct sequence spread spectrum*.

DSU/CSU   See *data service unit/channel service unit*.

Dynamic Host Configuration Protocol (DHCP)   Issues IP addresses automatically within a specified range to devices such as PCs when they are first powered on. The device retains the use of the IP address for a specific license period that the system administrator can define. DHCP is available as part of the many operating systems including Microsoft Windows NT Server and UNIX.

E

EDI   See *electronic data interchange*.

EIA   See *Electronics Industry Association*.

electronic data interchange (EDI)   A service that provides standardized intercompany computer communications for business transactions. ANSI standard X.12 defines the data format for business transactions for EDI.

Electronics Industry Association (EIA)   A domestic standards-forming organization that represents a vast number of electronics firms in the United States.

ESS   See *Extended Service Set*.

ethernet   A 10 Mbps LAN medium-access method that uses *CSMA* to allow the sharing of a bus-type network. *IEEE* 802.3 is a standard that specifies ethernet.

ethernet repeater   Refers to a component that provides *ethernet* connections among multiple stations sharing a common collision domain. Also referred to as a shared *ethernet* hub.

ethernet switch   More intelligent than a hub, having the capability to connect the sending station directly to the receiving station.

Extended Service Set (ESS)   A collection of *Basic Service Sets* tied together via a distribution system.

F

FDDI   See *Fiber Distributed Data Interface*.

FEC   See *forward error correction*.

FHSS   See *frequency hopping spread spectrum*.

Fiber Distributed Data Interface (FDDI)   An ANSI standard for token-passing networks. FDDI uses optical fiber and operates at 100 Mbps.

File Transfer Protocol (FTP)   A TCP/IP protocol for file transfer.

firewall   A device that interfaces the network to the outside world and shields the network from unauthorized users. The firewall does this by blocking certain types of traffic. For example, some firewalls permit only electronic mail traffic to enter the network from elsewhere. This helps protect the network against attacks made to other network resources, such as sensitive files, databases, and applications.

forward error correction (FEC)   A method of error control where the receiving *node* automatically corrects as many channel errors as it can without referring to the sending *node*.

fractional T-1   A 64 Kbps increment of a *T1* frame.

frame relay   A packet-switching interface that operates at data rates of 56 Kbps to 2 Mbps. Actually, frame relay is similar to X.25, minus the transmission error control overhead. Thus, frame relay assumes that a higher layer, end-to-end protocol will check for transmission errors. Carriers offer frame relay as permanent connection-oriented (virtual circuit) service.

frequency hopping spread spectrum (FHSS)   Takes the data signal and modulates it with a carrier signal that hops from frequency to frequency as a function of time over a wide band of frequencies. For example, a frequency-hopping radio will hop the carrier frequency over the 2.4 GHz frequency band between 2.4 GHz and 2.483 GHz. A hopping code determines the frequencies it will transmit and in which order. To properly receive the signal, the receiver must be set to the same hopping code and "listen" to the incoming signal at the right time at the correct frequency.

FTP   See *File Transfer Protocol*.

fully-connected topology   A *topology* where every *node* is directly connected to every other *node* in the network.

G

gateway   A network component that provides interconnectivity at higher network layers. For example, electronic mail gateways can interconnect dissimilar electronic mail systems.

Gaussian frequency shift keying   A frequency modulation technique that filters the *baseband* signal with a Gaussian filter before performing the modulation.

Global Positioning System (GPS)   A worldwide, satellite-based radio navigation system providing three-dimensional position, velocity, and time information to users having GPS receivers anywhere on or near the surface of the Earth.

GPS   See *Global Positioning System*.

H

HDLC   See *High-level Data Link Control.*

hierarchical topology   A *topology* where *nodes* in the same geographical area are joined together, and then tied to the remaining network as groups. The idea of a hierarchical topology is to install more links within high–density areas and fewer links between these populations.

High-level Data Link Control (HDLC)   An *ISO* protocol for link synchronization and error control.

HTML   See *Hypertext Markup Language.*

Hypertext Markup Language (HTML)   A standard used on the World Wide Web for defining hypertext links between documents.

I

IBSS Network   See *Independent Basic Service Set Network.*

IEEE   See *Institute of Electrical and Electronic Engineers.*

Independent Basic Service Set Network (IBSS Network)   An *IEEE 802.11*–based wireless network that has no backbone infrastructure and consists of at least two wireless stations. This type of network is often referred to as an *ad hoc network* because it can be constructed quickly without much planning.

industrial, scientific, and medicine bands (ISM bands)   Radio frequency bands that the Federal Communications Commission (FCC) authorized for wireless LANs. The ISM bands are located at 902 MHz, 2.400 GHz, and 5.7 GHz.

infrared light   Light waves having wavelengths ranging from about 0.75 to 1,000 microns, which is longer (lower in frequency) than the spectral colors but much shorter (higher in frequency) than radio waves. Therefore, under most lighting conditions, infrared light is invisible to the naked eye.

Institute of Electrical and Electronic Engineers (IEEE)   A U.S.-based standards organization participating in the development of standards for data transmission systems. IEEE has made significant progress in the establishment of standards for LANs, namely the *IEEE 802* series of standards.

Integrated Services Digital Network (ISDN)   A collection of *CCITT* standards specifying WAN digital transmission service. The overall goal of ISDN is to provide a single physical network outlet and transport mechanism for the transmission of all types of information, including data, video, and voice.

integration service   Enables the delivery of MAC frames through a portal between an *IEEE 802.11 distribution system* and a non–802.11 LAN.

integration testing   Type of testing that verifies the interfaces between network components as the components are installed. The installation crew should integrate components into the network one-by-one and perform integration testing when necessary to ensure proper gradual integration of components.

interframe space   Defines spacing between different aspects of the *IEEE 802.11* MAC access protocol to enable different transmission priorities.

Intermediate System-to-Intermediate System Protocol   An *OSI* protocol for intermediate systems exchange routing information.

International Standards Organization (ISO)   A non-treaty standards organization active in the development of international standards such as the *Open System Interconnection (OSI)* network architecture.

International Telecommunications Union (ITU)   An agency of the United States providing coordination for the development of international standards.

International Telephone and Telegraph Consultative Committee (CCITT)   A defunct international standards organization (Comité Consultatif International Téléphonique et Télégraphique) that was part of the *ITU* and dedicated to establishing effective and compatible telecommunications among members of the United Nations. CCITT developed the widely used V-series and X-series standards and protocols.

internetwork   A collection of interconnected networks. Often it is necessary to connect networks together, and an internetwork provides the connection between different networks. One organization having a network may want to share information with another organization having a different network. The internetwork provides functionality needed to share information between these two networks.

inward interference   Interference coming from other devices, such as microwave ovens and other wireless network devices, that will result in delay to the user by either blocking transmissions from stations on the LAN, or by causing bit errors to occur in data being sent.

ISDN   See *Integrated Services Digital Network*.

ISM Bands   See *industrial, scientific, and medicine bands*.

ISO   See *International Standards Organization*.

isochronous transmission Type of synchronization where information frames are sent at specific times.

ITU See *International Telecommunications Union*.

J–K

JAD See *joint application design*.

joint application design (JAD) A parallel process simultaneously defining requirements in the eyes of the customers, users, sales people, marketing staff, project managers, analysts, and engineers. You can use the members of this team to define requirements.

L

LAP See *Link Access Procedure*.

laser A common term for Light Amplification by Stimulated Emission of Radiation, a device containing a substance where the majority of its atoms or molecules are put into an excited energy state. As a result, the laser emits coherent light of a precise wavelength in a narrow beam. Most laser MANs use lasers that produce infrared light.

LED See *light emitting diode*.

light emitting diode (LED) Used in conjunction with optical fiber, it emits incoherent light when current is passed through it. Advantages to LEDs include low cost and long lifetime, and they are capable of operating in the Mbps range.

Link Access Procedure (LAP) An *ITU* error correction protocol derived from the *HDLC* standard.

LLC See *Logical Link Control Layer*.

local bridge A bridge that connects two LANs within close proximity.

Logical Link Control Layer (LLC) The highest layer of the IEEE 802 Reference Model, providing similar functions of a traditional data link control protocol.

M

MAC Layer See *Medium Access Control Layer*.

MAC protocol data unit (MPDU) The unit of data in an IEEE 802 network that two peer MAC entities exchange across a *Physical Layer*.

mail gateway   A type of *gateway* that interconnects dissimilar electronic mail systems.

management information base (MIB)   A collection of managed objects residing in a virtual information store.

MAU   See *multistation access unit.*

medium   A physical link that provides a basic building block to support the transmission of information signals. Most media are composed of either metal, glass, plastic, or air.

medium access   A Data Link Layer function that controls the use of a common network medium.

Medium Access Control Layer (MAC Layer)   Provides medium access services for *IEEE* 802 LANs.

meteor burst communications   A communications system that directs a radio wave, modulated with a data signal, at the iono-sphere. The radio signal reflects off the ionized gas left by the burning of meteors entering the atmosphere and is directed back to Earth in the form of a large footprint, enabling long-distance operation.

MIB   See *management information base.*

middleware   An intermediate software component located on the wired network between the wireless appliance and the application or data residing on the wired network. Middleware provides appropriate interfaces between the appliance and the host application or server database.

MIDI   See *Musical Instrument Digital Interface.*

Mobile IP   A protocol developed by the *Internet Engineering Task Force* to enable users to roam to parts of the network associated with a different IP address than what's loaded in the user's appliance.

mobility   Ability to continually move from one location to another.

mobility requirements   Describe the movement of the users when performing their tasks. Mobility requirements should distinguish whether the degree of movement is continuous or periodic.

modulation   The process of translating the *baseband* digital signal to a suitable analog form.

MPDU   See *MAC protocol data unit.*

multiplexer A network component that combines multiple signals into one composite signal in a form suitable for transmission over a long-haul connection, such as leased 56 Kbps or *T1* circuits.

multistation access unit (MAU) A multiple-port wiring hub for *token-ring* networks.

Musical Instrument Digital Interface (MIDI) A standard protocol for the interchange of musical information between musical instruments and computers.

N

narrowband system A wireless system that uses dedicated frequencies assigned by the FCC licenses. The advantage of narrowband systems is that if interference occurs, the FCC will intervene and issue an order for the interfering source to cease operations. This is especially important when operating wireless MANs in areas having a great deal of other operating radio-based systems.

NetBIOS See *Network Basic Input Output System.*

Network Basic Input Output System (NetBIOS) A standard interface between networks and PCs that allows applications on different computers to communicate within a LAN. It was created by IBM for its early PC Network, was adopted by Microsoft, and has since become a de facto industry standard. It is not routable across a WAN.

network file system (NFS) A distributed file system enabling a set of dissimilar computers to access each other's files in a transparent manner.

network ID See *Basic Service Set Identification.*

network interface card (NIC) A network adapter inserted into a computer so that the computer can be connected to a network. It is responsible for converting data from the form stored in the computer to the form transmitted or received.

Network Layer Provides the routing of packets from source to destination. See *Open System Interconnection.*

network management Consists of a variety of elements that protect the network from disruption and provide proactive control of the configuration of the network.

network management station Executes management applications that monitor and control network elements.

network monitoring   A form of operational support enabling network management to view the inner-workings of the network. Most network monitoring equipment is nonobtrusive and can determine the network's utilization and locate faults.

network re-engineering   A structured process that can help an organization proactively control the evolution of its network. Network re-engineering consists of continually identifying factors influencing network changes, analyzing network modification feasibility, and performing network modifications as necessary.

network service access point (NSAP)   A point in the network where *OSI* network services are available to a transport entity.

NFS   See *network file system*.

NIC   See *network interface card*.

node   Any network-addressable device on the network, such as a *router* or *network interface card*.

NSAP   See *network service access point*.

O

ODBC   See *Open Database Connectivity*.

ODI   See *Open Data-Link Interface*.

Open Database Connectivity (ODBC)   A standard database interface enabling interoperability between application software and multiple-vendor *ODBC*-compliant databases.

Open Data-Link Interface (ODI)   Novell's specification for *network interface card* device drivers, allowing simultaneous operation of multiple protocol stacks.

Open Shortest Path First (OSPF)   Routing protocol for TCP/IP *routers* that bases routing decisions on the least number of hops between the source to the destination.

open system authentication   The *IEEE 802.11* default authentication method, which is a very simple, two-step process. First the station wanting to authenticate with another station sends an authentication management frame containing the sending station's identity. The receiving station then sends back a frame alerting whether it recognizes the identity of the authenticating station.

Open System Interconnection (OSI)   An ISO standard specifying an open system capable of enabling the communications between diverse systems. OSI has the following seven layers of distinction: *Physical*, *Data Link*, *Network*, *Transport*, *Session*, *Presentation*, and *Application*. These layers provide the functions necessary to allow standardized communications between two application processes.

OSI   See *Open System Interconnection*.

OSPF   See *Open Shortest Path First*.

P

packet radio   Uses packet switching to move data from one location to another across radio links.

PCF   See *point coordination function*.

PCM   See *pulse code modulation*.

PCMCIA form factor   See *Personal Computer Memory Card International Association form factor*.

PCS   See *Personal Communications Services*.

peer-to-peer network   A network where there are communications between a group of equal devices. A peer-to-peer LAN does not depend on a dedicated server, but allows any *node* to be installed as a non-dedicated server and share its files and peripherals across the network. Peer-to-peer LANs are normally less expensive because they do not require a dedicated computer to store applications and data. They do not perform well, however, for larger networks.

performance modeling   The use of simulation software to predict network behavior, enabling you to perform capacity planning. Simulation enables you to model the network and impose varying levels of utilization to observe the effects. Performance monitoring addresses performance of a network during normal operations. Performance monitoring includes real-time monitoring, where metrics are collected and compared against thresholds that can set off alarms; recent-past monitoring, where metrics are collected and analyzed for trends that may lead to performance problems; and historical data analysis, where metrics are collected and stored for later analysis.

Personal Communications Services (PCS)   A spectrum allocation located at 1.9 GHz, a new wireless communications technology offering wireless access to the World Wide Web, wireless email, wireless voice mail, and cellular telephone service.

Personal Computer Memory Card International Association form factor (PCMCIA form factor)   A standard set of physical interfaces for portable computers. PCMCIA specifies three interface sizes: Type I (3.3 millimeters), Type II (5.0 millimeters), and Type III (10.5 millimeters).

Physical Layer   Provides the transmission of bits through a communication channel by defining electrical, mechanical, and procedural specifications. See *Open System Interconnection*.

physical layer convergence procedure sublayer (PLCP)   Prepares *MAC protocol data units (MPDUs)* as instructed by the *MAC Layer* for transmission and delivers incoming frames to the *MAC Layer*.

physical medium dependent sublayer (PMD)   Provides the actual transmission and reception of *Physical Layer* entities between two stations via the wireless medium.

plain old telephone system (POTS)   The original common analog telephone system, which is still in wide use today.

PLCP   See *physical layer convergence procedure sublayer*.

PMD   See *physical medium dependent sublayer*.

point coordination function (PCF)   An *IEEE 802.11* mode that enables contention-free frame transfer based on a priority mechanism. Enables time-bounded services that support the transmission of voice and video.

Point-to-Point Protocol (PPP)   A protocol that provides router-to-router and host-to-network connections over both synchronous and asynchronous circuits. PPP is the successor to *SLIP*.

portability   Defines network connectivity that can be easily established, used, and dismantled.

portal   A logical point where *MSDUs* from a non-*IEEE 802.11* LAN enter the *distribution system* of an *Extended Service Set* wireless network.

POTS   See *plain old telephone system*.

PPP   See *Point-to-Point Protocol*.

Presentation Layer   Negotiates data transfer syntax for the *Application Layer* and performs translations between different data types, if necessary. See *Open System Interconnection*.

Primitive   An abstract representation of an interaction between two layers of the *OSI* Reference Model. See *Open System Interconnection*.

processing gain   Equal to the data rate of the spread direct sequence signal divided by the data rate of the actual data. See *direct sequence spread spectrum*.

project charter   Formally recognizes the existence of the project, identifies the business need that the project is addressing, and gives a general description of the resulting product.

prototyping   A method of determining or verifying requirements and design specifications. The prototype normally consists of network hardware and software that support a proposed solution. The approach to prototyping is typically a trial-and-error experimental process.

pseudo-noise   An actual signal having a long pattern that resembles noise.

pulse code modulation (PCM)   A common method for converting analog voice signals into a digital bit stream.

pulse position modulation (PPM)   The varying of the position of a pulse to represent different binary symbols. The changes in pulse positions maintain the information content of the signal.

Q

QPSK   See *Quadrature Phase Shift Keying*.

Quadrature Phase Shift Keying (QPSK)   A modulation technique that changes the phase of a signal to represent different, four-bit binary words.

R

reassociation service   Enables an *IEEE 802.11* station to change its association with different access points as the station moves throughout the facility.

Red Book   A document of the United States National Security Agency (NSA) defining criteria for secure networks.

relay node   Implements a routing protocol that maintains the optimum routes for the routing tables, forwarding packets closer to the destination.

remote bridge   A bridge that connects networks separated by longer distances. Organizations use leased 56 Kbps circuits, *T1* digital circuits, and radio waves to provide long-distance connections between remote bridges.

repeater   A network component that provides internetworking functionality at the *Physical Layer* of a network's architecture. A repeater amplifies network signals, extending the distance they can travel.

requirements analysis   A process of defining what the network is supposed to do, providing a basis for the network design.

ring topology   A *topology* where a set of *nodes* are joined in a closed loop.

RIP   See *Routing Information Protocol*.

router   A network component that provides internetworking at the *Network Layer* of a network's architecture by allowing individual networks to become part of a WAN. It routes using logical and physical addresses to connect two or more separate networks. It determines the best path by which to send a packet of information.

Routing Information Protocol (RIP)   A common type of routing protocol. RIP bases its routing path on the distance (number of hops) to the destination. RIP maintains optimum routing paths by sending out routing update messages if the network *topology* changes. For example, if a *router* finds that a particular link is faulty, it will update its routing table, and then send a copy of the modified table to each of its neighbors.

RS-232   An *EIA* standard that specifies up to 20 Kbps, 50 foot, serial transmission between computers and peripheral devices.

RS-422   An *EIA* standard specifying electrical characteristics for balanced circuits (that is, both transmit and return wires are at the same voltage above ground). RS-422 is used in conjunction with RS-449.

RS-423   An *EIA* standard specifying electrical characteristics for unbalanced circuits (that is, the return wire is tied to ground). RS-423 is used in conjunction with *RS-449*.

RS-449   An *EIA* standard specifying a 37-pin connector for high-speed transmission.

RS-485   An *EIA* standard for multiple-point communications lines.

S

SAP   See *service access point*.

Serial Line Internet Protocol (SLIP)   An Internet protocol used to run IP over serial lines and dial-up connections.

server-oriented network   A network architecture where the network software is split into two pieces, one each for the client and the server. The server component provides services for the client software; the client part interacts with the user. The client and server components run on different computers, and the server is usually more powerful than the client. The main advantages of a server-oriented network is less network traffic. Therefore, networks having a large number of users will normally perform better with server-oriented networks.

service access point (SAP)   A point at which the services of an *OSI* layer are made available to the next higher layer.

service primitive   A communications element for sending information between network architectural layers.

Session Layer   Establishes, manages, and terminates sessions between applications. See *Open System Interconnection*.

shared key authentication   A type of authentication that assumes each station has received a secret shared key through a secure channel independent from an *802.11* network. Stations authenticate through shared knowledge of the secret key. Use of shared key authentication requires implementation of the *802.11 Wireless Equivalent Privacy* algorithm.

Simple Mail Transfer Protocol (SMTP)   The Internet electronic mail protocol.

Simple Network Monitoring Protocol (SNMP)   A network management protocol that defines the transfer of information between *management information bases (MIBs)*. Most high-end network monitoring stations require the implementation of SNMP on each of the components the organization wishes to monitor.

SLIP   See *Serial Line Internet Protocol*.

SMDS   See *Switched Multimegabit Digital Service*.

SMTP   See *Simple Mail Transfer Protocol*.

SNA   See *Systems Network Architecture*.

SNMP   See *Simple Network Monitoring Protocol*.

SONET   See *Synchronous Optical NETwork*.

spectrum analyzer   An instrument that identifies the amplitude of signals at various frequencies.

spread spectrum   A modulation technique that spreads a signal's power over a wide band of frequencies. The main reasons for this technique are that the signal becomes much less susceptible to electrical noise and interferes less with other radio-based systems.

SQL   See *Structured Query Language*.

ST connector   An optical-fiber connector that uses a bayonet plug and socket.

star topology   A *topology* where each *node* is connected to a common central switch or hub.

station   In *IEEE 802.11* networks, any device that contains an *IEEE 802.11*-compliant *Medium Access Control* and *Physical Layers*.

Structured Query Language (SQL)   An international standard for defining and accessing relational databases.

Switched Multimegabit Digital Service (SMDS)   A packet switching connectionless data service for WANs.

Synchronous Optical NETwork (SONET)   A fiber-optic transmission system for high-speed digital traffic. SONET is part of the B-*ISDN* standard.

synchronous transmission   Type of synchronization that sends information frames within certain time periods. It uses a clock to control the timing of bits being sent.

system testing   Type of testing that verifies the installation of the entire network. Testers normally complete system testing in a simulated production environment, simulating actual users to ensure that the network meets all stated requirements.

Systems Network Architecture (SNA)   IBM's proprietary network architecture.

T

T1   A standard specifying a time division multiplexing scheme for point-to-point transmission of digital signals at 1.544 Mbps.

TCP   See *Transmission Control Protocol*.

TDR   See *time-domain reflectometer*.

Technical Service Bulletin 67 (TSB 67)   Describes how to test category 5 twisted-pair cable. TSB 67 was published by the Link Performance Task Group, a subcommittee of the Telecommunications Industry Association's TR41 Standards Committee.

technology comparison matrix   A documentation method that compares similar technologies based on attributes such as functionality, performance, cost, and maturity.

telecommuting   The concept of electronically stretching an office to a person's home.

Telnet   A virtual terminal protocol used in the Internet, enabling users to log on to a remote host.

terminal node controller (TNC)   Interfaces computers to ham radio equipment. TNCs act much like a telephone modem, converting the computer's digital signal into one that a ham radio can modulate and send over the airwaves using a packet switching technique.

test case   An executable test with a specific set of input values and a corresponding expected result.

thick ethernet   See *10Base-5*.

thin ethernet   See *10Base-2*.

time-domain reflectometer (TDR)   Tests the effectiveness of network cabling.

TNC   See *terminal node controller*.

token ring   A medium access method that provides multiple access to a ring-type network through the use of a token. *FDDI* and *IEEE 802.5* are token-ring standards.

top-down design   First defines high-level specifications directly satisfying network requirements, and then defines the remaining elements in an order that satisfies the most specifications already determined.

topography   A description of the network's physical surface spots. Topography specifies the type and location of *node*s with respect to one another.

topology   The description of a network's geographical layout of *node*s and links.

TP0   *OSI* Transport Protocol Class 0 (Simple Class), useful only with very reliable networks.

TP4   *OSI* Transport Protocol Class 4 (Error Detection and Recovery Class), useful with any type of network. The functionality of TP4 is similar to TCP.

transceiver   A device for transmitting and receiving packets between the computer and the medium.

Transmission Control Protocol (TCP)   A commonly used protocol for establishing and maintaining communications between applications on different computers. TCP provides full-duplex, acknowledged, and flow-controlled service to upper-layer protocols and applications.

Transport Layer   Provides mechanisms for the establishment, maintenance, and orderly termination of virtual circuits, while shielding the higher layers from the network implementation details. See *Open System Interconnection*.

TSB 67   See *Technical Service Bulletin 67*.

twisted-pair wire   Type of medium using metallic type conductors twisted together to provide a path for current flow. The wire in this medium is twisted in pairs to minimize the electromagnetic interference between one pair and another.

U

UDP   See *User Data Protocol*.

unacknowledged connectionless service   A datagram-style service that does not involve any error-control or flow-control mechanisms.

unit testing   Type of testing that verifies the accuracy of each network component, such as servers, cables, hubs, and bridges. The goal of unit testing is to make certain the component works properly by running tests that fully exercise the internal workings of the component.

User Data Protocol (UDP)   A connetionless protocol that works at the *OSI Transport Layer*. UDP transports datagrams, but does not acknowledge their receipt.

user profile requirements   Identify the attributes of each person who will be using the system, providing human factors that designers can use to select or develop applications.

V

V.21   An *ITU* standard for asynchronous 0–300 bps full-duplex modems.

V.21 FAX   An *ITU* standard for facsimile operations at 300 bps.

V.34   An *ITU* standard for 28,800 bps modems.

W

WBS   See *work breakdown structure*.

WEP   See *Wired Equivalent Privacy*.

Wired Equivalent Privacy (WEP)   An optional *IEEE 802.11* function that offers frame transmission privacy similar to a wired network. The Wired Equivalent Privacy generates secret shared encryption keys that both source and destination stations can use to alter frame bits to avoid disclosure to eavesdroppers.

wireless metropolitan area network Provides communications links between buildings, avoiding the costly installation of cabling or leasing fees and the downtime associated with system failures.

wireless network interface Couples the digital signal from the end-user appliance to the wireless medium, which is air.

wiremap test Ensures a link has proper connectivity by testing for continuity and other installation mistakes, such as the connection of wires to the wrong connector pin.

work breakdown structure (WBS) Shows how the team will accomplish the project by listing all tasks the team will need to perform and the products they must deliver.

X–Z

X.12 An *ITU* standard for *EDI*.

X.21 An *ITU* standard for a circuit switching network.

X.25 An *ITU* standard for an interface between a terminal and a packet switching network. X.25 was the first public packet switching technology, developed by the *CCITT* and offered as a service during the 1970s and still available today. X.25 offers connection-oriented (virtual circuit) service and operates at 64 Kbps, which is too slow for some high-speed applications.

X.75 An *ITU* standard for packet switching between public networks.

X.121 An *ITU* standard for international address numbering.

X.400 An *ITU* standard for *OSI* messaging.

X.500 An *ITU* standard for *OSI* directory services.

Index

Symbols